LINGUISTIC SURVEYS OF AFRICA

Volume 19

THE SOUTHERN BANTU LANGUAGES

THE SOUTHERN BANTU LANGUAGES
Handbook of African Languages

C. M. DOKE

LONDON AND NEW YORK

First published in 1954 by Dawsons of Pall Mall

This edition first published in 2018
by Routledge
2 Park Square, Milton Park, Abingdon, Oxon OX14 4RN

and by Routledge
711 Third Avenue, New York, NY 10017

Routledge is an imprint of the Taylor & Francis Group, an informa business

© 1954 International African Institute

All rights reserved. No part of this book may be reprinted or reproduced or utilised in any form or by any electronic, mechanical, or other means, now known or hereafter invented, including photocopying and recording, or in any information storage or retrieval system, without permission in writing from the publishers.

Trademark notice: Product or corporate names may be trademarks or registered trademarks, and are used only for identification and explanation without intent to infringe.

British Library Cataloguing in Publication Data
A catalogue record for this book is available from the British Library

ISBN: 978-1-138-08975-4 (Set)
ISBN: 978-1-315-10381-5 (Set) (ebk)
ISBN: 978-1-138-09807-7 (Volume 19) (hbk)
ISBN: 978-1-138-09814-5 (Volume 19) (pbk)
ISBN: 978-1-315-10454-6 (Volume 19) (ebk)

Publisher's Note
The publisher has gone to great lengths to ensure the quality of this reprint but points out that some imperfections in the original copies may be apparent.

Disclaimer
The publisher has made every effort to trace copyright holders and would welcome correspondence from those they have been unable to trace.

Due to modern production methods, it has not been possible to reproduce the fold-out maps within the book. Please visit www.routledge.com to view them.

THE
SOUTHERN BANTU
LANGUAGES

BY
C. M. DOKE

Published for the
INTERNATIONAL AFRICAN INSTITUTE
by
DAWSONS OF PALL MALL
LONDON
1967

First published for
International African Institute 1954
Reprinted 1967

SBN: 7129 0201 5

Dawsons of Pall Mall
16, Pall Mall, London, S.W.1

PRINTED BY PHOTOLITHOGRAPHY
UNWIN BROTHERS LIMITED, WOKING AND LONDON

CONTENTS

INTRODUCTION	7
ABBREVIATIONS	9
I. THE HISTORY AND GROWTH OF KNOWLEDGE CONCERNING THE SOUTHERN BANTU LANGUAGES	11
II. THE CLASSIFICATION OF THE SOUTHERN BANTU LANGUAGES	20
III. THE PHONETICS AND PHONOLOGY OF THE SOUTHERN BANTU LANGUAGES	26
IV. THE MORPHOLOGY OF THE SOUTHERN BANTU LANGUAGES	47
V. THE NGUNI GROUP	91
VI. THE SOTHO GROUP	119
VII. VENDA	154
VIII. THE TSONGA GROUP	180
IX. THE SHONA GROUP	205

APPENDIXES

I. Chopi Tables	231
II. Phuthi Tables	234
III. Ngoni Tables	237
IV. Lozi Tables	240
V. Kgalagadi Tables	243
VI. Pai Tables	246
VII. Pulana and Kutswe Tables	249
VIII. Kalanga Tables	252
INDEX	255
MAP	*at end*

INTRODUCTION

IN 1937 the Inter-University Committee for African Studies, in South Africa, appointed a small committee to undertake the preparation of a work on the languages of South Africa. Originally it was planned to include Bushman and Hottentot languages in the survey, but this ambitious project was reduced when difficulties were encountered over appointments to the various sections. Then even the allocation of chapters for the Bantu languages proved difficult; and, with the outbreak of the war in 1939, only four chapters had been prepared by the present writer and 'vetted' by Professor G. P. Lestrade. The project then went into 'cold storage'. But in 1948 the writer was approached by the International African Institute to write a monograph on the Southern Bantu languages as one of the special studies supplementary to the Handbook of African Languages, on the preparation of which the Institute was engaged. Shortly after agreeing to this request severe illness made it necessary to ask to be relieved of the task. Meanwhile, a constant demand had been growing in South Africa for the preparation of a textbook on Comparative South African Bantu Philology for university studies. With the insistence of these demands and with an improvement in health, the task was tackled again, and the present publication is the result.

The author realizes considerable shortcomings in the work: the treatment of tone is one that needs attention in all the areas considered; syntax has scarcely been dealt with; many dialectal forms in each of the groups need special study. Nevertheless he feels that this survey contains a large amount of detailed information that will be of value to students, and that it will serve to put in perspective the various groups and languages constituting the Southern Bantu and thus serve a dual purpose.

The grammatical classification followed is that used in Bantu studies in the universities of South Africa. No one system of treatment can claim to be the only right one; but this has proved of practical value for understanding the structure of the languages and for carrying out comparative work in them. An ideal treatment would have been to reduce all the orthographies to a common phonetic or phonological form. To use a common phonetic orthography, however, would have required such a multiplicity of symbols that each language would have been effectively disguised and unrecognizable by the ordinary reader. The success of a phonological alphabet is only possible within an individual language group, and could not be applied to a comparative study of this magnitude. In the circumstances it has been felt best to employ the various accepted orthographies, using phonetic equivalents merely as 'handmaids' for explanation. On one point, however, the writer maintains that it is absolutely necessary to have uniformity, and that is on the question of word-division. The word is the basis of grammatical classification, and a rational approach to this is impossible apart from a clear understanding of the constitution of the word in Bantu. The writer has no hesitation in stating that the disjunctive writing used in a number of Bantu languages has no relationship whatever to the constitution of the word. For this reason a system of hyphening together the disjointed parts of words in examples from the Sotho, Venda, and Tsonga groups has been followed. The current orthographical divisions may be detected in this; but a common basis for description, classification, and comparison is achieved.

In the appendixes certain detailed information, for comparative purposes, is given on some striking dialectal forms. The writer would have liked to have included more of this dialectal study, but lack of sufficient exact information and considerations of space have prevented more than the eight appendixes given. The Inhambane group might well have occupied a chapter by itself, but here again detailed information is meagre, and these languages, apart from their use in Scripture translations and mission publications, are not being developed as ordinary literary media. For this reason the most important member, Chopi, is treated as an appendix.

I wish to place on record my gratitude for help from a number of quarters, given most readily.

I acknowledge with sincere thanks my indebtedness to my Cape Town colleague, Professor G. P. Lestrade, M.A., for help, particularly in the original preparation of Chapter IV on the general morphology of the languages, and also for helpful criticism and suggestions in the early drafts of Chapters I, V, and IX. Professor Lestrade's keen insight into details and grasp of comparative implications have always been a stimulus in any work on which we have co-operated.

For the material in Chapter VII I am greatly indebted to Mr. E. O. Westphal, M.A., of the School of Oriental and African Studies, London, who generously permitted me to make use of his unpublished M.A. thesis, 'A Scientific Analysis of the Phonetics Morphology and Syntax of the Venda Language' (1946).

To my colleague in Johannesburg, Mr. D. T. Cole, M.A., I am grateful for help in the general Sotho field, and more particularly for access to his material on Tswana grammar, which made my task on the preparation of Chapter VI the easier. In regard to this chapter also, I owe much to long research work carried out some years ago with Mr. S. M. Mofokeng, M.A., Sotho language assistant in the Department of Bantu Studies, University of the Witwatersrand.

I also record grateful thanks to Dr. D. Ziervogel, of Pretoria University, for allowing me to use his *Grammar of Swazi (siSwati)* then in the press, for comparative work in Chapter V; and for all the trouble he went to in providing me with the material for the *Pai Tables* (App. VI) and the *Pulana and Kutswe Tables* (App. VII), which constitute most valuable information hitherto unpublished.

To the Rev. G. Fortune, S.J., M.A., of the Department of African Studies, University of Cape Town, I am grateful for supplying me with material for the *Kalanga Tables* (App. VIII); these verified what I had prepared, and filled in certain gaps in my information.

And to my niece, Miss Ilva Meier, I record my warmest thanks for the difficult job of typing an intricate manuscript so splendidly. If printers always had such manuscripts as this one to work from, their troubles would be immensely lightened.

C. M. DOKE

LIST OF ABBREVIATIONS

A.C.	Adjectival Concord	med.	medial
adj.	adjective, adjectival		
affric.	affricative	neg.	negative
alv.	alveolar	N.P.	Noun Prefix
asp.	aspirated		
auxil.	auxiliary	obj.	object, objectival
bilab.	bilabial		
		p.	(1) page, (2) plural
caus.	causative	P.C.	Possessive Concord
cd.	concord	perf.	perfect
cf.	compare	pers.	person
ch(s).	chapter(s)	phon.	phonetic
cl(s).	class(es)	pl.	plural
concd(s).	concord(s)	pos.	positive
cons.	consonant	poss.	possessive
contin.	continuant, continuous	posit.	positive
		positn.	position
def.	definite	potent.	potential
defic.	deficient	pp.	pages
demons.	demonstrative	pres.	present
denti-lab.	denti-labial	pron.	pronoun
E.C.	Enumerative Concord	Q.P.	Quantitative Prefix
e.g.	for example	quant.	quantitative
eject.	ejective		
enum.	enumerative	rad.	radical
et seq.	and following	R.C.	Relative Concord
expl.	explosive	rel.	relative
		rem.	remote
fric.	fricative		
fut.	future	s., sg., sing.	singular
		st.	stem
glott.	glottal	stat.	stative
		subj.	(1) subject, subjectival
ibid.	the same		(2) subjunctive
i.e.	that is	s-v.	semi-vowel
imm.	immediate	syll.	syllabic
indef.	indefinite		
indic.	indicative	tr.	transitive
infin.	infinitive		
intr.	intransitive	unv.	unvoiced
lat.	lateral	v.	verb
loc.	locative	voic.	voiced

Signs

< derived from
> forming, becoming
+ plus
= equals

ABBREVIATIONS

Abbreviated References to Languages

Jo	Jonga	Ro.	Ronga	Tg.	Tsonga
Kl.	Kalanga	Sh.	Shona	To.	Tonga
Ko.	Korekore	So.	Sotho	Ts.	Tswa
Kr.	Karanga	So.(N)	Northern Sotho	Ve.	Venda
Li.	Lilima	So.(S)	Southern Sotho	X.	Xhosa
Ma.	Manyika	So.(T)	Tswana	Z.	Zulu
Nd.	Ndau	S.S.	Southern Sotho	Ze.	Zezuru
Ng.	Nguni	Sz.	Swazi		
N.S.	Northern Sotho	T.	Tswana		

I

THE HISTORY AND GROWTH OF KNOWLEDGE CONCERNING THE SOUTHERN BANTU LANGUAGES

Early Landmarks

From the beginning of the sixteenth century Portuguese writers recorded considerable numbers of Bantu words, particularly from the languages of the eastern coast of Africa, where Sofala, Kilwa, Mozambique, and other places had been occupied by considerable forces; and many such words may be culled from the writings of Barbosa, De Barros, Silveira, Monclaro, dos Santos, and others. The first serious recordings from the Bantu languages of the western coast were in the *Report of the Kingdom of Congo* in 1591 by Pigafetta, an Italian who obtained his information from a Portuguese merchant named Lopes. The words recorded were from the Kongo language, and many of them are verifiable today.

The first Bantu publication, however, did not appear until 1624. In this year was printed at Lisbon Cardoso's translation into Kongo of Jorge's *Doutrina Christãa*, a little manual of Christian doctrine, in Portuguese with interlinear translation in Kongo. In 1643 appeared Pacconio and de Couto's *Gentio de Angola*, a 90-page book of Christian doctrine, in Ndongo[1] and Portuguese on opposite pages. This book underwent three subsequent editions: 1661, 1784, and the last as late as 1855.

There were several other publications and manuscripts prepared during the seventeenth century, but the outstanding work was that of Giacinto Brusciotto, an Italian Capuchin priest. In 1659 Brusciotto published in Latin at Rome a little book of 98 pages entitled *Regulae quaedam pro difficillimi Congensium idiomatis faciliori captu ad grammaticae normam redactae*, the first grammar of a Bantu language. This is a definite landmark in Bantu research. Brusciotto was the discoverer of the Bantu noun-class and concord system; he termed the classes 'principiations'; and he was the first recorder of Bantu verbal derivatives. When it is known that the principle of the noun-classes eluded many of his successors, even such comparatively recent writers as Lichtenstein and Burton (in 1860), Brusciotto's linguistic aptitudes are seen to be of no mean order.

The second Bantu grammar published, Dias's *Arte da lingua de Angola* of 1697, is also a meritorious piece of work. Though containing only 48 pages, it is a remarkably accurate record of Ndongo. Dias does not seem to have known Brusciotto's work, and later workers in Ndongo, such as de Cannecattim (1805), do not seem to have known his: de Cannecattim does not mention Dias and certainly has not profited from his work.

In 1776 the Abbé Proyart wrote a chapter on language in his *History of Loango, Kakongo and other Kingdoms in Africa*. In this he treated the Bantu noun-prefixes as 'articles', but nevertheless showed considerable understanding of Bantu language structure.

Classification and Comparative Studies

Though in the eighteenth century the Portuguese repeatedly referred in their writings to the similarity of speech between Angola and Mozambique, it was not until the beginning of the nineteenth century that any categorical statement was made regarding a classification of the languages of Southern Africa. It fell to Heinrich Lichtenstein in 1808, in his paper entitled 'Bemerkungen über die Sprachen der Südafricanischen wilden Völkerstämme', to

[1] Often referred to as Mbundu.

point out that 'the inhabitants of Southern Africa may be divided into two principal races, viz. the Hottentots and the Kaffirs. The two races may be clearly distinguished by their build, features, colour, customs and speech. . . . Although the above-mentioned characteristics sufficiently illustrate the difference in origin, yet even more proof of this is the most complete lack of affinity of the two languages to one another. . . . All linguistic types of the South African aborigines must be classified as dialects of either one or the other of these two principal classes.' He further stated that 'we are justified in considering all the inhabitants of the East Coast of Africa, from 10° or 12° S. to the frontiers of the Dutch Colony, as one nation . . . to which further research may perhaps compel us to add the inhabitants of the South-west Coast'.

This conclusion seems to have been arrived at by several other writers much about this time. William Marsden, the Orientalist, in his instructions to Tuckey's ill-fated expedition to the Congo in 1816, drew attention to the similarity between vocabularies collected on the east and west coasts of Africa; while in 1824 Dr. John Philip, the well-known L.M.S. missionary at Cape Town, wrote in the *Missionary Register*: 'I have been bestowing some attention on the affinity of several languages spoken in this angle of the continent of Africa; and have discovered that the languages spoken by the Cafres on the eastern coast of Africa, by the inhabitants of the Comoro Islands, and by the Bootsuannas, are different dialects only of the same language . . . and I have little doubt but that the different tongues spoken from the borders of our Colony to the confines of Abyssinia, and from the mouth of the Zembeza on the eastern coast of Africa to the mouth of the Congo on the western coast, will be found different dialects only of the same language.'

Knowledge had so far advanced that by 1837 William Boyce was able, in his introduction to Archbell's *Grammar of the Bechuana Language*, to make a clear distinction between the 'uncouth and inharmonious dialects' of the 'Namacqua, Korana and Bushmen' and 'the second division, or family, of the South African languages' comprising 'the sister dialects spoken by the Kafir and Bechuana tribes'. He included a table of 'Specimens of the Languages of South Africa resembling the Kafir and Sechuana', in which he gave examples of words from 'Delagoa Bay', 'Makoha' (Makua), 'Monjou' (Yao), and 'Sowaiel' (Swahili). He further linked up these languages with those of the Congo and Angola, and provided the foundation upon which Appleyard built. But perhaps Boyce's greatest contribution to Bantu language study was his discovery and naming of the alliterative concord in Xhosa, 'the key to the etymological structure of the language', as Davis termed it.

During 1847 J. W. Appleyard, a Wesleyan Missionary, contributed a series of articles on South African languages to the *S.A. Christian Watchman and Missionary Magazine*, in which he attempted a classification. These articles were evidently the basis of Lewis Grout's paper 'The Zulu and other Dialects of Southern Africa' which was published in America in 1849. In 1850 Appleyard elaborated them in the introduction to *The Kafir Language*. He classified the 'South African dialects' under two main heads: the 'click class' and the 'alliteral class'. In the former he placed two 'families', the Hottentot and the Bushman. The 'alliteral class' he divided into four families: Congo, Damara, Sechuana, and Kafir. He classified Sotho under 'Sechuana'; and further divided 'the Kafir family' into (1) 'the Kafir branch spoken by the Amaxosa', (2) 'the Zulu branch' with dialects of Natal and of 'the people of Umzelekazi', and (3) 'the Fingoe branch' including the 'Amafengu', the 'Amabaca', the 'Matabele' living in the neighbourhood of the Caledon River, and certain other tribes living to the south of the Swazi. In his comparative study Appleyard anticipated the later work of Bleek and Meinhof in giving certain tables of vowel and consonantal changes, illustrating the sound-shiftings between Tswana and Xhosa.

W. H. I. Bleek (1827–75) marked a new era in the study of South African languages. As interpreter to the High Commissioner and later as custodian of the Grey Library, Dr. Bleek used his opportunities to do an enormous amount of linguistic research, for which he was peculiarly fitted. In 1862 and 1869 he brought out the two published sections of his *Comparative Grammar of South African Languages*. Besides containing a valuable analysis of Hottentot speech, these volumes constituted a detailed study of the then-known Bantu languages, with a reasonable classification of their types and an arrangement of the noun-classes into eighteen categories. It was Bleek who first used the term *Bantu* (in the form 'Bâ-ntu') in connexion with these languages, though he recorded that Dr. H. Barth had called them 'Ba-Languages'. The work of Bleek has earned for him the title of 'the Father of Bantu Philology'. From 1870 to the time of his death, his researches were diverted to a study of Bushman, which he rescued from a threatened oblivion; and Bleek never completed his comparative work.

Shortly after this the Viennese scholar F. Müller made a sixfold classification of African languages, and this was adopted by R. N. Cust, who gave a comprehensive survey of the position in his *Modern Languages of Africa* in 1883. The classification adopted by Müller and Cust was as follows: (1) Semitic family, (2) Hamitic group, (3) Nuba-Fula group, (4) Negro group, (5) Bantu family, and (6) Hottentot-Bushman group. Later researches have to a certain extent modified this classification in recognizing four main language families in Africa—Semitic, Hamitic, Sudanic (with a Nilotic subdivision), and Bantu—and linking Hottentot to the Hamitic, though the position of Bushman is still a matter of debate amongst scholars.

In connexion with the comparative study of the languages, four other names should be mentioned: J. Torrend, S.J. (1861–1936), who in 1891 wrote his remarkable *Comparative Grammar of the South African Bantu Languages*, a book containing a vast amount of research material, but marred by wild etymological speculation; Sir H. H. Johnston (1858–1927), the author of *A Comparative Study of the Bantu and Semi-Bantu Languages*, a vast comparative vocabulary 'of 366 Bantu and 87 Semi-Bantu languages and dialects', published in two volumes (1919 and 1922), but unfortunately unreliable, as Johnston was too ready to publish information culled from any source or informant without adequate verification and checking; Dr. Alice Werner (1859–1935), Professor of Swahili and Bantu Languages at the London School of Oriental Studies, who popularized the study of African languages for the English reader in two excellent publications, *The Language-Families of Africa* (1915), and her *Introductory Sketch of the Bantu Languages* (1919); and Professor Carl Meinhof (1857–1944) of the Seminar für Afrikanische Sprachen, Hamburg.

The value of Professor Meinhof's contribution to our knowledge of African languages cannot be over-estimated. In the Hamitic field he wrote *Die Sprachen der Hamiten* (1912) and the *Lehrbuch der Nama-Sprache* (1909). But it was in connexion with Bantu that his greatest work was done. Apart from studies in East African languages and small monographs on Herero, Duala, and Swahili, Meinhof produced in 1899 his *magnum opus*, the *Grundriss einer Lautlehre der Bantusprachen* (2nd edition 1910, published in an English edition with the help of N. J. van Warmelo under the title of *Bantu Phonology* in 1932). In 1906 he published his *Grundzüge einer Vergleichenden Grammatik der Bantusprachen*;[1] but it was in the *Lautlehre* that Meinhof propounded his theory of Ur-Bantu, upon which basis he has constructed all his comparative phonological and grammatical work. Meinhof received his phonetic impulse from Lepsius, of whom he was an ardent disciple. Most German investigators of Bantu languages have followed Meinhof's system of analysis, and some, particularly O. Dempwolff and W. Bourquin, have elaborated his comparative study of Bantu roots. Meinhof had started in 1911 the *Zeitschrift für Kolonialsprachen*, later continued as the *Zeitschrift für Eingeborenen-Sprachen*. Of these publications, to which many of Meinhof's disciples have contributed, he was the editor until his death.

[1] 2nd ed. 1948.

The Southern Bantu Languages

The earliest records of the Southern Bantu languages are to be found in the shape of vocabularies appended to the accounts of travellers.[1] Most of these have proved to be of little value, often very inaccurate, with a weird method of spelling African words. The most serious of these travel vocabularies are those compiled by Heinrich Lichtenstein and appended to his *Travels in Southern Africa* (1803-6). Lichtenstein gives a long vocabulary of Xhosa, with sundry grammatical observations and numerous phrases, and a further section 'upon the Language of the Beetjuans', in which we have the earliest record of Tswana. Despite the fact that Lichtenstein had shown sufficient linguistic acumen to be able to classify broadly the language-grouping in Southern Africa, these records showed a very poor appreciation of the nature of Xhosa and Tswana; and their author completely failed to understand the principle of the noun-prefix and the concord—a principle fully recognized by Brusciotto 150 years before.

How this all-important principle of Bantu grammatical structure could elude any serious student is incomprehensible, and yet we find that John Bennie, who has been called 'the Father of Kafir literature', entirely missed discovering the 'alliterative concord', despite his long and serious contact, as a Presbyterian missionary, with Xhosa. Bennie published in 1826 *A Systematic Vocabulary of the Kaffrarian Language*, in which he included a 12-page grammatical portion. He also left a larger manuscript grammar dated 1832, and manuscript portions of an English–Xhosa and a Xhosa–English dictionary. Bennie actually divided the nouns into fourteen 'classes', and yet he failed to detect the principle of concord in the sentence-structure. That he was no mean student of the language, however, is evidenced by the fact that he actually recorded the existence of semantic tone.

The first published grammar of a Southern Bantu language was William B. Boyce's *Grammar of the Kafir Language* (1834). In this little treatise of 54 quarto pages Boyce clearly expounds the principle of what he terms 'the Euphonic or Alliteral Concord', the 'peculiarity upon which the whole grammar of the Language depends'. His colleague W. J. Davis, who edited the second and subsequent editions of Boyce's work, termed the alliterative concord 'the key to the etymological structure of the language'.

Boyce divided the nouns of Xhosa 'into twelve Classes or Declensions, eight of which comprise the singular prefixes, and four those of the plural'. Throughout the various editions of this work the term 'declension' was preferred to 'class'; later Davis replaced this by the term 'species', following Appleyard's example. Today, not only for Xhosa, but in Bantu language studies generally, whether comparative or individual, the term 'class' is used to denote the grouping of nouns according to their prefixes and concordial agreements.

The earliest grammar of a language of the Sotho group was that of J. Archbell (1837), but as this was almost a word-for-word adaptation of Boyce's work it marked no real advance. Eugène Casalis' *Études sur la langue séchuana* (1841) was also but a slight account.

John W. Appleyard (1814–74), however, brought real scholarship to the study of Southern Bantu languages. His 1847 contribution towards a classification of the languages has already been noticed. In 1850 he produced *The Kafir Language*, which, after 64 pages of preliminary comparative work, devoted 300 pages to a close grammatical study of Xhosa. In this he takes opportunity vigorously to attack disjunctive writing, which had then already begun to be used in Tswana. Throughout his grammatical work Appleyard displayed a true philological grip, and used very sane terminology. Altogether his grammar is a masterly piece of work and deserves to have seen more than the solitary 1850 edition. Boyce had classified the nouns into twelve classes, differentiating singular from plural, 1–8 being singular and 9–12 plural;[2]

---
[1] For instance Xhosa in Sparrman (1776), Barrow (1801), and Lichtenstein (1806); Tsonga in White (1800) and Boteler (1826); Tswana in Lichtenstein (1806) and Burchell (1824).

[2] 1 *um-*; 2 *i(li)-*; 3 *in-*; 4 *isi-*; 5 *u(lu)-*; 6 *um-*; 7 *ubu-*; 8 *uku-*; 9 *aba-*; 10 *ama-*; 11 *izi-*; 12 *imi-*; no difference being made between Bantu classes 8 and 10.

Archbell had followed suit for Tswana, as did Schreuder in 1850 for Zulu, making, however, thirteen classes. Appleyard, however, departed from this method, and classified according to eight 'species', bracketing singular and plural, and establishing an order of classes[1] which was used in all subsequent Xhosa grammars down to the second edition of McLaren's *Grammar of the Kaffir Language*, which appeared in 1917. Although Grout had adopted this same order in 1859 and even in his second edition of 1893, Bishop Colenso made a departure in class-order in his grammatical work of 1859, and was followed by subsequent Zulu writers. It was not until the publication of the second edition of Doke's *Text-book of Zulu Grammar* (1931) and Welsh's third edition of McLaren, under the revised title of *A Xhosa Grammar* (1936), that the two Nguni languages reverted again to a common class-numbering, this time based, as far as possible, upon the order adopted by Meinhof for comparative work. It still, however, brackets singular and plural into single classes, whereas Meinhof and other comparative workers separate singulars from plurals, keeping them as close together in order as possible.

Although phonetic principles had to a certain extent guided the reduction to writing of the South African vernaculars, the first great protagonist for the application of these principles in Southern Bantu languages was Lewis Grout, of the American Board Mission, who reached Natal in 1847, where among other things he developed a mission press. In 1852 Grout read a paper before the American Oriental Society in New York entitled 'An Essay on the Phonology and Orthography of the Zulu and Kindred Dialects in Southern Africa'.[2] Even as early as this the missionaries were exercised over orthography reforms and a Committee on Uniform Orthography had been set up, on which Grout served. In this early paper he introduced his subject by discussing Pickering's system of orthography as prepared for the North American Indian languages. Grout's proposals were, however, too detailed and revolutionary to commend themselves to his colleagues. For Zulu he actually deduced ninety-one fundamental sounds! And among his proposals were a number of special symbols.

In 1859 Grout printed his great work *The Isizulu: a Grammar of the Zulu Language* at the Mission Press, Umsunduzi. A large part of the introduction to this work deals with the Lepsius 'Standard Alphabet' which the mission had at that time decided to adopt. Grout boldly stood for this, which entailed the introduction into the Zulu alphabet of ten new symbols.

The Lepsius alphabet, which has had such a marked influence upon many Bantu orthographies elsewhere in Africa, was employed by C. H. Hahn in his *Grundzüge einer Grammatik des Hereró*, which appeared in 1857. This alphabet was modified by Carl Meinhof and used in his Bantu work. Meinhof's system was what K. Endemann employed in his Grammar and Dictionary of Sotho. In this orthography use is made of diacritic signs added to the letters to mark significant differences. A heritage of this method is still to be found in some of the symbols used in the latest Sotho orthographies. In 1927 the International Institute of African Languages and Cultures issued a pamphlet *The Practical Orthography of African Languages*, embodying recommendations based on the principles of the International Phonetic Association, which may be described as the 'monotype' school of phonetics. The whole question of orthography for the Southern Bantu languages was fully discussed by G. P. Lestrade in his paper 'Some Remarks on the Practical Orthography of the South African Bantu Languages'[3] in 1928.

Various orthography settlements had from time to time been reached in individual languages, as for instance those in Sotho arrived at in 1906, and those in Zulu which culminated in the findings of the Durban Conference of 1907. But with the formation of the Union Government Advisory Committee on Bantu Studies and Research, a Central Orthography Committee was set up to take charge of the question of reforms in the various

---

[1] Following the order of Boyce's eight singulars.
[2] Published in the *Journal of the American Oriental Society*, 1853, vol. iii, no. 2, pp. 421–72.
[3] *Bantu Studies*, vol. iii, no. 3, pp. 261–73.

orthographies. Later, on the formation of the Inter-University Committee for African Studies, the functions of the Central Orthography Committee were continued, and work was carried out through subcommittees. The result is that settlements were reached in Northern Sotho (1930),[1] Xhosa (1931), Zulu (1934), and Tswana (1937). In Southern Rhodesia, after a survey undertaken by C. M. Doke in 1929, an orthography approved by the International Institute of African Languages and Cultures was adopted by the Government in 1931 for Shona. This settlement also entailed far-reaching proposals for the unification of the various Shona dialects.

A preliminary to orthographic settlement was a thorough phonetic study of the languages involved. Foremost in this field of study was Professor Carl Meinhof, who published the first edition of his renowned book, *Grundriss einer Lautlehre der Bantusprachen*, in 1899. This contained, *inter alia*, a phonological analysis of the Pedi dialect of Northern Sotho. In 1901 appeared Meinhof's *Das Tši-venda*, a thorough piece of work; and in 1924 his *Zur Lautlehre des Zulu*, of which an English translation was later incorporated in his *Introduction to the Phonology of the Bantu Languages* (1932). In all these studies Meinhof followed a common method based on comparison with his hypothetical 'Ur-Bantu'. In 1914 Paul Passy of the International Phonetic Association published a short description of Tsonga sounds in *La Langue Thonga* (*Miscellanea Phonetica*); while later contributions on this subject were made by N. J. van Warmelo[2] and W. M. Eiselen.[3] Professor Daniel Jones, too, had published a 16-page pamphlet on the *Pronunciation and Orthography of the Chindau Language*, dealing with an eastern member of the Shona group of languages. In 1916 Jones, in collaboration with Sol. T. Plaatje, produced *A Sechuana Reader*, a scientific study based on I.P.A. script. In 1926 C. M. Doke published *The Phonetics of the Zulu Language*, a descriptive study developed from an earlier 'Dissertation on the Phonetics of the Zulu Language'.[4] A. N. Tucker followed this in 1929 with his *Comparative Phonetics of the Suto-Chuana group of Bantu Languages*. In 1931 C. M. Doke published two reports resulting from a linguistic survey in Southern Rhodesia: *Report on the Unification of the Shona Dialects* and *A Comparative Study in Shona Phonetics*, the former of which was presented to the Legislative Assembly; and made proposals regarding a unification of the dialects and standardization.

An important subject in phonetic studies is that of tone; and it is remarkable to find that, as early as 1661, de Couto, who edited the *Gentio de Angola*, recorded the existence of semantic tone, though admittedly he did not fully realize what it was.[5] Tone is a difficult subject for the untrained investigator, and its existence was not again recorded until John Bennie wrote his manuscript Xhosa Grammar in 1832. In this, however, he wrote: 'The rising or the falling inflexion of the accent gives to words, which correspond in letters, a different signification: *bona*, see, they; *umnyama*, dark, the rainbow; *tiya*, snare, hate.' This phenomenon was unpublished in Xhosa until Appleyard referred to it in his grammar of 1850 where he stated: 'In addition to the accent, some words are further distinguished by a peculiar intonation. . . . Thus *itanga, hlanza, umkombe*, &c. express two or three different ideas, according to the particular mode of their pronunciation.' After Appleyard, tone passed unnoticed in Xhosa until Godfrey and McLaren mentioned it in 1915 and 1917 respectively. Probably K. Endemann was the first Bantu grammarian to attempt an analysis of tone. In his *Versuch einer Grammatik des Sotho* (1876) he describes three tones, and uses certain diacritic accents to mark them throughout his book; these he expanded to five tones in his subsequent *Wörterbuch* (1911), where each entry was carefully marked. Endemann also contributed

---

[1] The present orthography is based on a further revision in 1950.
[2] 'Zur Gwamba-Lautlehre', *Zeitschrift für Eingeborenen-Sprachen*, 1927, vol. xx, no. 3, pp. 221–31.
[3] 'Nasalverbindungen im Thonga', *Festschrift Meinhof*, 1927
[4] *Bulletin of the School of Oriental Studies*, 1923, vol. ii, pp. 685–729.
[5] Cf. 'Early Bantu Literature', by C. M. Doke, in *Bantu Studies*, 1935, vol. ix, no. 2, pp. 91–92.

notes on the intonation-system of Northern Sotho in his paper, 'Beitrag zu dem Capitel von den Tönen in den sogenannten Bantu-Sprachen'.[1] Ch. Endemann also contributed to our knowledge of tone in Bantu in his paper, 'Der Tonfall in den südostafrikanischen Bantusprachen', which appeared in *Vox* in 1916. A general appreciation of the importance of tone in Bantu was now recognized in scientific circles. Daniel Jones and S. T. Plaatje dealt with it in *A Sechuana Reader* (1916), giving a careful analysis and marking the tones in their texts. Professor Jones further developed his tone-studies in Tswana in two papers subsequently published: 'Words distinguished by Tone in Sechuana',[2] and 'The Tones of Sechuana Nouns'.[3] Meanwhile this study was very considerably advanced in South Africa by D. M. Beach's paper, 'The Science of Tonetics and its Application to Bantu Languages'.[4] Dr. Beach brought his knowledge of tone in Chinese to bear on the subject, and drew his material mainly from Xhosa. Individual intensive tone-analyses also appeared in C. M. Doke's *Phonetics of the Zulu Language* (1926), and in A. N. Tucker's work on 'Suto-Chuana' (1929). The next step was the application of the data collected to the problem of orthography. This, however, has only been done in a preliminary fashion, and the only Southern Bantu languages where any practical indication of tone is included in ordinary books are Xhosa, Northern Sotho, and Tswana, in which, for the present, it was decided to indicate tone only in such cases as would otherwise prove ambiguous.

The earliest Bantu grammatical works had had a medieval approach, based upon Latin grammar; the grammars of Southern Bantu languages well into the twentieth century took the modern European languages as the basis of their classification, one of the best of these being E. Jacottet's *Grammar of the Sesuto Language* (1927); and it is only in recent studies that a serious attempt has been made to find a truly Bantu mode for grammatical work. C. M. Doke tried out this new approach in his *Text Book of Zulu Grammar* (1927); this method has since been to a certain extent applied in the third edition of McLaren's *Xhosa Grammar*, edited by G. H. Welsh (1936), and to a fuller extent in B. I. C. van Eeden's *Inleiding tot die Studie van Suid-Sotho* (1941),[5] in *A Comparative Study of Kgalagadi, Kwena and other Sotho Dialects*[5] (1943) by D. F. v. d. Merwe and I. Schapera, in G. I. M. Mzamane's *Concise Treatise on Phuthi with special reference to its Relationship with Nguni and Sotho* (1949), and in D. Ziervogel's *Noordsotho-Leerboek*[5] (1949) and his *Grammar of Swazi* (1952). This entailed, among other things, a recognition of the conjunctive word as constituting the part of speech, the discarding of the terms *case* and *preposition* as not being applicable to Bantu languages, and the classification of the Ideophone and the Copulative as separate parts of speech. In 1935 appeared Doke's *Bantu Linguistic Terminology*, containing mainly a descriptive and critical dictionary of terms used in Bantu linguistics. The Inter-University Committee for African Studies, too, took a hand in this question of terminology, and in the use of names in tribal and linguistic classification; a note upon their findings in regard to this latter was published in *Bantu Studies*, vol. xi, pp. 373–5, under the title of 'The Spelling of Names of Bantu Languages and Tribes in English', written by G. P. Lestrade (1937).

Grammatical studies have also benefited much from work upon individual subjects. Numerous studies have been made upon the model of Meinhof's Ur-Bantu analysis, as, for instance, N. J. van Warmelo's *Die Gliederung der süd-afrikanischen Bantusprachen* (1927). Mention might also be made of W. Bourquin's 'Adverb und adverbiale Umschreibung im

[1] *Mitteilungen des Seminars für Orientalische Sprachen*, 1901, vol. iv, Abt. iii, pp. 37–41.
[2] *Festschrift Meinhof*, 1927.
[3] Memorandum VI of the International Institute of African Languages and Cultures, 1929.
[4] *Bantu Studies*, 1924, vol. ii, pp. 75–106.
[5] Though in these three publications the disjunctive word-division prevalent in the Sotho Group has been retained.

Kafir', contributed to the *Zeitschrift für Kolonialsprachen* (1912–13), J. Engelbrecht's *Suffixbildung in den südafrikanischen Bantusprachen* (1925), and G. P. Lestrade's 'Locative-class Nouns and Formatives in Sotho' in *Bantu Studies* (1938).

Interesting attempts have been made to produce grammars for Native students in the vernaculars. In 1908 E. Jacottet wrote *Grammar e nyenyane ea Sesotho*, which has been in fair demand. In 1922 A. R. Kempe and H. K. Leisegang published *Igrama lesizulu*, which, however, did not meet with the success it really deserved. P. E. Schwellnus wrote *Thlalosa-Polêlô* in 1931 for Northern Sotho and *Phenḓa-Luambo*[1] for Venda schools, and the former of these is in considerable demand. He also wrote an interesting little book on 'accent, intonation and poetic diction' in Northern Sotho in 1942, entitled *Kima le Kxalô le Mešitô ya Dirêtô*. These attempts have meant the searching for vernacular terminology which has been undertaken in several areas by Native teachers. A comprehensive list of such terms has been agreed upon in Natal for Zulu, and published in the *Native Teachers' Journal* (vol. xviii, no. 2, 1939), under the heading 'Zulu Terminology' (pp. 81–87).

The question of terminology is rightly one for the lexicographer, and some of the finest analytical reasoning in this connexion was done by W. Wanger in his *Catholic Zulu Terminology* (1913), which contains a masterly discussion of Zulu words and their applicability to European ideas. Wanger published in 1917 a splendid *Konversations-Grammatik der Zulu-Sprache*, full of idiomatic material. His real forte was lexicographical, however, and this, unfortunately, led him in 1927 to publish his *Scientific Zulu Grammar*, vol. i, a number of extremely speculative attempts to prove the connexion, on a lexicographical basis, between Zulu and Sumerian—thus spoiling a work otherwise valuable for its close grammatical analysis of Zulu.

For many years the best dictionary of a Southern Bantu language was A. T. Bryant's *Zulu-English Dictionary* of 1905, now out of print. In this, entries are made under the stem and not under the prefixes as is the case in so many other dictionaries, e.g. Mabille's for Southern Sotho and van Warmelo's for Venda. Entry by stem has obvious advantages in Bantu, and this method had been followed by J. L. Döhne in his *Zulu-Kafir Dictionary* as early as 1857, and by A. Kropf in his *Kafir-English Dictionary* in 1899. Endemann followed the same principle with his *Wörterbuch der Sotho-Sprache* (1911), a work not confined to any one of the Sotho clusters, but rather comparative in form.

For Southern Sotho the present standard dictionary is that by A. Mabille and H. Dieterlen, revised by R. A. Paroz in 1950; this was first published by Mabille as early as 1878, entitled *Sesuto-English Dictionary*; edited later by Dieterlen it went through several editions, entries being under the prefixes; the latest reclassification by Paroz is under stems, and is entitled *Southern Sotho-English Dictionary*. The most detailed Zulu-English Dictionary is that of C. M. Doke and the late B. W. Vilakazi, published in 1948, a book of 900 pages double-column.

The only really good English–Bantu dictionary dealing with a South African language is J. McLaren's *Concise English-Kafir Dictionary* of 1923. Most of the others are merely large vocabularies.

Bantu language study has profited by the careful collection of textual material which has gone on from time to time, and Bishop H. Callaway's contribution in this connexion must not be overlooked. He printed at Springvale Mission two outstanding books: *Nursery Tales, Traditions and Histories of the Zulus* (1866–8) and *The Religious System of the Amazulu* (1870). These publications are of the highest value for their language content. C. Hoffman also did valuable service in his *Sotho-Texte* (Northern Sotho) which appeared from time to time in the

---

[1] T. M. H. Endemann and E. F. N. Mudau issued a later book under similar title in 1940.

Zeitschrift für Eingeborenen-Sprachen. J. Stuart's Zulu readers, *uThulasizwe*, *uBaxoxele* and others, are also a valuable contribution. A variety of Tswana dialectal forms is illustrated in I. Schapera's *Mekgwa le Melaô ya Batswana* and his *Ditirafalô tsa Merafe ya Batswana*. In all the languages, today, African writers are beginning to make their contribution to Southern Bantu literature, and an increasing field for linguistic research is being provided thereby.

REFERENCES

R. N. CUST: *A Sketch of the Modern Languages of Africa*, vol. ii, pp. 289–434. Trubner & Co., London, 1883.

H. H. JOHNSTON: *A Comparative Study of the Bantu and Semi-Bantu Languages.* Oxford, vol. i, 1919; vol. ii, 1922.

I. SCHAPERA: *Select Bibliography of South African Native Life and Problems*, pp. 209–31. Oxford, 1941.

Papers by C. M. DOKE:

'A Preliminary Investigation into the State of the Native Languages of South Africa with Suggestions as to Research and the Development of Literature', *Bantu Studies*. Johannesburg, March 1933.
'The Earliest Records of Bantu', *Bantu Studies*. Johannesburg, June 1938.
'Early Bantu Literature', *Bantu Studies*. Johannesburg, June 1935.
'Bantu Language Pioneers of the Nineteenth Century', *Bantu Studies*. Johannesburg, Sept. 1940.
'The Growth of Comparative Bantu Philology', *African Studies*. Johannesburg, March 1943.
Bantu: Modern Grammatical, Phonetical and Lexicographical Studies since 1860. International African Institute, London, 1945.

II

THE CLASSIFICATION OF THE SOUTHERN BANTU LANGUAGES

FOR the purposes of this study two southern zones of Bantu have been included, viz. the important South-eastern zone, found in the Union of South Africa, Southern Mozambique, and the three Protectorates (of Bechuanaland, Basutoland, and Swaziland), and the South-central zone, comprising the Shona group of Southern Rhodesia and some contiguous areas. This roughly means the Bantu languages south of the Zambesi and east of the Kalahari Desert. It is a fairly compact area, but, naturally individual offshoots from the languages of these zones are found farther afield, as, for instance, the Ngoni of Nyasaland and of Tanganyika, dialects of Zulu, and the Lozi of Barotseland, Northern Rhodesia, a dialect of Southern Sotho. The Bantu languages of South-west Africa, though they might be considered 'southern' from the geographical point of view, are not included, as they belong to the Western Bantu and reveal characteristics strikingly distinct from those of the two zones included. In the northern portions of Bechuanaland, still south of the Zambesi, are certain isolated members of both Western (e.g. Yeye) and Central (e.g. Subiya) zones, and these have naturally been excluded.

The phonetic and morphological characteristics of these two southern zones will be discussed in succeeding chapters. Here it remains merely to give a classification of the groups, clusters, and dialects which fall within our survey. It will be found that there are individual languages which bridge between different groups, as Phuthi and Sotho-Ndebele, which show characteristics, and have historical connexions, derived from both Nguni and Sotho, or Lozi, a Sotho offshoot heavily influenced by Central Bantu. It will further be found that there are the remnants of extreme types, the exact relationship of which to the main groups has not yet been determined; such are Kutswe, Pai, and Lovedu, hitherto classed with Northern Sotho. Other languages, though definitely belonging to certain groups or clusters, have developed or become influenced away from the norm in such a way that they tend to stand apart from the other members of their grouping; some may even be survivors of a much earlier form; among these are such a dialect of Karanga as Mhari, and the Tavara and Budya dialects of Korekore, and perhaps the Kgalagadi dialect of Tswana.

The term 'zone'[1] is really a geographical term applied in a special way to a language area characterized by uniform or similar linguistic phenomena. In using this term it must be realized that individual members of a particular zone may today be living among members of a different zone owing to tribal migrations, but the zone label is taken from the habitat of the majority. This is the case with such languages as Lozi and Ngoni. While languages belonging to one zone differ in certain essential phenomena from languages belonging to another zone, yet languages belonging to the same zone need not be mutually understood.

The term 'group'[2] indicates an aggregation of languages possessing common salient phonetic and grammatical features, and having a high degree of mutual understanding, so that members can, without serious difficulty, converse with one another. Naturally individual cases may arise (as with Western Shona, which could not join the Shona literary unification) in which one section of the group has developed historically out of great mutual intelligibility with the

---

[1] *Bantu Linguistic Terminology*, p. 221.
[2] Ibid., p. 67, where the term 'cluster' is, however, used with this connotation.

other members, and yet must still be considered as belonging to that group. Between the clusters within the group there is always some possibility of language unification. The name given to a group has often to be of an artificial type, as in the case of Nguni, Shona, Tsonga, &c., since each dialect usually has its distinctive name, and no common group name exists.

A language 'cluster'[1] is an aggregation of dialects which contribute to, or use, a common literary form, e.g. the Tswana cluster comprises Tlhaping, Kgatla, Ngwato, Rolong, Kwena, and several other dialects. Several such clusters may be found within a language group; and the advisability of the literary unification of the clusters belonging to the same group must not be lost sight of.

'Dialect'[2] indicates the local form of language. In Bantu it is applicable to the language of a tribe, and more particularly of a clan section of a tribe. It is best to reserve this term for such ultimate local vernaculars as are recognized by the Native speakers under special names; hence Qwabe, Ngoni, and Ndebele (of Rhodesia) are dialects of Zulu, and Nohwe, Harava, Mbire, &c., are dialects of Zezuru. Generally a number of dialects contribute to a common literary form. Artificial barriers may, however, bolster up dialectal literary variants; for instance the fact that Ndebele in Southern Rhodesia is under different governmental administration from the main literary form, Zulu, has resulted in the sponsoring of a separate Ndebele literature. Much the same influences have led to the relatively recent development of Northern Sotho as a literary and educational medium distinct from Southern Sotho, though in this case the distinction is between clusters and not mere dialects.

South-central Zone

This zone comprises a single Bantu group, viz. Shona. This group is divided into six clusters as follows:

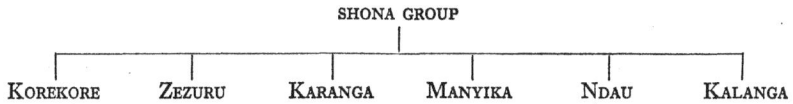

The six clusters have dialectal forms as hereunder:

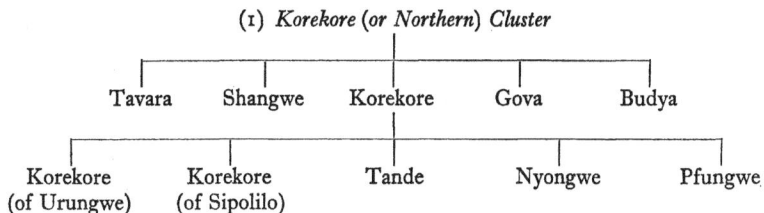

This makes a total of nine dialectal varieties, of which five are typical, and four display certain definite divergencies from the central forms.

[1] Ibid., p. 113, where the term 'group' is, however, used with this connotation.
[2] Ibid., p. 91.

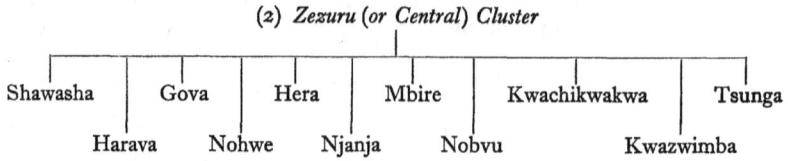

There is no great variation between these dialects.

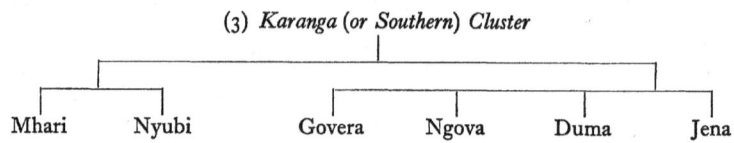

Duma and associated dialects constitute typical Karanga, while Mhari and Nyubi are extreme types.

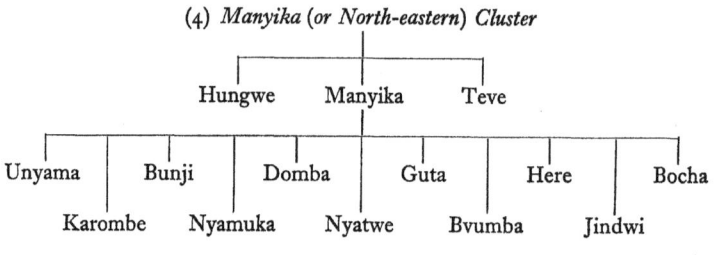

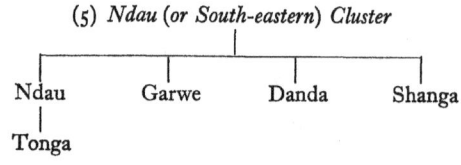

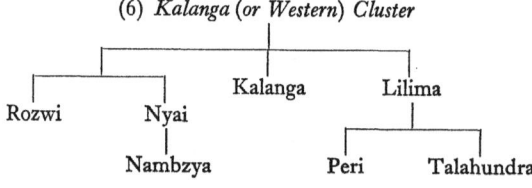

THE SOUTHERN BANTU LANGUAGES

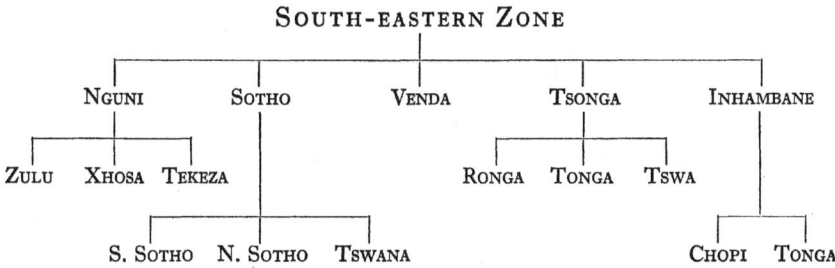

In the above table the groups are represented by Nguni, Sotho, Venda, Tsonga, and Inhambane. The clusters are Zulu, Xhosa, and Tekeza; Southern Sotho, Northern Sotho, and Tswana; Venda; Ronga, Tonga, and Tswa; Chopi and Tonga.

Subdivision according to dialects is as follows:

(A) NGUNI GROUP

(1) *Zulu Cluster*

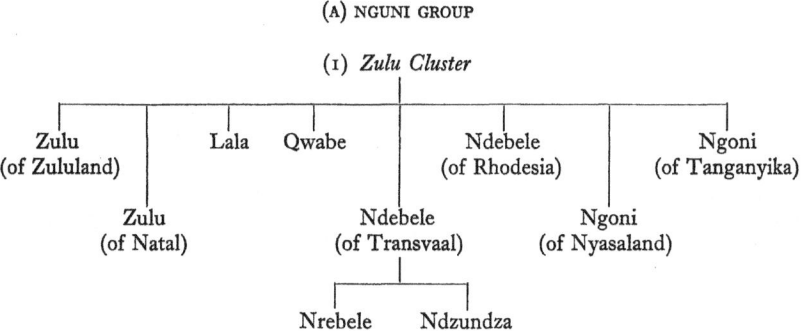

Rhodesian Ndebele has been developed considerably as a separate literary form from standard Zulu, based on the Zululand and Natal types; some literary work has been done in Nyasaland Ngoni.

(2) *Xhosa Cluster*

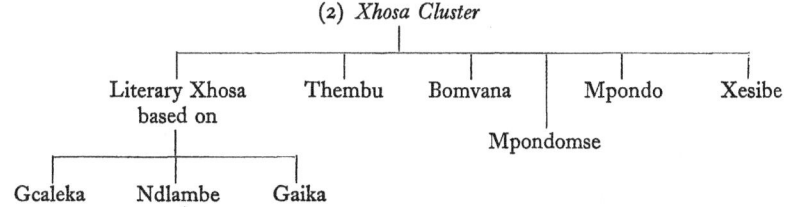

Xesibe tends towards the Tekeza cluster, and Mpondo is considerably different from standard Xhosa.

THE CLASSIFICATION OF

(3) *Tekeza Cluster*

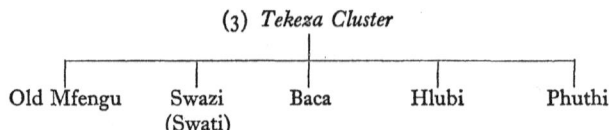

'Old Mfengu' is extinct; the modern 'Fingoes' speak Xhosa. Swazi is the most important member, and Phuthi is very heavily influenced from Sotho.

(B) SOTHO GROUP

(1) *Southern Sotho Cluster*

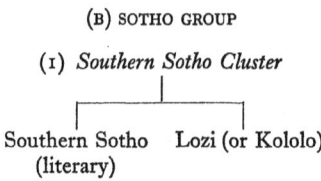

Lozi (of Barotseland) is considerably influenced by Central Bantu. There are no distinctive dialectal types of Southern Sotho.

(2) *Northern Sotho Cluster*

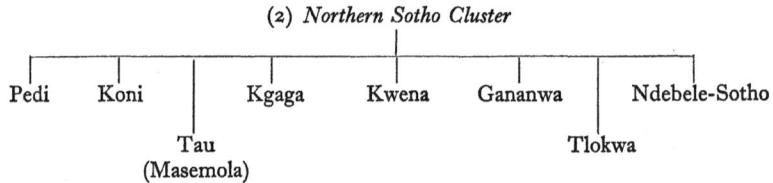

In addition the languages of (1) Lovedu, (2) Phalaborwa, and (3) Pai, Kutswe, and Pulana, spoken in northern and eastern Transvaal, differ very considerably from Northern Sotho, but their classification has not yet been definitely determined.[1]

(3) *Tswana Cluster*

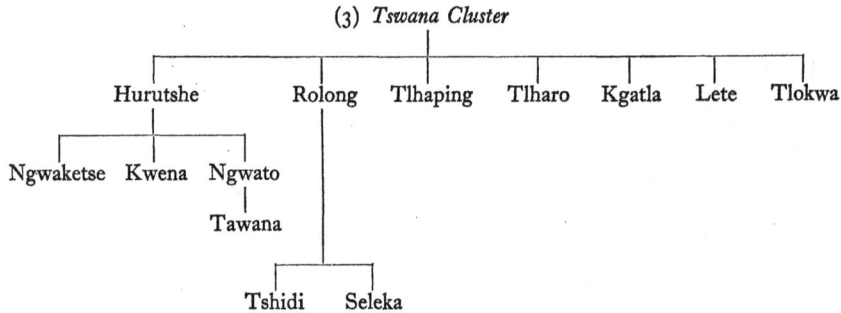

Kgalagadi[2] is sufficiently distinct from Tswana to warrant a separate classification, but more information is necessary before this can be done satisfactorily.

---

[1] N. J. v. Warmelo in his *Preliminary Survey* (pp. 108–16) classifies the Pedi, Tau, Kwena, and Koni as 'Central Sotho', the Pai, Kutswe, and Pulana as 'Eastern Sotho', the Phalaborwa and Lovedu as 'North-eastern Sotho', and the Kgaga, Tlokwa, Gananwa, and Birwa (as well as some Koni elements) as 'Northern Sotho'.

[2] D. F. v. d. Merwe gives the following dialects of Kgalagadi: Ngologa, Koma, and Kuwe.

THE SOUTHERN BANTU LANGUAGES

(C) VENDA

There is little distinctive dialectal variation in Venda, the literary form being based on the Phani and Tavhatsindi dialects.

(D) TSONGA GROUP

(1) *Ronga Cluster*

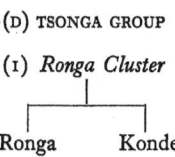

Konde is a southern dialect influenced by Zulu.

(2) *Tonga Cluster*

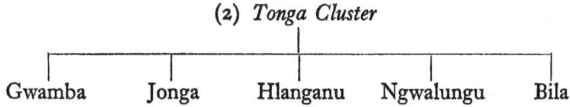

Gwamba has been built up of elements of the other four dialects of this cluster with accretions from Ronga. Bila seems to be a buffer with the Tswa cluster.

(3) *Tswa Cluster*

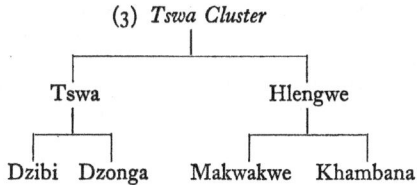

(E) INHAMBANE GROUP

(1) *Chopi Cluster*

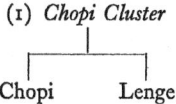

(2) *Tonga Cluster*

(no distinctive dialectal forms)

REFERENCES

H. H. JOHNSTON: *A Comparative Study of the Bantu and Semi-Bantu Languages*, vol. ii, pp. 1–13. Oxford 1922.

N. J. v. WARMELO: *A Preliminary Survey of the Bantu Tribes of South Africa*. Native Affairs Dept. Ethnographical Publications, vol. v, 1935.

C. M. DOKE: *Modern Grammatical, Phonetical and Lexicographical Studies since 1860*. International African Institute, 1945.

M. GUTHRIE: *The Classification of the Bantu Languages*. International African Institute, 1948.

III

THE PHONETICS AND PHONOLOGY OF THE SOUTHERN BANTU LANGUAGES

A. The Vowels

1. The Southern Bantu languages are typical of Bantu in having a perfectly balanced system with one low vowel, **a**, and an equal number of equally positioned front and back vowels. Shona has the simplest system with the three basic vowels **a, i, u,** and one mid-forward vowel, **e,** and one mid-back vowel, **o**: a simple five-vowel system. Chopi, of the Inhambane group, has similar vowels. Most of the language groups, however, Nguni, Venda, and Tsonga, have two varieties each of mid-forward and mid-back vowels, viz. e and ɛ, o and ɔ. As these pairs constitute single phonemes in each case, their differentiation being dependent upon the quality of the vowel in a succeeding syllable, it is unnecessary to distinguish them in a practical orthography. The Sotho group is clearly distinguished from the others in having, in addition to the seven vowels, two extremely 'close' types of **i** and **u,** which might be indicated by the symbols **î** and **û**. Orthographically it is necessary to represent the Sotho vowels by seven separate symbols, here again the vowels **e** and **o** each having an open and a close member of the phoneme. Strangely enough the Lozi and Kgalagadi dialects of Sotho differ from the main groups in employing only five-vowel phonemes, as in Nguni; and the Nguni (Tekeza) dialect of Phuthi is so influenced by Sotho that it employs the seven phònemes of that group.

2. On page 27 are typical vowel charts to illustrate the positions of the vowels in the three types found in Southern Bantu, in comparison with the cardinal vowel positions, as used by the International Phonetic Association.[1]

3. In most Southern Bantu groups vowels occur both long and short; in most cases the vowel is lengthened in penultimate position in the word, and especially so in the case of the penultimate syllable of a sense-group. In Shona, however, long vowels are rarely found, and certainly not as typical penultimates; several cases of recorded long vowels have proved to be in fact double syllables.

All Southern Bantu vowels are tense; lax vowels are not recorded apart from occasional occurrence in emotional ideophones. All vowels are oral; nasalized vowels (apart from ideophonic occurrence) are only found as assimilations between nasal consonants. All vowels are pure; typically there are no diphthongs in Southern Bantu, though a slurring of juxtaposed vowels is found in Shona and sometimes in Sotho, particularly in verse composition.

In those languages which have an open and a close member of the mid-forward and mid-back vowels it is a general rule that the close member is used when the vowel of the succeeding syllable is close, **i** or **u,** or when the succeeding syllable is composed of a syllabic consonant implying a suppressed close vowel, e.g. m̩, in Zulu, < **mu,** or ŋ̍ in Sotho < Bantu **ni.** Examples:

Z. ɓɔːna (see) > perf. -ɓoniːlɛ; lɛːlɔ (that, cl. 5), but leːli (this, cl. 5); nom̩faːna (and the boy).

S.S. kiaɓɔːna (I see) > hakiɓoːni (I do not see); fɛːla (finish) > caus. fediːsa; tsɛːbɛ (ear) > loc. tsebeːŋ̍.

---

[1] A full explanation of the Cardinal Vowel Chart system is given in Westermann and Ward's *Practical Phonetics for Students of African Languages*, pp. 20–28.

THE SOUTHERN BANTU LANGUAGES

(a) Type 1, five vowels, five phonemes, illustrated by Shona:

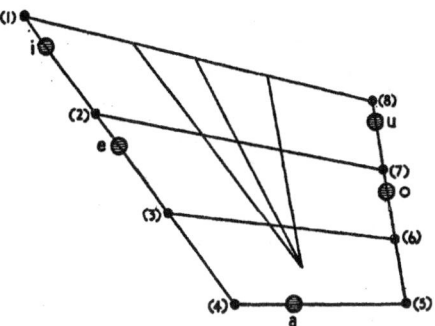

(b) Type 2, seven vowels, five phonemes, illustrated by Nguni:

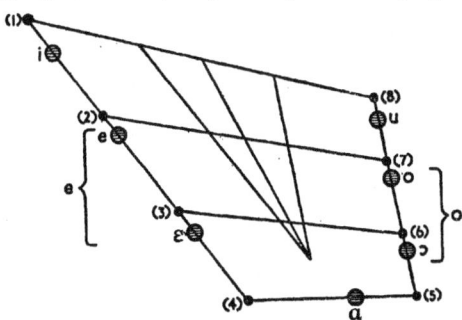

(c) Type 3, nine vowels, seven phonemes, illustrated by Sotho:

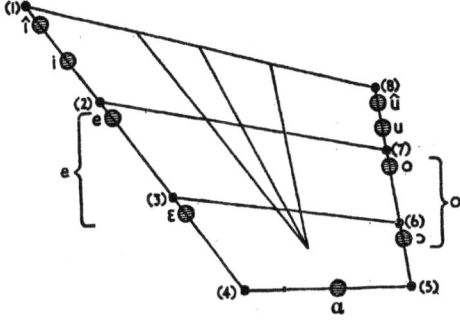

B. Phenomena Associated with the Vowels

1. THE INITIAL VOWEL. The five main language-groups of the Southern Bantu are remarkably diverse in regard to the feature of an initial vowel with the noun prefixes. The Sotho and Venda groups lack the initial vowel entirely, having monosyllabic prefixes typically, e.g. S.S. *mō-*, *ba-*, *lē-*, *sē-*, Ve. *mu-*, *vha-*, *ma-*, *zwi-*. In these languages the phenomena of elision and coalescence of vowels are practically non-existent. In Nguni, on the other hand, an initial vowel, similar to the vowel of the prefix, is found regularly with all ordinary[1] nouns, the noun prefixes being typically disyllabic, e.g. Z. *umu-*, *aβa-*, *isi-*, *uβu-*. Shona is unique in that, while no initial vowel appears with the nouns in isolation, there is latent an initial vowel, similar to the vowel of the prefix, which exerts an influence upon prefixal formatives ending in -*a*, and, in the Karanga cluster, upon preceding words ending in -*a*; this influence is to cause coalescence over most of the Shona area and substitution of *e* in the Manyika cluster. The prefixes in Shona, therefore, are best represented as follows: (*u*)*mu-*, (*a*)*va-*, (*i*)*mi-*, (*u*)*ru-*, &c. Tsonga presents quite another feature in regard to the initial vowel; the Tonga cluster uses an initial *e-* with all ordinary classes, while the Ronga and Tswa clusters use the vowel *a-*. The employment of these initials in Tsonga has been, for many years, neglected in the writing and seems to be, to a certain extent, falling into desuetude in the languages. The general effect of the vowel, however, is to influence formatives such as *na-* and *ha-*, changing them to *ni-* and *hi-* by substitution of *i*.

Much has been written and discussed concerning the function and grammatical rôle of the initial vowel in Bantu; by some it has been termed an 'article', owing to its lapsing in certain constructions, such as with vocatives, axiomatic negatives, and after demonstratives. Other considerations, however, operate in Bantu languages to distinguish between definite and indefinite uses of nouns, and it is best still to refer to this feature by the non-committal term 'initial vowel'.

In Zulu the initial vowel is generally retained and exerts coalescing influence on the final -*a* of a preceding formative, except:[2]

(a) After pronouns of the 1st and 2nd persons, e.g. *mina-muntu* (I the person).
(b) After demonstrative pronouns, e.g. *lowo-muntu* (that person).
(c) In axiomatic negatives and positives, e.g. *angiβoni-muntu* (I see nobody); *uβona-muntu na?* (do you see anybody?). This principle is extended to apply to qualificatives, e.g. compare *ngiβona umuntu omkhulu* (I see a big person) and *angiβoni-muntu-mkhulu* (I see no big person).
(d) When nouns are inflected to form: (i) vocative interjectives, e.g. *muntu!* (O man!); (ii) locatives with prefix *ku-*, e.g. *kumuntu* (to the person); (iii) compound nouns, e.g. *umnini-muntu* (the owner of the person).

Similar rules obtain in Tsonga. It is noteworthy that, in this group, an initial vowel is assumed in certain morphological instances, as when qualificatives are used pronominally, e.g. To. *etihomu ta-mina* (my cattle) but *eta-makweru* (those of my brother), and may occur with locatives, e.g. Ro. *amisaβeni* (on earth).

2. ELISION OF VOWELS. This feature is practically confined to the languages which employ an initial vowel, and is of two kinds: initial elision, the elision of the first vowel of a word, and final elision, that of the last vowel of a word. Initial elision is a compulsory morphological process, as illustrated in the previous section. Final elision, on the other hand, is optional and consequent upon quick or fluent speech, as in Zulu: *βonk'aβantu* for *βonke aβantu* (everybody); *asifun'ukuziβon'izinkaβ'ezimnyama* for *asifuni ukuziβona izinkaβi ezimnyama*

---

[1] Nouns of cls. 1a and 2a are excluded from this consideration.
[2] The noun *umuntu* is the test example used.

(we do not want to see the black oxen). Such elisions sometimes involve a semi-vowel as well, as in *lod'ukhuni* (only firewood) for *lodwa ukhuni*, since a mere contraction to *dw'u* is an impossible pronunciation in Zulu.

A type of internal elision, which is compulsory, is that of the vowel of formatives preceding vowel-verb stems, of which the vowel is always secondary and potentially strong, e.g. *sala* (we refusing) < *si-*+*ala*; *ɓayenza* (they are doing) with aux. *-ya-*; *ngizoyosa* (I shall roast it) with obj. concd. *yi-*.

3. COALESCENCE OF VOWELS. Here again, this feature is dependent almost entirely upon the existence of an initial vowel with the noun-prefix. Coalescence, however, is a feature of Shona also, where the latent initial vowel exerts its influence. Though there are varying subsidiary cases of coalescence, the typical Bantu instances are of the basic vowel α when followed by another basic vowel, with the following result: $\alpha+i > e$; $\alpha+\alpha > \alpha$; $\alpha+u > o$, in each case the resulting vowel being secondary, and usually having a potentiality stronger than the basic vowels.

In Zulu, coalescence occurs with the possessive concords, with the conjunctive formative *na-*, and with the adverbial formatives *nga-*, *kuna-*, *njenga-*, and *nganga-*, e.g. poss. *wa-*+*umuntu* > *womuntu*, *wa-*+*imithi* > *wemithi*, *wa-*+*amakhosi* > *wamakhosi*; similarly: *naɓantu*, *nenkosi*, *nomame*, with the conjunctive formative. The pronominal possessive stems *-ithu* and *-inu* (1st and 2nd persons plural respectively) cause coalescence, giving *wethu*, *wenu*, &c.

In Shona the instances are very similar to those in Nguni, being as follows: (*a*) in possessive formation, e.g. *mŋana womukadzi* (the woman's child < (*u*)*mukadzi*), *mŋana wemhuka* (the young of the animal < (*i*)*mhuka*); (*b*) after *na-* (conjunctive or instrumental), e.g. *nomusikana* (and the girl), *navanhu* (and people); (*c*) after *sa-*, e.g. *sehuku* (like a fowl), *somunhu* (like a person). Manyika does not share this feature with the other Shona clusters, but features substitution of *e*.

In the Karanga cluster of Shona, coalescence is carried still farther, and is normal after verbs ending in the vowel *-a* (where in Nguni elision would take place), the resultant being a compound expression: e.g. *ndinodo-munhu*, Ze. *ndinoda munhu* (I like a person), *vanorise-mbudzi*, Ze. *vanorisa mbudzi* (they are herding goats).

Coalescence of vowels is not found in Tsoŋga and Sotho apart from that with possessive pronominal stems of the 1st and 2nd persons plur., Ts. *-iru* and *-inu*, S.S. *-ēsō* and *-ēnō*. In Venda the only traces are in certain verbal auxiliary formations, e.g. *-to-* < *ita*+*u-* (infin.); this sort of formation is common in Shona, e.g. *-garo-* < *gara*+(*k*)*u-*.

4. SUBSTITUTION OF VOWELS. In the Manyika cluster of Shona, coalescence does not ordinarily take place; instead, substitution of the vowel *e* occurs before all nouns other than those of cls. 1a and 2a (which have no latent initial vowel), when the formatives *na-* (conjunctive), *nga-* (instrumental), *sa-* (comparative) and the possessive concords are prefixed, e.g. *kashiri kemupxere* (the child's little bird < (*u*)*mupxere*); *newanhu* (and people < (*a*)*wanhu*); *ŋgemutsa* (graciously < (*u*)*mutsa*).[1]

Tsonga employs substitution of *i* in two of the above instances, viz. with conjunctive *na-* and instrumental *ha-*, e.g. *na-tatana* (and my father), where there is no initial vowel; *ni-ʋanhu* (and the people < To. *e-ʋanhu*); *hi-nsati* (by the woman < Ro. *a-nsati*).

5. PENULTIMATE *i*. In Southern Bantu, apart from the emotional speech of ideophones and interjections, monosyllabic words are not favoured; there are monosyllabic demonstratives in Nguni, e.g. in Z. *lo*, *le*, *la*; and, in the Karanga of Shona, monosyllabic nouns, such as *she* (headman), *ɓge* (stone), *go* (wasp) are found; but most of the languages avoid the monosyllabic word by adding a prefix or a suffix. When the prefix is used it is *i-* (in Sotho the open type, written *e*, Jacottet *ē*); when the suffix is used, it is generally *-na* as in Zulu *dlana*,

---

[1] In the Bemba group of Central Bantu, while the main member, Bemba, employs coalescence, Lamba, another member of the group, employs substitution of *e* in these circumstances.

imperative of *-dla* (eat), and with the absolute pronouns *mina*, *zona*, &c. When prefixal, *i-* takes the stress and is therefore called 'penultimate *i*'.

In Nguni (Z.) penultimate *i* occurs in imperative singulars of monosyllabic verbs, e.g. *-dla* > *idla* or *yidla*, *-sho* (say) < *isho* or *yisho*. In X. this becomes *-si-* in the participial mood, e.g. *ndisiva* (I hearing) < *va*.

In Sotho penultimate *e* occurs in certain tenses with monosyllabic verbs, e.g. in S.S. participial *kē-ē-tla* (I coming), imperative *ē-ja*, *ē-jang* (eat!).

In Shona penultimate *i* occurs: (i) with certain nouns of monosyllabic stem, e.g. *ishe* (cl. 1a, headman), *iŋgwe* (cl. 9, leopard), *ibge* (cl. 5, stone); (ii) with monosyllabic adjectives agreeing with cls. 5, 9, and 10, e.g. *ina* (four), *itṣa* (new); (iii) with absolute pronouns of the 3rd person,[1] e.g. *iye* (cl. 1), *idzo* (cl. 10); and (iv) with the imperative (sing. and plur.) of monosyllabic verbs, e.g. *idya* (eat), pl. *idyai*.

C. The Consonants

The Consonantal Systems of the six main groups of Southern Bantu differ considerably in general complexion. Nguni has plain consonants and click consonants. Sotho has plain

PHONETIC CHART OF PLAIN CONSONANTS FOR SOUTHERN BANTU

		Bilabial	Denti-labial	Dental	Alveolar	Retroflex	Labio-alveolar	Prepalatal	Palatal	Prevelar	Velar	Glottal
Explosive	rad. eject. asp. voic.	p p' ph b		ṭ' ṭh ḍ	t t' th d	ṭ' ṭh ḍ			c' ch ɟ		k k' kh g	
Implosive		ɓ			ɗ							
Nasal	contin. syll.	m m̩	(ɱ)	n̪ n̪̩	n n̩	ɳ	(ɲ̪)	ɲ ɲ̩	(ɲ)		ŋ ŋ̩	
Rolled	contin. syll.				r r̩	ɽ						
Flapped	voic.				ɾ							
Lateral	contin. syll.			ḻ	l l̩	ɭ						
Fricative	med. unv. voic.	ɸ β	f v		s z		ṣ ẓ	ʃ ʒ		ɧ	x ɣ	h ɦ
	lat. unv. voic.				ɬ ɮ							
Affricate	med. rad. eject. asp. voic.	pf ɸf' ɸfh bv ɓv			ts ts' tsh dz		tṣ dẓ	tʃ tʃ' tʃh dʒ			kx' kxh	
	lat. eject. asp. voic.				tɬ' tɬh dɮ						(kɬ') kɬh	
Semi-vowel		(w)	β̆						j		w	

[1] Pronouns of the 1st and 2nd persons in Shona have a static *i*; note *iye* > *naye*, but *isu* (we) > *nesu*.

consonants and certain compounds, only S.S. employing clicks. Shona has plain consonants and a large range of velarized forms. Venda, in addition to plain consonants, has limited palatalized and velarized forms; while Tsonga has only plain consonants. Forms with velar glide and palatal glide are frequent in Chopi (Inhambane group).

REMARKS ON SOUTHERN BANTU PLAIN CONSONANTS

1. Certain general features of Southern Bantu consonantal charts stand out, for instance the distinction between ejective and aspirated explosives and affricates, the use of lateral fricatives and lateral affricates, the presence of implosives in certain groups and similarly of the so-called 'whistling fricatives', and the wide employment of affricates. Certain other features, typical of Central Bantu and perhaps of Bantu as a whole, are also found here: the flapped lateral, the bilabial voiced fricative, the range of homorganic nasals, and the general aversion from heterorganic combinations. While there are marked distinctions between the different groups dealt with, the greatest division is found to be between Shona, representing South-central Bantu, and the languages of the South-eastern zone. This is only to be expected.

2. Four main types of EXPLOSIVE CONSONANTS are found in Southern Bantu: radical, ejected, aspirated, and voiced. Radical explosives are unvoiced forms without either ejection or aspiration. These are found in Shona, but not in South-eastern Bantu, except in the insufficiently investigated Kgalagadi. In Zulu the *k* appearing in such words as *kahle*, *ukuthi*, &c., has a slight degree of voicing. Ejectives are a typical South-eastern feature. They are articulated with simultaneous glottal closure and compression of the air-passage above the glottis; this gives a characteristic sharpness to the enunciation. All the South-eastern groups use ejective explosives and affricates, often in sharp distinction from the aspirated forms. Aspirates are featured by the audible rush of air following the release. In Shona generally both ejection and aspiration are unknown, but in Ndau (Eastern Shona) both occur regularly with explosives and affricates, and in Western Shona, especially Kalanga and Lilima, aspiration of explosives occurs. The following examples of semantic distinction, from Zulu, may be given: **k'a:k'a** (encircle), **kha:kha** (be acrid), **t'ɛ:ŋga** (wave about) **thɛ:ŋga** (barter), **p'et'u** (of turning inside out), **phethu** (of crowding over). Voiced explosives do not occur as regularly as the unvoiced, unless accompanied by the homorganic nasal, as **mb, nd, ŋg**, &c., although this combination is unknown in the Sotho group. In Sotho **b** is very softly pronounced and gives way to the fricative (β) in N.S. In Shona **b** and **d** are very rare, implosive forms being commonly used. The explosives **b, d,** and **g** are regularly used in Nguni. Alveolar **d** is seldom used in its simple form in the other groups, however. Sotho uses the flapped lateral (**l**), or in S.S. a type of velar-stop explosive. Venda more commonly employs the dental (ḓ). Tsonga has the alveolar type in To. and Ts., but Ro. uses the retroflex form (ḍ). The voiced velar, **g**, is regular in all the groups except Sotho, where it only occurs in a few borrowed words. Venda is unique in its use of dental explosives (ṱ', ṱh, and ḓ) phonemically distinct from the alveolars; dental consonants also extend to the nasal and lateral types. On the other hand, the Ronga cluster of Tsonga is unique in its employment of retroflex explosives (ṭ', ṭh, and ḍ), a feature similarly extended to the nasal and rolled consonants; Venda has a retroflex lateral. Palatal explosives (c', ch, and ɟ) are found in Xhosa of the Nguni group, in Tonga of the Tsonga group, and in Kgalagadi of the Sotho group.

3. IMPLOSIVE CONSONANTS have a certain limited range in Eastern and Southern Bantu areas, and in Southern Bantu are confined to Shona, Nguni, and Inhambane. Implosives may be described as closure sounds in the production of which there is a simultaneous closure of the glottis, the air between the two points of closure being rarefied by increasing the volume of the oral and pharyngeal cavities, so that when the front release takes place

an inrush of the air results to fill the cavity. This speech-sound is usually voiced because of the pressure of the breath from the lungs on the vocal lips by the downward moving larynx.[1] Nguni has only the bilabial implosive (ɓ); Shona and Chopi have both bilabial and alveolar (ɗ). Semantic distinction from explosives is clear: note in Zulu, bɛ:kɑ (look), ɓɛ:kɑ (put), bu:zɑ (buzz), ɓu:zɑ (ask); and in Shona (Ze.) dededza (toddle), ɗeɗedza (bite). Under homorganic nasal influence implosives become explosive, e.g. Shona: mbato (pincers) < ɓata (grasp). The implosives are unknown in Sotho, Venda, and Tsonga.

4. Southern Bantu affords a fairly full range of NASAL CONSONANTS. In addition to such nasals as have individual standing, there are homorganic forms used in association with denti-labial, labio-alveolar, and palatal consonants. Generally the languages are strict in observing homorganic choice, but Shona, Tsonga, and Chopi are peculiar in using the heterorganic compounds mv or mbv, where Nguni and Venda, for instance, use ɱɟbv. A full range of syllabic nasals, m̩, n̩, ṉ, and ŋ̍, is used in Sotho, with an additional one ṋ in Venda. Nguni and Chopi use only the bilabial syllabically. Syllabic nasals are not used in Tsonga[2] and Shona. Nasal consonants may be accompanied by the voiced glottal fricative in Tsonga (mɦ, nɦ, ŋɦ), in Shona and Kgalagadi (mɦ, nɦ), and in Xhosa (mɦ, ɲɦ, ŋwɦ).

5. In Bantu generally, ROLLED, FLAPPED, AND LATERAL CONSONANTS have a certain interconnexion. The flapped consonant, produced by a single flap of the tongue, with varying lateral or medial expression, is not a continuant, as are the other two. It is commonly found in association with the forward vowels i and e, or in quick speech. In Sotho (N.S. and T.) the flapped lateral belongs to the l phoneme, and occurs when that phoneme is followed by either of the close vowels î and û. [In S.S. a velar-stop explosive, resembling alveolar d, occurs in this position.] In N.S., for instance, m̩mɑ:lî (reader) is derived from the verb βɑ:lɑ (read). In Shona the flapped lateral (ɹ) is a member of the r phoneme, and in the Karanga cluster invariably occurs before the vowel i and sometimes before e, e.g. ru.limi (tongue), ɗu.li (mortar). Nguni typically uses the l phoneme, whereas Shona typically uses the r phoneme. Western Shona, however, uses l. The word 'sit' appears as follows: Nguni ɬɑ:lɑ, Central Shona gara, Kalanga gala. Sotho, Venda, Tsonga, and Chopi all use both l and r as different phonemes. In the Tsonga group Ro. uses ʈ (retroflex), while Venda differentiates between dental and retroflex laterals (ḷ and ɭ). The Sotho group is unique in using syllabic lateral and rolled consonants: S.S. and N.S. have ḷ (a reduction from li or lu), e.g. S.S. huḷ:lɑ (to cry, T. xuli:lɑ); S.S. bofuḷ:lɑ (outspan, T. xulu:lɑ). Tswana and Kgalagadi have r̩, e.g. r̩:rɛ (my father).

6. There is a good range of FRICATIVE CONSONANTS in the Southern Bantu languages, voiced forms corresponding fairly to the unvoiced, though Sotho, particularly S.S. and T., is almost devoid of voiced fricatives. The bilabial fricatives (ɸ and β) are noteworthy; both occur in Northern Sotho, Kutswe (a Sotho dialect), and Venda; the unvoiced form is found in Tswana; while the voiced form (β) is much more widespread, being common in Shona, Tsonga, Chopi, Pai (a Sotho dialect), and Lozi—it is very common in Central Bantu languages. The unvoiced form is much the sound made when blowing out a candle. The denti-labial fricatives (f and v) are practically universal in the area, though v is rare in Sotho and Tsonga. The alveolar fricatives (s and z) occur regularly, except that z is rare in Sotho. The prepalatal fricatives (ʃ and ʒ) are similarly common, but the voiced form does not occur in Nguni apart from the affricate dʒ, and apart from that is only found in N.S. in the Sotho group. The velar fricatives (x and ɣ) are found in Nguni (the latter only in Xhosa and Phuthi) and Venda, the unvoiced form (x) occurring also in Tswana, Pai, and Kgalagadi, the voiced form (ɣ) in Northern Sotho and Kutswe. In Zulu only are both unvoiced and voiced forms of glottal fricative (h and ɦ) used as separate phonemes. Elsewhere, languages

---

[1] From a definition by Professor P. de V. Pienaar.
[2] Except in the contraction of a final -ni.

vary in usage between the voiced and the unvoiced form; for instance h is used in Xhosa, Tswana, Tonga, Ronga, Chopi, Kgalagadi, Lozi, and Ndau, while ɦ is used in Northern and Southern Sotho, Shona, Venda, Tswa, Pai, and Kutswe. In Zulu h and x are often interchangeable with different speakers or for emphasis. Northern Sotho and the Kutswe dialect of Sotho are unique in having an unvoiced prevelar fricative (ḣ) in place of the velar form.

Two important types of fricatives which occur among the Southern Bantu are the labio-alveolars and the laterals. Labio-alveolar fricatives (ṣ and ʐ), commonly called 'whistling fricatives', are pronounced with a flattening of the tongue and considerable lip-rounding. Generally the enunciation is accompanied with a degree of hissing, but in certain languages and with certain speakers a whistling note is to be detected. In Southern Bantu these fricatives are confined to the Shona, Venda, and Tsonga groups. Outside these groups this feature does not seem to be found beyond the Sena and Nyungwe, bordering on the Shona to the north-east; though some of the compounds, such as pʃ' and bʒ (with variants) in Sotho, and bzj and psj in Nyanja, probably have their origin in the labio-alveolar fricatives. Lateral fricatives also have a definitely limited range in Bantu languages. In Southern Bantu they occur in Nguni, Sotho, and Tsonga, but are not found in Venda and Chopi. Both unvoiced and voiced forms (ɬ and ɮ) occur in Nguni and Tsonga; in Sotho the unvoiced form is found, and unvoiced affricates (tɬ' and tɬh), but no voiced forms. Affricates both voiced and unvoiced occur in Nguni, and the unvoiced affricate in Tsonga. Typically, Shona does not have this feature, but in the Western dialect of Kalanga both ɬ and ɮ are used, and in Manyika palatalized forms, ɬj and ɮj, are found. It is noteworthy that the Sotho dialects of Kgalagadi and Lozi are without lateral fricatives, the latter having obviously lost them from contact with Central Bantu neighbours; the former might never have had them.

7. AFFRICATES are certainly a feature of Southern Bantu; all the languages of both the zones concerned employ them. They are not typically a feature of Bantu as a whole, being noticeably absent from a large number of Bantu languages, and Meinhof did not postulate any for his Ur-Bantu reconstruction. Affricates are composite sounds resulting from a compounding of an explosive consonant and its homorganic fricative; this may be brought about by a slow release of the explosive. With true affricates the two elements are fully homorganic, and this is the case generally in Southern Bantu, where, in such forms as tṣ, tʃ, dʐ, dʒ, the explosive element is not alveolar but of the same organic position as the fricative. Shona, Tsonga, and Chopi, however, have labial affricates which are not fully homorganic,[1] viz. pf and bv, in which the explosive is bilabial and the fricative denti-labial. Fully homorganic denti-labial affricates occur in Venda and Nguni. In the latter the affricate is only found in association with the homorganic nasal, viz. ɱpf' and ɱbv, but in Venda it occurs without the nasal, as in ɸfhu:mɔ (spear). Naturally the digraphs pf and bv are sufficient representation in a practical orthography. The unvoiced affricates in Shona are radical, but in the South-eastern Bantu groups they are ejective, and there aspirated forms often occur distinctively. In Nguni the effect of the homorganic nasal upon fricatives is to produce affricates; thus current orthography ns, mv, nz represents nts', ɱbv, and ndz respectively. In Shona, on the other hand, nasals readily precede voiced fricatives without effecting change, e.g. mv, nz, nʐ.

In the case of the labio-alveolar affricates, the common forms used are tṣ and dʐ with the emphasis upon the alveolar in the explosive element. In the Tswa cluster of Tsonga and in most of the Manyika dialects of Shona, however, the lip-rounding is so extreme that the acoustic effect of the explosive element is far more that of a bilabial, and would be more correctly recorded as pṣ and bʐ. In fact in Northern Tavara, under the influence of Nyungwe of the Sena group, the affricates actually become pṣ and bʐ, heterorganic compounds.

[1] These might be termed heterorganic.

Lateral affricates occur in Nguni, Sotho, and Tsonga, tɬ', tɬh, and dɮ being found. In addition, the Tswa cluster of Tsonga has velar lateral affricates, written *kl* and *khl*, which I represent in broad phonetic script by kɬ' and kɬh respectively. The former of these two is found in Zulu as a variant of the velar affricate with medial release, kx'. This affricate, and especially its aspirated equivalent, kxh, are very widely used in the various types of Nguni and Sotho languages.

8. The SEMI-VOWELS, j and w, occur in all the languages, the latter having both bilabial and velar aspects. Under nasal influence, the velar ŋ or ŋg often appears; on the other hand, in such a cluster as Manyika, w is often the equivalent of the more typical Shona β, e.g. **wana waŋgu** for **βana βaŋgu** (my children). The Zezuru cluster of Shona and a number of Eastern and Northern forms have the distinction of using a peculiar denti-labial type of semi-vowel in place of the bilabial voiced fricative. This might be represented by β̞. The semi-vowels j and w have their origin in the consonantalization of the vowels i and u respectively; β has its origin in the abnormal vowel ɯ, which is formed with the tongue in the position of u but with the lips spread as for i. When ɯ is normally consonantalized, i.e. pronounced with such tensity and proximity of the vocal organs as to constitute a consonant, it is found that the upper teeth just touch the lower spread lip, giving very much the position for normal v; for this reason β̞ has sometimes been mistaken for v, but it is entirely frictionless.

HETERORGANIC COMPOUNDS

It is a general feature of Southern Bantu, as of Bantu as a whole, to favour homorganic compounds, and it is not surprising to find heterorganic compounds confined to the Sotho group, Chopi, and the Phuthi dialect. In Sotho bilabial explosives are found in association with prepalatal fricatives forming pʃ', pʃh, and bʒ; the denti-labial unvoiced fricative is also found associated with ʃ in fʃ, Northern Sotho has bilabial fricatives associated with the prepalatal fricatives, forming Φʃ and βʒ. Chopi uses the combination ps (bilabial+alveolar); this is probably a development from the labio-alveolar affricate pş. Phuthi (Sothoized Nguni) is distinctive in having alveolar explosives associated with denti-labial fricatives in the compounds tfh and dv.

COMPOUNDS WITH THE SEMI-VOWELS

In typical Central Bantu languages compounds with the prepalatal and velar semi-vowels are commonly found with practically every other consonant; for instance in Lamba are found pj, mbj, βj, fj, tj, ndj, mj, nj, and lj, in addition to actual palatal consonants; also pw, bw, tw, ndw, kw, ŋgw, mw, nw, ɲw, ŋw, fw, sw, lw, and jw. In Southern Bantu, however, such occurrences are not found with that regularity: the use of the prepalatal 'glide' is very limited, and the use of the velar 'glide' with bilabials strictly avoided. A result of this avoidance in the case of bilabials (and seemingly by analogy with certain other consonants) is the emergence of velar or prepalatal (or palatal) consonants in place of the bilabials: these phenomena are termed velarization and palatalization respectively.

(*a*) THE INCIDENCE OF PREPALATAL GLIDES. These occur most fully in Chopi where pj', mbj, dj, gj, hj, and others have been recorded. In the Tsonga group, Ronga has t̪j', t̪jh, and d̪j, while the bilabial forms pj' and bj seem to be general, **labji:wa**, for instance, being the passive of **la:βa** (seek) in Tswa; in the case of the bilabials, however, there is usually a modification of the glide, Tswa having a tendency to use the labio-alveolar fricative, pş and bʐ resulting. Northern Sotho varies the pronunciation of bʐ to that of bj in some dialects, and in the extreme eastern types of Kutswe and Pai the prepalatal glide occurs quite frequently: Kutswe, pj', pjh, tjh, and dj; Pai, pjh, bj, and dj. In Venda the forms tj' and dj occur.

(b) THE INCIDENCE OF VELAR GLIDES. In considering the distribution of velar glides, consonants may conveniently be divided into three sections: (i) labials, (ii) those with position between labial and velar, and (iii) velars and those with post-velar position.

(i) In regard to labials, the velar glide is generally avoided.[1] In passive formation, for instance, instead of the suffix -wa being used, some, such as Karanga, use the suffix -iwa (e.g. **rapa** > **rapiwa**), or interpose a prepalatal glide, as in Tsonga; but in other cases a phenomenal change takes place, such as that of palatalization in Nguni and Sotho, or velarization in Shona, Venda, and in certain cases in Sotho. In Shona the resultant forms are **px** (**pk**), **bɣ** (**bg**), and **mŋ** for bilabials, and in the Zezuru dialect **ɲŋ**, **tʃk**, and **dʒg** for prepalatals. In Venda they are **px'**, **pxh**, **bɣ**, and **mŋ** for bilabials only. With denti-labials there is generally the same avoidance, though Zulu may use alternatively -**fi:ni** and -**fwi:ni**, for instance, in locative formation.

(ii) For positions between labial and velar, such as alveolar, labio-alveolar, prepalatal, velar glides are commonly used in Nguni, Sotho, Venda, and Tsonga; but in Shona, velarization takes place along with the semi-vowel; thus in Zulu **lɛ:tha** (bring) > **lɛ:thwa**, but in Shona **ɓata** (hold) > **ɓatxwa**. It is common, then, to find **tw, dw, nw, sw, zw, lw, rw, ʃw**, even **jw**, as well as with affricates, e.g. **tsw, dzw, dɦw, tʃw**, &c.

(iii) It is normal to all the languages to use the velar glide with velar and glottal consonants, e.g. **kw, k'w, khw, gw, ŋw, xw, ɣw, hw, fiw**.

The phenomena of palatalization and velarization as phonological processes will be considered later.[2]

THE CLICK CONSONANTS

A click is an injected consonant produced by a rarefaction between two points of closure, one of these points always being velar. There is little doubt that the Bushman languages provide the fountain-head of clicks in Africa. Typical Bushman languages such as !*kuŋ* (Northern) or /*kam* (Southern), each employ five positional types of click[3] (/, ʇ, ≠, //, /// and /, ʇ, ≠, //, ⊙ respectively). Of these, the Hottentot languages acquired four positional types, viz. /, ʇ, ≠, and //. With the Bantu, clicks are distinctly a foreign element, acquired either by direct contact with the Bushman or additionally by Hottentot influence. It is the Nguni group which has been most affected by click influence, three positional types, /, ʇ, and //, being found in most Nguni languages. Southern Sotho has acquired one positional type, viz. /, clicks being very rare in the other Sotho clusters. Certain Northern Kalahari languages, such as Yeye, use clicks, but they do not belong to the Southern Bantu. Yeye belongs to the Western Bantu zone, and the clicks used are directly derived from the Bushman in the vicinity; it is interesting to note, however, that even in Yeye it is only the three positional types of /, ʇ, and // which are found. Of the Nguni group, Xhosa is the most heavily influenced cluster, and this influence is shared by the Phuthi dialect despite its connexion with Sotho. Tsonga has to a certain extent been affected by click words borrowed from Zulu.

The three positional types found in Southern Bantu are: (i) dental, / (phonetic ʇ), (ii) palato-alveolar, ʇ (phonetic ʗ), and (iii) lateral, // (phonetic ʖ). These are represented in the current Bantu orthographies by the basic symbols *c*, *q*, and *x*, respectively.

In the formation of each of the clicks, the back of the tongue is raised to touch the soft palate (in the position for **k**). To form the dental click the tip of the tongue is then placed lightly against the upper front teeth and gums; the centre of the tongue is depressed forming a space of rarefaction above it, and then the tip of the tongue is drawn backwards; the radical form of the resulting click resembles the 'click of annoyance' written 'tut-tut' in English.

---

[1] Except with certain dialects of Korekore (Northern Shona).
[2] See section D below, pp. 39 and 40.
[3] The symbols here given are those used in current Nama Hottentot orthography and in Bushman transcriptions.

To form the palato-alveolar click the upper part of the tongue-tip is pressed tightly against the division between the teeth-ridge and hard palate; the centre of the tongue is depressed, and then the tip of the tongue is drawn sharply downwards; the radical form of the resulting click resembles the sound of the drawing of a cork from a bottle. The lateral click has the tongue position much as for the palato-alveolar, but the tongue-tip is not released. It is one side of the tongue against the upper side teeth which is withdrawn; the radical form of the resulting click resembles the sound made by a cabby when urging his horses.

PHONETIC CHART OF SOUTHERN BANTU CLICKS

	Dental	Palato-alveolar	Lateral
Radical	ʇ	C	ʖ
Rad. preceded by homorganic nasal	{ɲʇ}	{ɲC}	{ɲʖ}
Rad. preceded by syllabic velar nasal		(ŋC)	
Aspirated	ʇh	Ch	ʖh
Asp. preceded by syllabic velar nasal		(ŋCh)	
Voiced	ʇg	Cg	ʖg
Voic. preceded by homorganic nasal	ɲʇg	ɲCg	ɲʖg
Nasal	ʇŋ	Cŋ	ʖŋ
Nasal followed by voic. glottal fric.	[ʇŋɦ]	[Cŋɦ]	[ʖŋɦ]
Nasal preceded by syllabic velar nasal		(ŋCŋ)	

[ ] occurring in Xhosa and Phuthi only.   ( ) occurring in Southern Sotho only.
{ } occurring in Xhosa, but rare in Zulu.

TABLE OF INCIDENCE OF CONSONANTAL TYPES[1]

	Nguni	Sotho	Venda	Tsonga	Chopi	Shona
ejectives	×	×	×	×	×	
aspirates	×	×	×	×	×	(×)
distinctive dentals			×			
retroflex cons.			(×)	×		
palatal expl.	×			×		
implosives	×				×	×
syll. nasals	×	×	×		×	
rolled contin.		×	×	×	×	×
lateral contin.	×	×	×	×	×	(×)
flapped lat.		×				×
syll. lats. and rolled		×				
bilab. fric. unv.		×	×			
,, ,, voic.		×	×	×	×	×
lat. frics. and affrics.	×	×		×		(×)
heterorganic affrics.				×	×	×
labio-alv. frics.			×	×		×
prevelar fric.		(×)				
voic. velar fric.	×	×	×			
velar affric. (med.)	×	×				
velar affric. (lat.)	(×)			×		
denti-labial s-v.						×
palatal glide cons.		(×)		×	×	
velarized cons.			×			×
click cons.	×	×		(×)		

(×) = dialectal or limited.

[1] Types normal to all groups are not included.

D. Phonological Phenomena with Consonants

Nasalization, or the effect of the prefixing of a homorganic nasal, is a consonantal phenomenon common to all Bantu languages, and it occurs in varying forms with all the Southern languages. Other phenomena, much more restricted among Bantu languages, and some of which are peculiar to the Southern zones, are Palatalization, Velarization, Alveolarization, and Vocalization. These will now be dealt with in turn.

1. NASALIZATION. A common word in Bantu provides a key to the type of phonological change to be found in each language: this is the word for 'person', the stem of which is postulated by Meinhof to be, in Ur-Bantu, -ntu, i.e. N+tu.[1] An examination of the form this word assumes in each of the languages reveals the type of nasal change operating upon primitive explosives. The following table reveals four types of change, two of which, strangely enough, are found within one group—the Inhambane group. The languages are arranged according to type.

	Ur-B. mu-ntu	Ur-B. p.	t.	k.
1. N+eject. expl.				
Nguni	umu-nt'u	mp'	nt'	ŋk'
2. (N)+asp. expl.				
Sotho	mu-thu	ph	th	kh(kxh)
Venda	mu-thu	ph	th	kh
3. N+voic. glott. fric.				
Shona	mu-nɦu	mɦ	nɦ	ɦ
Tsonga	mu-nɦu	mɦ	nɦ	h(ɦ)
4. N+voic. expl.				
Lenge	mu-ndu	mb	nd	ŋg

Note 1: Tonga (of Inhambane) differs sharply here from Lenge in following the No. 2 pattern with **m-thu**.

Note 2: In Western Shona there is a variety of formations, e.g. Rozwi and Nambzya have typical Shona forms with the key word: **u-nɦu**.

Kalanga has **ṇ-nu** (a variety of the above).
Talahundra has **ṇ-dhu** (cf. Lenge).
Lilima has **ṇ-thu** (cf. Sotho).

In all the Southern Bantu languages nasalization occurs in the formation of nouns of cls. 9 and 10 and usually with adjectives in agreement therewith. The hypothetical prefix involved is **ni-** in Ur-Bantu. In the cases of Sotho and Venda, in addition, nasalization occurs when the 1st pers. s. objectival concord is used before a verb-stem; and in the case of Sotho it occurs further when the reflexive prefix is so used. Tsonga has, also, a different type of nasalization due to the operation of the prefix **mu-**, particularly in cl. 3. This feature is shared by Lenge of the Inhambane group, and certain Western Shona languages.

Following is a summary of the main changes effected by the use of the homorganic nasal in the different groups.[2]

---

[1] N (capital) is used to represent the varying homorganic nasal.

[2] The changes given here are from the bases found in each language, not from the Ur-Bantu sources, unless specifically stated. Details are to be found in the succeeding chapters.

(a) NGUNI (ZULU)
   (i) aspirated explosives become ejective, e.g. **ph** > **mp'**.
   (ii) aspirated clicks become nasal clicks, e.g. ʇh > ʇŋ.
   (iii) radical clicks become voiced, e.g. ʇ > ŋʇg.
   (iv) unvoiced fricatives become ejective affricates, e.g. **s** > **nts'**.
   (v) voiced fricatives become voiced affricates, e.g. **z** > **ndz**.
   (vi) bilabial implosive becomes voiced bilabial explosive, i.e. **ɓ** > **mb**.
   (vii) before **l, w, j,** and **h** the nasal drops without effecting change, except that on rare occasions **l** > **nd**.

(b) SOTHO (SOUTHERN)
   (i) vowels and semi-vowels become **(ṇ)k'**.
   (ii) voiced explosives become ejective, e.g. **b** > **(m̱)p'**.
   (iii) fricatives become aspirated explosives or affricates, e.g. **f** > **(m̱)ph, s** > **(ṇ)tsh**.
   (iv) voiced affricate becomes ejective, i.e. **dʒ** > **(ṇ)tʃ'**. [*N*- when used is syllabic.]

(c) VENDA
   (i) vowel-stems preplace either ɲ or ṇ.
   (ii) the equivalents of the primitive Bantu unvoiced explosives, viz. Φ, r, ɦ, become aspirated explosives, i.e. **ph, th, kh**.
   (iii) the equivalents of the primitive Bantu voiced fricatives, viz. β and l̪, become *N*-+voiced explosives, i.e. **mb** and **nd**.
   (iv) unvoiced fricatives become aspirated affricates, e.g. **s** > **tsh**.
   (v) voiced fricatives become *N*-+voiced affricates, e.g. **z** > **ndz**.
   (vi) denasalized sounds regain nasalization, the unvoiced being aspirated, the voiced preplacing *N*-, e.g. **p'** > **ph, pf'** > **pfh; b** > **mb**.

(d) SHONA
   (i) unvoiced explosives become voiced glottal fricatives, generally preceded by a significant nasal, i.e. **p** > **mɦ, t** > **nɦ, k** > **ɦ**.
   (ii) implosives become explosives, e.g. **ɓ** > **mb**.
   (iii) rolled consonant becomes explosive, i.e. **r** > **nd**.
   (iv) unvoiced fricatives and affricates generally remain unchanged, though the former at times become affricative, e.g. **s** > **s** (sometimes **ts**).
   (v) voiced fricatives preplace the homorganic nasal, e.g. **v** > **mv**; but β > **mb**, and in the Karanga cluster *N*-+z > ʒ, elsewhere **nz**.

(e) TSONGA
Here there are two types of nasalization: from original **ni-**, and one of probably later formation from original **mu-**.
From original **ni-**:
   (i) all consonants may assume the homorganic nasal, e.g. **mp, nɦ, ns, ŋg** [but Ts. omits the nasal before unvoiced fricatives and v].
   (ii) the equivalents of the primitive Bantu unvoiced explosives become voiced glottal fricatives, generally preceded by a significant nasal, as in Shona, i.e. **mɦ, nɦ,** and **ɦ**.
   (iii) the equivalents of the primitive Bantu voiced fricatives, viz. β and l, become *N*-+voiced explosives, i.e. **mb** and **ɳɖ** (Ts. **nz**).
   (iv) vowel-stems preplace either ɲ or ŋ.

From original **mu-**:

(i) explosive consonants become *N*-+consonant, e.g. **mu-+t' > nt', mu-+d > nd**.
(ii) fricative consonants generally remain unchanged, the nasal dropping away, e.g. **mu-+ s > s, mu-+ɬ > ɬ** (To. and Ro. often have **ns, nɬ**).
(iii) special changes are: **mu-+β > mb; mu-+r > ṇḍ; mu-+l > n**.

Similar rules of formation from original **mu-** are found in Lenge (Inhambane group), e.g. **ɲtʃ'i:ma** (moon) pl. **mitʃ'i:ma**; also in Western Shona, where one finds in Kalanga **nlume** (man) pl. **βalume**, in Rozwi **ŋkuru** (big) for **mu-kuru**, and so on.

2. PALATALIZATION. This is generally more strictly 'prepalatalization', though in Xhosa both palatals and prepalatals are used in the process. Palatalization is a phonological process, occurring among Southern Bantu languages in Nguni and Sotho, by which a palatal (or prepalatal) consonant is substituted for one of another organic position. In these languages palatalization is generally due to the incompatibility of bilabial consonants with the semi-vowel **w**, and is exhibited most clearly in the formation of passives, when the suffix **-wa** might succeed a bilabial consonant, e.g. Zulu **lɔ:βa** (write) > **lɔ:tʃ'wa**; S. Sotho **rɔ:ba** (break) > **rɔ:dʒwa** or **rɔ:bʒwa**. That the process, however, is not entirely due to the incompatibility of **w** with a bilabial is shown by the fact that the diminutive suffix **-ana** has a similar effect upon bilabials and even upon certain alveolars, e.g. in Zulu **int'a: βa** (mountain) > **int'atʃ'a:na** (hill), and **i:k'a:t'i** (cat) > **i:k'atʃ'a:na** (little cat).

While this process is confined to the two groups, Nguni and Sotho, among Southern Bantu languages, it operates elsewhere in Bantu also. For instance, in Tetela,[1] a Middle-Congo language, nouns of Bantu cl. 19 (Meinhof's prefix *pĭ-*) undergo regular palatalization as follows:

(i) palatal semi-vowel precedes vowel stems, e.g. **-amba > jamba**.
(ii) palatal glide follows labial, velar, and glottal consonants, e.g. **p > pj, m > mj, k > kj** or **c; dipeŋge > dimin. pjeŋge**.
(iii) alveolar consonants give place to palatals, e.g. **t > tʃ, d > dʒ, n > ɲ; ulua > dimin. dʒua**.
(iv) palatals remain unchanged.
(v) **β** and **w** are not subject to palatalization.

In Nguni the process occurs in four main instances: (*a*) with verb passives, (*b*) with locatives when a bilabial consonant is followed by **-ɔ** or **-u**, (*c*) with diminutives of nouns and qualificatives when the final syllable has a bilabial or an alveolar consonant, and (*d*) with certain special words with prefixes of cls. 1 (or 3), 9, and 14. A comparison of words in this last category is interesting:

Ur-Bantu	Xhosa	S. Sotho	Shona	Venda	Tsonga	Lenge
muana (child)	**uɲa:na**	**ŋwa:na**	**mɲana**	**ŋwa:na**	**ŋwa:na**	**mwana:na**
imbwa (dog)	**i:ɲdʒa**	**n:tʃ'a**	**imbya**	**m:bɣa**	**mbja:na**	**i:mbwa**
buala (beer)	**uc'wa:la**	**dʒwa:la**	**byabɣa**	**(ha:lwa)**	**bja:la**	**wa:dwa**

Xhosa has palatalization in each case; S. Sotho has velarization in the first instance, palatalization in the others; Shona and Venda have velarization throughout (except for the non-committal **ha:lwa**); Tsonga has velarization in the first (as Sotho) and uses a palatal glide in the other cases; Lenge conforms to the Ur-Bantu postulation. It is seen from this that the processes of palatalization and velarization are complementary processes, similar in origin. It is not surprising, then, to find that in Sotho they are to a certain extent intermingled.

---

[1] Information from a MS. *Otetela Grammar*, supplied to me by the Rev. E. B. Stilz of the M.M.C.C., Wembo Nyama, Congo Belge.

So, too, are palatalization and alveolarization in Sotho, for, where **ts** by alveolarization occurs in S.S., palatalization in **tʃ** occurs in N.S.

The phenomenon occurs in Sotho in the case of passives of verbs with a bilabial consonant in the final syllable (though **m > ŋ** here by velarization), and in the formation of diminutives of nouns and adjectives, where alveolarization and velarization also feature.

The changes which take place in Nguni are as follows:

p' and t' > tʃ'
ph and th > Z. ʃ, X. tʃh
b and d > dʒ
ɓ > Z. tʃ', X. c'
m and n > ɲ.

For the changes in Sotho (S.S. and T.) reference may be made to Chapter VI.[1]

3. VELARIZATION. There are two aspects of velarization which occur in Southern Bantu: the one involves the substitution of a velar consonant for one of another organic position, as when in Sotho the passive of **ru:ma** is **ru:ŋwa**; and the other is a process, particularly common in Shona, brought about by an abnormal raising of the back of the tongue towards the soft palate (velum) instead of the usual slight raising effected in pronouncing the velar semi-vowel **w**.

(*a*) *Velarization by substitution.* Sotho provides a good example of this, which occurs in passive formation, with suffixal diminutive formation, and with nouns of cls. 1 and 3. In each case the result is the velar nasal **ŋ**. In passives **m > ŋ** and **ɲ > ŋŋ** (e.g. **si:ɲa**, spoil > **siŋ:ŋwa**); with diminutives **m > ŋ**; and with nouns **mu-**+vowel **> ŋw** (e.g. **mu-**+**-ets'i > ŋwe:ts'i**, daughter-in-law). Tsonga has examples of the last, e.g. **ŋwa:na** (child) < **-ana**, and in Ro. **ŋwi:ɲi** (master), pl. βe:ɲi < **-iɲi**.

(*b*) *Velarization due to abnormal raising of the back of the tongue when using the velar semi-vowel.* Shona provides the classic example of this. The division of consonants into three sections—labial, those between labial and velar, and velars and post-velars[2]—was observed when dealing with the incidence of velar glides. In Shona, under the influence of velarization, (i) labials substitute a velar consonant (explosive or fricative) for the semi-vowel; (ii) sounds between labial and velar positions assume the velar consonant as well as the semi-vowel; (iii) sounds that are velar or post-velar merely use the semi-vowel. Hence in Shona are found: (i) **pxa, bɣa, mŋa** (Zezuru: **pka, bga, mŋa**); (ii) **txwa, sxwa, ʒɣwa, rɣwa**, &c. (Zezuru: **tkwa, ʃkwa**, &c. when unvoiced); (iii) **kwa, gwa, ŋwa, fiwa**, &c. In the various dialectal types of Shona there are varying degrees of intensity of velarization, from the most intense explosive type (**pk, bg**), to the common fricative type (**px, bɣ**), then the resonated type (**pŵ, bŵ**), down to the simple use of the semi-vowel, as in Northern Korekore (**pw, bw**). The commonest occurrence of velarization is in passive formation, but it is found with nouns of cls. 1 and 3 and in certain noun-stems, e.g. **mŋana, imbɣa, βusxwa** (grass).

Venda is similar to, though less regular than, Shona in this type of velarization. The general changes, which include substitutions, are as follows:

Φ > xw   p' > px'
β > ɣw   ph > pxh
m > mŋ or ŋw   b > bɣ

and the glottal fricative **ɦ > ɣw**, an unusual change, since **ɦ** is 'post-velar'.

4. ALVEOLARIZATION. This process, the substitution of an alveolar affricative sound for one of some other organic position, or the transference thereto of some other alveolar sound, occurs only in the Sotho group among the Southern Bantu; and in this group N.S. is

[1] p. 124.
[2] Here used to indicate positions farther back in the mouth than velar, e.g. glottal.

excluded, as palatalization takes its place there. The resulting sounds are **ts'** or **tsh** (N.S. **tʃ'**, **tʃh**). The process occurs in the formation of noun and adjective diminutives, where **p, b, l, d > ts'**; and **ph, f,** and **r > tsh**. In addition, in Tswana **t > ts'** and **x > tsh** (or **s**). The formations are often irregular and intermingled with palatalization. A common form of alveolarization is that of transference of **l > ts'**, as in concords of cls. 8 and 10, and in verb derivative forms. Further details may be found in Chapter VI.[1]

5. VOCALIZATION. Shona again provides the classic example of this. It may be defined as the substitution of a voiced for an unvoiced consonant, and it takes place in the formation of nouns of cl. 5 and adjectives in agreement therewith. It is due to the suppression of the prefix **ri-** in this class, the concords and pronouns only retaining the *ri-* form. With nouns and adjectives, only a vocalizing effect of the suppressed prefix remains. This vocalizing is exerted upon explosive consonants and hence (to a certain extent) upon affricates, but not upon fricatives: it is noteworthy that the vocalizing effect upon **p** and **t** results in implosives. The changes then are: **p > ɓ, t > ɗ, k > g, tʃ > dʒ, tṣ > dẓ**, e.g. **-paŋga > ɓaŋga** (cl. 5), pl. **mapaŋga** (cl. 6). Further examples are given in Chapter IX.[2]

In Venda this process has become somewhat irregular, so that while the pattern of changes is based on vocalization, certain of the mutations are not 'voicings' at all. The unvoiced explosives change regularly, i.e. **p', ʈ', t'**, and **k' > b, ḍ, d,** and **g** respectively; but with the fricatives a variety of changes is encountered, e.g. **ɸ > f** or **b, ɦ > f, v,** or **s, β > v** or **b**; while **r > ʃ, d,** or **dz**, and **ḷ > d,** or **dz**. Examples are to be found in Chapter VII.[3]

E. SOUND-SHIFTING

From what has gone before in this chapter there is abundant evidence that the languages under review belong to a single 'family' and have a high percentage of roots and formatives of common origin. It is also plainly evident that a diversity of phonetic form has come into being among them. Consonantal changes are particularly in evidence. As observed in Chapter I,[4] Appleyard was the first to draw attention to this 'sound-shifting', taking as his basis of comparison Xhosa.[5] Bleek followed the lead of Appleyard, developing comparison more fully in his 1862 *Comparative Grammar*.[6] He also took Xhosa ('Kafir' as it was called in those days) as his basis for comparison. Bleek realized that there was danger in this, for he observed: 'It need not be remarked that the Kafir by no means always exhibits a more original form of consonant.' Torrend, in his 1891 *Comparative Grammar*, took Tonga, a middle-Zambesi Central Bantu language, as his basis, and again gave a bias to his comparative studies. It was Carl Meinhof who boldly proceeded, in his *Grundriss einer Lautlehre der Bantusprachen*, first published in 1899, to propound a hypothetical 'Ur-Bantu', an attempted 'reconstruction of the prototype of Bantu speech', in order to provide a basis for the comparison of the Bantu languages of today. This work, which is of the greatest importance to students of Bantu, is available in an English translation, entitled *Introduction to the Phonology of the Bantu Languages*.[7]

In this Meinhof postulates as primary vowels, *a*, *i*, and *u*; composite vowels, *e* and *o*; and, in addition, what he calls 'close' vowels and indicates by the symbols *î* and *û*, showing that they have palatal and labial effect respectively upon preceding consonants.

In regard to consonants, Meinhof makes the following postulations:

(i) primary explosives (unvoiced): **p, t, k.**
(ii) primary 'fricatives' (voiced): **β, l, ɣ.**
(iii) primary nasals: **m, n, ŋ.**

[1] p. 124.   [2] p. 208.   [3] p. 157.   [4] p. 12.
[5] See his *Kafir Language* (1850), pp. 51 et seq.; he had foreshadowed this in his 1847 articles.
[6] See pp. 82 et seq.
[7] Translated and enlarged by N. J. v. Warmelo.

(iv) palatalized forms of alveolar and velar primaries: tj, kj ; lj, ɣj.[1]
(v) semi-vowels: w, j.

In addition, Meinhof worked out forms under nasal influence, and under the influence of varying vowels.

SPECIMEN CHART OF THE MOST IMPORTANT
SOUND-SHIFTINGS FOR SOUTHERN BANTU

Ur-Bantu		Nguni[2] (Zulu)	Sotho[3] (Northern)	Venda[4]	Tsonga[5] (Gwamba)	Shona[6] (Karanga)
1. Primary:						
explosive	k	kh, k	x, ɣ	ɦ (ɣ, ')	k	k
	t	th	r	r	r	t
	p	ph	ɸ	ɸ	ɦ	p
fricative	ɣ	j (w)	—, j	—, (ɦ)	—, j	—, w
	l	l	l	ḽ	l	r
	β	ɓ	β	β	β	β
nasal	(ŋ)	(ŋ)		(ŋ)		
	n	n	n	n	n	n
	m	m	m	m	m	m
2. Palatal:						
	kj	} ɬ	} ɬ	t'	} ɬ	} s, ts, ʃ
	tj					
	ɣj	} ɦ	} tɬ'	ḓ	} tɬ, t	z
	lj					ʒ? [7]
3. Nasal compounds:						
primary	ŋk	ŋk'	(ŋ) kxh	(ŋ) kh	h (ɦ)	ɦ
	nt	nt'	(n) th	(n) th	nɦ	nɦ
	mp	mp'	(m) ph	(m) ph	mɦ	mɦ
	ŋg	ŋg, ŋ	(ŋ) k'	ŋg (ɲ)	ŋg, ŋ	ŋg, ŋ
	nd	nd	(n) t'	nd	nd	nd
	mb	mb	(m) p'	mb	mb	mb
palatals	ŋkj	ntɬ'	ɬ, (n) tɬh	ṱh, ṋṱ'	nɬ	s, ts, ʃ
	ntj					s, ʃ
	ŋgj	} ndɦ	(n) tɬ'	ṋḓ	} nɦ	} nz, ʒ
	ndj					
4. Through 'heavy' vowel influence:		(î) (û)	(î) (û)	(î) (û)	(î) (û)	(î) (û)
	k	s f	ʃ 'h	ts' f, pf	s f	s f
	t	s f	ʃ r	s, ts' f, pf	s f	s pf
	p	f f	ɸ ɸ	ṣ f	f f	ṣ f
	ɣ	z v	— —	d —	t pf	ʐ bv
	l	z v	ɮ ɮ	dz bv	t pf	dz bv
	β	v v	β β	ʐ v, bv	pf pf	ʐ bv

Following are a few examples of this sound-shifting:

Ur-Bantu: -tatu (three): Ng. -thathu ; So. -raru ; Ve. -raru ; Tg. -raru ; Sh. -tatu.
Ur-Bantu: -pa (give): Ng. pha ; So. ɸa, fa ; Ve. ɸa ; Tg. ɦa ; Sh. pa.
Ur-Bantu: -tjano (five): Ng. -ɬanu ; So. -ɬanu ; Ve. -ṱanu ; Tg. -ntɬhanu ;[8] Sh. ʃanu.

---

[1] Meinhof indicated these by underlining the primary symbols; here I have used the palatal glide, j, to mark them.
[2] Meinhof and v. Warmelo, *Bantu-Phonology*, pp. 82–110.
[3] Ibid., pp. 58–81.   [4] Meinhof, 'Das Tši-Venḓa', pp. 607–42.
[5] v. Warmelo, *Die Gliederung der südafrikanischen Bantusprachen*, pp. 18–41.
[6] Ibid., pp. 51–57.   [7] Probably also z, but no example found.
[8] Here under nasal influence.

Ur-Bantu: -βili (two): Ng. -ɓili, -ɓini (X.); So. -βeli; Ve. -βiḽi; Tg. -βiri; Sh. -βiri.
Ur-Bantu: mbûla (rain): Ng. iɱɔ̄vu:la; So. p'û:la; Ve. mvu:la; Tg. mpf'u:la; Sh. mvura.
Ur-Bantu: mukîpa (sinew): Ng. um̱si:pha; N.S. muʃî:Φa; Ve. luts'i:ŋga; Tg. si:ɦa.

F. THE PROSODIC ELEMENTS

Three prosodic elements in Southern Bantu speech will be briefly noticed here; they are stress, length, and tone. To a certain extent they are interdependent; certain types of tone, in Nguni for instance, are associated with long syllables; again, in some cases stress is associated with length.

1. STRESS. This is the 'dynamic accent' by which one syllable is made more prominent than others. Every complete word in Bantu has a main stress on one of its syllables, secondary stresses falling at intervals on other syllables of polysyllabic words. The main stress is then a great factor in word-building in Bantu and proves the incorrectness of the disjunctive methods of word-division employed in many orthographies. In all the Southern Bantu languages the main stress is typically on the penultimate syllable of each word, though its presence is more noticeable in some languages than others owing to the interrelationship of the type of tone used. The position of the stress may be checked from a study of Bantu hymns, where stress is often violated by the employment of European tunes and metrical systems. When words are lengthened by the addition of suffixes, the stress continually moves forward to remain on the penultimate syllable, e.g. in Zulu: ˈɓɔ:na, ɓoˈni:sa, ɓɔnaˈka:la, ɓɔnakaˈli:sa, ɓɔnakaliˈsi:sa. These examples show the stress associated with the long penultimate syllable in each case. In Shona the same thing takes place without accompanying length, e.g. kutaˈura, kutauˈrira, kutauriˈrana. Some Bantu languages, on the other hand, retain the main stress on the root syllable of the word, e.g. Ganda of the Northern zone, ˈjaga > ˈjagala. This is not done in Southern Bantu; though some students of Venda think it is done there, it is probably a psychological recognition of the word-root among the many prefixes and suffixes that gives this impression. There are, of course, seeming exceptions to the penultimate position of the stress. In both Nguni and Tsonga stress is on the last syllable of 3rd position demonstratives, e.g. Z. laɓaˈja:; and in Nguni is also final on inflected monosyllabic demonstratives, e.g. Z. kuˈlɔ (to this one), in contrast to ˈku:lɔ (to it). In Nguni contracted verb perfects have stress on the final syllable, e.g. in Z. ɓaɓɔˈnɛ: (they saw, contr. < ɓaɓoˈni:lɛ) in contrast to the subjunctive baˈɓɔ:nɛ. In Tsonga, when the final vowel of the locative suffix is elided (as an alternative pronunciation) the stress 'seems' to be ultimate, but the final nasal is syllabic, and the stress is really still penultimate, e.g. faˈmba:ni > faˈmba:n̩; the same is the case with Sotho locatives and imperative plurals, e.g. raˈta:n̩ (love ye), ŋwaˈne:n̩ (to the child).

Ideophones in Southern Bantu have their own rules regarding stress position: here it is normally initial, e.g. in Zulu: ˈbaɓa, ˈmikithi, ˈbhɔkɔlozi, ˈgɛmbɛlɛkɛçɛ. This ideophonic stress position is not so clearly marked in all the languages, and there are cases of ideophones with ultimate stress.

2. LENGTH. Generally speaking three lengths of syllables are to be distinguished in Southern Bantu: the short syllable, the long syllable, and the abnormally or emotionally lengthened syllable. In the languages of the South-western zone the penultimate syllable of the word, when isolated or when final in a sentence, is long. When not final in a sense-group the long penultimate syllable generally becomes 'half-long', e.g. in Zulu: aˈɓa·ntu ɓajam̱ˈɓɔ:na. This principle of penultimate length does not apply in the South-central zone, Shona being differentiated by its lack of long syllables—a lack which gives it a peculiar staccato effect. Abnormal length occurs in emotional speech and ideophones, e.g. Z.

la::pha‖ja:: (right over there!), u‖kuˑthi ‖dʒa:: (to be stretched out). Even in Shona abnormal length occurs with ideophones, e.g. si:: (of darkness).

Length of syllable may be of grammatical significance in Nguni. For instance, in Xhosa the remote past indicative tense (as in **sa:ɓɔ:na**)[1] is distinguished from the past subjunctive (as in **saɓɔ:na**) by the length of the initial syllable. Contractions of certain nounprefixes result in long vowels, e.g. in Zulu **i:hu:ɓo** (song) for **ilihu:ɓo**, **u:khu:ni** (firewood) for **ulukhu:ni**; in Xhosa **i:nt'ɔ:nga** (sticks) for **izint'ɔ:ŋga**. Xhosa uses length with greater significance than does Zulu, especially in the case of demonstratives.

Nevertheless, Southern Bantu does not use length semantically as it is used in Central Bantu, where, for instance, in Ila **maŋga** is 'kindness', but **ma:ŋga** 'twins'; **kuβola** (to rot), **kuβo:la** (to return to the village).

In Southern Bantu all syllables of ideophones, other than monosyllabic ones, are typically short: there are cases of final syllable length, but this is exceptional. Thus in Zulu the verb **badaˈla:la** (lie sprawling) is distinguished from the corresponding ideophone **ˈbadalala**, not only in the position of the stress, but also in the lack of vowel length in the latter.

3. TONE. In all the Southern Bantu languages tone is a significant feature. Apart from a characteristic intonation, varying from group to group, tone has its function as a semantic factor differentiating the meanings of words, and as a grammatical factor reflecting morphological inflexion; further, as an emotional factor, tone plays a big part in the formation of ideophones and interjectives. The full pattern of tones on a word is revealed when the word is isolated or when final in a sense-group. When a word is used initially or medially in a sense-group its tones undergo modification due to surrounding circumstances. A study of these tone-changes is a very complicated affair and, as yet, has not been systematically undertaken for any of the Southern Bantu languages.[2]

Of the Southern Bantu, Shona (South-central) probably provides the simplest of the tonal systems. As with the Central Bantu languages, the tone range in Shona is not very marked; there are three level tones in normal speech and no gliding tones; of these three tones, two only are significant, a high and a low, the third being a tone-fall, more emotional than significant. If, therefore, the low tones are left unmarked, only the high tones need be indicated, and they provide peaks of tone in the sentence. The following, from a Korekore text will illustrate this: **tsuro jakasáŋgana nebvéne, ikati, watatéguru muˌlikutsá̱geni? bvene ˌlikati, ndiˌlikùtsaga kudʒá̱**.[3] Numerous cases of semantic differentiation by tone occur in Shona, e.g. Manyika: **ɓetó** (dew), **ɓéto** (tax); **pfunda** (chew), **pfúnda** (bachelor); **rudzi** (bark rope), **rúdzi** (tribe). The common Southern Bantu differentiation between the subjectival concord of the 2nd pers. s. and that of cl. 1 is found in Shona, e.g. Ma. **wakauja** (thou camest) and **wákauja** (he came), the higher tone being on the cl. 1 concord. A much greater tone range is used, however, when emotion influences the speech as in ideophones and interjectives; here intermediate tone positions and gliding tones are used.

In Venda, Sotho, and Tsonga two main tone heights are recognized tonemically, though there may be variants due to the type of consonant being used, and to various factors of assimilation and tone-stepping. Though much more study is necessary in regard to tone in these languages, it seems most probable that rules may be formulated under which the marking of relatively high tones only will suffice to indicate the tones. A differentiation between the three following words in Venda, for instance, may be made in this way: **pha:-ŋgá̱** (travel under difficulties), **pha:ŋga** (desert), **phá̱:ŋgá̱** (knives). Actually the isolated pronunciations of words in these languages reveal a variety of tonal nuances as the following examples from Southern Sotho demonstratives reveal:

---

[1] Tone differences also occur between these forms.
[2] Sectional studies have been done by Daniel Jones and A. N. Tucker.
[3] A hare met a baboon, and said, 'What are you looking for?' The baboon said, 'I am looking for food.'

(1st position)		(2nd position)		(3rd position)	
boːu	boːnɑ	boːu	boːnu	bɑːni	boːlɑ
_ ⁻	⁻ \	⁻ _	⁻ \	⁻ \	⁻ _

These reveal, however, only two tonemic patterns, low+high, and high+low. Absolute pronouns all follow the first pattern above. Tense differentiations are made often by tone, for instance **kiboːni** indicative is $\_\ ^-\ \_$, but subjunctive $^-\ ^-\ \_$. Rules governing the falling tones will no doubt be found, so that a recognition of two tones only will also here suffice.

In Nguni, tone recording for practical purposes is certainly more complicated. The tone range here is much greater: nine pitch points have been recorded with rising, falling, and rising-falling tones in addition to level tones. It is probable that in Nguni three tone heights will have to be recognized for tonemic purposes. Though a considerable amount of recording has been done, no conclusion has yet been reached on the tonemic question in Nguni.[1] Xhosa is the only Southern Bantu language which attempts to mark tone in a practical orthography, and it only does so in order to avoid possible ambiguities, as for instance: *waɓazˈisa* (he made known to them) and *waɓazˌisa* (he brought them); *ingˌachithwa* (let it be not dissolved) and *ingˈachithwa* (it may be dissolved). These are but expediencies used to label words and are not really serious tone markings. For instance, the difference between the first pair of words above could have been achieved by a doubling of the second vowel of the first word, i.e. *waɓaazisa*. The intricate system of the absolute tones used in Zulu is illustrated in Chapter V.[2]

G. ORTHOGRAPHY

The orthographies of the Southern Bantu languages may be described as 'phonetic', and for that reason are serviceable vehicles with a minimum of difficulties for the learner. Except in the case of the Sotho group the vowels are written phonemically. A discussion of the Sotho vowel implications is given in Chapter VI.[3] For consonants, in Nguni the twenty-six letters of the English alphabet were applied as far as needed, and surplus symbols, *c*, *q*, and *x* were applied to the clicks. In Southern Sotho French tradition was followed, and for the semi-vowels the symbols *o* and *e* were used instead of *w* and *y*; the latter are used in Tswana and Northern Sotho. In recent orthography revisions certain phonetic symbols *ɓ*, *ʃ*, and *ʈ* (a specially created symbol) were introduced into Xhosa. The Lepsius alphabet was the guiding one in the orthography of Venda, and certain diacritics are used to differentiate certain sounds, such as the dentals and the velar nasal. Diacritics are still more frequent in Tsonga, where they are used with retroflex consonants, and labio-alveolar and prepalatal fricatives. The various types of orthography are discussed at the commencement of each chapter V–IX. In contradistinction to the use of diacritics, according to the Lepsius system, Shona uses several phonetic symbols of the system as advocated by the International Phonetic Association, viz. *ɓ*, *ɗ*, *s̨*, *z̨*, *v*, *ŋ*. These are not all I.P.A. symbols, but have been devised on the principle of 'one sound one symbol'.

The biggest divergence between the different orthographies lies, however, in the word-division. Basing their deductions upon the grammatical forms applicable to the European language they were used to, the early missionaries, in reducing the different Bantu tongues to writing, divided up the words according to a non-Bantu conception—according to a disjunctive method, separating each grammatical conception without realizing the great difference existing in Bantu between what are words forming 'parts of speech' and what are

---

[1] Tucker has made a valuable contribution in his *Sotho-Nguni Orthography and Tone-Marking*.
[2] See p. 95.
[3] See p. 120.

non-isolatable formatives. Since that time revision of orthographies has brought fully conjunctive writing to Zulu and Shona, and an almost full conjunctive form to Xhosa; but the three Sotho literary forms, the three Tsonga literary forms, and Venda all still adhere to disjunctive writing. It is to be hoped that this non-Bantu imposition upon these languages will be done away with before long. In two pamphlets, *The Problem of Word-Division in Bantu, with special reference to the languages of Mashonaland* (1929), and *Conjunctive Writing for Bantu Languages* (1944), I drew attention to the problems involved in this, basing my conclusions upon the natural speech of the people and the function of stress. Approaching the subject from a different angle, Malcolm Guthrie came to the same conclusion in his paper, *Bantu Word Division* (1948). It is now beginning to be generally recognized that the conjunctive method is the correct one for Bantu.

REFERENCES

(a) *Phonetics and Phonology*

C. M. DOKE: *The Phonetics of the Zulu Language*. Johannesburg, 1926.
A. N. TUCKER: *The Comparative Phonetics of the Suto-Chuana Group of Bantu Languages* (1929.).
C. M. DOKE: *A Comparative Study in Shona Phonetics*. Johannesburg, 1931.
D. WESTERMANN and I. C. WARD: *Practical Phonetics for Students of African Languages*. Oxford, 1933.
C. MEINHOF: 'Das Ṱṣi-venḓa' (pp. 607–82 of *Zeitschrift der Deutschen Morgenländischen Gesellschaft*, Heft iv, 1901).
N. J. VAN WARMELO: *Die Gliederung der südafrikanischen Bantusprachen*. Berlin, 1927.
C. MEINHOF and N. J. VAN WARMELO: *Introduction to the Phonology of the Bantu Languages*. Berlin, 1932.

(b) *Tonetics*

D. JONES and S. T. PLAATJE: *A Sechuana Reader*. London, 1916.
D. M. BEACH: 'The Science of Tonetics and its Application to Bantu Languages' (pp. 75–106 of *Bantu Studies*, vol. i, 1924).
D. JONES: *The Tones of Sechuana Nouns*. London, (1928).
A. N. TUCKER: *Suggestions for the Spelling of Transvaal Sesuto*. London, (n.d.).
—— 'Sotho-Nguni Orthography and Tone-Marking' (pp. 200–24 of the *Bulletin of the School of Oriental and African Studies*, vol. xiii, 1949).

(c) *Word-division*

C. M. DOKE: *The Problem of Word-Division in Bantu, with special reference to the languages of Mashonaland*. S. Rhodesia, 1929.
—— *Bantu Linguistic Terminology*. London, 1935.
—— *Conjunctive Writing for Bantu Languages*. Livingstone, 1944.
MALCOLM GUTHRIE: *Bantu Word Division*. London, 1948.

(d) *Orthography*

International Institute of African Languages and Cultures: *Practical Orthography of African Languages*. London, 2nd ed. 1930.
W. G. BENNIE: *A Practical Orthography for Xhosa*. Union Govt. Advisory Committee on Bantu Studies and Research, 1931.
D. McK. MALCOLM: *A Practical Orthography for Zulu*. Union Govt. Advisory Committee on Bantu Studies and Research, 1931.
G. P. LESTRADE: 'A Practical Orthography for Tswana' (pp. 137–48 of *Bantu Studies*, vol. xi, 1937).

IV

THE MORPHOLOGY OF THE SOUTHERN BANTU LANGUAGES

Main Morphological Characteristics of the Bantu Family of Languages

THE Bantu languages are clearly distinguished from all others by a unique combination of morphological characteristics. Certain of these features appear to be found in the Bantu languages alone, others are found in other languages as well: but their association, as well as their particular forms, constitute the primary morphological *differentia* of the Bantu family. Following are the most important of the characteristics.

1. Bantu languages are mainly *inflexional*, making use of prefixes, suffixes, and, at times, internal vowel-change. Though they afford instances of agglutination, these are neither numerous nor marked enough to justify us in terming the languages agglutinating, as has been done by some writers.[1] Traces of isolating structure are also found, but these are very slight. It should be remembered that, of the other great African language families, the Hamitic is inflexional and the Sudanic is mainly isolating; and it may well be that in these several respects the Bantu language family is genealogically as well as structurally allied to these languages.

2. Bantu languages employ *grammatical class-gender*. The sex-gender found in Hamitic and other inflexional languages is only a particular instance of this general feature, which, incidentally, occurs sporadically in some Sudanic languages. But Bantu class-gender is not on a sex-basis: sex, when indicated at all, is shown in quite different ways.

3. Bantu languages employ a *concordial agreement* in their sentence structure. All pronouns, qualifying words, and predicates relating to a noun assume a prefixal element in agreement with that noun, and related in form to its prefix. These concords are usually called *alliterative*, since they are apt to contain the characteristic 'letter' of the noun-prefix; although in some cases, for various reasons, this 'letter' is either not found or is much disguised. Concordial agreement as such is not confined to the Bantu languages:[2] but its particular form, and the way in which it is employed, are distinctively Bantu.

4. Typical Bantu languages have a *quinary system of numeration*. There are root words for the numbers from 1 to 5 in all these languages, and words for 10 in most. But the words for the numbers from 6 to 9, in many languages, are on a quinary basis, i.e. they mean $5+1$, $5+2$, &c. Some languages have, however, advanced towards a decimal basis even here, by employing for 6 to 9 distinctive non-quinary root words, either borrowed or evolved.

5. Bantu languages show an *extraordinarily high development in the conjugation of the verb*, including separate positive and negative conjugations, and a great variety of moods, implications, aspects, and tenses, as well as a great wealth of derivative verbal forms. In this respect there is considerable similarity to the Hamitic languages, and sharp contrast with what occurs in the Sudanic family.

6. Bantu languages have the *ideophone as a distinct part of speech*, only one such language[3]

---

[1] e.g. by the late Dr. Alice Werner in her *Structure and Relationship of African Languages*, p. 15; and by A. Capell in his article 'Bantu and North Australian: a Study in Agglutination' (*African Studies*, vol. x, 1951). Naturally it depends upon the width of the definition of agglutination adopted.

[2] It is also a feature of a number of North Australian languages, as is revealed by the recent researches of Dr. A. Capell of the University of Sydney.

[3] Viz. Swahili; and even here ideophones are now recognized.

being known not to possess this feature to any marked extent. Many Sudanic languages share this feature with Bantu.

In addition to the above positive features, certain negative characteristics of the Bantu languages may be noted.

1. Bantu languages, though inflexional, do not admit of 'case'. No formal distinction is made between substantives, whether they are subject or object of the sentence. Nouns are in some Bantu languages inflected to form the vocative: but vocatives are syntactically interjectives. Similarly, nouns may in some Bantu languages assume a locative form: but such locatives are syntactically adverbs, and in some cases may be used as subject or object of sentences.

2. There is no preposition, properly so called, in the Bantu languages. What many writers have called prepositions are not separable words, but morphological elements forming adverbs. Disjunctive orthography is largely responsible for these elements often having been regarded as prepositions.

3. The article does not exist in Bantu languages. Some writers have tried to identify the article in the initial vowel of the noun-prefix: but this shows a misunderstanding of the true nature of this initial vowel, which, incidentally, is found only in the minority of Bantu languages.

As in other language families, we find an *underlying unity of word roots*,[1] e.g. the word for 'see'—Nguni *ɓona*, Sotho (S) *bòna*, Shona *vona*, Kongo *mona*, Herero *muna*, &c.; the word for 'water'—Nguni *amanzi*, Sotho (S) *metsi*, Swahili *maji*, Kongo *maza*, Konde *amisi*, Ila *menzhi*, &c.; the word for 'person'—Nguni (Xhosa) *umntu*, Sotho (S) *mōthō*, Shona *munhu*, Bemba *umuntu*, Swahili *mtu*, Konde *umundu*, Kongo *muntu*, Herero *omundu*, Duala *moto*, Ganda *omuntu*, Komoro *mndru*, &c.[2] Such examples are to be found in hundreds in the Bantu languages.[3]

This unity of roots is, however, not always so easily perceived as in the above examples. The sound shiftings which operate between certain groups, and even between languages in the same group, tend to obscure the similarity of forms. For instance, in the Southern Bantu languages one original root is responsible for the Nguni *thanda*, the Tsonga (To.) *raṇḍa*, and the Sotho *rata*, all meaning 'to love'; and similarly with Nguni *uɓuthongo*, Tsonga (To.) *ʋurongo*, and Sotho (N) *borôkô*, the noun 'sleep'. These differences are found according to the rules that (*a*) Nguni *th* appears as *r* in Tsonga and Sotho, (*b*) Sotho *t* and *k* appear as *nd* and *ng* respectively in Nguni and Tsonga, (*c*) Nguni *ɓ* = Tsonga *ʋ* = Sotho *b*.

Special Morphological Characteristics of the Southern Bantu Languages

The languages with which we are particularly concerned in this book belong to the South-eastern zone of the family, with the exception of Shona. The latter, comprising the South-central zone, is of considerable value here on account of its geographical nearness to the South-eastern zone and its affinities with Venda, but genealogically and otherwise it stands definitely apart from the languages of the South-eastern zone and, while sharing certain of their features, shares perhaps more with languages of the Central, and, to a smaller extent, with those of the Eastern zone. Special reservations in connexion with Shona will therefore

[1] The most detailed work on this subject has been carried out by Prof. Carl Meinhof and his Hamburg school: cf. Meinhof and v. Warmelo, *Introduction to the Phonology of the Bantu Languages*, pp. 185–233; Bourquin, *Neue Ur-Bantu-Wortstämme*, and Dempwolff, 'Ostbantu-Wortstämme' (*Ztschr. f. Kolonialsprachen*, vii). Much material is also to be found in Johnston, *Comparative Study of the Bantu and Semi-Bantu Languages*.

[2] In this chapter, when references are specifically to Southern Sotho or to Tswana, the vowel markings used by Jacottet and Cole respectively are employed. In all other languages, vowels are indicated as in the current orthographies. [3] See also the examples given in the previous chapter, pp. 42–43.

have to be made from time to time in discussing the morphological characteristics of the languages dealt with as a whole. These languages have, of course, the general features common to Bantu languages; but in addition the following special points deserve notice.

1. *Both monosyllabic and disyllabic noun prefixes are found.* Sotho and Venda have monosyllabic prefixes; Shona has monosyllabic prefixes, with, however, a latent initial vowel, whose phonological influence is discernible in certain words preceding nouns and on a number of other occasions; Tsonga has both monosyllabic and disyllabic forms of the same prefixes, employing now the one and now the other, according to certain rules as yet obscure. In Nguni, Zulu and Xhosa have disyllabic prefixes, while Swazi has disyllabic forms for some classes and monosyllabic forms for others.

2. *The formation of locatives is by suffix.* Shona has the Central Bantu construction in these cases, using prefixes of cls. 16, 17, and 18, i.e. *pa-*, *ku-*, and *mu-* respectively, as prefixal locative formatives. Traces of this construction appear also in the South-eastern groups.[1] But the general type of locative formation in these latter languages is by suffix, though certain nouns in Nguni and Sotho do not take a suffix, and most nouns in Nguni take a special prefixal formative—not, however, connected with the prefixes of cls. 16, 17, or 18—in addition to the suffix.

3. *Noun diminutives are formed by suffix.* Nguni, Tsonga, and Sotho employ exclusively a suffix, *-ana* (or some variant thereof), in the formation of noun diminutives. In Venda, and in certain Karanga dialects of Shona, a suffix similar to the above may be used; but in the other Shona dialects, and as an alternative in Venda, prefixal diminutive formation is found. Venda has a diminutive noun class with prefix *ku-*, pl. *zwi-*; while the various Shona dialects employ one or other of the sets of diminutive noun-prefixes *ka-* pl. *tu-*, *ka-* pl. *vu-*, or *ṣi-* pl. *vu-*.

4. *Deficient verbs are widely used.* This is especially the case in Nguni and Sotho; but they are also frequent in Shona, and occur, though less frequently, in Tsonga and Venda.

Bantu Grammatical Classification

Students of Bantu languages have experienced the difficulty of trying to use unaltered the moulds of classical and modern European grammatical systems, and considerable harm has been done to the study of Bantu languages by forcing foreign nomenclatures upon Bantu structure. Perhaps nowhere has this been more evident than in the methods of word-division which have been applied to some Bantu languages. Reference has been made elsewhere to the part played by stress in all these languages, where one of the main phonetic characteristics is that each word has one and only one main stress: elements, therefore, which carry no main stress must be but formative parts of words, and should not be written separately. This rule is today incorporated more or less correctly in the so-called conjunctive method of word-division, which is now accepted for Nguni and Shona; but it is not accepted in Tsonga, Sotho, and Venda, which write disjunctively. In order to consider the morphology of the languages treated here from a comparative point of view, it has been found necessary to hyphen, in examples taken from languages written disjunctively, those elements which comprise the real words according to the point of view just set out.

The first main classification of the words is according to the work which they do in the sentence. In this respect we find in Bantu languages six fundamental parts of speech—the same number as in other inflexional languages. These are: the *Substantive*, the *Qualificative*, the *Predicative*, the *Descriptive*, the *Conjunctive*, and the *Interjective*. It is in the subdivision of these parts of speech that the Bantu languages reveal their special genius.

The Substantive comprises the *Noun* and the *Pronoun*, each further subdivided; the

[1] For this phenomenon in Sotho, cf. Lestrade: 'Locative Noun-Classes and Formatives in Sotho', *Bantu Studies*, xii.

Qualificative is divided, according to the type of concord assumed, into the *Adjective*, the *Relative*, the *Enumerative*, and the *Possessive*;[1] the Predicative is of two types, the *Verb* and the *Copulative*, the latter being a predicative formed from some other part of speech by inflexion; the Descriptive is also of two types, the *Adverb* and the *Ideophone*. The varieties of the Conjunctive are of syntactical and etymological rather than morphological importance in the Bantu languages. The Interjective also need not be morphologically subdivided for our present purpose; but it should be remembered that it contains vocatives of nouns in addition to other words of an exclamatory nature. In all, then, the languages with which we are here dealing have twelve parts of speech, as follows:

I. Substantive: (*a*) Noun (divided into classes) . . . . . (1)
 (*b*) Pronoun (i) Absolute
  (ii) Demonstrative
  (iii) Quantitative . . . . (2)
  (iv) Qualificative
  (v) Relative[2]
II. Qualificative: (*a*) Adjective . . . . (3)
 (*b*) Relative . . . . (4)
 (*c*) Enumerative . . . . (5)
 (*d*) Possessive . . . . (6)
III. Predicative: (*a*) Verb . . . . (7)
 (*b*) Copulative . . . . (8)
IV. Descriptive: (*a*) Adverb . . . . (9)
 (*b*) Ideophone . . . . (10)
V. Conjunctive . . . . (11)
VI. Interjective . . . . (12)

In addition to classifying the parts of speech in their entirety, it is possible to classify the formative elements which enter into their composition. These formative elements may be: (1) *Roots*, the primary semantic bases of individual words; (2) *Stems*, which are derived from roots by inflexion, and which constitute secondary semantic word-bases; or (3) *Affixes*, the inflexional elements proper. Affixes may be (*a*) *Prefixes*, (*b*) *Infixes*, or (*c*) *Suffixes*; and, according to their functions and the types of words in which they are found, may be further subdivided into (i) *Substantival Prefixes*, nominal and pronominal; (ii) *Concords*, qualificative and predicative; (iii) *Adverbial Prefixes*; (iv) *Proclitics*; (v) *Auxiliary Verbal Prefixes*; (vi) *Substantival Suffixes*, nominal and pronominal; (vii) *Verbal Suffixes*; (viii) *Verbal Infixes*; and (ix) *Enclitics*.

We shall now proceed to treat of the individual parts of speech in some detail.[3]

THE NOUN

The noun consists normally of two distinguishable parts, stem and prefix, e.g. Ng.(X) um/fazi[4] (woman), Ve. tshi/thu (thing). In some cases the prefix may have disappeared, e.g.

[1] Swahili possesses a fifth type of qualificative, the *Invariable*, which assumes no concord at all.
[2] Found only in Venda.
[3] From this point, in this chapter, the names of the five main groups will be abbreviated as follows: Nguni = Ng., Tsonga = Tg., Sotho = So., Venda = Ve., Shona = Sh. In Tsonga, unless otherwise specified, only Tonga (Gwamba) forms will be cited; in Venda similarly only the standard literary forms, and in Shona only forms in Unified Shona. In Nguni, Zulu or Xhosa forms will be cited, designated by the letters Z. and X. respectively; in Sotho, either Northern Sotho or Southern Sotho or Tswana forms, designated by N.S., S.S., and T. respectively, or by So.(N), So.(S) and So.(T). When no letter follows the abbreviations Ng. and So., it is to be assumed that the form cited appears in both Nguni languages or all three Sotho languages, as the case may be.
[4] The sign / is used here to separate prefix and stem. It does not appear in the orthographies of the languages.

Tg. *ǔoko* (arm) (originally *ri/ǔoko*), Sh. *shoko* (word) (originally *ri/shoko*); or it may be phonetically disguised, e.g. Ng.(Z) *utshwala* (beer) (originally *uβu/ala*), So.(N) *kgoši* (chief) (originally *N/goši*). There are a number of such prefixes, and nouns are divided into classes according to the prefix they take. Some twenty-three such prefixes have been identified in the Bantu language-family, some having only singular function, some only plural function, while others have an intermediate function, neither singular nor plural. Of these 23 prefixes, Ng. regularly uses 13, Tg. 13, So. 13, Ve. 15, Sh. 18; while Sh. sporadically uses 1 more and the other languages each 3 more.

In some classes the nouns are linked together semantically as well as morphologically: that is, they have a common element in their meaning as well as in their form. Thus there is one set (cls. 1 and 2 in the table below) containing exclusively nouns denoting human beings or personified animals or objects; another (cl. 14) containing only nouns denoting abstractions and certain other semi-abstract nouns; another (cl. 15) containing only verbal infinitives; and so on. But in the greater number of classes it is difficult to find a single unifying semantic basis, and in some it is virtually impossible to find any semantic connexions at all. Further, it happens not infrequently that nouns found in certain classes in a given language occur in different classes in other languages, either through the disappearance of some classes in such languages, with the consequent transfer of their nouns to other classes, or for other more obscure reasons.

It was indicated above that some classes contain only singulars, and others only plurals; and it should now be mentioned that many of the classes are grouped in pairs, one of which regularly acts as plural to the other. Some nouns occur only in the singular, such as the word for 'smoke', Ng.(Z) *umu/si*, So.(S) *mō/si*, and most nouns of the abstract class and all of the infinitive class; while other nouns occur only in the plural, such as the word for 'water', Ng. *ama/nzi*, Tg. *ma/ti*, So.(N) *me/etse*,[1] Ve. *ma/ḍi*. In some other cases, when nouns have to be pluralized they are put into a class which does not regularly serve as plural of the singular class to which they belong, e.g. with the word for 'garden', Ng.(Z) *in/simu*, where we would expect the plural form *izin/simu*, but actually find *ama/simu*, So.(S) *tšimō*,[2] pl. *ma/simō*, not *li/tšimō*.[3] Further, cases occur where a singular noun has two plural forms, frequently with slightly different meanings, e.g. So.(S) *lē/lēmē* (tongue), pl. *ma/lēmē* (tongues), or *li/tēmē* (rumours). But all such cases are comparatively rare, the regular thing being that every singular noun has a corresponding plural of the same meaning in a class regularly associated with it for the purpose of forming plurals only.

But a change of prefix may mean something much more far-reaching than a mere change of number: it may also indicate a more or less fundamental change in the meaning of the noun; and by this process a series of nouns may be found in a given language, with the same stem but with different prefixes, of connected but differentiated meaning, e.g. Ng.(X) *um/thi* (tree), *ulu/thi* (stick), *uβu/thi* (poison); So.(T) *mo/nna* (man), *se/nna* (manliness), *bo/nna* (manhood); Ve. *tshi/thu* (thing), *ku/thu* (tiny thing), *ḍi/thu* (huge thing).

The prefix of the noun is a governing element in the sentence, determining the form of the concords which appear in many words brought into grammatical relationship with it. This phenomenon may be illustrated from the following examples:

Ng.(Z)   *Isi/zwe sa/mi esi/khulu si/thulile*,
                 (lit. Tribe my great it-is-peaceful;
                 i.e. My great tribe is at peace).

                 Ama/khosi a/mi ama/khulu a/file,
                 (lit. Chiefs my great they-have-died;
                 i.e. My great chiefs are dead).

[1] From **ma/etse*, with assimilation of *a* to the following *e*.
[2] From **N/simō*, with disappearance of the nasal and strengthening of *s* to *ts*.
[3] From **liN/simō*.
[4] From **liN/lēmē*.

Here the two prefixes *isi-* and *ama-* respectively require different forms of the possessive concord (*sa-*, *a-*), the adjectival concord (*esi-*, *ama-*), and the subjectival concord (*si-*, *a-*). Similarly:

Tg. *V̌a/na v̌a-mina v̌a-tele, a-nḍi-v̌a-tiv̌i hikwa/v̌o,*
(lit. Children my they-abound, not-I-them-know all;
i.e. I have many children, I do not know them all).

Ti/homu ta-mina ti-tele, a-nḍi-ti-tiv̌i hikwa/to,
(lit. Cattle my they-abound, not-I-them-know all;
i.e. I have many cattle, I do not know them all).

Sh. *Ua/sikana va/viri va/kuru va/kaenda kumusha kwa/vo,*
(lit. Girls two big they-have-gone to-village their;
i.e. The two big girls have gone to their village).

Ẓi/garo ẓi/kuru ẓi/viri ẓi/ri-po,
(lit. Chairs big two they-are-there;
i.e. The two big chairs are there).

The table which follows gives a list of the noun classes and their prefixes in the five language groups, arranged and numbered according to Meinhof's classification, and with their main morphological function, together with the hypothetically reconstructed Ur-Bantu form from which they presumably derive.

COMPARATIVE TABLE OF NOUN PREFIXES[1]

No.	Function	Ur-B.	Ng.(Z)	Tg.	So.(T)	Ve.	Sh.
1	s. of 2	*mu-*	*umu-*	*mu-*	*mo-*	*mu-*	*(u)mu-*
2	p. of 1	*βa-*	*aβa-*	*v̌a-*	*ba-*	*vha-*	*(a)va-*
3	s. of 4	*mu-*	*umu-*	*mu-*	*mo-*	*mu-*	*(u)mu-*
4	p. of 3	*mi-*	*imi-*	*mi-*	*me-*	*mi-*	*(i)mi-*
5	s. of 6	*li-*	*ili-*	*[ri]-*	*le-*	*[li]-*	*(i)[ri]-*
6	p. of 5[2]	*ma-*	*ama-*	*ma-*	*ma-*	*mâ-*	*(a)ma-*
7	s. of 8	*ki-*	*isi-*	*ši-*	*se-*	*tshi-*	*(i)ci-*
8	p. of 7	*βi-*	*izi-*	*ši-*	*di-*	*zwi-*	*(i)zi-*
9	s. of 10	*ni-*	*iN-*[3]	*yi[N]-*	*[N]-*	*[N]-*	*(i)[N]-*
10	p. of 9, 11	*lini-*	*iziN-*	*ti[N]-*	*di[N]-*	*dzi[N]-*	*(i)[N]-*
11	s. of 10	*lu-*	*ulu-*	*ri-*	*lo-*[4]	*lu-*	*(u)ru-*
12	p. of 13	*tu-*	—	—	—	—	*(u)tu-*
13	s. of 12	*ka-*	—	—	—	—	*(a)ka-*
14	see[5]	*βu-*	*uβu-*	*v̌u-*	*bo-*	*vhu-*	*(u)vu-*
15	see[6]	*ku-*	*uku-*	*ku-*	*go-*	*u-*	*(u)ku-*
16	see[7]	*pa-*	*pha-*	*ha-*	*fa-*	*fha-*	*pa-*
17	see[7]	*ku-*	*ku-*	*ku-*	*go-*	*hu-*	*ku-*
18	see[7]	*mu-*	—	*mu*	*mo-*	*mu-*	*mu-*
19	s. of 14	*pî-*	—	—	—	—	*(i)ṣi-*[8]
20	see[9]	*ɣu-*	—	—	—	*ku-*	—
21	see[10]	*ɣi-*	—	—	—	*ḍi-*	*zi-*

[1] The prefixes given in this table are the full and basic forms. Some of these forms may in certain cases undergo contraction or other phonetic change. Prefixes in square brackets are found only rarely, or not at all, their original presence in the language being deducible from their phonetic influence on the initial phones of the stem or from the concords employed with them. Vowels in parentheses in Sh. are not found with the nouns, but their original presence may be deduced from certain changes in final vowels of words preceding nouns.

[2] Also occasionally pl. of 14, esp. in Tg. and So.

[*For notes 3–10 see opposite.*]

GENERAL OBSERVATIONS ON THE TABLE OF PREFIXES

The prefixes in Ng.—except those of cls. 16, 17, 18, and (in Swazi only) certain other classes—are disyllabic, showing an initial vowel which may fall away in certain constructions, but which in the vast majority of cases is retained, either appearing unchanged or giving rise to coalescence with final vowels of formative elements preceding the nouns in which they appear. Tg. employs an initial vowel (*e* in To., *a* in the other forms of the language) not shown in the table: the rules for its employment are rather obscure and were discussed in Chapter III.[1] So. and Ve. have no initial vowel. Sh. has latent initial vowels, which seldom appear as such, but whose phonological influence is discernible in certain constructions.

CLASSES 1 AND 2 contain only nouns denoting human beings. There are sub-classes of these, which are called 1a and 2a respectively, with prefixes different from those of cls. 1 and 2, but employing the same concords as these classes. These contain proper names of persons, many terms of relationship, and certain miscellaneous words, including names of personified animals and objects. The prefixes are:

(Class)	(Ng.(Z))	(Tg.)	(So.(T))	(Ve.)	(Sh.)
1a	*u-*	—	—	—	—
2a	*o-*	*v̌a-*	*bó-*	*vho-*	*va-*

It will be seen that in Tg., So., Ve., and Sh. cl. 1a differs from cl. 1 in the entire absence of any prefix; while the prefix of cl. 2a in Tg. and Sh. is identical with that of cl. 2.

Examples of words in these classes are the word for 'my father', Ng.(Z) *uɓaɓa*, pl. *oɓaɓa*; Tg. (To.) *tatana*, pl. *v̌atatana*; So.(T) *rrê*, pl. *bó-rrê*; Ve. *khotsi*, pl. *vho-khotsi*; Sh. *ɓaɓa*, pl. *vaɓaɓa*.

While the prefixes of cls. 1 and 3 are identical in form, the concords used with them are different, sometimes very much so.

CLASSES 3 AND 4 contain, besides one or two personal nouns, a variety of non-personals, including names of spirits, diseases, trees and plants, some animals, some parts of the body, sometimes rivers, and a certain number of abstract nouns.

CLASS 5 is noteworthy phonologically, firstly for the frequent disappearance of the prefix, and secondly for the varying forms of the prefix and the phonological influence it exerts on the initial phones of the noun-stems. In Tg., Ve., and Sh. the prefix rarely appears, if at all; while in Ng. it varies from the full *ili-* through *li-* to *i-*; in Tg. from *ri-* (To.) to *li-* (Ro.). In Ve., and to an even greater degree in Sh., it is in this class that we meet with the phenomenon of vocalization of the initial phone of the noun-stem—cf. Sh. *gore* (cloud), from an original *ri/kore* (the plural is *ma/kore*). Cl. 5, besides miscellaneous names, tends to contain the majority of names of fruits.

CLASS 6, which, besides serving as plural for cl. 5, can also serve as plural for cls. 11, 14,

---

[1] See p. 28, also Chapter VIII, pp. 183, 203.

[3] The symbol *N* in these tables indicates a variable nasal, homorganic to the initial phones of the stems, and almost invariably exerting strong phonological influence on these phones. Its original presence is mostly deducible only from such phonological changes, which are usually very marked.

[4] This class has disappeared in So. (N and S), the nouns therein being transferred to cl. 5.

[5] This class contains many nouns found in the singular only; it also serves as singular to certain cl. 6 nouns; in Sh. it serves as plural to cl. 9 in Mhari, a dialect of Karanga.

[6] This class contains only verb infinitives.

[7] Only a few words are found in these classes; nearly all of these have lost their nounal function, and are now adverbs.

[8] Only in the Mhari dialect of Karanga, in place of 13.

[9] Cl. 8 is used as the plural of this class. The prefix *ku-* frequently exerts phonological influence on the initial phones of the stem of the noun.

[10] This prefix is treated concordially like cl. 5, and nouns of this class have cl. 6 plurals; but the prefix of this latter class is always added to, and not substituted for, the singular prefix.

and 21, contains primarily a number of nouns denoting things occurring in pairs or in parallel, such as certain parts of the body; a number of fluids or semi-fluids, e.g. the words for 'water', milk', and 'fat'; a number of abstract nouns, such as the words for 'strength', 'wisdom', &c.; and finally, a number of collective nouns. In So. this class occurs as a sort of quantitative plural for words which have other plural forms, e.g. (N.S.) *nku* (sheep), pl. *dinku*, quantitative pl. *manku* (many sheep); *kgoši* (chief), pl. *dikgoši* (chiefs), quantitative pl. *magoši* (many chiefs). In Ve. and Sh. in the case of cl. 21 always, and in So. in the case of cl. 14 frequently, this plural prefix is added to, and not substituted for, the singular prefix, e.g. Ve. *ḍikolomo* (huge head of cattle), pl. *maḍikolomo*; So. (N) *bothata* (difficulty), pl. *mabothata*.

CLASSES 7 AND 8 contain many names of material objects and instruments, e.g. Ng.(X) *isitya* (dish), Tg. *šilo* (thing); also of acts, e.g. Ng.(Z) *isililo*, So.(S) *sēllò* (weeping): and of persons regarded in some way as inferior, either on account of their size, their trade, or some physical defect, e.g. Ng.(Z) *isithunywa* (messenger); Tg. *šimunhu*[1] (manikin); So.(T) *sefôfu* (blind person). In all Southern Bantu languages, cl. 7 contains the name referring to the language and customs of people, e.g. Ng.(X) *isiXhosa* (the Xhosa language, customs, &c.); and similarly *šiṬonga, seSotho, tshiVenḍa, ciShona*.

CLASSES 9 AND 10, which are specially remarkable for the phonological influence of the nasal in their prefixes upon the initial phones of the stems of nouns, contain many names of animals, e.g. Ng.(Z) *ingwe* (leopard), So. *tau* (lion), Sh. *mhou* (ostrich). It is noteworthy that the prefix of cl. 10 is that of cl. 9 preceded by another element, which is not substituted for but added to it; and that the cl. 9 prefix is monosyllabic even in languages with disyllabic prefixes in other cases, and tends to disappear entirely in languages with monosyllabic prefixes, leaving only phonological traces of its former presence. In So., except in words with monosyllabic stem, and in one or two isolated cases elsewhere, the cl. 9 prefix is never found as such. In Sh., and often in Ve., the distinguishing element of the cl. 10 prefix is dropped, its former presence being deducible only from the concords of the nouns, the nouns themselves being indistinguishable in form in singular and plural.

CLASS 11 is remarkable for the tendency of its nouns to pass over, in some languages, into cl. 5, and to assume the prefix and concords of the latter class. This has happened in Tg., and in So.(N and S). In Tg., So., Ve., and Sh. there is a tendency for nouns of this class to take their plural in cl. 6, instead of in cl. 10; and in So. a number of such nouns have two plural forms, one in cl. 6 and another in cl. 10, often with slightly different meanings. It is only Ng. which has kept this class distinct in prefix, concords, and plural formation.

CLASSES 12 AND 13 occur commonly in the Central Bantu languages: among the Southern Bantu, however, it will have been observed that they are found only in Sh., and there only in certain dialects. The nouns in these classes are all diminutives.[2] Diminutive formation by prefix is not typical in the South-eastern Bantu languages, being found only in Ve. and in the way in which the cl. 7 prefix may be used in Tg. and, very occasionally, in So.; and so we find the nouns of the Sh. cls. 12 and 13 represented in the South-eastern languages, as well as in some Sh. dialects, by nouns with the same stems but showing diminutive suffixes: cf. Ng.(Z) *imbuzi* (goat), *imbuzana* (little goat); Tg. *mbuti, mbutana*; So.(N) *pudi, putšana*; Ve. *mbudzi, mbudzana*; Sh. *mbudzi, kambudzi* (but, e.g. in Karanga, *mbudzana*). Ve., however, also uses cl. 20 as a diminutive class, e.g. *luhuni*, cl. 14 (piece of wood), *kukuni*, cl. 20 (small piece of wood).

CLASS 14 contains mainly abstract nouns, though there are a few non-abstracts, mostly collective, in this class, which may take a plural;[3] cf. Ng.(Z) *uɓuntu* (humanity); Tg. *byalwa* (beer), pl. *mabyalwa* (kinds of beer, beer-drinks); So.(N) *bothata* (difficulty), pl. *mabothata*.

[1] Tg. uses this prefix frequently to form diminutives from nouns; and in such cases, as in the example given, the prefix is added to, and not substituted for, the existing prefix of the noun.
[2] In Central Bantu non-diminutives are also found in these classes.   [3] Not in Ng. or Sh.

CLASS 15 contains exclusively verbal infinitives, which may, however, appear with affixes, negative, objective, &c., e.g. Tg. *ku-tirisa* (to cause to work); *ku-ṅwi-tirisa* (to cause him to work); *ku-nga-tirisi* (not to cause to work); *ku-nga-ṅwi-tirisi* (not to cause him to work).

CLASSES 16, 17, AND 18 are locative classes, found in full force only in Sh.; and occurring in the South-eastern zone in a few isolated cases only. These will be dealt with more fully in connexion with the locative construction.

CLASS 19, among our languages, again occurs only in Sh., and there only in one dialect. Like cls. 12 and 13, it contains exclusively diminutives.

CLASS 20, which elsewhere (e.g. in Northern Bantu languages such as Ganda) occurs as an augmentative class, occurs in our languages as a diminutive class, and there only in Ve., e.g. *kuhothi* (little door), cf. *vothi* (door).

CLASS 21 occurs as an augmentative class, as in the Northern Bantu zone—but, among our languages, only in Ve. and Sh. The peculiar plural formation of this class has already been noted, e.g. Ve. *ḓikolomo* (huge head of cattle), pl. *maḓikolomo*; cf. *kholomo*, pl. (*dzi*)*kholomo* (cattle).

THE DERIVATION OF NOUNS

A large number of nouns are primitive in their stems, i.e., as far as can be seen they are not derived from other words. This is particularly so in the case of nouns with monosyllabic stems, e.g. Ng.(Z) *umuntu* (person), Tg. *rito* (word), So.(T) *motse* (village), Ve. *mmbwa* (dog), Sh. (*i*)*she* (chief); and there are also a large number of nouns with disyllabic and polysyllabic stems which are primitive, e.g. Ng.(X) *inkomo* (head of cattle), So.(S) *lēnaka* (horn), Sh. *vusiku* (night).

Many nouns are, however, derivative, being formed from various parts of speech, principally nouns and verbs, by different inflexional processes. There are also many compound nouns, of various types.

DERIVATION OF NOUNS FROM NOUNS

This occurs principally by suffix, and usually for the purpose of forming (*a*) feminines, (*b*) augmentatives, and (*c*) diminutives.

FEMININES are formed very sparingly; and for this purpose a suffix is employed, Ng. *-kazi*: *imbuzi* (goat), *imbuzikazi* (ewe); So.(S) *-hali*: *tau* (lion), *tauhali* (lioness); Sh. *-kadzi*: *imbga* (dog), *imbgakadzi* (bitch).

AUGMENTATIVES may be formed in Ve. and Sh. by putting nouns into cl. 21, as has been seen; but in So., and occasionally in Ng., a suffix identical in form with the feminine suffix may be employed for this purpose, e.g. So.(T) *mosadi* (woman), *mosadigadi* (huge woman); Ng.(Z) *itshe* (stone), *itshekazi* (huge boulder).

DIMINUTIVES may be formed in Ve. by putting nouns into cl. 20, and in Sh. by putting them into cls. 12 and 13. But, alternatively in Ve. and Sh., and regularly in the three other groups, diminutives are formed by employing a suffix, usually *-ana*, with the alternative *-anyana* in Tg. and So. The addition of this suffix usually gives rise to marked phonological changes in the final phones of the basic noun-stem, e.g. Ng.(Z) *impuphu* (meal), *impushana*; *intamo* (neck), *intanyana*; *isikhathi* (time), *isikhashana*; So.(N) *mosadi* (woman), *mosatšana*; *kgomo* (head of cattle), *kgongwana*.[1]

---

[1] So., curiously enough, sometimes employs the diminutive ending *-ana* to indicate feminines, by attaching it to the adjective qualifying a noun, e.g. in So.(N) *kgomo e-thšweu* (white male beast), *kgomo e-thšwana* (white cow).

NOUNS DERIVED FROM VERBS

There are numerous ways of deriving nouns from verbs, most of them occurring but sporadically. Two regular and extremely frequent ways, however, may be noted here.

PERSONAL NOUNS are formed by adding an appropriate prefix to the stem of the verb, and changing the final vowel -*a* to -*i*, e.g. Ng.(Z) *umhambi* (traveller), from *hamba* (travel): Tg. *mutiri* (worker), from *tira* (work); So.(S) *mōeti* (traveller), from *èta* (travel); Ve. *mufuli* (smith), from *fula* (forge); Sh. *mufambi* (traveller), from *famba* (travel).[1]

NON-PERSONAL NOUNS may be formed similarly by adding an appropriate prefix, and by changing the final -*a* of the verb-stem to -*o*, e.g. Ng.(Z) *uhambo* (journey), from *hamba* (travel); Tg. *ntiro* (work), from *tira* (work); So.(T) *loêtô* (journey), from *êta* (travel); Ve. *luambo* (language), from *amba* (speak); Sh. *rwendo* (journey), from *enda* (travel).

COMPOUND NOUNS

These may be formed in a great variety of ways, of which the following are typical, all from Ng.(Z):

Noun+Noun: *umninimuzi* (kraal-head), from *umnini* (owner) and *umuzi* (kraal).
Noun+Pronoun: *umniniyo* (its owner), from *umnini* and *yo*(*na*) (it).
Noun+Qualificative: *amanzimtoti* (sweet water), from *amanzi* (water) and -*mtoti* (sweet).
Verb+Noun: *impumalanga* (east), from *phuma* (come out) and *ilanga* (sun).
Verb+Pronoun: *uvumazonke* (yes-man), from *vuma* (assent) and *zonke* (all things).
Verb+Descriptive: *umlalandle* (wild animal), from *lala* (lie) and *endle* (outside).

THE PRONOUN

There are five types of pronouns in the languages under discussion: the Absolute, the Demonstrative, the Quantitative, the Qualificative, and the Relative.

1. THE ABSOLUTE PRONOUN merely indicates the substantive to which it refers, and in no way limits or qualifies it as do the other types of pronouns. The following table illustrates its forms:

		(Ng.(Z))	(Tg.)	(So.(N))	(Ve.)	(Sh.)
1st pers.	s.	*mina*	*mina*	*nna*	*nṇe*	*ini*
1st pers.	p.	*thina*	*hina*	*rena*	*riṇe*	*isu*
2nd pers.	s.	*wena*	*wena*	*Wêna*	*iwe*	*iwe*
2nd pers.	p.	*nina*	*ṅwina*	*Lena*	*inwi*	*imi*
3rd pers. cl.	1	*yena*	*yena*	*yêna*	*ene*	*iye*
	2	*bona*	*v̌ona*	*bôna*	*vhone*	*ivo*
	7	*sona*	*šona*	*sôna*	*tshone*	*ico*
	8	*zona*	*šona*	*tšôna*	*zwone*	*izo*
	9	*yona*	*yona*	*yôna*	*yone*	*iyo*
	10	*zona*	*tona*	*tšôna*	*dzone*	*idzo*

It will be noticed that the Ng., Tg., and So. forms have, in all cases, the final syllable -*na*;[2] and Ve. the corresponding -*ne*, -*ṇe*[3] in the forms of the 1st and 3rd pers.; while Sh. has an initial *i*-, found also in the 2nd pers. forms in Ve.[4]

---

[1] Personal nouns formed from verb passives, or followed by a cognate adjunct, do not change the final vowel of the verb-stem, e.g. Ng.(Z) *isithunywa* (messenger), from *thunywa*, passive of *thuma* (send); So.(S) *mōetsalibè* (sinner), from *etsa* (do) and *libè* (sins).

[2] Some Ronga dialects of Tsonga, and some Tswana dialects of Sotho, have -*ne* instead of -*na*.

[3] These are purely phonological variants.

[4] Venda is morphologically and otherwise strongly reminiscent of Shona, with which it is genealogically related.

THE SOUTHERN BANTU LANGUAGES

These pronouns may be used instead of, or in apposition to, a noun.

Tg. *Hina hi-ta-famba: ku-ta-sala ṅwina;*
(lit. We we-shall-go: there-will-stay you;
i.e. As for us, we shall go: you will stay).

Nḍi-ṅwi-v̌onile yena;
(lit. I-him-have-seen him;
i.e. As for him, I have seen him).

So.(N) *Ke-ra' Wêna. Nna, kgoši?*
(I-mean you. Me, chief?)

Barwa bóna ga-se-batho byale-ka-rena;
(lit. The Bushmen, they, it-is-not-people like-us;
i.e. The Bushmen are not people like ourselves).

Ve. *Hu-ḍo-ḍivha ene muṇe;*
(lit. There-will-know he master;
i.e. He himself will know).

VhaLemba vhone a-vha-na-dzikhosi dzavho;
(lit. The Lemba, they, they-have-not-chiefs of-theirs;
i.e. The Lemba have not got their own chiefs).

2. DEMONSTRATIVE PRONOUNS. There are four real demonstrative positions indicated in Bantu, originally divided into two contrast pairs, lit. 'this' and 'that', 'this one here' and 'that one yonder'. Among the Southern Bantu, all four are found in Shona; they are indicated in Sotho, though only fully used in Tswana; while only the 1st, 2nd, and 4th forms occur in Nguni, Tsonga, and Venda. In all the groups except Nguni the three forms are expanded with varieties of each to indicate a large number of intricate distinctions. This is especially the case in Venda. The following are examples from cls. 1 and 2 for each of the positions:

		(Ng.(Z))	(Tg.)	(So.(T))	(Ve.)	(Sh.)
1st position	1	lo	loyi	yô	uyu	uyu
	2	laƀa	lav̌a	ba	avha	ava
2nd position	1	lowo	lo, lweyo	yôo	uyo	uyo
	2	laƀo	lav̌o	bao	avho	avo
3rd position	1	—	—	yôno	—	uno
	2	—	—	bano	—	vano
4th position	1	lowayá	loya	yôlê	uḽa	uya
	2	laƀayá	lav̌aya	balê	vhaḽa	vaya

In the above table cl. 2 gives the forms typical for all the other classes, viz. in the 1st position the typical consonant and vowel of the noun-prefix appear, in the 2nd position the final vowel is changed to -o, in the 3rd position there is a suffixed -no, and in the 4th position a suffixed -ya or -la.

Demonstrative pronouns may be used (a) standing alone in place of the noun, (b) following the noun and in apposition thereto, or (c) before the noun in apposition, in which case one word group results, the initial vowel of the noun in Nguni being elided. So. (except for a few instances in S.S.) does not employ this last.

Examples:

Ng.(Z) *Asisifuni isitsha lesi;*
(lit. Not-we-it-want dish this;
i.e. We do not want this dish).

Asisifuni lesi-sitsha;
(lit. Not-we-it-want this-dish).

Asisifuni lesi;
(lit. Not-we-it-want this-one—referring to a noun of cl. 7 such as *isitsha*).

Ve. *Tshithu itshi, hetshi, tshenetshi, tshenehetshi;*
(This, this very, this same, this selfsame thing).

Tshithu itsho, hetsho, tshenetsho, tshenehetsho;
(That, that very, that same, that selfsame thing).

Tshithu tshiḽa, hetshiḽa, tshenetshiḽa, tshenehetshiḽa;
(Yonder, yonder very, yonder same, yonder selfsame thing).

3. QUANTITATIVE PRONOUNS are of two kinds, differing in concord: the *simple* and the *inclusive*.

The simple quantitative pronouns are derived from stems meaning respectively (i) *all* or *the whole of*, and (ii) *only* or *alone*, which have the following forms in the various language-groups:

	(Ng.)	(Tg.(Ts))	(So.(T))	(Ve.)	(Sh.)
all:	-nke	-nkle	-tlhê	-ṱhe	-se
only:	-dwa	-ce	-si	-ṱhe	-ga[1]

It is noteworthy that in the Tsonga group, To. and Ro. have no quantitative stem for 'all': only the Tswa cluster has such a stem, viz. *-nkle*; for 'only' To. and Ro. use the Jonga form *-še*, which is *-ce* in Ts. In place of the quantitative stem for 'all', Ro. and To. use an obsolete noun **hiku* with possessive suffixes, e.g. *hikweru* (all of us), *hikwav́o* (all of them), &c.

Examples of the use of these forms are Ng.(X) *mna ndonke* (the whole of me), *thina sonke* (all of us); Tg.(Ts) *žihari žonkle* (all the animals); Ve. *shango ḽoṱhe* (the whole of the country); So.(T) *wêna wêsi* (only you); Sh. *biza roga* (only the horse). Contrast Tg.(To) *v́anhu hikwav́o* (all the people).

Alternative constructions, where adverbs are used instead of quantitative pronouns, are employed to express 'all' in So.(N. and S.), and 'only' in Ng., So., Ve., and Sh., e.g. N.S. *batho ka-moka* (lit. the-people by-entirety, i.e. all the people), S.S. *bathō kaōfèla* < *ka-hō-fèla* (lit. the-people by-to-finish, i.e. all the people); So.(T) *batho fèla* (the people only), Ve. *vhathu fhedzi*. The derivatives from *-si* in So. may be employed participially, e.g. (T) *nna nôsi* or *nna ke-le-nôsi* (I only).

The inclusive quantitative pronouns are found only in Ng. and So., and in So. only in Tswana. They are derived from the stems of numerals, and mean 'both', 'all three', 'all four', &c. The derivatives from these stems use concordial elements similar to those of the simple quantitative pronouns. Note the following table:

		(both)	(all three)
Ng.(Z):	1st pers. p.	soɓaɓili	soɓathathu
	2nd pers. p.	noɓaɓili	noɓathathu
	3rd pers. cl. 2	ɓoɓaɓili	ɓoɓathathu
	6	omaɓili	omathathu
	8	zo(zi)mbili	zo(zi)ntathu

---

[1] The stems for 'all' are etymologically related, and prefix the concordial element in the derivative forms. The Tg. and So. stems for 'only' are etymologically related, but stand apart from the stems in Ng. and Sh., the etymological connexion between which is doubtful. In So., only T. has a full range of derivatives from *-si*, while N.S. has but one derivative from this stem (*noši*) and S.S. has but two derivatives (*notši* and *inotši*, the latter but a variant of the former), which are used invariably for all persons and classes. Ve. uses for 'only' the same forms as for 'all', preceded, however, by the copulative participial concords, e.g. *vhathu vhoṱhe* (all the people), *vhathu vhe-vhoṱhe* (the people only).

So.(T): 1st pers. p.   róóbabêdi   róóbararó
2nd pers. p.   lóóbabêdi   lóóbararó
3rd pers. cl. 2   bóóbabêdi   bóóbararó
6   óómabêdi   óómararó
8   tšóópêdi   tšóótharó

Examples of the use of the inclusive quantitative pronoun are: Ng.(Z) *thina soBaBili* (both of us), *nina noBathathu* (all three of you); So.(T) *lona lóóbabêdi* (both of you), *dikgómo tšóótharó* (all three head of cattle).

TABLES OF QUANTITATIVE PRONOUNS

all[1]	(Ng.)	(Tg.(Ts))	(So.(T))	(Ve.)	(Sh.)
1st pers. s.	ndonke(X)	nzonkle	—	—	ndose, ndese
	wonke(Z)	—	yôtlhê	—	—
p.	sonke	honkle	rôtlhê	rothe	tose, tese
	—	—	bôtlhê	—	—
2nd pers. s.	wonke	wenkle	—	—	wose, wese
	—	—	yôtlhê	—	—
p.	nonke	ṅwenkle	lôtlhê	nothe	mose, mese
	—	—	bôtlhê	—	—
3rd pers. cl. 1	wonke	yenkle	yôtlhê	wothe	wose, wese
2	Bonke	bonkle	bôtlhê	vhothe	vose, vese
5	lonke	gonkle	lôtlhê	lothe	rose, rese
6	onke	wonkle	aôtlhê	othe	ose, ese

only[2]	(Ng.(X))	(Tg.(To))	(So.(T))	(Ve.)	(Sh.)
1st pers. s.	ndodwa	ndoše	nôsi	ndothe	ndoga
	ndedwa	ndeše	—	—	ndega
p.	sodwa	—	rôsi	rothe	toga
	sedwa	heše	—	—	tega
2nd pers. s.	—	—	—	wothe	woga
	wedwa	weše	wêsi	—	wega
p.	nodwa	—	lôsi	nothe	moga
	nedwa	ṅweše	—	—	mega
3rd pers. cl. 1	—	woše	—	—	woga
	yedwa	—	êsi	ethe	wega
2	Bodwa	voše	bôsi	vhothe	voga
	—	—	—	—	vega
5	lodwa	roše	lôsi	lothe	roga
	—	—	—	—	rega
6	odwa	woše	ôsi	othe	oga
	—	—	—	—	ega

4. QUALIFICATIVE PRONOUNS are qualificatives, e.g. adjectives, possessives, &c., used substantivally as subject or object of a sentence. There is no change of form with this change of function except in the case of possessives in Ng.[3] Compare the following sentences, all of the same meaning:

Ng.(X) *Umfazi wakhe ukhona, kodwa owam uhambile*
(lit. Wife his she-is-here, but mine she-has-gone),
where *owam*, an inflected form, is used substantivally instead of *umfazi wam*.

---

[1] The existence and incidence of special 1st and 2nd pers. forms should be noted. They are given in the first line under the respective person. Where such special forms do not exist, 3rd pers. forms, given in the second line, are employed. Note also that Sh. has alternative vowels in the concordial element in all cases.

[2] The incidence of alternative vowels in the concordial element in the forms in this table should be noted: forms with *o* are given in the first line, forms with *e* in the second.

[3] Ng. possessives in this case (i.e. where they are used substantivally) assume an initial vowel. This is due to the fact that Ng. noun substantives have initial vowels; cf. Lamba, another language having initial vowels in its nouns, where the parallel sentence would run *Umukasi wakwe alipo, sombi uwanji waya*, where *uwanji*, an inflected substantival form, stands instead of the ordinary possessive *wanji*.

So.(S) *Mōsali ŏa-haĕ ō-teng, ēmpa ŏa-ka ō-tsamaile*, where *ŏa-ka* stands for *mosali ŏa-ka*.

Sh. *Mukadzi wake aripo, asi waŋgu wafamba*, where *waŋgu* stands for *mukadzi waŋgu*.

No change of form takes place in any of the languages when adjectives, relatives, or enumeratives are used pronominally, e.g. in Zulu:

Aɓakhulu ɓayeza (The elders are coming < *aɓantu aɓakhulu*), adjective.
Sifuna eziyisithupha (We want six < *izinkomo eziyisithupha*), relative.
Ngifuna inye (I want one < *into inye*), enumerative.

5. RELATIVE PRONOUNS are found only in Ve., and are there used, in one of the two alternative relative constructions employed by the language, to link the antecedent to the relative clause. These relative pronouns always refer to and agree with the antecedent. There are two series, the first employed when the verb in the relative clause is in a present or future tense, the second employed when the verb in the relative clause is in a past tense. Examples for various classes, with the present and future series given first in each case, are: 1. *ane, we*; 2. *vhane, vhe*; 5. *ḽine, ḽe*; 6. *ane, e*; 7. *tshine, tshe*; 8. *zwine, zwe*; 9. *ine, ye*; 10. *dzine, dze*. Examples of their use are: *munna ane a-ḓo-amba* (lit. man who he-will-speak, i.e. the man who will speak); *vhasadzi vhe vha-ita ngaurali* (lit. women who they-did thus, i.e. the women who acted thus); *zwithu zwe nda-(zwi)-vhona* (lit. things which I-(them)-saw, i.e. the things which I saw).

THE QUALIFICATIVE

Four types of qualificatives, differentiated according to the concords they employ, occur in the languages under treatment: the *Adjective*, the *Relative*, the *Enumerative*, and the *Possessive*. Qualificatives as such accompany and follow the substantive they qualify. If used apart from or preceding such substantives, they become functionally qualificative pronouns. In word order, possessives normally take precedence over other qualificatives, e.g. Ng.(Z) *inja yami enhle* (lit. dog my fine, i.e. my fine dog).

1. ADJECTIVES are comparatively rare in the Bantu languages. Ng. appears to have somewhat less than twenty, Tg. but eight, So. rather more than twenty, Ve. and Sh. just over thirty apiece. This comparative scarcity is made up for in various ways, by the employment of other qualificatives. The lists of adjectival stems in the various languages tally only to a restricted extent. Some such stems are confined to certain languages only, e.g. Tg. *-ṽisi*, Ve. *-vhisi*, Sh. *-mbishi* (green, raw); while others are found as adjectives in some languages and as other qualificatives, or even as other parts of speech, in others, e.g. the So.(N) stem *-botse* (good, nice), which is an adjectival stem in some dialects and a relative stem in others, while its Ve. counterpart *-vhuḓi* is a possessive stem.

The forms of the concords used with adjectival stems differ greatly in the various languages, not only phonetically, but also morphologically. In all the languages they contain an element which is closely related to the prefix of the noun class with which the concord agrees. In some cases, as in Ve. and Sh., the adjectival concords and the noun-prefixes are virtually identical. In Ng. the adjectival concords are derived from the noun-prefixes by preplacing a formative element *a-*, which coalesces with the initial vowel of the prefix, giving rise to distinctive adjectival concords. In Tg. and So. the adjectival concord proper (which is never used alone in Tg., and only rarely so used in So.) is once again practically identical with the noun-prefixes; but in these languages a compound adjectival concord, which is the concord commonly used, is made by preplacing to these forms demonstrative pronouns. The comparative table of select concords below shows the nature of such forms.

The Ng. forms are derived as described above, *a+um(u)-* giving *om-*, *a+ili-* giving *eli-*, &c. The symbol *N*, as before, indicates a homorganic nasal, which not only adapts itself to the succeeding phone, but also influences it.

THE SOUTHERN BANTU LANGUAGES 61

(Class)	(Ng.(X))	(Tg.)	(So.(T))	(Ve.)	(Sh.)
1	om-	lo'n-	yô-mo-	mu-	mu-
2	aβa-	la'v̌a-	ba-ba-	vha-	va-
5	eli-	le'ri-	lê-le-	ḷi-	(ri)-
6	ama-	la'ma-	a-ma-	ma-	ma-
7	esi-	le'ši-	sê-se-	tshi-	ci-
8	ezi-	le'ši-	tsê-di(N)-	zwi-	zi-
9	eN-	le'yi-	ê-(N)-	(N)-	(N)-
10	eziN-	le'ti-	tsê-di(N)-	(N)-	(N)-

The Tg. forms consist of the first position simple demonstrative pronouns plus the noun-prefixes[1] except in the case of cl. 14[2], where the subject concord takes the place of the noun-prefix. The two components coalesce through the elision of the final syllable of the demonstrative, e.g. cl. 2. lav̌a+v̌a gives la'v̌a; cl. 5. leri+ri gives le'ri; cl. 14. lebyi+byi gives le'byi.

The So. forms consist of first position simple demonstrative pronouns plus the noun-prefixes, except in the case of cl. 8, where an element is used identical with the prefix of cl. 9. In So. the homorganic nasal appears with monosyllabic stems, but disappears elsewhere—in all cases, however, influencing the initial phone of the stem. It should be added that in S.S. universally, in N.S. often, and even in T. sporadically, the non-nasal element in the concords of cls. 8 and 10 disappears.

In Ve. and Sh. the nasal acts in the same way as in So. In Sh., further, ri- does not appear in the concord of cl. 5, its previous presence being, however, deducible from the influence exercised by it upon the initial phone of the stem.

The following may serve as examples of adjectives and their concords: Ng.(X) aβantu aβadala (old people); Tg. ribye le'rikulu (a big stone); So.(T) basadi ba-bantšho (black women); Ve. tshithu tshiṭuku (a small thing); Sh. ɓaŋga guru (a big knife).

2. A RELATIVE is a qualificative differentiated from other qualificatives by the relative concord. Three kinds of relative stem occur: (a) Primitive stems, found mainly in Ng., and to a smaller extent in So., e.g. Ng.(Z) -ze (naked); So.(S) -thata (hard); (b) Nominal stems, mainly in Ng. and So. (with, in Ng., loss of the initial vowel of the noun-prefix), e.g. Ng.(Z) -makhaza (cold), from amakhaza (coldness); So.(T) -molemô (good), from molemô (goodness); (c) Verbal stems (which, except in Sh., under most circumstances take a distinctive relative ending), e.g. Ng.(X) -zayo (coming), from -za (come); Tg. -tiraka (working), from -tira (work); So.(T) -buang (speaking), from -bua (speak); Ve. -tshimbilaho (walking), from -tshimbila (walk).

The following is a comparative table of some selected forms of the relative concord:

		(Ng.(Z))	(Tg.)	(So.(N))	(Ve.)	(Sh.)
1st pers.	s.	engi-	ndi-	ke-	ndi-	ndi-
	p.	esi-	hi-	re-	ri-	ti-
2nd pers.	s.	o-	u-	O-	U-	u-
	p.	eni-	mi-	Le-	ni-	mu-
3rd pers. cl.	1	o-	a-	a-	a-	a-
	2	aβa-	v̌a-	ba-	vha-	va-
	5	eli-	ri-	le-	ḷi-	ri-
	6	a-	ma-	a-	a-	a-
	7	esi-	ši-	se-	tshi-	ci-
	8	ezi-	ši-	di-	zwi-	zi-
	9	e-	yi-	e-	i-	i-
	10	ezi-	ti-	di-	dzi-	dzi-

[1] The form n- of the prefix of cl. 1 is not the commonest form, which is mu-; but it occurs in quite a number of cases, e.g. nsati (woman) for *musati, nkata (spouse) for *mukata.

[2] And also, dialectally, in cl. 4.

The Ng. forms are derived by preplacing the formative *a*- to the indicative subjectival concords, with resultant vowel coalescences. The forms in the other languages are identical with the participial subjectival concords. These forms are used, singly in Ng., and preceded by a demonstrative pronoun in So., in the formation of relatives from primitive or nounal stems. They are also used in all the languages in the construction of relative clauses, where they refer to the antecedent, expressed or implied. It should be added that, in such clauses, the concords may change their form according to the tense of the verb in the relative clause. Only the present tense forms have been given above.

The construction of relative clauses is treated in detail in the chapters on the individual groups[1] and will not be gone into here. It should, however, be noted at this stage that (i) in Tg. and So., (ii) in one of the two alternative relative constructions in Ve., and (iii) in cases where the antecedent is not subject of the relative clause in Sh., the antecedent is followed by a word which serves as a connective between it and the relative clause, but which, unlike the relative concord (which refers to and agrees with the subject of the relative clause only), refers to and agrees with the antecedent. This word is or was originally a demonstrative pronoun in Tg. and So., a relative pronoun in Ve., and a possessive concord in Sh.

The following examples illustrate the relative and its concord:

Ng.(Z) *umfundisi oǫotho* (a reliable teacher)
  izinguɓo ezimanzi (wet clothes)
  aɓantu aɓahambayo (people who-walk)
  aɓantu engihamba naɓo (lit. people I-who-walk with-them, i.e. people with whom I walk)
  aɓantu engahamba naɓo (lit. people I-who-walked with-them, i.e. people with whom I walked).

So.(T) *mosêbêtsi ó-o-thata* (lit. work this-it-difficult, i.e. difficult work)
  batho ba-ba-molemô (lit. people these-they-goodness, i.e. good people)
  dikgosi tsê-di-busang sentlê (lit. chiefs these-they-rule well, i.e. chiefs who rule well)
  dithipa tsê-ke-sêgang ka-tšônê (lit. knives these-I-cut with-them, i.e. knives with which I cut).

3. The term ENUMERATIVE is used here to denote a category of qualificatives which are miscellaneous in character, but most of which have some numeral significance. The lists of enumeratives differ from language to language, and in some cases even from dialect to dialect. While the enumerative concord is generally of one type, it may be of two types, which will here be called a strong and weak respectively, in each of cls. 1, 3, 4, and 6; and the enumerative stems in each language have to be divided into three series according to the concords they assume in these classes, i.e. strong only, weak only, or either strong or weak. The incidence of the various stems, whether they are etymologically connected or not, again differs in the three series, both from language to language and in some cases from dialect to dialect. The following table gives most of the enumerative stems which occur.[2]

	(strong only)	(weak only)	(strong or weak)
Ng.(Z)	-*nye* (one)		
	-*ni?* (what?)		
	-*phi?* (which?)		
	-*mbe* (other)		
(X)		-*phi-na?* (which?)	
		-*mbi* (other)	

[1] Cf. Chs. V, p. 117; VI, p. 152; VII, p. 178; VIII, p. 204; and IX, p. 229.
[2] Ng. -*nye* means either 'some, other' (when it is treated as an adjective) or 'one' (when it is treated as an adjective in X. and as an enumerative in Z.). It has a full range of enumerative derivatives in Z. but only a limited range in X. All the languages have non-enumerative as well as enumerative derivatives from their enumerative stems, and in some even enumerative derivatives may be used non-enumeratively.

	(strong only)	(weak only)	(strong or weak)
Tg.	-ṽiri, -mbiri (two)	-hi? (which?)	
	-raru, -nharu (three)	-mbe (other)	
	-ngani? (how many?)	-ni?[1] (what?)	
	-nyingi (many) (cl. 6)		-nyingi (many) (cl. 4)
	-ṅwana, -ṅwanyana	-ṅwana, -ṅwanyana	-ṅwana, -ṅwanyana
	(some, other) (cl. 6)	(some, other) (cls. 1, 3)	(some, other) (cl. 4)
So.	-ng? (what?)	-fe? (which?), -sele (different), -pē (T. only) (any), -tee (N. only) (one)	
Ve.	-ṇe (self) (cl. 1)	-ṇe (self) (cls. 3, 4, 6)	
		-fhio? (which?)	
		-sili (different)	
Sh.	-mṇe (one, some, other)	-pi? (which?)	

The forms of the enumerative concord are:[2]

A. *Classes with one type*

(Class)	(Ng.(Z)	(Tg.)	(So.(T))	(Ve.)	(Sh.)
2	ɓa-	ṽa-	ba-	vha-	va-
5	li-	ri-	le-	ḽi-	ri-
7	si-	ši-	se-	tshi-	ci-
8	zi-	ŝi-	di-	zwi-	zi-
9	i-	yi-	e-	i-	i-
10	zi-	ti-	di-	dzi-	dzi-

B. *Classes with two types*[3].

I. Strong:

	mu-	mu-	mo-	mu-	mu-
1	mu-	mu-	mo-	mu-	mu-
3	mu-	mu-	mo-	—	mu-
4	mi-	mi-	me-	—	mi-
6	ma-	ma-	ma-	—	ma-

II Weak:

1	wu-	u-	o-	u-	u-
3	wu-	wu-	o-	u-	u-
4	yi-	yi-	e-	i-	i-
6	wa-	wa-	a-	a-	a-

Examples of the use of enumeratives with the above concords are Ng.(Z) *umfazi munye* (one woman), *izwe liphi?* (which country?), (X) *umntu wumbi* (another person), *isitya siphi-na?* (what dish?); Tg. *ṅwana muni?* (what child?), *marito maṅwana* (some words), *miri minyingi* or *yinyingi* (many villages), *nsati uṅwana* (some woman); So.(T) *ngwana mong?* (what child? i.e. of what sex?), *leina lesele* (a different name); Ve. *ene muṇe* (he himself), *vhone vhaṇe* (they themselves), Sh. *musikana mumṇe* (one girl), *shoko ripi?* (which word?).

4. A POSSESSIVE is a qualificative differentiated from other qualificatives by the possessive concord. The stems of possessives are of two types: (i) pronominal possessive stems, and (ii) nouns, pronouns, or adverbs. Of the two components of the possessive, the concord refers to and agrees with the possessee, the stem either indicates the possessor directly, or refers to and agrees with a possessor implied though not directly expressed.

There are, however, two aspects of the possessive which must be differentiated in Bantu,

---

[1] In Ronga dialect; in To. an immutable form *muni* is used.

[2] Stems of singular meaning are found only with singular nouns, and stems of plural meaning only with plural nouns. In the case of plural nouns with singular meaning, however, enumerative stems of singular meaning may be found with plural concords, e.g. Ng.(Z) *ngifuna amanzi manye* (I want one kind of water).

[3] In Ng. the strong forms occur in Z. only, the weak forms in X. only.

as also in European languages: (1) the direct possessive, which indicates the possessor of the antecedent, e.g. Z. *indlu yenkosi* (the house of the king), and (2) the descriptive possessive, which indicates some attribute, quality, content, &c., of the antecedent, e.g. Z. *indlu yamatshe* (a house of stone) or *indlu yesonto* (a house of worship). Direct possessives have as their basis nouns or pronouns; descriptive possessives have as their basis nouns or adverbs. A pronominal base will almost always indicate a direct possessive; an adverbial base always a descriptive possessive; while a noun base may function in either case.

The following table illustrates comparatively certain selected forms of the pronominal possessive stems:

	(Ng.(Z))	(Tg.) (a)	(Tg.) (b)	(So.(N)) (a)	(So.(N)) (b)	(Ve.)	(Sh.)
1st pers. s.	-mi	-nga	-mina	-ka[1]	—	-nga	-ŋgu
p.	-ithu	-iru	-hina	-ešo	-rena	-shu	-idu
2nd pers. s.	-kho	-ku	-wena	-go[2]	—	-u	-ko
p.	-inu	-inu	-ṅwina	-eno	-lena	-ṋu	-inyu
3rd pers. cl. 1	-khe	-kwe	-yena	-gwê[3]	—	-we	-ke
2	-ɓo	-ǒo	-ǒona	-bô	-bôna	-vho	-vo
5	-lo	—	-rona	—	-lôna	-ḽo	-ro
6	-wo	—	-wona	—	-ôna	-o	-wo
7	-so	—	-šona	—	-sona	-tsho	-co
8	-zo	—	-šona	—	-tšôna	-zwo	-ẓo
9	-yo	—	-yona	—	-yôna	-yo	-yo
10	-zo	—	-tona	—	-tšôna	-dzo	-dzo

The forms in the *b*-columns in Tg. and So., which are identical with the forms of the absolute pronouns in these languages, are used exclusively for all classes (except 1 and 2) of the 3rd pers. In the 1st and 2nd pers., and in the 3rd pers. cls. 1 and 2, these languages use both the *a*-forms and the *b*-forms, though with differentiated significance. In Tg. the *a*-forms and the *b*-forms are used alternatively, though the *a*-forms are disappearing, particularly in To. In So., only *a*-forms are used in the 1st and 2nd pers. s., and in the 3rd pers. cl. 1: the *a*-forms of the 1st and 2nd pers. pl., and of the 3rd pers. cl. 2, are used alternatively with the corresponding *b*-forms, though with differentiated meaning, the *a*-forms indicating communal possession, the *b*-forms possession not necessarily communal.

Possessive concords are of two kinds.

(*a*) The first kind may be illustrated by the following table of selected forms:

(Class)	(Ng.)	(Tg.)	(So.(N))	(Ve.)	(Sh.)
1	wa-	wa-	wa-	wa-	wa-
2	ɓa-	ǒa-	ba-	vha-	va-
5	la-	ra-	la-	ḽa-	ra-
6	a-	ya-	a-	a-	a-
7	sa-	ša-	sa-	tsha-	ca-
8	za-	ša-	tša-	zwa-	ẓa-
9	ya-	ya-	ya-	ya-	ya-
10	za-	ta-	tša-	dza-	dza-

This is the commonest kind of possessive concord found. It is the only one used in Sh.;

---

[1] -ka is also found in S. and in some eastern dialects of T.; but in most T. dialects it is replaced by -me, except in certain compound nouns ending in a possessive element, where -ka is found. In such compound nouns -ka frequently undergoes phonological change, sometimes of a fundamental nature, being often changed to -kê and occasionally even to -ê, e.g. T. *nnakê* (my younger brother), *rrê* (my father).

[2] -go is spelt -gô in T.; and appears as -ō in S., and in certain compound nouns ending in a possessive element, e.g. T. *kgantsadiô* (your sister).

[3] -gwê appears as -ê in S., and in certain compound nouns ending in a possessive element, e.g. T. *kgantsadiê* (his sister).

and in the other languages it is used in all those cases where the second kind is out of place—i.e. in the vast majority of possessive constructions. Examples are: Ng. *umfazi wakho* (your wife), So.(N) *lefase la-lena* (your country), Ve. *zwanḍa zwashu* (our hands).

(*b*) The second kind is of two types, found respectively only in Ng. and So. The following table shows selected forms of these two types:

(Class)	(Ng.)	(So.(T))
1	ka-	wa-ga-
2	ɓaka-	ba-ga-
5	lika-	la-ga-
6	ka-	a-ga-
7	sika	sa-ga-
8	zika-	tsa-ga-
9	ka-	ya-ga-
10	zika-	tsa-ga-

It will be observed that the Ng. type consists of the formative *ka-* alone for those classes whose prefix contains no consonant other than a nasal, and of *ka-* preceded by the subject concord for all other classes. The So. type consists of the formative *ga-* preceded in all cases by the first kind of possessive concord. The forms in Ng. are used when the possessor is a noun of cl. 1a, and necessitates the dropping of the prefix of that noun, e.g. (X) *umfazi kaɓawo* (my father's wife), *iinkomo zikaSandile* (Sandile's cattle). When this concord is used referring to proper nouns of cl. 1a, it has the meaning 'son of', e.g. (Z) *uNtengo kaJojo* (Ntengo the son of Jojo). The forms in So. are used (i) in N., S., and T., with pronominal possessive stems of the 2nd pers. s., and of the 3rd pers. cl. 1[1], as well as (sporadically in certain T. dialects) of the 1st pers. s.; and (ii) in T. only, with noun-stems of cl. 1a. Examples are (i) (N) *kgoši ya-ga-go*[2] (your chief), (S) *mōsali ŏa-ha-ē* (his wife), and (T) *dikgómo tsa-ga-me* (my cattle)—the last a rare form; and (ii) (T) *ntlo ya-ga-rrê* (my father's house).

When a possessive concord of the first kind is followed by a possessive pronominal stem commencing in *i-* (i.e. Ng. *-ithu*, *-inu*; Tg. *-iru*, *-inu*; Sh. *-id'u*, *-inyu*), or by a noun whose prefix begins with a vowel (i.e. in Ng.) or contains a latent vowel (i.e. in Sh.), vowel coalescence takes place, and we get e.g. Ng. *wethu* (our) from *wa-+-ithu*, *lomfana* (of the boy) from *la-+umfana*; Tg. *renu* (your) from *ra-+-inu*; Sh. *cenyu* (your) from *ca-+-inyu*, *dzomunhu* (of the person) from *dza-+(u)munhu*. The vowel of this kind of concord is dropped before the So. stems *-ešo* (*-esō*, *-etšho*) and *-eno*, and we get e.g. (N) *wešo* (our) from *wa-+-ešo*.

Wa-, the possessive concord of the first kind for cls. 1 and 1a, enters into a number of compound nouns as part of a possessive element affixed to a noun of one of these classes[3] to form the compound. In most such cases coalescence and contraction between the various elements in the compound take place, frequently resulting in the reduction of *wa-* to *a-*, and occasionally in its total disappearance. Thus we have e.g. Ng.(Z) *umntanami* from *umnt(w)ana wami*, Tg. and Ve. *ṅwananga* from *ṅwana wanga*, So.(N) *ngwanaka* from *ngwana wa-ka* (my child); and So.(T) *kgantsadiô*, *kgantsadiê*, and *morwa-kgósi* (chief's child) for *kgantsadi wa-ga-gô*, *kgantsadi wa-ga-gwê*, and *morwa wa-kgósi* respectively.

---

[1] Some exceptions to this rule are at times found. We occasionally get such forms as (N) *wa-go* (yours) for *wa-ga-go*, *tša-gwê* (his) for *tša-ga-gwê*. But such forms are rare.

[2] The current fashion of writing possessives containing pronominal stems of the 2nd pers. s. and of the 3rd pers. cl. 1 as e.g. *ya gago*, *ŏa haē*, disguises the real nature of the formative *ga-* (*ha-*), especially as the same formative, when used in T. with cl. 1a noun-stems, is written separately, e.g. *tsa ga rrê*. If So. were written conjunctively, such forms would have to read *yagago*, *ŏahaē*, *tsagarrê*; as it is, they should be written *ya ga go*, *ŏa ha ē*, on the model of the present *tsa ga rrê*; and are so written here, with the addition of the hyphens whose justification is explained earlier in this chapter.

[3] Occasionally in Ng. nouns of cl. 9, with concord *ya-*, appear in such compounds, when *ya-* is similarly reduced to *a-*, e.g. (X) *Nkosam!* (my chief!) from *nkosi yam*.

Wa-ga-, the possessive concord of the second kind for cls. 1 and 1a in So., enters in T. into phrases whose semantic formula is 'X. the son of Y.', and is there always reduced to *a-*, e.g. *Ratshidi a-Tauê.*

THE VERB

The verb in the South African Bantu languages may be studied under two main headings: (i) its varieties, including its derivatives, and (ii) its conjugation, including its compound forms. The languages differ considerably from each other in both these respects, especially in the latter.

Further it is of significance to consider Bantu verbs according to their IMPORT; this governs, to a great extent, their syntactical use. Generally speaking there are six types of verbs according to import: (1) Intransitive verbs, which are self-contained in their action, including many stative verbs and neuter forms, e.g. Z. *gula* (be ill), *hleka* (laugh). (2) Transitive verbs, which need an object to complete their action, including causative and most applied forms of the verb, e.g. Z. *shaya* (hit), *seɓenzela* (work for). (3) Locative verbs, which need a locative adverb to complete their action, including certain applied forms of verbs of motion, e.g. Z. *vela* (come from, originate in), *gijimela* (run to). (4) Agentive verbs, which need an agentive adverb to complete their action, including verb passives, e.g. Z. *ɓonwa* (be seen). (5) Conjunctive verbs, which need a conjunctive expression to complete their action, including reciprocal forms of the verb, e.g. Z. *fana* (resemble). (6) Instrumental verbs, which require an instrumental adverb to complete their action, e.g. Z. *hamba* (travel).

VARIETIES OF THE VERB

According to form, verbs may be divided into two categories: (i) those with primitive stem, and (ii) those with derivative stem.

The stems of primitive verbs are usually disyllabic, beginning in a consonant and ending in the vowel -*a*[1], e.g. Ng. *ɓona* (see), Tg. *raṇḍa* (love), So. *leka* (try), Ve. *ḍivha* (know), Sh. *tora* (take). But (i) a number of monosyllabic verbs occur, e.g. Ng. *pha* (give), *dla* (eat); So. (N) *ga* (draw water), *fsa* (burn); Sh. *bva* (come out), *d'a* (love); (ii) a number of stems begin with a vowel, e.g. Ng. *enza* (do), *akha* (build); So.(N) *ēma* (stand), *ila* (hate, taboo); Sh. *enda* (travel), *imba* (sing); and (iii) there are a few verbs whose stems end in vowels other than -*a*, e.g. Ng. *azi* (know), (*t*)*sho* (say), So.(T) *itse* (know), *re* (say), *lēre* (bring).

The stems of derivative verbs are usually polysyllabic. Three main varieties occur: (i) verbal derivatives, formed from other verb-stems generally by suffix; (ii) ideophonic derivatives, e.g. Ng.(Z) *ɓihlika* (fall apart), *ɓihlila* (knock apart), *ɓihliza* (scatter about), from the ideophone *ɓihli* (of sliding apart); (iii) nominal and qualificative derivatives, formed from noun- and adjective-stems,[2] e.g. So.(T) *tlhalefa* (become wise), from *botlhale* (wisdom); Ve. *vhifhala* (become bad), from -*vhi* (bad).

TABLE OF COMMON VERBAL DERIVATIVE SUFFIXES

(Species)	(Ng.(Z))	(Tg.)	(So.(T))	(Ve.)	(Sh.)
1. Passive	-*wa*	-*iwa*	-*wa*	-*wa*	-*wa*
2. Applied	-*ela*	-*ela*	-*êla*	-*ela*	-*ira*, -*era*
3. Neuter	-*eka*	-*eka*	-*êga*	-*ea*, -*eka*	-*ika*, -*eka*
	-*ala*	-*ala*	-*ala*	-*ala*	—
	-*akala*	-*akala*	-*agala*	—	—
4. Causative	-*ya*	-*ya*	-*ya*	-*ya*	-*ya*
	-*isa*	-*isa*	-*isa*	-*isa*	-*isa*, -*esa*

[1] That is, in the positive conjugation, indicative mood. In the negative conjugation, and in other moods, the stem may end in other vowels. In some languages of the Congo zone and elsewhere the final vowel is assimilated to the stem-vowel: this is not the case in Southern Bantu.

[2] Termed 'denominative verbs'.

	(Species)	(Ng.(Z))	(Tg.)	(So.(T))	(Ve.)	(Sh.)
5.	Intensive	-isa	-isa	-isa	-esa	-isa, -esa
		-isisa	-isisa	-isisa	-esesa	-isisa, -esesa
6.	Extensive	—	—	-aka	—	—
7.	Reciprocal	-ana	-ana	-ana	-ana	-ana
8.	Reversive	-uka	-uka	-oga	-uwa, -owa	-uka, -oka
		-ula	-ula	-ola	-ula, -ola	-ura, -ora
		-uluka	-uluka	-ologa	-uluwa, -olowa	-uruka, -oroka
		-ulula	-ulula	-olola	-ulula, -olola	-urura, -orora
9.	Perfective	-elela	-elela	-ĕlĕla	-elela	—
10.	Stative	-ama	-ama	-ama	-ama	-ama
11.	Contactive	-atha	-ata	-ama	-ara	-ata
12.	Repetitive or Diminutive	reduplication	reduplication/or diminutive ending	reduplication/or diminutive ending	reduplication	—

Certain of these suffixes may be compounded to form fresh suffixes with meanings resulting from those of the several members of the compound. Examples are So.(T) -*ĕlwa* (applied+passive), -*anya* (reciprocal+causative), -*isana* (causative+reciprocal), -*agana* (neuter+reciprocal), -*osa* (reversive+causative), -*isanya* (causative+reciprocal+causative), -*aganwa* (neuter+reciprocal+passive). It should also be remarked here that many of the suffixes shown in the above table are themselves already compound, e.g. Ng. -*akala* (-*eka*+-*ala*), So. -*ologa* (-*ola*+-*oga*), Ve. -*elela* (-*ela*+-*ela*). The etymology and phonology of such suffixes are, however, as yet obscure, and cannot be gone into in any detail here. The primary semantic characteristic of a suffix, however, appears to be its consonant, and the vowel or vowels, which are often evolved independently, and sometimes may not belong to the suffix proper at all, appear to be secondary characteristics, though they do play some semantic part. It is interesting, in this connexion, to compare, for example, such a series as the So. -*oga*, -*ola*, -*ologa*, -*olola*, with the series -*ĕga*, -*ĕla*, -*ĕlĕga* (not shown in the table), and -*ĕlĕla*, where the meanings of the several words in each series run in parallel, and in which, as it were, the vowels *o* and *ĕ* respectively are fitted into the consonantal framework ..*ga*, ..*la*, ..*l*..*ga*, ..*l*..*la*, whose final vowel serves merely as stem-terminal, not as suffix.

The PASSIVE species indicates that the action expressed by the verb is performed upon, not by, the grammatical subject. The commonest form of the suffix is -*wa*, e.g. Ng. *ɓonwa* (be seen), from *ɓona* (see); but this form appears to be absent from Tg., which seems to use -*iwa* on all occasions, e.g. *vŏniwa*, from *vŏna*. The form -*iwa* is also found in Ng., So.(T) and N), Ve. and Sh., with varying incidence: chiefly with monosyllabic stems, e.g. Ve. *fhiwa* (be given), from *fha* (give); and in Ng. with stems beginning with a vowel, e.g. *enziwa* (be done), from *enza* (do). In So. (S) we find also -*ewa*, -*owa*, and -*uwa* (there spelled -*ĕŏa*, -*ŏŏa*, and -*uŏa* respectively), with varying incidence: all three appearing, under different circumstances, instead of -*iwa* elsewhere, and the last appearing also in certain cases beside -*wa* (there spelled -*ŏa*), e.g. *jĕŏa* (be eaten), from *ja* (eat); *nĕŏa* (be drunk), from *nŏa* (drink); -*uŏa* (be gone), from *ĕa* (go); and *ratuŏa* beside *ratŏa* (be loved), from *rata* (love).

In Ng., So., Ve., and Sh. the suffix -*wa* may under given circumstances exert phonological influence upon the final consonant of the verb-stem, and in Ng. this influence may even affect retrogressively consonants preceding the final. This influence acts in three ways: in Ng., palatalization takes place, e.g. *ɓanjwa* (be seized), from *ɓamba* (seize), and (with retrogressive palatalization) *ɓanjiswa* (be caused to seize). In Ve. and Sh., velarization takes place, e.g. Sh. *rumɲa* (be bitten), from *ruma* (bite). In So. both palatalization and velarization occur, as well as a third process, labialization, e.g. So.(N) *tsebya*[1] (be known), from *tseba* (know); *rongwa* (be sent), from *roma* (send); and *rĕkwa*[2] (be bought), from *rĕka* (buy).

The APPLIED species indicates that the action is done on behalf of, or with regard to, or proceeding towards a person, or that it moves towards, or takes place on or at an object or place.

[1] Pronounced **tsiβja** (with palatalization) or **tsibɥɑ** (with front labialization).
[2] Pronounced with back labialization.

Its force may generally be rendered in English by such prepositions or prepositional phrases as 'for', 'on behalf of', 'towards', 'at', &c. The general form of the suffix is of the type *-ela*, e.g. So. (T) *rêkêla* (buy for), from *rêka* (buy). In Sh. we find vowel variation, *-ila* being used when the stem-vowel is primary, i.e. *i*, *a*, or *u*, and *-ela* when the stem-vowel is secondary, i.e. *e* or *o*; e.g. *ɓikira* (cook for), from *ɓika* (cook); *sorera* (spy for), from *sora* (spy). In So. the suffix is *-etsa* (S), *-êtsa* (T), *-etša* (N) for verb-stems containing non-primitive suffixes, e.g. (T) *bilêtsa* (call for), from *bitsa*—originally *bil-*+causative suffix *-ya*—(call). In Ve. the suffix is *-tshela* for verb-stems which have lost an original *k*, e.g. *setshela* (laugh at), from *sea*— originally *seka*—(laugh).

The NEUTER species indicates an intransitive state or condition, and its force can often be rendered in English by the suffixes '-able' or '-ible'. It will be seen that there are three types of suffix in this species, the last being compounded of the first two, e.g. So.(T) *-agala*, from an earlier *-êgala* (= *-êga*+*-ala*). The three suffixes are of varying incidence in the different languages: in some, e.g. Ng., the suffix *-ala* is rare, its place being taken by the compound suffix *-akala*. There appears to be a slight difference in meaning between the suffixes of the type of *-eka* and those of the type of *-ala*, the first being rather passive, the second rather active in force, e.g. So.(N) *bônêga* (be visible), and *bônala* (show oneself), from *bôna* (see). But the third suffix, of the type *-akala*, seems to be identical in force with the second, and so we find in So.(N) *bônagala* (show oneself). Sh. agrees here and elsewhere with the Central type of Bantu languages in varying the vowel, using *-ika* when the stem-vowel is primary, and *-eka* when it is secondary, e.g. *rasika* (get lost), from *rasa* (lose), but *voneka* (be visible), from *vona* (see). Tg. possesses a fourth form, *-aka*, not shown in the table, e.g. *v̊onaka* (be visible), from *v̊ona* (see); but it also uses the other three suffixes, e.g. *dyeka* (be edible), from *dya* (eat), *twala* and *twakala* (be audible), from *twa* (hear).

The CAUSATIVE species indicates that the grammatical subject of the derivative verb causes another agency to perform the action denoted by the stem verb. Its force may therefore generally be rendered in English by 'cause to', 'make to', 'oblige to', &c. In special cases this species, particularly when formed from verbs implying communal action, has the meaning 'help to', 'assist in'. Examples are e.g. Ng.(Z) *khulumisa* (cause to speak), from *khuluma* (speak); So.(N) *agiša* (help to build), from *aga* (build). Ng. also uses the causative species in a special idiom meaning 'act like', e.g. *ukuhambisa okwaɓanye* (to walk like others), a contraction of *ukuhambisa ukuhamba kwaɓanye* (to cause to walk the walking of others).

Of the two types of suffix shown, *-isa* is the commoner in all the languages and is a still living suffix, while *-ya* is rarer and is no longer living. This *-ya* is, however, the primary and basic causative suffix, while *-isa* is secondary and composite; and it is the suffix *-ya* which is in most cases responsible for the many contracted forms of the causative species which are found in the various languages, sometimes alongside uncontracted forms ending in *-isa*, and sometimes with slightly different meaning from these latter forms. Thus we have Ng.(Z) *fudumeza* and *fudumalisa* (heat up), from *fudumala* (be hot); So.(T) *letsa* (ring), and *ledisa* (cause to cry), from *lela* (cry); Sh. *pinza* and *pindisa* (cause to enter), from *pinda* (enter).

The INTENSIVE species indicates that the action denoted by the stem verb is performed intensively, quickly, or, in some cases, to an excessive degree, e.g. Ng.(Z) *ɓonisisa* (see well), from *ɓona* (see), *hambisisa* (travel fast), from *hamba* (travel)· Ve. *vhibvesa* (be too soft), from *vhibva* (be soft). Sh. here once more shows vowel variation. All the languages have two suffixes, with differing incidence and occasionally different meaning in each: a simple suffix, identical—except in Ve.—with the commoner form of the causative suffix, and a compound suffix, consisting—again except in Ve.[1]—of the causative suffix reduplicated. The difference between the two suffixes appears to be usually one of incidence rather than of meaning; but

---

[1] The vowel differentiation of Ve., like the vowel variation of Sh., is a secondary phenomenon: primarily, in spite of the difference in vowel, the causative and intensive suffixes are here also identical. The same holds for So.(N).

slight differences of meaning may occasionally be found, e.g. Ve. *pfesa* (hear well), *pfesesa* (hear very well indeed), from *pfa* (hear). This identity of form between the causative and the intensive suffixes is responsible for the fact that sometimes the same derivative verb may have two meanings, e.g. So.(S) *utlŏisisa*, from *utlŏa* (hear), may mean either 'hear very well indeed' (compound intensive) or 'cause to hear well' (simple intensive+compound causative). So.(N) in most of its dialects agrees with Ve. in having a distinctive intensive suffix, *-éša*, e.g. *rêrêša* (speak to the point, speak the truth), from *rêra* (discourse).

The EXTENSIVE species indicates that the action of the stem verb is performed extensively in space or time. The extensive is found fairly commonly in the Central Bantu languages, with suffixes *-aula, -aila, -ala* (transitive), *-auka, -aika, -aka* (intransitive), &c. In Southern Bantu it occurs only sporadically, except in So. where it is still frequently found. The suffix is *-aka* in So., e.g. (T) *rêmaka* (chop about), from *rêma* (chop), *rŏgaka* (curse up and down), from *rŏga* (curse). This suffix, however, is etymologically connected with the Bantu continuous, appearing in Yao, Kinga, Sango, &c., as *-ga*, in Ganda and Kongo as *-nga*, and is obviously not connected with the Central Bantu extensive.

The RECIPROCAL species indicates that the action of the stem verb is performed reciprocally or mutually by the subject, which is normally plural. It is formed in all the languages, with the suffix *-ana*, e.g. Tg. *ǎanhwana ǎa-randana* (the girls love each other), from *randa* (love); Sh. *varume vanotaurirana* (the men are talking to each other), from *taurira* (talk to). In Tg. the suffix is *-anana* when the verb-stem is monosyllabic, e.g. *twanana* (hear each other), from *twa* (hear). The reciprocal species may also be used with a singular subject, in which case the second associated subject follows the verb, with the conjunctive formative, e.g. Ng.(Z) *uzondana nenkosi* (he and the chief hate each other, lit. he-hates-mutually and-the-chief).

The REVERSIVE species indicates the undoing or reversal of the action denoted by the stem verb. Four types of suffixes are found: (i) simple intransitive, (ii) simple transitive, (iii) compound intransitive, and (iv) compound transitive. In Ng. these suffixes occur only inactively and sporadically; in the other languages they are to varying degrees active, and less sporadic. They have varying incidence in the different languages; and a considerable number of cases occur where no simple stem is extant corresponding to a given derivative stem. Ve. in this species agrees with Sh. in showing vowel variation, though with differing incidence. Miscellaneous examples of this species are Ng.(Z) *sombuluka* (come unwound), *thukulula* (untie); Tg. *simula* (uproot), from *sima* (plant); So.(N) *tloga* (go away), from *tla* (come), *lapologa* (rest), from *lapa* (become tired); Ve. *vhofolola* (untie), from *vhofha* (tie); Sh. *suŋgura* (untie), from *suŋga* (tie).

The PERFECTIVE species indicates the performance to the full or to completion of the action denoted by the stem verb. In the Central Bantu languages this is still an active species, but in those of the South the species is no longer active, only occasional verbs of this sort being found, while in Sh. it does not appear to exist at all. The suffix is of one type only, *-elela*, and is in form a reduplication of the applied suffix.[1] It is contracted to *-ella* in So.(S and N) and in certain Tswana dialects. Examples are Ng.(Z) *yekelela* (let go altogether), from *yeka* (let go); Tg. *hetelela* (finish right off), from *heta* (finish); So.(S) *qètèlla* (end altogether), from *qèta* (end).

The STATIVE species indicates that the subject is in a given position or posture. This species is no longer an active one, though a number of examples of it are found in all the languages. The suffix is *-ama*. Most of the verbs in this species do not appear to have corresponding simple forms. Examples are Ng.(Z) *khothama* (kneel); So.(T) *siama* (become straight); Ve. *gwadama* (kneel).

[1] It is noteworthy that intensity of action of one type or another is achieved by a reduplication of certain suffixes: the 'intensive' is formed by reduplicating the causative; this perfective is formed by reduplicating the applied; in some languages intensification is achieved by reduplicating the reversive.

The CONTACTIVE species indicates touching or contact of some sort. This species, also, is no longer active, though all the languages afford examples of it. The suffix generally is *-ata* (*-ara* in So. and Ve.). Simple stems corresponding to these verbs are no longer extant. Examples: Ng.(Z) *thaɓatha* (take), *namatha* (stick); Ve. *ambara* (dress oneself); So.(S) *tšŏara* (seize), *fupara* (grasp in the hand); Sh. *ɓata* (catch), *fuŋgata* (embrace).

In most Bantu languages there are derivative species in which the simple verb-stem is reduplicated. These species have not always the same force. Sometimes they are REPETITIVE, indicating that the action is done again and again, e.g. So.(T) *bua-bua* (speak again and again), from *bua* (speak); Ve. *buḍa-buḍa* (ramble about), from *buḍa* (go through); and sometimes they are DIMINUTIVE, indicating that the action is done only to a limited extent, e.g. Ng.(Z) *ɓona-ɓona* (see indistinctly), from *ɓona* (see), *hamba-hamba* (take a little walk), from *hamba* (walk). But there is a certain amount of confusion in meaning between these two species. Tg., and to a smaller extent So., may also form a diminutive species by adding the diminutive suffix *-anyana* to the simple verb-stem, e.g. Tg. *tiranyana* (work a bit), from *tira* (work); So.(N) *tsebanyana* (know a little), from *tseba* (know).

There are many other verbal suffixes occurring in the various languages. Such suffixes, however, are no longer active, and the stems they form are difficult to classify under distinctive species; space precludes any discussion of them here.

THE CONJUGATION OF THE VERB

With the exception of the Infinitive and the Imperative, all verbal forms consist of at least two parts: subjectival concord and stem. The latter may undergo certain inflexions, as in the formation of the perfect, certain negative forms, the relative form, &c., as well as in the formation of the various derivative species, as discussed above. The former is also capable of change in certain instances, notably for tense and mood. Various auxiliary formatives may also be brought in in the formation of certain tenses and moods, some of these appearing before and some after the subjectival concord. The objectival concord may also play a part; and in the formation of compound tenses deficient verbs may enter into the various verbal forms.

There are two distinct conjugations: the *Positive* and the *Negative*; and a number of different mechanisms for building up the forms found in each of these conjugations. There is no general method of deriving negative from positive forms; thus in Ng.(Z) we have *ngiyaɓona* (I see), neg. *angiɓoni*, but *ɓengiɓona* (I saw), neg. *ɓengingaɓoni*; Ve. *ndi-vhona* (I see), neg. *a-thi-vhoni*, but *ndo-vhona* (I have seen), neg. *a-thongo-vhona*. This variation in the form of negatives, *vis-à-vis* their corresponding positives, is found throughout the whole range of verbal forms. The incidence of the different mechanisms varies from language to language: cf. Ng.(Z) *ngithandile* (I have loved), neg. *angithandanga*, with So.(S) *kē-ratile* (I have loved), neg. *ha-kēa-rata*; and Tg. *nḍi-ta-tiv̌a* (I shall know), neg. *nḍi-nga-ka nḍi-nga-tiv̌i*, with Sh. *ndicaziva* (I shall know), neg. (Ze.) *handicaziva*. Even different dialects of the same language may employ different mechanisms in building up the same verbal forms: thus we have e.g. for 'I shall love' and its negative the following forms in So.(N) *ke-tl'o-rata*, *nka-se-rate*; (S) *kē-tla-rata*, *ha-kē-tl'o-rata*; (T) *ke-tla-rata*, *ga-nke-tla ke-rata*. Although, in general, to every positive form there is a corresponding negative, and vice versa, this is by no means always the case, e.g. all the languages, except Ng. and (under Ng. influence) So.(S), have only negative forms of the exclusive implication. Further, forms which morphologically are negatives of a given positive may semantically function as negatives of a different positive, e.g. Ve. *a-thi-nga-ḍivhi* (lit. I cannot know), a negative potential, is used as the negative of the positive indicative *ndi-ḍo-ḍivha* (I shall know).

Within each conjugation there is a considerable variety of modal forms. Apart from the *Infinitive* and *Imperative* forms, which, since they employ no subjectival concords, it is better not to call 'moods', the term *Mood* is applied to the *Indicative*, the *Subjunctive*, the *Conditional* (or *Contingent*), and to others having no direct equivalents elsewhere, such as the *Potential, Participial*, the *Temporal*, and the *Dependent*.

Within some of the main modal forms there may be further subdivisions: thus e.g. there may be various *Implications*—a *simple* (unspecified), a *progressive* (indicating action progressing from the past), and an *exclusive* (indicating action not going on previously); and various *Aspects*—an *indefinite* (unspecified), a *continuous* (indicating continuity), and a *perfect* (indicating a completed state of the action). The normal division of *Tenses* into *Past, Present,* and *Future* is also found, and it should be noted that most languages divide the past and the future tenses into an Immediate and a Remote, the dividing line between these varying, however, from language to language.

The number and incidence of the modal forms, the manner of their formation, and their meanings and functions, all vary greatly from language to language, and even in some cases from dialect to dialect. It is accordingly impossible here to give more than an outline of some of the commonest and most typical of these phenomena. It must also be noted that this aspect of Bantu morphology is the one in which the greatest chaos prevails in the existing literature as to the classifications adopted and the nomenclature used. What is set out hereunder must therefore still be regarded as suggestive and tentative.

The INFINITIVE, though a noun in form and partly in function, yet possesses a certain amount of verbal function. Positive forms are e.g. Ng. *ukuthanda*, Tg. *ku-randa*, Ve. *u-funa* (to love); and there are also negative forms, e.g. Ng. *ukungathandi*, So.(S) *hō-sa-ratē*, Sh. *kusada* (not to love). Tg. and So.(S) also have future forms, e.g. *ku-ta-randa*, *hō-tla-rata* (to be about to love); and So.(S) further has a potential form, *hō-ka-rata* (to be able to love); but these do not appear to have corresponding negatives. In all the languages the infinitive, positive or negative, is capable of taking an object, nominal, pronominal, or concordial, or some other extension, e.g. Ng.(Z) *ukuthanda aβantu* (to love people), *ukuthanda laβa* (to love these, i.e. people), *ukuβathanda* (to love them, i.e. people), *ukuthanda kakhulu* (to love greatly); and similarly in the negative forms *ukungathandi-βantu, ukungathandi laβa, ukungaβathandi*,[1] *ukungathandi kakhulu*.

The IMPERATIVE has an interjectional character and function, but is essentially verbal. It has singular and plural forms. The positive singular generally consists of the plain stem of the verb,[2] e.g. Ng. *βona*, Tg. *v̌ona*, Ve. *vhona*[3] (see); and the plural is formed by adding a suffix, e.g. Ng. *βonani*, Tg. *v̌onan(i)*, Ve. *vhonani*; though Ve. has an alternative singular form *vhonai*, which also uses a suffix.[4] Monosyllabic stems, except in Tg., assume a vowel, *e-* in So., *i-* in the other languages, e.g. Ng.(Z) *idla, idlani*—also *yidla, yidlani*—(eat); and similarly in So. *è-ja, e-jang*, Ve. *iḽai, iḽani*, Sh. *idya, idyai*. In Tg., and alternatively in Ng., they may assume a suffix, e.g. Tg. *dyana, dyanan(i)*, Ng.(Z) *dlana, dlanini*.[5] When the positive imperative takes an object or extension after it, it does not change its form: but when the objectival concord or reflexive prefix is used before it, the terminal *-a* is changed to *-e*, e.g. So.(S) *mō-thusè, mō-thuseng*, Ve. *mu-farise, mu-fariseni* (help him), Sh. *ẓivone* (look at yourself). It should be noted that subjunctive and hortative forms are frequently used instead of the imperative positive.

The negative imperative may be formed in various ways. So. has a distinctive form, which may be derived from the positive by preplacing *se-* and changing the terminal *-a* to *-e*, e.g.

---

[1] The Ng. negative is either definite, e.g. Z. *ukungaβathandi aβantu* (not to love the people) or axiomatic, e.g. Z. *ukungathandi-βantu* (not to love people at all, not to love anybody). In the latter case there is elision of the initial vowel of the noun object, and a single word group results.

[2] Sh. has also a more immediate imperative, formed with the prefix *ci-*, e.g. *cisara* (just you remain), pl. *cisarayi*.

[3] *vhona* is used when an object or extension follows.

[4] *vhonai* is used when the imperative stands alone.

[5] Also *yidlanini*.

se-rate, se-rateng (do not love). In Ng. and Sh. the imperative positive of a negativing verb is combined with the infinitive of the verb to be negatived, e.g. Ng.(Z) *musa ukuthanda*, *musani ukuthanda*, Sh. *rega kuɗa, regai kuɗa* (do not love), where *musa* and *rega* both mean 'leave', 'abstain from'. Tg. and Ve. use conjugated forms of certain verbs, usually deficient, with the infinitive or some other form of the verb to be negatived, e.g. Tg. *u-nga-ǔi-ǔona* (lit. you may not be seeing), *u-nga-thuki u-ǔona* (lit. you may not happen to be seeing), Ve. *u-songo-vhona* (lit. you must not be able to see); all equivalent to 'do not see'. Negative subjunctive, hortative, or potential forms may be used instead of the negative imperative.

Both objects and other extensions may be used with the imperative, e.g. Ng.(Z) *thanda aβantu* (love the people), *thanda laβa* (love these, i.e. people), *thanda kakhulu* (love greatly), *βathande* (love them, i.e. people); and similarly in the negative, e.g. Ve. *ni-songo-ɖisa vhathu* (do not bring the people), *ni-songo-vha-ɖisa* (do not bring them), *ni-songo-ɖisa zwino* (do not bring now).

The INDICATIVE MOOD shows the greatest number and variety of forms, including the fullest development of implications and aspects, and the fullest range of tenses.

The three typical implications may be illustrated by the following forms of the present tense, indefinite aspect:

(Implication)		(Ng.(Z))	(So.(S))	(Meaning)
Simple:	Pos.	*ngithanda*	*kē-rata*	I love
	Neg.	*angithandi*	*ha-kē-ratē*	I do not love
Progressive:	Pos.	*ngisathanda*	*kē-sa-rata*	I still love
	Neg.	*angisathandi*	*ha-kē-sa-rata*	I no longer love
Exclusive:	Pos.	*sengithanda*	*kē-se kē-rata*	Now I love
	Neg.	*angikathandi*	*ha-kē-e-s'o-ratē*	I do not yet love[1]

The three typical aspects may be illustrated by the following forms of the immediate future tense, simple implication:

(Aspect)		(Ng.(Z))	(So.(S))	(Meaning)
Indefinite:	Pos.	*ngizokuthanda*	*kē-tla-rata*	I shall/shall not love
	Neg.	*angizukuthanda*	*ha-kē-tl'o-rata*	
Continuous:	Pos.	*ngizokuβe ngithanda*	*kē-tla-be kē-rata*	I shall/shall not be loving
	Neg.	*ngizokuβe ngingathandi*	*kē-tla-be kē-sa-ratē*	
Perfect:	Pos.	*ngizokuβe ngithandile*[2]	*kē-tla-be kē-ratile*	I shall/shall not have loved
	Neg.	*ngizokuβe ngingathandanga*	*kē-tla-be kē-sa-rata*	

The five typical tenses may be illustrated by the following examples of the simple implication, continuous aspect:

---

[1] In Tg. the formative for the progressive implication is *-ha-*, e.g. *nḍa-ha-ranḍa* (I still love), neg. *a-nḍa-ha-ranḍi*; but only a negative form of the exclusive is used, e.g. *a-ndi-si-ranḍa* (I do not yet love). In Ve. the progressive implication is formed with *-tsha-*, but is seldom used in the positive, where another construction takes its place. In the negative, however, there is *a-thi-tsha-vhoni* (I no longer see). No forms for the exclusive implication appear to exist in Ve., though other constructions conveying the exclusive idea are found, e.g. *a-thi-athu u-vhona* (I do not yet see). In Sh. the progressive implication is formed with *-ca-*, e.g. *ndicavona* (I still see), neg. *handicavoni*; but the exclusive idea can only be indicated by means of another construction, and only in the negative, e.g. *handisati ndavona* (I do not yet see).

[2] This tense in Ng. is much more commonly used with stative verbs, &c.: *-lambile* (be hungry), from *lamba* (become hungry).

(Tense)[1]		(Ng.(Z))	(So.(S))	(Meaning)
Rem. Past:	Pos.	ngangithanda	kē-ile ka-ne kē-rata	I was/was not loving (formerly)
	Neg.	ngangingathandi	kē-ile ka-ne kē-sa-ratē	
Imm. Past:	Pos.	ɓengithanda	kē-ne kē-rata	I was/was not loving (recently)
	Neg.	ɓengingathandi	kē-ne kē-sa-ratē	
Present:	Pos.	ngiyathanda	kēa-rata	I am/am not loving (now)
	Neg.	angithandi	ha-kē-ratē	
Imm. Fut.:	Pos.	ngizokuɓe ngithanda	kē-tla-be kē-rata	I shall/shall not be loving (soon)
	Neg.	ngizokuɓe ngingathandi	kē-tla-be kē-sa-ratē	
Rem. Fut.:	Pos.	ngiyokuɓe ngithanda	kē-ĕ'o-ba kē-rata	I shall/shall not be loving (some time hence)
	Neg.	ngiyokuɓe ngingathandi	kē-ĕ'o-ba kē-sa-ratē	

The following examples, from So.(N), illustrate some of the time-action sequences in the simple implication, continuous aspect:

(Sequence)		(Immediate Past Tense)	(Meaning)
Imm. Past+	Pos.	ke-be ke-be ke-rata	I had/had not been loving
Imm. Past	Neg.	ke-be ke-be ke-sa-rate	
Imm. Past+	Pos.	ke-be ke-rata	I was/was not loving
Present	Neg.	ke-be ke-sa-rate	
Imm. Past+	Pos.	ke-be ke-tl'o-rata	I was/was not about to love
Imm. Fut.	Neg.	ke-be nka-se-ke ka-rata	

In Ng. there is a further tense distinction in present and immediate past time, which might be called that between the definite and the indefinite, depending in some cases upon the employment of a definite or an indefinite object. Thus in Ng.(Z) *ngiɓona* is used when a descriptive extension or an indefinite object follows, e.g. *ngiɓona umuntu* (I see a person), *ngiɓona kaɓi* (I see badly); while *ngiyaɓona*[2] is used when no descriptive follows, or when the object is definite, in which case an object-concord is also employed, e.g. *ngiyaɓona* (I see), *ngiyamɓona umuntu* (I see the person). Similar distinctions exist between the immediate past forms *ngiɓonile* (I saw; definite) and *ngiɓoné* (I saw; indefinite). In Tg., So., and Ve. similar distinctions of form are found, but only in the present, e.g. Tg. *ṇḍi-ǒona* and *ṇḍa-ǒona*, So.(N) *ke-bóna* and *ke-a-bóna*, Ve. *ndi-vhona* and *ndi-a-vhona*. In these groups, however, the nature of the object or extension does not appear to be of importance, only the fact of its presence, the indefinite forms being used when there is an object or extension, and the definite forms when there is none.

The SUBJUNCTIVE MOOD has, in comparison with the indicative, a restricted number of forms. There are no implications, and aspects are recognized only in some tenses. Of the forms of this mood we shall cite only one[3] which is common in incidence and formation in all the languages, i.e. the simple indefinite present[4] tense:

	(Ng.(Z))	(Tg.)	(So.(S))	(Ve.)	(Sh.)
Pos.	ngihambe	ṇḍi-fambe[5]	kē-tsamaĕè	ndi-tshimbile	ndifambe
Neg.	ngingahambi	ṇḍi-nga-fambi	kē-sē-tsamaĕè	ndi-si-tshimbile	ndisafambe

The meanings of these forms are '(that) I (may) travel' and '(that) I (may) not travel' respectively. Their most common uses are: (i) in clauses of purpose, (ii) hortatively or

---

[1] The dividing lines between the two past and the two future tenses vary. In Ng. the dividing line for the past tenses is between the day before yesterday and yesterday; that for the future tenses is more vague, but generally lies between today and tomorrow. In the other languages both lines are vague and subjective.

[2] This form is also used for emphasis, e.g. *ngiyaɓona umuntu* (I do see a person).

[3] Other subjunctive tenses will be referred to in the individual studies.

[4] As its function commonly covers future action, the term 'present-future' is sometimes used.

[5] The subjunctive ending -e is becoming obsolete in Tg., being replaced by -a.

permissively, (iii) in consecutive construction, and (iv) after certain deficient verbs. Examples are Ng.(Z) *Woza uɓone* (lit. Come that you may see, i.e. Come and see); Tg. *Ndi-ta-ta ndi-ŏone/a* (lit. I shall come that I may see, i.e. I shall come and see); So.(N) *Tsebiša monna gore a-tlê* (lit. Let-know the man that he-come, i.e. Tell the man to come); Ve. *Ndi-vhone!* (Let me see!); Sh. *Ndifambe?* (Must I go?).

A variant of the subjunctive mood is the HORTATIVE, usually formed therefrom by prefixing some hortative formative, *ma-* or *a-* in Ng., *a-* in Tg., *a-* (*ha-*) in So., *a-*, *nga-*, or *kha-* in Ve., *a-* or *ŋga-* in Sh. It has only one tense in common use, the present, e.g. Ng.(Z) *Mangiɓone* (Let me see); So.(S) *A-rē-bònè* (dual)[1], *A-rē-boneng* (plural) (Let us see). Its negative forms are like those of the subjunctive, e.g. *Mangingaɓoni*, *A-rē-sē-bonē*, *A-rē-sē-bonēng*. More polite hortatives may be formed by preplacing other hortative formatives: *ka-* in Ng.(Z), e.g. *Kawungiphe* (Please give me); *a-nkê-* in So.(N), e.g. *A-nkê-O-sepelê* (Please go away).

A number of forms of a *Conditional* or *Contingent Mood* are found in some of the languages, but the variety of their incidence, manner of formation, meaning, and use precludes adequate treatment here. In addition to their conditional meaning ('I should', &c.) they often have an optative meaning ('would that I . . .', &c.) and a past potential meaning ('I could have', &c.); but in form, though not in meaning and use, they are readily distinguishable from the forms of the potential mood.[2] Where they occur, they are usually marked by a distinctive introductory conjunctive, e.g. Tg. (*i*)*ngi*, e.g. (*i*)*ngi ndi-ŏona*, (*i*)*ngi ndi-nga-ŏoni* (I would/would not see); Sh. *d'ayi*, e.g. *d'ayi usinakwenda* (if you had not gone).

In Ng. the contingent is indicated by the use of tenses of past-future sequence, implying unfulfilled intention, e.g. in Z. *ɓesiyohamba* . . . (we would have travelled, but . . .). A similar usage is found in So., e.g. in T. *re-nê re-tla-tsamaya* . . . (we would go, but . . .).

All the languages have a POTENTIAL MOOD indicating ability to act. It is characterized by an infixed formative, -*ka-* in So., -*nga-* in the other languages, e.g. Tg. *hi-nga-tira*, So.(N, T) *re-ka-dira* (we can work). The negatives of this mood are of varied construction, e.g. Tg. *hi-nge-tiri*, So.(N) *re-ka-se-dire*, (T) *ga-re-ka-ke ra-dira* (we cannot work). The range and incidence of implications, aspects, and tenses vary greatly, being very restricted in Ng. on the one hand, and very wide in So. on the other. The following are examples of forms of this mood in So.(N): *nka-be ke-rata* (I may be loving); *nka-be ke-ratile* (I may have loved); *nka-be ke-tl'o-rata* (I may be about to love); *ke-be nka-be ke-rata* (I was able to be loving); *ke-be nka-be ke-tl'o-rata* (I was able to be about to love); *ke-tl'o-ba nka-be ke-rata* (I shall be able to be loving). The forms of this mood have conditional and optative, as well as purely potential, meaning, and are frequently used in conditional and optative constructions.

The PARTICIPIAL MOOD has been so called because its forms have, *inter alia*, meanings and functions akin to those of the participles of other languages. The range of participial forms is wide: they are found in various implications, aspects, and tenses.

Participial forms are distinguished from others in one or more of three different ways, whose nature and incidence vary in the different languages: (i) Tone: e.g. So.(N) *ke-dutše* ‿ ¯ ‿ (I have sat down), *ke-dutše* ¯ ‿ ‿ (I having sat down); (ii) Concord: e.g. Ng.(Z) *ɓakhala* (they speak), *ɓekhala* (they speaking); and (iii) Formative elements other than concords: e.g. Ve. *ndi-amba* (I speak), *ndi-tshi-amba* (I speaking); *a-thi-ambi* (I do not speak), *ndi-sa-ambi* (I not speaking).

Participial forms appear as constituents of many indicative and potential tenses, and as

---

[1] Tg., So., and Ve. in this mood show dual as well as plural forms next to the singular, at least in the first person, probably also in the other two persons. Thus we have a series of dual forms in, e.g. Tg. *a-hi-ŏone*, *a-mi-ŏone*, *a-ŏa-ŏone*, and a parallel series of plural forms *a-hi-ŏonen*, *a-mi-ŏonen*, *a-ŏa-ŏonen*; and similarly in So. and Ve.

[2] There appears to be no hard-and-fast demarcation in these moods between the ideas of contingency, desirability, and potentiality.

the basis of relative forms, e.g. Ng.(Z) *uɓethanda*, from *uɓe*+*ethanda* (lit. he-was+he-loving, i.e. he was loving); Tg. *ndi-nga-v̌a ndi-tirile* (lit. I-may-be I-having-worked, i.e. I may have worked); So.(N) *a-tlilego* (he who has come), from *a-tlile* (he having come). Apart from these circumstances, participial forms appear chiefly in constructions corresponding more nearly to participial clauses in other languages, both after certain verbs and after certain conjunctives e.g. Ng.(X) *Ndiɓaɓonile ɓehleli* (I have seen them sitting); So.(N) *O-šetše a-tlile* (lit. He-has-stayed he-having-come, i.e. He has already come); Ve. *Arali vha-tshi-funa* (If they wish).

The forms of the RELATIVE, a variant of the participial mood, are used in the construction of relative clauses.[1] As indicated previously, they are built up on a participial basis. In Ng. they consist of participial forms, with a relative concord substituted for the participial concord, and a relative suffix *-yo* frequently added, e.g. (Z) *aɓangathandiyo* (those who do not love)—cf. the participial *ɓengathandi* (they not loving). In Tg. they consist of participial forms with a relative suffix added, the suffix varying in form and place with the conjugation and the tense, e.g. *a-tiraka* (he who works), *a-nga-tiriki* (he who does not work), *a-tireke* (he who has worked), *a-nga-tirangiki* (he who has not worked). In So. they consist of participial forms with a relative suffix added, *-ng* in Tswana, So.(S), and some So.(N) dialects, *-go* in most So.(N) dialects, the place of the suffix varying with the conjugation and the tense, e.g. (N) *ke-ratago* (I who love), *ke-sa-ratego* (I who do not love), *ke-bego ke-rata* (I who was loving), *ke-bego ke-sa-rate* (I who was not loving), *ke-tl'o-go-rata* (I who will love), *nka-se-kego ka-rata* (I who will not—lit. cannot—love). In Ve. they are formed from participial forms by the addition of the relative suffix *-ho*, as in the case of So., e.g. *ndi-vhonaho* (I who see), *ndi-sa-vhoniho* (I who do not see), *ndo-vhonaho* (I who have seen), *ndo-vhaho ndi-sa-vhoni* (I who have not been seeing).

There are two further moods which are peculiar to individual languages: the TEMPORAL MOOD found in Xhosa (of the Nguni group), and what I have termed the DEPENDENT MOOD found in Venda. The former has but one tense, characterized by infixed *-aku-*, and expressing an action preceding that of the main verb. The latter, with both positive and negative forms, is characterized by infixed *-a-* in the positive (*-asa-* in the negative), and is used in a variety of constructions. Details are given in the individual language sketches.[2]

DEFICIENT VERBS

It will have been noticed that a good many forms occurring in the conjugation of the verb consist of two or more verb-stems, each with its own concord[3] and perhaps its own auxiliary formatives, functioning together as a compound predicate, e.g. So.(S) *kė-ne kė-sa-ratė* (lit. I-was I-not-loving, i.e. I was not loving), *kė-tla-be kė-sa-rata* (lit. I shall-be I-still-loving, i.e. I shall still be loving); Ve. *ndo-vha ndi-tshi-amba* (lit. I-have-been I-speaking, i.e. I have been speaking), *ndi-ḍo-vha ndo-amba* (lit. I-shall-be I-having-spoken, i.e. I shall have spoken). All such forms are but particular instances of a general phenomenon which is very widespread in the Southern Bantu languages. But the compound predicates we have met so far have contained only a restricted number of the deficient verbs[4] which

---
[1] Ve. uses the relative variant of the participial mood in one of its two types of relative construction, the participial mood in the other; and in some cases in So. the participial mood is used in relative clauses. The individual language sketches must be consulted for details.

[2] For the temporal mood, see Chapter V, p. 109; and for the dependent mood, see Chapter VII, p. 174.

[3] Except when one of the constituents of the compound predicate is an infinitive, in which case there is of course no concord, but an infinitive prefix.

[4] These have long been known as 'auxiliary verbs'. They are, however, always in fact syntactically the main verb in the constructions in which they appear. Some of them are used only deficiently, i.e. with incomplete predication and necessarily followed by another verb to complete such predication. Others, however, may regularly be used independently, and only function deficiently in special cases. The term 'deficient' must therefore be understood as applying only to their function when appearing in compound predicate constructions.

habitually enter into such expressions, and the range of meanings that we have come across has consequently been relatively small. The number of these verbs in any given language is, however, considerable,[1] and the range of meanings which they help to express is very wide. Moreover, these compound predicates are so frequent in their occurrence, and so typical of Bantu idiom, that they must receive some further attention.

Most of the deficient verbs we have met so far have helped to give some temporal shade of meaning to the compound predicate; but there are many of them which help to express non-temporal ideas. Most such verbs, further, are like those we have met already, defective, i.e. they possess only a restricted number of forms. Syntactically, they are variable: some are followed by the subjunctive mood of the complementary verb, others by the participial, yet others by the infinitive.

In Ng.(Z), most deficient verbs are also defective, and end irregularly, mostly in *-e*, e.g. *-ɓuye* (do thereupon): *ɓaɓuye ɓasinde* (they thereupon recover); *-ze* (do at last): *waze wafa* (at last he died, or until he died); *-damene* (do always): *udamene ehleka* (he always laughs); *-lokhu* (do continually): *ngilokhu ngiɓaɓona* (I continually see them). Others, mostly those which are followed by the infinitive, end regularly in *-a*, e.g. *-vama* (do habitually): *sivama ukuzingela* (we habitually hunt); and such verbs are not generally defective. But there are quite a number of defective verbs in *-e* which take the infinitive, e.g. *-cishe* (do·almost): *ɓacishe ukuzwa* (they almost hear).

In So. most of the verbs used deficiently also regularly function independently, e.g. (N) *-féla* as in *di-fedile* (they have come to an end), but *di-féla di-e-hwa* (they keep on dying); (T) *-lala* as in *ke-a-lala* (I am going to lie down), but *ke-létse ke-tsilé* (lit. I-have-lain-down I-came, i.e. I came last night). Accordingly few of these verbs are defective or end irregularly. A number of them take the infinitive, whose prefix coalesces with the final *-a* of the deficient verb, resulting in the contraction *o*, e.g. (N) *-nyak'o-*, for *-nyaka go-* (be on the point of); *ke-nyak'o-sepela* (I am on the point of going); *-f'o-* for *-fa go-* (do just): *ke-f'o-bóna* (I just look). Many, however, take the participial mood, e.g. (S) *-hlòla* (do continually): *kē-hlòla kē-bua* (I keep on talking).

In Sh. most deficient verbs are followed by the infinitive, the final *-a* of the verb coalescing with (*u*)*ku-*, the infinitive prefix, resulting in the contraction *o*, e.g. *-natso-* (do well) from *-natsa+*(*u*)*ku-*. This *o* is not influenced by subjunctive or negative changes, e.g. *handinatso-vona*—not *handinatsi-*(*u*)*kuvona*—(I do not see well). Sh. has a wide range of such forms, including a considerable number of monosyllabic ones, e.g. *-go-* (be able), *-ndo-* (go and do), *-karo-* (do almost), *-garo-* (do always); and such forms can even be combined into fresh compounds, e.g. *-gondo-* (be able to go and do). Sh. has also, however, some deficient verbs followed by the participial mood, e.g. *-bva* (do thereupon); *ndabva ndoenda* (thereupon I went); *-ŋge* (appear to do): *vakaŋge vakapeŋga* (they appeared to be mad).

PREDICATIVE CONCORDS

In Southern Bantu languages all tenses of the various moods have, in their essential construction, a subjectival concord; in addition an objectival concord may also be found with them. These two types of concord, which may be called predicative,[2] must now be further noticed.

The SUBJECTIVAL CONCORD is a predicative prefixal formative which is used in verbal and copulative constructions, and which indicates the person, the number, and (in the third person only) the noun class to which the expressed or implied grammatical subject[3] of the

---

[1] The numbers of such verbs, and their meanings, vary considerably in the different languages: Ng. appears to have the greatest range; Tg., as far as our present state of knowledge of this group shows, the smallest.

[2] The term 'predicative' is used rather than 'verbal', since the subjectival concords are used in copulative as well as in verbal constructions.

[3] This we call the 'concordial subject'. There are constructions of an indefinite nature in which a cl. 17

predicate belongs. It is invariably used in verbal constructions, and appears also in most of the copulative constructions, although in the latter case its incidence varies in the different languages. Its position relative to the predicative stem varies: in some forms it directly precedes the stem, in others it is separated from the stem by other formatives.

The forms of the subjectival concord undergo various modifications, partly functional (for conjugation, mood, tense, &c.) and partly phonological (depending upon the initial phone of the succeeding element). The following table of selected forms of the subjectival concord in Ng.(Z) will illustrate these variations:

		(1)	(2)	(3)	(4)	(5)[1]
1st pers.	s.	ngi-	ngi-	ngi-	ngi-	ng-
	p.	si-	si-	si-	si-	s-
2nd pers.	s.	u-	(w)u-	u-	u-	w-
	p.	ni-	ni-	ni-	ni-	n-
3rd pers. cl.	1	u-	(k)a-	a-	e-	w-
	2	ɓa-	ɓa-	ɓa-	ɓe-	ɓ-
	3	u-	(w)u-	u-	u-	w-
	6	a-	(k/w)a-	a-	e-	—

The following table illustrates comparatively the forms of the subjectival concord of the first of the above types in the various languages.[2] Each language has variants from this type in the same way as Ng.

		(Ng.(Z))	(Tg.)	(So.(T))	(Ve.)	(Sh.)
1st pers.	s.	ngi-	ndi-	ke-	ndi-	ndi-
	p.	si-	hi-	re-	ri-	ti-
2nd pers.	s.	u-	u-	O-	U-	u-
	p.	ni-	mi-	lo-, le-	ni-	mu-
3rd pers. cl.	1.	u-	u-, o-, a-	o-	u-	u-
	2.	ɓa-	ʋa-	ba-	vha-	va-
	3	u-	wu-	o-	u-	u-
	4	i-	yi-	e-	i-	i-
	5	li-	ri-	le-	ḽi-	ri-
	6	a-	ma-	a-	a-	a-
	7	si-	ši-	se-	tshi-	ci-
	8	zi-	ši-	di-	zwi-	zi-
	9	i-	yi-	e-	i-	i-
	10	zi-	ti-	di-	dzi-	dzi-

concord with the predicate refers to an indefinite subject represented by a noun of a different class; such a subject is termed the 'logical subject', e.g. Ng.(Z) kuyeza aɓantu (people are coming), in contrast to aɓantu ɓayeza (the people are coming).

[1] The forms in the first four columns are used when the immediately succeeding formative element begins with a consonant; those in the fifth column are used when that element begins with a vowel. Formative elements may be either verb-stems or verbal auxiliaries. The sounds indicated in brackets in column (2) are secondary, intervening between the vowel a of certain formatives and the concord proper.

Besides differences in phones and morphology, these forms also exhibit differences in intonation, which are not indicated above. The concords under (1) are used in positive indicative forms, e.g. (2nd pers. s.) uɓonile; those under (2) in negative indicative forms, e.g. (cl. 6) (k)awaɓoni and in hortative forms, e.g. makaɓone; those under (3) in subjunctive forms, e.g. (cl. 1) aɓone; those under (4) in participial forms, e.g. (cl. 2) ɓeɓona; and those under (5) whenever a vowel follows, e.g. (1st pers. s.) ngaɓona.

[2] A few points in connexion with the tones of these forms—not indicated in the table—should be noted. The forms for the 1st and 2nd persons have low tone, those for the 3rd person have high tone. As the current orthographies of the languages do not in general indicate tone, some orthographic devices have been introduced to distinguish similar forms in some cases: thus in Tg. cl. 1 is often written o instead of u to distinguish it from 2nd pers. s.; in So. and Ve. 2nd pers. s. is capitalized to distinguish it from cl. 1; and this also happens sometimes in So. in the case of the forms of 2nd pers. pl., which are capitalized to distinguish them from cls. 11 and 5 respectively.

The OBJECTIVAL CONCORD indicates the person, the number, and (in the 3rd person only), the noun class to which the expressed or implied grammatical object of the predicate belongs. It is naturally found only in verbal constructions; and it always immediately precedes the verb-stem. The following comparative table shows its forms in the various languages:

		(Ng.(Z))		(Tg.)	(So.(T))	(Ve.)	(Sh.)
1st pers.	s.	ngi-	ng-	ndi	N-	N-	ndi-
	p.	si-	s-	hi-	re-	ri-	ti-
2nd pers.	s.	ku-	kw-	ku-	Go-	U-	ku-
	p.	ni-	ni-	mi-	lo-, le-	ni-	mu-, ku-...-yi, mu-...-yi
3rd pers.	cl. 1	m-	m-	ṅwi-, mu-	mo-	mu-	mu-
	2	ɓa-	ɓ-	ča-	ba-	vha-	va-
	3	wu-	w-	wu-	o-	u-	u-
	4	yi-	y-	yi-, mi-	e-	i-	i-
	5	li-	l-	ri-	le-	ḽi-	ri-
	6	wa-	w-	ma-, a-, ya-	a-	a-	a-
	7	si-	s-	ši-	se-	tshi-	ci-
	8	zi-	z-	ŝi-	di-	zwi-	zi-
	9	yi-	y-	yi-	e-	i-	i-
	10	zi-	z-	ti-	di-	dzi-	dzi-

Ng. has two series, the first used with consonantal verb-stems, the second with vowel verb-stems, e.g. (Z) *uyangiɓona* (you see me), but *uyangazi* (you know me).

The variants found in certain cases in Tg. are dialectal.

The symbol *N* appearing in the 1st pers. s. in So. and Ve. denotes a nasal, which is homorganic to the initial phone of the verb-stem, and which produces strengthening in this initial phone, according to the laws indicated in the previous chapter, and which will be found treated of in somewhat more detail in the individual sketches devoted to So. and Ve. respectively. In the current orthographies, these sounds are written *m-* before labials, *n-* in all other cases. Thus e.g. in So.(T) *N-*(= **m-**)+*bóna* becomes *mpóna* (see me), *N-*(= **n-**)+*rata* becomes *nthata* (love me), *N-*(= **ŋ-**)+*araba* becomes **ŋkaraba**, written *nkaraba* (answer me), *N-*(= **ɲ-**)+*nyatsa* becomes **ɲɲatsa**, written *ṅṅyatsa* (despise me). Similar examples from Ve. are *mbudza* (tell me), from *vhudza*; *ngwana* (find me), from *wana*; *nthuma* (send me), from *ruma*; *ndaṱa* (abandon me), from *laṱa*.

The form *mo-* found in cl. 1 in So. becomes *m-* when prefixed to a verb-stem beginning with *b-*, and changes that *b-* to *m-*, e.g. (N) *mo-*+*bóna* becomes *mmóna*. This always happens in So.(N) and in So.(T) and usually in So.(S) as well, although there the uncontracted form is also frequently heard.

Sh. has three forms for the 2nd pers. p. The first of these, used in Karanga and Manyika, is on the model of the other forms. The second and third, used in the other Sh. dialects, suffix *-yi* to the verb-stem, as well as prefixing *ku-* or *mu-*: thus 'I see you (pl.)' may be either *ndinomuvona*, *ndinokuvonayi*, or *ndinomuvonayi*.

All the languages have a further objectival prefix, the REFLEXIVE, which is invariable in each language. It is used in the same way as the objectival concords. Its forms are Ng. *zi-*, e.g. (Z) *ukuziɓona* (to see oneself); Tg. *ti-*, e.g. *ku-titiṽa* (to know oneself); So. *i-*, e.g. (N) *go-ineêla* (to give oneself up to); Ve. *ḓi-*,[1] e.g. *u-ḓi-sumbedza* (to show oneself); Sh. *zi-*, e.g. *kuzitaurira* (to speak for oneself). In So. the reflexive objectival prefix causes strengthening[2] of the initial phones of the verb-stem, e.g. (S) *-ipòna* (see oneself) from *bòna*, *-ithata* (love oneself) from *rata*, *-ikaraba* (answer oneself) from *araba*; and so on.

[1] Always hyphened to the verb-stem.   [2] Or nasalization; see Chapter VI, p. 123.

The Copulative

'Copulative' is the term applied to all predicatives formed from other parts of speech. In English the verb 'to be' is used for this purpose; for instance, when using an adjective predicatively, 'a big person' becomes 'the person *is* big'. In such direct predication of an adjective in most Southern Bantu languages, however, no verb[1] is employed, but an inflexion of the adjective is carried out to form a predicate from it, such predicate being called 'the copulative'; and we have, e.g., in So.(S) *mōthō e-mōhōlō* becoming *mōthō ō-mōhōlō* (the person is big); or in Ng.(Z) *umuntu omkhulu* becoming *umuntu mkhulu*. In the same way if one noun is predicated of another it undergoes inflexion to form a copulative, e.g. 'John is a man'; So.(S) *Johanne kē-mōnna*, Ng.(Z) *uJohane yindoda*.

When, however, more than mere predication is indicated, when the copulative is conjugated in order to express mood or tense modification, an auxiliary verb, a type of copulative verb, is brought in. All the Southern Bantu languages employ one or more such verbs, though their incidence and treatment vary considerably from language to language.

All of them possess a verb whose primary stem is derived from Ur-Bantu *-βa (Ng. -ɓa, Tg. -ṽa, So.(N and S) -ba, Ve. -vha, Sh. -va), a copulative verb giving the general idea of 'become'; and all except Ng. possess living forms of another such verb *-li (Tg. -ri, So. -le, Ve. -re, Sh. -ri), a stative perfect giving the general idea of 'be'; while some (including Ng.) show the phonological influence of now disused forms of this latter verb in certain formative elements used in copulative constructions. So., further, also possesses a third copulative verb -na. No attempt can here be made to detail all the forms and uses of these verbs, which are defective and peculiar in their morphology, and whose syntax is governed by intricate rules. But the following points might be borne in mind at this stage.

In all the languages except Ng., copulative verbs and copulatives[2] are mutually exclusive in any copulative construction. Thus in So.(N) the copulative *ké-motho* (it is a person) is not used in the construction *O-tl'o-ba motho* (you will be a person), which contains a copulative verb; but the Ng.(X) equivalent *ngumntu* appears in the parallel construction *uzokuɓa ngumntu*.

In each language there is a division of functions between the *-βa-forms (with which, in So., -na is grouped as well) and the *-li-forms. In Ng., only traces of now disused *-li-forms are found in the copulative formatives *-nge-*, *-se-*, and *-si-*—(X) *ndingekho* (I not being there), cf. *ndingaɓoni* (I not seeing); *ndisekho* (I am still here), cf. *ndisaɓona* (I still see); *asimntu* (it is not a person), where *-si-* is the negative of *-li. Tg. *-ri* is used only in certain participial constructions, and this language possesses a special form for the positive relative, viz. *-nga* or *-nge*, e.g. *la'ṽa-nge ṽanhu* (those who are people). So. *-le* is used only participially, e.g. *ke-le motho* (I being a person), and has a negative *-se*, from *-sa-*+*-li, e.g. *ke-se motho* (I not being a person), cf. *ke-sa-rate* (I not loving). Ve. *-re* is used only as a relative stem, e.g. *mmbwa i-re yanga* (the dog which is mine), and shows the influence of a now disused form of *-li in (i) the negative participial stem *-si*, e.g. *ndi-si muthu* (I not being a person), (ii) the progressive formative *-tshee* e.g. *ndi-tshee-ho* (I am still here), and (iii) the special forms of the participial subjectival concords used with copulative verbs, e.g. *e-muthu* (he being a person), where *e-* is the ordinary participial concord *a-* changed under the influence of *-li. Sh. *-ri* appears in nearly all 1st and 2nd pers. copulative constructions, e.g. *tiri vanhu* (we are people), and in past, future, and negative constructions in all persons, e.g. *waŋga ari muvezi* (he was a carpenter), *handisirini* (it is not I); also before adverbs, e.g. *vari pano* (they are here). In all the languages *-βa-forms (or in So. alternatively forms of *-na*) are

---

[1] This is not universal; there are, for instance in Shona, cases of plain predication in which a copulative verb is used.
[2] This does not mean 'copulative base', for it is evident that even with copulative verbs a copulative base (not the full copulative form) is used in the other languages.

used in cases where *-li-forms are not available or cannot be employed; and it should be remembered that *-βa-forms are often used as auxiliary formatives in ordinary verb-tenses, e.g. Ng.(X) *ndiβe ndithetha* (I was speaking), contracted into *βendithetha*, Tg. *nḍi-ta-ʋa nḍi-ranḍile* (I shall have loved).

Copulatives may therefore be defined as non-verbal predicatives, formed from other parts of speech (substantives, qualificatives, adverbs, and conjunctives) by inflexion through modification of prefix or concord, by addition of formative elements, or by some other mechanism. The various languages differ considerably in the ways in which they form copulatives; and even in the same language various mechanisms may be employed for forming copulatives from different parts of speech, or from the same part of speech under different circumstances.

In addition to their function as predicates, copulatives in most of the languages of the South-eastern zone may function as agentive adverbs, e.g. Ng.(Z) *ngaβonwa ngumuntu* (I was seen by a person); in So.(S) *kē-ile ka-bònŏa kē-mōthō*. Such use of the copulative is not found in Shona[1] or Venda, where the conjunctive formative *na-* is used. Following is an outline of the morphology and use of the copulative in the various groups.

Nguni

The formation of copulatives from nouns is best illustrated from Xhosa, which prefixes *ng-* to nouns of certain classes, *y-* to those of certain other classes, and the characteristic consonant of the prefix to nouns of the remaining classes, in all cases lowering the basic high tone on the initial vowel of the prefix. Thus we have e.g. *ngumntu* (it is a person), *yimithi* (it is trees), *kukutya* (it is food). When such forms stand alone, their significance is positive, indicative, present. But they may also enter as stems into compound copulatives, or as complements into copulative constructions; and then these meanings are variously changed. Thus we have e.g. *ndingumntu* (I am a person); *kwakungumntu* (there was a person); *βendingengumntu* (I was not the person). In sentences indicating absolute negation, these copulatives change their form, and consist of the nouns minus their initial vowels, e.g. *asimntu* (it is not a person at all), *akamntu* (he is nobody).

The simplest type of copulative formed from pronouns is that in Zulu from the absolute pronouns (which may in all cases lose their final *-na*) by prefixing *ngu-* to those of 2nd pers. s. and cl. 1, and *yi-* to the others, e.g. *yimina* or *yimi* (it is I), *nguyena* or *nguye* (it is he). Such forms may stand alone or be subject to conjugation, e.g. *nginguye* (I am he), *asiyiβo* (we are not they), *ningeyithi* (you not being we). In absolute negation, no copulative formative appears, e.g. *akusimi* or *akusomina* (it is not I at all).

Copulatives are formed from adjectives by dropping the initial vowel of the adjectival concord, except in cl. 9, which substitutes *i-* for that vowel. Thus we have e.g. (X) *umthi mkhulu* (the tree is big), cf. *umthi omkhulu* (the big tree); *ihaſi lidala* (the horse is old), cf. *ihaſi elidala* (the old horse); *intonga inde* (the stick is long), cf. *intonga ende* (the long stick). These forms may also be conjugated, e.g. *umthi awumkhulu* (the tree is not big), *ihaſi lingelidala* (the horse not being old).

Impersonal non-adverbial copulatives may be formed from adverbs and conjunctives by prefixing *i-* or *yi-*, e.g. (Z) *yikhona* (it is there), *yingokuβa* (it is because). The syntactical uses of such forms are, however, restricted. Other forms, in which the plain adverb enters as stem into personal copulatives, or adverbial impersonal ones, are more common and fulfil a large number of syntactic functions, e.g. *ngikhona* (I am there), *βengikhona* (I was there), *ngingekho(na)* (I not being there); *kukhona* (there is), *βekukhona* (there was), *kungekho(na)* (there not being). Such forms can, however, be derived only from adverbs of place.

Mention must finally be made of the locative demonstrative copulatives meaning 'here

[1] Except in the Manyika cluster, where one finds, for instance, *ndakapiwa ndiβaβa wangu* (it was given to me by my father).

is/are', 'there is/are', 'yonder is/are', which are allied morphologically to the demonstrative pronouns, having distinctive forms for each of the demonstrative positions, and for each noun-class. They are formed with the prefixal element *na-* and an appropriate stem of concordial colouring, e.g. (Z) *nangu* (here he is), *nampo* (there they are), *nantiyá* (yonder is). They are used either alone, as in the preceding examples, or with the related noun following, e.g. *nangu umfundisi* (here is the teacher), *nampo aɓafazi* (there are the women), *nantiyá izwe* (yonder is the country).

TSONGA, SOTHO, AND VENDA

These languages resemble each other in their manner of forming and using copulatives, and differ from Ng. in possessing a very much smaller range of them and in using them to a much smaller extent. As already mentioned, copulative verbs and copulatives are mutually exclusive in any given copulative construction in these languages; and it may now be added that copulatives here are used only in plain predication, i.e. in present indicative copulative constructions: in all other cases, copulative verbs are used.

Non-adverbial impersonal copulatives are formed from nouns by means of a prefixal element which has two forms, positive and negative, but which is otherwise invariable. These elements are respectively *i-* (or *hi-*) and *a-hi-* in Tg., *ké-* and *ga-se-* in So.(N), *ndi-* and *asi-* in Ve.[1] Thus we have e.g. Tg. *i-munhu* (it is a person), *a-hi-munhu* (it is not a person), *i-ʋanhu* (it is people), *a-hi-ʋanhu* (it is not people).[2] All such forms are used as the predicative element in constructions whose subject is in the 3rd pers., e.g. Ve. *murena ndi-musadzi* (the chief is a woman), *vhone asi-vhafunzi* (they are not teachers).

Adverbial impersonal copulatives are formed from nouns in So. only, by means of the subjectival concord of cl. 17, e.g. (T) *go-motho* (there is a person), *ga-go-motho* (there is nobody).

Personal copulatives are formed from nouns by prefixing the subjectival concords agreeing with the subject of the copulative construction. They exist for the 1st and 2nd pers. only, except in T., where 3rd pers. forms are also found as alternatives to the non-adverbial impersonal copulatives mentioned above. Thus we have e.g. in Ve. *ndi-muthu* (I am a person), *a-ri-vhathu* (we are not people); and (in T. only) *o-motho* (he is a person), *ga-ba-batho* (they are not people).

Only impersonal non-adverbial copulatives are formed from absolute pronouns, in the same way as from nouns, e.g. Tg. *hi-mina* (it is I), *a-hi-yena* (it is not he). No copulatives are formed from the Ve. relative pronouns; but both impersonal and personal copulatives are formed from the other types of pronoun, personal ones (for the 1st and 2nd pers. only, except in T.) with the appropriate subjectival concord, impersonal ones (non-adverbial and for the 3rd pers. only) with the invariable copulative formatives, e.g. So.(T) *re-ba-gagwê* (we are his), *ga-se-bauô* (it is not those).

The simplest copulative formations from adjectives are found in Ve. where personal copulatives (for the 1st and 2nd pers. only) are formed by prefixing the appropriate subjectival concords, e.g. *ndi-muṭuku* (I am small), *a-ri-vhanzhi* (we are not many); and impersonal copulatives (for the 3rd pers. only) are formed with the invariable copulative formatives, e.g. *ndi-muhulwane* (he is important), *asi-vhanzhi* (they are not many). In Tg. and So. the rules for forming such copulatives are somewhat more complicated: examples are Tg. *ndi-nkulu* or *ndi-lo'nkulu* (I am big), *ʋanhu ʋakulu* or *i-ʋakulu* or *mbakulu* or *i-la'ʋakulu* (the people are

---

[1] The copulative formatives *hi-*, *ke-*, and *ndi-*, have basic high tone, while the 1st pers. s. subjectival concords *hi-* (pl.), *ke-*, and *ndi-* have basic low tone. These tones, which are in any case subject to change, are not indicated except in the new Tswana and So.(N) orthographies, where the copulative formative is usually now written *ké-* as above.

[2] There are some instances of an earlier nasal formative in Tg., in such copulatives as *nžito* (it is a word), from *rito* (word), *mbaʋanuna* (they are men) from *ʋaʋanuna* (men); but this formation is obsolescent in Tg., and does not occur in So. or Ve.

big), the corresponding So.(S) forms being *kē-mōhōlō* or *kē-ē-mōhōlō*, *bathō ba-bahōlō* or *kē-ba-bahōlō*.[1]

Impersonal copulatives are formed from adverbs and conjunctives by means of the invariable copulative formatives, e.g. Tg. *hi-kusuhi* (it is near), *hikuʋa* (it is because). Personal copulatives are formed from adverbs of place only, by prefixing the appropriate subjectival concords, e.g. So.(S) *kē-mona* (I am here), *ha-ba-teng* (they are not there).

In addition to the demonstrative pronominal copulatives, So.(N) and Ve. also possess locative demonstrative copulatives,[2] similar in meaning, and somewhat similar in formation, to those found in Ng. They are arrived at by prefixing *se-* in So.(N), and *kha-*, *nga-*, or *asi-* in Ve. to the respective demonstrative pronouns, the final vowel of the prefixal formative being subject to assimilation to a succeeding vowel. They may be used alone, e.g. So.(N) *šo*, (here he is), *šebaɓ* (there they are), *šobyolê* (yonder it is); Ve. *khoyu* (here he is), *ngevho* (there they are), *asuvhuḽaa* (yonder it is); or with the related noun preceding, e.g. So.(N) *mosadi šo* (here is the woman), *bašemane šebaɓ* (there are the boys), *byang šobyolê* (yonder is the grass); Ve. *mufu khoyu* (here is the deceased), *vhatukana ngevho* (there are the boys), *vhuswa asuvhuḽaa* (yonder is the porridge).

Shona

This language resembles Ng. in using tone-change as a factor in the formation of copulatives from nouns; and resembles Tg., So., and Ve. in the use of an invariable copulative formative, which, however, has only a positive form. It also resembles the latter languages in possessing a restricted number of copulatives, and in using them in relatively few cases only. Here, too, copulatives and copulative verbs are mutually exclusive in any given copulative construction. It may be added that these verbs, *-va* and *-ri*, with functions rigorously divided between them, are much more used in Sh. than in any other Southern Bantu language.

From nouns, except those of cl. 1a, and from adjectives, impersonal non-adverbial copulatives are formed, and used as predicative elements in 3rd pers. copulative constructions in the present indicative positive. The forms are arrived at by prefixing *i-* to nouns or adjectives of cls. 5, 9, and 10, and by raising the basic middle tone on the prefix or concord, as the case may be, in the remaining classes, e.g. *iɓaŋga* (it is a knife), *ishumba* (it is a lion), *iŋombe* (it is cattle), *cigaro* (it is a chair), *mùnhu* (it is a person); *ɓaŋga irefu* (the knife is long), *shumba isharu* (the lion is old), *ŋombe inhete* (the cattle are thin), *cigaro cikuru* (the chair is big), *munhu mùrefu* (the person is tall). There are no negative forms of these copulatives: in negative constructions, copulative verbs are employed.

From nouns of cl. 1a, from pronouns, and from adverbs and conjunctives, impersonal non-adverbial copulatives are formed with the prefixal element *ndi-*, whose vowel may assimilate to succeeding vowels, e.g. *ndiMutasa* (it is Mutasa), *ndiɓaɓa* (it is father), *ndini* (it is I), *ndivo* (it is they), *ndouyu* (it is this one; cl. 1), *nedziya* (it is those yonder; cl. 10), *ndowaŋgu* (it is mine; cl. 3), *ndipano* (it is here), *ndokuti* (it is because).

Personal copulatives are formed from adverbs containing the prefixal element *na-* (with), by prefixing the subjectival concords agreeing with the subject of the construction, e.g. *ndinehope* (lit. I-with-eyelids, i.e. I am sleepy), *unesimba* (lit. you-with-strength, i.e. you are strong), *vanokudya* (lit. they-with-food, i.e. they have food), *handinehope* (I am not sleepy), *haunesimba* (you are not strong), *havanokudya* (they have no food), In constructions other

---

[1] The Ve. forms, as well as Tg. *nḓi-lo'nkulu*, *i-la'ʋakulu*, and So. *ke-e-moholo* and *ke-ba-baholo*, can also be regarded as having been formed from the corresponding qualificative pronouns instead of from the adjectives. In meaning these copulatives are in fact more pronominal, i.e. 'I am the big one', 'they are the big ones', &c.

[2] Locative demonstrative copulatives are unknown in Tsonga and in the other clusters of the Sotho group; similarly they do not occur in Shona.

than the present indicative various other forms of this type of copulative may be found, e.g. *ndainehope* (I was sleepy); though usually in these cases copulative verbs followed by this type of adverb replace copulatives made from such adverbs, e.g. *ndaiva nomusoro* (lit. I-was with-head, i.e. I had a headache).[1]

THE ADVERB

The adverb in the Southern Bantu languages may be defined as a word which describes a predicative in respect of time, place, or manner, or describes a qualificative or other adverb in respect of manner. It is functionally distinct from the other type of descriptive, the ideophone, in that the latter does not indicate time or place, but only manner, and in addition indicates qualities such as colour, sound, smell, &c., or describes actions such as walking, running, &c., or states such as sitting, lying, &c. Formally, many adverbs differ from ideophones in containing grammatical formative elements, which the latter lack; though a number of such elements are not exclusively or primarily adverbial, and a small proportion of adverbs contain no such elements at all.

The adverb shows close affinity with the conjunctive. The forms of the two parts of speech run on parallel lines, and are often identical. They are also closely allied functionally, and cases where the same word functions alternatively as an adverb and as a conjunctive are frequent.

Although the morphology of many adverbs is a matter of etymology rather than accidence, it will be convenient here to discuss the forms of all adverbs without discriminating between the two aspects of their formation. In this way, the following types may be identified:

1. Primitive adverbs, not consisting of, or derivable from, other parts of speech, although some show formative elements which also occur in other words: their number is relatively small. Examples are Ng.(Z) *futhi* (again), *le* (far away), *nini?* (when?), cf. the enumerative stem *-ni?* (what?); Tg. *khwaṭi* (gently), *tano* (thus), *khale* (long ago); So.(T) *jaana* (now, thus), *kae?* (where?), *kwa* (there); Ve. *tsini* (near), *ṭaḍulu* (above), *ḍasi* (below), cf. the noun *fhasi*, used adverbially, with the same meaning; Sh. *cete* (only), *seri* (behind), *nhasi* (today), cf. the noun *musi* (day).

2. Other parts of speech, used unchanged in form, but with adverbial function,[2] e.g. Ng. *izolo* (yesterday: noun); Tg. *munḍuku* (tomorrow: noun), *hi-ku-biha* (badly: copulative); So.(N) *nthse* (there: noun); Ve. *vhusiku* (at night: noun), *zwino* (now: pronoun), *zwavhuḍi* (well: possessive); Sh. *masikati* (by day: noun), *ẓikuru* (greatly: adjective), *ẓakadaro* (thus: verb). Many adverbs of this type are nouns belonging to one of the locative cls. 16, 17, 18, or other parts of speech showing locative class concords, e.g. Ng.(X) *phandle* (outside: noun cl. 16), *apha* (here: demons. pron. cl. 16), *kudala* (long ago: noun cl. 17), *khona* (there: absolute pron. cl. 17); Tg. *hansi* (below: noun cl. 16), *kuṅwana* (elsewhere: adjective cl. 17), *lomu* (inside: demons. pron. cl. 18); So.(S) *fatše̩* (down: noun cl. 16), *hòna* (there: absolute pron. cl. 17), *mona* (here: demons. pron. cl. 18); Ve. *afha* (here: demons. pron. cl. 16), *hunzhi* (in

---

[1] Constructions containing copulatives formed from adverbs incorporating a prefixal element meaning 'with' are the normal Bantu equivalent for English constructions containing some form of the verb 'to have'. In addition to the Sh. examples given above, note Ng.(X) *ndinehafi* (I have a horse), *andinalo* (lit. not-I-with-it, i.e. I haven't got it); Tg. *nḍi-ni-matimba* (I am strong), *a-hi-na-tihomu* (we have no cattle); Ve. *ndi-na-mbudzi* (I have a goat), *a-hu-na-tshithu* (lit. not-there-with-thing, i.e. there is nothing). So. in these cases uses the copulative verb *-na*, followed by such adverbs, whose prefixal element is *le-*, or in certain cases its variant *na-*, e.g. (S) *kē-na lē-thipa* (lit. I-am with-knife, i.e. I have a knife), *kē-ne kē-na lē-pōli* (lit. I-was I-being with-goat, i.e. I had a goat), *kē-na na-eô* (I have it). In the negative, *le-* is dropped (or, in So.(N) leaves only a trace of its former presence), e.g. (S) *ha-kē-na pōli*, (N) *ga-ke-n'e-pudi*: *na-*, however, remains, as in *ha-kē-na na-eô* (I have not got it).

[2] Cf. in English the use of 'yesterday' as noun and adverb respectively in the phrases 'Yesterday was a fine day' and 'I saw him yesterday'.

many places, frequently: adjective cl. 17), *murahu* (behind: noun cl. 18); Sh. *pamberi* (before: noun cl. 16), *apo* (there: demons. pron. cl. 16), *pose* (everywhere: quant. pron. cl. 16), *kunze* (outside: noun cl. 17), *kwesekwese* (everywhere: quant. pron. cl. 17), *mukati* (in the middle: noun cl. 18), *umo* (inside: demons. pron. cl. 18).

3. Other parts of speech, modified by omission, addition, or change of formative elements: only the chief types of such adverbs can be mentioned here.

(*a*) *Word-stems*. These occur chiefly in So., e.g. (T) *pele* (before: noun cl. 16), *thata* (very much: relative), *fêla* (only, just: verb);[1] Ng.(X) *nyakomnye* (the year before last), from *umnyaka omnye* (another year); Sh. *siku nesikati* (by night and day), from *usiku nesikati* (a night and a day).

(*b*) *Nouns minus the initial vowel of their prefix*. This type is naturally confined to Ng., but is frequent in that group, e.g. (Z) *kuqala* (at first), from *ukuqala* (to begin); *ntambama* (in the afternoon), from *intambama* (the afternoon). The formation is also met in compound expressions, e.g. *nhliziyonye* (with one accord), from *inhliziyo inye* (one heart); *mpondozankomo* (at dawn), from *izimpondo zenkomo* (the horns of the cattle, i.e. when the horns of the cattle first become visible).

(*c*) *Substantives or qualificatives or their stems, or adverbs, preceded by non-locative adverbial formatives*. The chief of these are formed:

(i) with Ng. *nga-*, e.g. (Z) *ngomusa* (kindly), from *umusa* (kindness); *ngaɓo* (by them), from *ɓona* (they); *ngokuhle* (nicely), from *okuhle* (nice one); *ngokwami* (on my own accord), from *okwami* (mine); *ngezinkomo* (about the cattle), from *izinkomo* (cattle); *ngaphezulu* (upwards), from *phezulu* (above); So. *ka-*, e.g. (S) *ka-thipa* (with a knife), *ka-èòna* (with it), *ka-kŏanō* (hereabouts), *kantlè* (outside), *ka'ng?* (with what?); Ve. *nga-*, e.g. *nga-maanḓa* (with strength, i.e. very much), *nga-ngoho* (with truth, i.e. certainly), *nga-nṇe* (by me), *ngayo* (about it). Compounds of this formative are found in Ng. *njenga-* (like), *nganga-* (as big as), e.g. (Z) *njengawe* (like you), *ngangendlu* (as big as a house); and in Ve. *vhunga-* (like), e.g. *vhunga-riṇe* (like us).

(ii) with Ng. *ka-*, e.g. (X) *kahle* (well), *kakhulu* (very much), *kaɓini* (twice); Tg. *ka-*, e.g. *kanwe* (once), *kanyingi* (often); So.(N) *ga-*, e.g. *ga-botse* (well), *ga-raro* (three times); Ve. *ka-*, e.g. *katanu* (five times), *kanzhi* (often); Sh. *ka-*, e.g. *kashoma* (seldom, little by little), *kazhinji* (often).

(iii) with Ve. and Sh. *sa-* (like), e.g. Ve. *sa-inwi* (like you), *sa-lungano* (like—i.e. according to—the fable); Sh. *somurume* (like a man), *sezo* (like those), from *sa-+murume* and *sa-+izo*);

(iv) with Ng. *na-*, e.g. (Z) *nenkosi* (with the chief), *nani* (with you); Tg. *na-*, and its variant *ni-*, due to substitution of *i*, e.g. *ni-mišo* (with the dawn), *na-yena* (with him); So. *le-*, and its variant *na-* in certain forms, e.g. (N) *le-mosadi* (with the woman), *le-tšŏna* or *natšŏ* (with them); Ve. *na-*, e.g. *na-mbudzi* (with the goat), *navho* (with them); Sh. *na-*, e.g. *nemvura* (with the water), *nesu*, from *na-+isu* (with us). In Sh. this formative has also instrumental or agentive meaning, e.g. *nomurume* (by the man), *nezo* (by these). Compounds of this formative are found in the Ng. *kuna-* (compared with), e.g. *kunawe* (compared with you); and in the Sh. *pana-*, *kuna-*, and *muna-*, which will be mentioned later.

(v) with the various copulative formatives, which may be regarded as adverbial when the copulatives are used as agentive adverbs, e.g. Ng. *yindoda* (lit. it is the man, i.e. by the man).

---

[1] Most noun-stems used in So. in this way belong to one of the locative cls. 16, 17, and 18, and are frequently preceded by a locative demonstrative adverb, or by a locative class demonstrative pronoun, e.g. (T) *kwa pele* (there in front), *fa gare* (here in the middle).

(*d*) *Substantives with prefixal locative formatives allied concordially to the locative noun classes 16, 17, and 18.* This type is very common in Sh. but occurs to some extent also in the other languages.

In Sh. the prefixes of these three classes, respectively *pa-*, indicating 'at, on, by, near', *ku-*, indicating 'to, towards' and 'from', and *mu-*, indicating 'in, among' and 'out from, from among',[1] may be prefixed to nouns of all classes except 1a and 2a, resulting in fresh nouns with locative adverbial meaning and function, e.g. *pamusha* (at the village), *kumusha* (to or from the village), *mumusha* (in or out of the village), from *musha* (village); and similarly *pagomo* (on the hill), *kumusoro* (to or from the top), *mumba* (in the house). These prefixes become respectively *pana-*, *kuna-*, and *muna-* when used with nouns of cls. 1a and 2a, and with pronouns, e.g. *kunaɓaɓa* (to the father), *munavo* (among them). Such adverbs may, however, continue to function as nouns, taking full noun concords, e.g. *pamusha paŋgu pakuru* (at my big village)—sometimes, with the concords of *musha*, *pamusha waŋgu mukuru*; *kumusoro kwegomo kwakaipa* (towards the top of the hill it is bad), (Ma.) *mumba medu munevanhu* (in our house there are people).

In Ng. *pha-*, the prefix of cl. 16, is used with the nouns *izulu* (heaven) and (X) *izolo* (yesterday) to form the adverbs *phezulu* (above), and (X) *phezolo* (yesterday evening), as well as with a few obsolete nouns, e.g. *phansi* from obs. noun *insi*. *Ku-*, the prefix of cl. 17, is used with nouns of cls. 1, 1a, 2, and 2a (and in Xhosa only, with nouns of all the other classes also), as well as with pronouns, e.g. (X) *kumfundisi* (to or from the teacher), *kuɓelungu* (to or from the Europeans), *kuɓawo* (to or from my father), *komaa* (to or from my mothers), *kwinkosi* (to or from the chief), *kuɓo* (to or from them), *kuló* (to or from this one). *Kwa-*, which is identical in form with the possessive concord of cl. 17,[2] is also used, with nouns minus their initial vowel, and with possessive stems, e.g. (Z) *kwaMpande* (at Mpande's place), *kwamfundisi* (at the teacher's place), *kwethu* (at my mother's place).

In Tg. *ha-*, the prefix of cl. 16, is used with the noun *yini?* (what?) to form the adverb *ha-yini?* (why?). *Ku-*, parallel to Ng. *ku-* above, appears only in Ro. Elsewhere in Tg. *ka-*, parallel to Ng. *kwa-*, functions like both Ng. *ku-* and Ng. *kwa-*, e.g. *ka-mfund̦isi* (to or from the teacher, or at the teacher's place), *ka-mina* (to or from me, or at my place).

In So. the prefix of cl. 17, (S) *hō-*, is used with nouns of cls. 1, 1a, 2, and 2a, and with pronouns, e.g. *hō-mōrèna* (to or from the chief), *hō-Saōle* (to or from Saole), *hō-bathō* (to or from the people), *hō-bo-ntate* (to or from my fathers), *hō-ěena* (to or from him), *hō-eō* (to or from this one). *Ha-*, parallel with Ng. *kwa-* and Tg. *ka-*, is used with nouns and possessive stems, e.g. *ha-Masōpha* (at Masopha's place), *ha-mōrèna* (at the chief's place), *habò* (at their place). It is sometimes found reduplicated, e.g. *ha-habò* (at their place).

In Ve., as in most Tg. dialects, the prefix of cl. 17, *hu-*, is not found, but *ha-*, parallel to Ng. *kwa-*, Tg. *ka-*, and So.(S) *ha-*, is used like *ka-* in To., e.g. *ha-Tshivhasa* (to or from Tshivhasa or at Tshivhasa's place), *hashu* (our place), and, reduplicated, *ha-hashu* (to, from, or at our place).

(*e*) *Nouns with suffixal locative formatives.* Such adverbs have a generalized locative meaning, which is particularized by the context, e.g. So.(S) *kē-ahile mōreneng* (I live at the chief's), *kē-ĕa mōreneng* (I am going to the chief), *kē-tsŏa mōreneng* (I come from the chief). The formative in Ng. is *-ini*, or *-eni*, according to the final vowel of the noun, and it may affect the last consonant of the noun-stem; it is also accompanied by change of the initial vowel of the noun-prefix to *e-* in all classes except 11, where it becomes *o-*. Nouns of cls. 1a and 2a

---

[1] In Central Bantu the difference in significance between the prefixes *pa-* and *ku-* is one of relative distance, *pa-* signifying rest at or motion to or from a relatively near place, *ku-* having the same significances in regard, however, to a relatively distant place. Shona does, to a certain extent, show this differentiation also.

[2] The possessive concord proper appears in such constructions as *phandle kwendlu* (outside the house), *emva kokho* (after that).

(and, in Zulu only, of cls. 1 and 2) do not employ this formation; while some nouns employ only the initial change of vowel. Examples are (Z) *entaβeni*, from *intaβa* (hill); *emlonyeni*, from *umlomo* (mouth); *engutsheni*, from *inguβo* (blanket); *esiβanjeni*, from *isiβambo* (handle); *othini*, from *uthi* (stick); *ekhanda*, from *ikhanda* (head); *oβala*, from *uβala* (open place). In Tg. the formative is also *-ini*, sometimes *-in* (with syllabic *n*), and affects the final vowel and may affect the last consonant of the noun-stem, e.g. *misaβen(i)*, from *misaβa* (earth); *masinwin(i)*, from *masimu* (gardens); *mombyen(i)*, from *mombo* (forehead). In So. the formative is *-ng* (syllabic), a suffix which affects the final vowel and may affect penultimate vowels and final consonants, e.g. (N) *thabeng*, from *thaba* (hill); *kgorong*, from *kgôrô* (council-place); *dikgonyeng*, from *dikgong* (firewood). In Ve. the formative is *-ni*, which may influence final and penultimate vowels, but does not influence consonants, e.g. *ḍakani*, from *ḍaka* (forest); *nnḍuni*, from *nnḍu* (hut); *khoroni* (phon. **khoroni**), from *khoro* (phon. **khɔrɔ**) (council-place). The suffixal formation does not occur in Sh.

The Ideophone

The ideophone in the Southern Bantu languages may be described as an interjectional descriptive. It differs from the adverb (i) functionally, in describing action, state, intensity, colour, sound, smell, &c., in addition to manner, but not describing time or place; (ii) semantically, in its interjectional and emotional nature, which adverbs lack, and (iii) morphologically, in a complete absence of grammatical formative elements, which are present in the majority of adverbs. On the other hand, its descriptive nature and functions differentiate it from the interjective. Its closest analogy in European languages consists in onomatopoeic interjections such as English 'bang', 'whizz', 'splash', &c.; and many Bantu ideophones are in fact onomatopoeic. All the languages are rich in these words, though perhaps Ng. and Tg. possess, or at least habitually use, more than So., Ve., or Sh.

Since ideophones lack grammatical formative elements, only certain non-morphological characteristics of this part of speech can be noted here. They generally have their own special phonetic laws, employing special prosodic rules of length, stress, and tone, and even sounds (e.g. pressed vowels, and consonants abnormal in any particular language), not found outside this part of speech.

Two possible formal classifications of ideophones would be: (*a*) according to the number of their syllables, and (*b*) according to the nature and succession of their tones. According to the first classification ideophones are: (i) Monosyllabic, e.g. Ng.(Z) *du*, Tg. *duu*, So.(T) *tuu* (of quiet); Ve. *te* (of hardness); Sh. *ďoo* (of setting of the sun). (ii) Disyllabic, e.g. Ng.(Z) *βénye* (of glinting); Tg. *nyúpe* (of diving); So.(S) *kápe* (of spilling); Ve. *tshéte* (of silence); Sh. *tabvu*[1] (of bouncing). (iii) Trisyllabic, e.g. Ng.(Z) *cháphasha* (of crossing a river); Tg. *gédlele* (of the hare's gait); So.(N) *kápata* (of a horse running); Ve. *pípiti* (of starting up from sleep); Sh. *cácaca* (of heavy rain). (iv) Quadrisyllabic, e.g. Ng.(Z) *xhókolozi* (of jabbing in the eye); Tg. *šúlululu* (of falling backwards), Ve. *ṭikinini* (of squatting flat). (v) Quinquesyllabic, e.g. Ng.(Z) *gómbolokoqo* (of turning upside down), Tg. *pfóngologohlo* (of breaking in). According to the second classification, there is, e.g. in Ng.(Z), the following tonal series of monosyllabic ideophones: (i) rising-falling, (ii) low-falling, (iii) low-rising, (iv) high-level, (v) high-falling; and similar series for ideophones with more than one syllable.

There is remarkably little phonetic or semantic correspondence in ideophones from language to language, or even from dialect to dialect in the same language. Few such words resemble each other phonetically at all; and even where some phonetic similarity exists, and a phonological and etymological connexion might consequently be supposed, the words

[1] The stress accent on ideophones indicates a short stressed syllable; since this is normal to Shona in penultimate position it is not marked; in the other languages, however, the penultimate syllable is normally *long* and stressed, hence it is marked when short for ideophones.

are often used with totally different meanings. Conversely, though there is more similarity in the range and nature of the ideas expressed by ideophones in the various languages, the same idea is in the vast majority of cases expressed by ideophones having radically different forms. These phenomena are in striking contrast to the phonetic and semantic similarities, and the phonological and etymological correlations, existing from language to language, and still more, of course, from dialect to dialect, between the roots and formative elements of all the other parts of speech, except the interjective. It is the emotional content of the ideophone which differentiates it and the interjective from other parts of speech.

Within each language, however, numbers of nouns and verbs are etymologically connected with ideophones. Reference was made earlier in this chapter to verbs derived from ideophones, e.g. Ng.(X) *dazuka* (be split), from *dázu* (of splitting); So.(N) *taboga* (jump), from *tábo* (of jumping); Sh. *tabvuka* (bounce), from *tábvu* (of bouncing). Nouns are also similarly derived, e.g. Sh. *nhabvu* (ball), from *tábvu* (bounce); and similarly *citabvu, katabvu, runhabvu*, indicating various sizes and kinds of balls. Nouns derived from ideophones are comparatively rare, but verbs so derived are very numerous. Conversely, ideophones may be derived from verbs, in Ng.(Z) by adding *-iyani*, e.g. *bóniyani* (of seeing), from *bona* (see), *xóxiyani* (of relating), from *xoxa* (relate); in So.(N) by changing the final *-a* of the verb-stem to *-i*, e.g. *emí* (of standing up), from *éma* (stand up), *rerí* (of speechifying), from *rêra* (make a speech).

Ideophones frequently follow a verb meaning originally 'say', but by extension 'do, act, make, demonstrate', and even 'be', and which in fact may take semantic colouring from the ideophone. In Ng. this verb is *-thi*, e.g. (Z) *yathi phéshe* (lit. it-made flashing-past, i.e. it went past in a flash); So. *-re*, e.g. *ba-re tuu* (lit. they-say silence, i.e. they are silent); Sh. *-ti*, e.g. *yati tása* (lit. it-does running-straight, i.e. it runs straight). Tg. has three such verbs, *-ku, -ti*, and *-li*, e.g. *a-ku ntse* (he was silent), *ku-ti mohu* (it is gloomy), *yi-li baa* (it is bright). Ve. has *-ri* (which often coalesces with the preceding subjectival concord, resulting in such forms as *vhe'*, from *vha-+-ri*), *-pfi* (the passive of *-ri*), and *-tou'*;[1] e.g. *ra-ri gidi-gidi* (we ran), *vhe' du* (they are quiet), *a-pfi gávhi* (he was snatched), *o-tou' pilivhili* (he was red). All such verbs may take an objectival concord, e.g. Ng.(Z) *walithi phóqo* (lit. he-it-made smash, i.e. he smashed it); So.(N) *ka-e-re kwilikwiti* (lit. I-it-did swallow, i.e. I swallowed it). Often, however, other verbs are used, whose meaning may sometimes be allied to that of the ideophone, e.g. So.(T) *pitse e-siana kápata-kápata* (the horse hurries galloping); Ve. *u-sokou' dono* (lit. he just-does staring, i.e. he just stares). Frequently no verb is used at all, e.g. Ve. *mulambo pha* (the river (is) quite full); *maḍi vhili-vhili* (the water (is) hot). The ideophone, as will have been noted from the examples above, is often reduplicated; and triplicated forms are not rare, e.g. Ng.(Z) *báni-báni-báni* (of flashing continually), So.(N) *gwdša-gwdša-gwdša* (of continual rustling). Sometimes two, three, or more ideophones follow each other, as in the So.(N) *gwdša-gwdša emí, gwdša-gwdša emí, tábo*, which may be freely translated *There was a continuous rustling movement, which stopped, and went on again, and stopped again; and then there was a sudden jump.*

The Conjunctive

The conjunctive in the Southern Bantu languages may be briefly described as a word which joins other words, or links phrases, clauses, or sentences. Conjunctives are closely allied to adverbs, and in some cases show affinity to the deficient verbs.

There are three main groups: (*a*) primitive conjunctives, which may be called conjunctions; (*b*) other parts of speech, used unchanged in form, but with conjunctive function; and (*c*) other parts of speech, modified by omission, addition, or change of formative elements.

---

[1] *-tou'* consists of an apocopated form of the verb-stem *-ita* (do, make), plus the infinitive prefix *u-* of a verb whose stem is omitted but here represented by the apostrophe. The omitted verb-stem is probably *-ri*.

Under (a) may be mentioned Ng. *futhi* (furthermore), *kanti* (nevertheless); Tg. *hambi* (though), *kasi* (whereas); So.(N) *mme* (and, but), *ge* (if); Ve. *mathina* (whereas), *kana* (if); Sh. *kana* (if, whether), *asi* (but, only).

Under (b) we have e.g. (i) nouns—verb-infinitives like Ng. *ukuthi, ukuɓa,* So.(S) *hōrē, hōba* (that), e.g. (Z) *ngicaɓanga ukuthi ɓazofika* (I-think that they-will-arrive), and other nouns like So.(S) *mōhla* (the day when), *ngŏaha* (the year when), e.g. *mōhla a-tlang* (the day when he comes); (ii) pronouns, like Ng. *kodwa* (but, only), Tg. *loko* (if, when), *leŝi* (provided that), *leŝaku* (that), e.g. *loko v̌a-fambile* (when they-have-gone), *nd̩i-lav̌a leŝaku mi-famba* (I-wish that you-go); (iii) verbal forms, like So.(S) *ēmpa* (but), *ētsŏe* (since), *ēsita* (even), and the series containing the stem *-ba* (*ēba, ēbe, ēbile, ěaba, ētlaba*, &c), meaning 'then', and similar series containing the stems *-rē* and *-ka*, meaning respectively 'then' and 'as if' or 'perhaps', e.g. *ēbile ba-tsamaĕa* (then they-went-away), *ētlarē kē-bua* (then I-shall-speak), *ēke lē-lula* (as if you-are-sitting); (iv) copulatives, like So.(T) *ké-gôna* (then), e.g. *ké-gôna ba-tloga* (then they-left); Ve. *ndi-uri* (that is), e.g. *ndi-uri ndi-mutshena* (that is, I-am-white); (v) adverbs, like Ng.(Z) *manje* (now), Tg. *kambe* (again, on the other hand), e.g. *nd̩i-ri kambe* (again, I say); (vi) ideophones and interjectives, like Ve. *fhedzi* (only), e.g. *fhedzi a-si-nn̩e* (only it is not I), Sh. *ko* (well), e.g. *ko, ari-pi?* (well, where is he?).

Under (c) we may note: (i) noun derivatives, like Ng.(X) *kuɓa, kukuɓa, ngakuɓa, ngokokuɓa, ekuɓeni,* all meaning 'since', *nakuɓa* and *nokuɓa,* both meaning 'although'; *njengokuɓa* and *ngangokuɓa,* both meaning 'inasmuch as'—all derived from the verb-infinitive *ukuɓa*; and such derivatives as (X) *mhla, mhlana, mhlenikweni, mhlenikwezeni* (the day when), from *umhla* (day); (ii) pronominal derivatives, e.g. Ng.(X) *kaloku* (now), *kuloko* (but that), *kukhona* (the more), *kungoko* (wherefore), *okanye* (otherwise), *ngangoko* (as much as), *njengoko* (according as), *koko* (but that); (iii) verbal derivatives, like Ng. *funa* and *hleze* (lest), and (Z) *ahle* (perhaps), *ake* (just), *anduɓa* (and then).

Conjunctives may further be classified according to the construction they govern, as follows:

(a) Non-influencing conjunctives, which do not affect the mood of a succeeding verb. Such are Ng. *kodwa* (but), (Z) *ngakhoke* (therefore); Sh. *bva, asi* (but); Tg. *hambi* (though).

(b) Conjunctives followed by the subjunctive mood. The commonest are those indicating purpose, e.g. Ng.(Z) *ukuthi, ukuɓa,* and *ukuze*: *ngifuna ukuɓa ahambe* (I-want that he-go; i.e. I want him to go).

(c) Conjunctives followed by the participial mood. Such are those meaning 'if, when' (Ng. *uma, inxa*; So. *ha*), 'although' (Ng. *noma*; So. *leha*), and 'because', Ng.(Z) *ngokuɓa*: *ngokuɓa efuna* (because he wants).

The Interjective

The interjective in the Southern Bantu languages may be described as a word of an exclamatory nature, used to express various emotions, or to convey assent or negation, a call or a command. It comprises two main types of words: (a) primitive interjectives, which may be called interjections, and (b) other parts of speech used interjectively. Primitive interjectives, like ideophones, are characterized by certain phonetic peculiarities, but lack distinctive morphological characteristics. Examples are Ng.(X) *wou!* (of wonder), *hawu!* (of surprise), (Z) *yeɓo!* (yes), *cha!* (no); So.(N) *mmalo!* (of wonder), *joo!* (of pain or sorrow), *ee!* (yes), *aowaa!* (no); Sh. *hiŋga!* (of wonder), *hokoyo!* (of warning), *hoŋgu!* (yes), *ɓodo!* (no). Other interjectives may again be subdivided into (i) those used without change of form, and (ii) those which undergo a formal change. Interjectives of the first of these subdivisions need not detain us here; it will be sufficient to say that practically every part of speech may, under certain circumstances, be used interjectively. The interjectional aspect of verbal imperatives particularly, which have already been dealt with, should be remembered in this connexion. Two main kinds of interjectives are found under the second subdivision: these are vocatives, the only interjectives which have characteristic morphological features. Noun vocatives of this kind exist in Ng., and to a limited extent in So.(T) and Ve. In Ng., where they may be formed from all nouns, the initial vowel of the prefix is elided in all classes except 2a, 5, and 11, e.g. *madoda!* (men!), from *amadoda*, *nkosi!* (chief!), from *inkosi*. In cl. 2a, *ɓo-* is substituted for the prefix *o-*, e.g. *ɓodadewethu!* (our sisters!), from *odadewethu*. In cls. 5 and 11, *l-* is prefixed to the short form of the prefix, when the stem is monosyllabic, e.g. *lizwe!* (country!), from *i(li)zwe*, *luthi!* (stick!), from *u(lu)thi*. A suffixal formative *-ndini* may be added to such forms, rendering them derogatory or familiar, e.g. *magwalandini!* (you wretched cowards!), from *magwala!* (cowards!). A similar formative, *-tena*, may be used with all nouns in So.(N), e.g. *lešilo-tena!* (you silly fool!), from *lešilo* (fool). In So.(T only) and Ve., proper names have different final vowels according to whether they are used vocatively or non-vocatively; but it should be noticed that the vocative forms are the basic ones, e.g. *Kgama!, Tau!, Mafoko!* (non-vocative *Kgamê, Tauê, Mafokwê*) from the common nouns *kgama* (hartebeest), *tau* (lion), and *mafoko* (words), respectively: and similarly in Ve. *Tshivhasa!, Sinthumula!* (non-vocative *Tshivhase, Sinthumule*). In Ve. there are special vocative forms for 2nd pers. absolute pronouns, viz. *diwe!* (you there!, sing.) and *dinwi!* (you there!, pl.), cf. the non-vocative absolute forms *iwe, inwi*.

Enclitic and Proclitic Formatives

Among the formatives are to be found some that are but loosely knit to the words to which they are joined, and do not alter the grammatical function of those words. It is very probable that they were originally separate words: some can be definitely shown to have been so. They are termed *enclitics* when suffixed to other words, and *proclitics* when prefixed. They have no characteristic morphological features, and no formal distinction exists between them. Among enclitics, many are interjectional, like Ng.(Z) *-ke* (so, then), e.g. *ɓahambáke* (and so they went away), *-ɓo* (now, I say), e.g. *thuláni-ɓo!* (keep quiet, now!); So.(N) *-hlê* (please), e.g. *dúla-hlê!* (sit down please!), *-gê* (I say), e.g. *é-kwa-gê!* (listen, I say!); Ve. *-ha* (so, now), e.g. *idáni-ha!* (come now!), *-vho* (also), e.g. *ndi-do-yá-vho* (I shall also go); others are pronominal or descriptive, like Ng.(Z) *-ni?* (what?), e.g. *ufunáni?* (what do you want?), *-phi?* (where? whence? whither?), e.g. *uveláphi?* (where do you come from?), *-ze*, naked, e.g. *wahambáze* (he travelled naked, i.e. without impedimenta), *-nje* (merely), e.g. *umúntu-nje* (merely a person); So.(S) *-'ng?* (what?), e.g. *u-ratá'ng?* (what do you wish?); Ve. *-de?* (what kind of?), e.g. *muláyo-de?* (what kind of a law?), *-ni?* (what?), e.g. *vha-khou-ambá-ni?* (what are they saying?); Sh. *-nyi?* (what sort of?), e.g. *múnhu-nyi?* (what sort of a person?), *-yi?* (what?), e.g. *munodé-yi?* (what do you want?), *-pi?* (where? whence? whither?), e.g. *wabvépi?* (where have you come from?), *-po*[1] (there), e.g. *ndáva-po* (I was there), *-ko* (thence, thither), e.g. *íbva-ko* (come away from there), *-mo* (inside, inwards, out from), e.g. *yísa-mo* (put it inside). It will have been noticed that some of the above enclitics leave the normal penultimate stress on the preceding word unaltered, while others shift it forward, as indicated by the stress accents which have been inserted.

Some particles may function as enclitics in one language and as separate words in another language, or even in the same language under different circumstances. Thus in Ng., *phi?* (where?) is an enclitic in Z. *uveláphi?* (where do you come from?), but a separate word in X. *uvéla phi?* On the other hand, *na?* (of interrogation) is an enclitic in X. *uyahámba-na?* (are you going?), but a separate word in Z. *uyahámba na?* Again, in Ng.(X) *ke* (and so)

[1] This and the two following are typical of Central Bantu usage; they are based on the pronominal forms of the three locative classes (16, 17, and 18).

may be an enclitic or a separate word, e.g. *ɓahambá-ke* or *ke ɓahámba* (and so they went); in Sh. *ko?* (well?) is similar, e.g. *arí-pi-ko?* or *ko arí-pi?* (well, where is he?).

The conjunctive formative Ng. *na-*, Tg. *na* (or *ni-*), So. *le-* or *na-*, Ve. *na-*, Sh. *na-* (and, with) is a proclitic, forming a single word with the word following it. In Ng. its vowel coalesces with any immediately following vowel, e.g. (Z) *nomfana* (with the boy), from *na-*+*umfana*; *nenkosi* (with the chief), from *na-*+*inkosi*; in Sh. its vowel coalesces with a following vowel expressed or latent, e.g. *nomurume* (with the man), from *na-*+(*u*)*murume*, *nesu* (with us), from *na-*+*isu*; in Tg. substitution of *i* for *a* takes place when *na-* precedes a noun which may take an initial vowel, thus *na-tatana* (with father; where *tatana* is of cl. 1a without possibility of an initial vowel), but *ni-ṅwana* (with the child; where *ṅwana* might be *eṅwana* in To.).

REFERENCES

J. TORREND: *A Comparative Grammar of the South African Bantu Languages.* 1891.
C. MEINHOF: *Grundzüge einer vergleichenden Grammatik der Bantusprachen.* 2nd ed. 1948.
A. WERNER: *Introductory Sketch of the Bantu Languages.* 1919.

V

THE NGUNI GROUP

Geographical Position of the Group

The Nguni group belongs to the South-eastern Bantu zone, and the Nguni-speaking peoples formed the head of the eastern coastal migration which had reached the vicinity of the Fish River when the first contact was made with Europeans. Today three main Nguni clusters are recognized: (1) *Zulu* (Z.) in Natal and Zululand, where the Qwabe and Lala dialects are found. Owing to the Shaka disturbances, Zulu has flung dialects far and wide, e.g. Ngoni in Nyasaland and Tanganyika, Ndebele in Southern Rhodesia, and Transvaal Ndebele; (2) *Xhosa* (X.) found in the Ciskei and in the Transkeian Territories of the Cape Province, up to the Natal border; standard Xhosa being based on the Ngqika, Ndlambe, and Gcaleka dialects, and being generally spoken today by Thembu, Bomvana, and Mpondomse as well, while more distinct dialectal variants are found in Mpondo and Xesibe; and (3) *Tekeza* with Swazi (Sz.) of Swaziland as its most important form, and associated with it Baca and Hlubi, and according to Appleyard the original Mfengu dialect.[1] Large numbers of Zulu and Xhosa speakers are to be found in the industrial centres, particularly the Witwatersrand, and the total number of those speaking one form or another of Nguni must be in the vicinity of five millions, Xhosa having over two and a quarter million, Zulu (with its dialects) two and a half millions, and Swazi considerably over a quarter of a million.

Literary work has been developed in Xhosa and Zulu, in which languages the whole Bible has long been available; and there is a growing devotional and educational literature. Xhosa has produced a number of novelists, while recently in both languages poetry has been published. Swazi has not been used as a literary form, educational work in Swaziland being through the medium of Zulu. An attempt has been made to develop a literature in Rhodesian Ndebele; the New Testament has been translated and a few small books; the paucity of readers militates, however, against any probable extension here.

Orthography

In 1931, owing to steps taken by the Union Government Advisory Committee on Bantu Studies and Research,[2] a new orthography was adopted for Xhosa, in which three new symbols were agreed to, viz. *ɓ* for implosive *b*, *f* for the voiceless prepalatal fricative, hitherto represented by *sh*, and *ɣ* for the voiceless velar fricative, hitherto indicated by *r*. It was further decided to use *h* instead of the old breathing-mark to indicate the aspiration of consonants; and the doubling of vowels to mark length was introduced where necessary. Lastly a closer approach to full conjunctive writing was made.

Zulu orthography was not settled until 1934. This settlement differed from that arrived at in Xhosa in that *sh* was retained (there not being such necessity for a change as there was in Xhosa), and that *h* was made to serve the purpose of both velar and glottal fricatives, as these are not significantly distinct in Zulu. Doubling of vowels was not agreed to, but full conjunctive writing was adopted. No standardization has yet been made in the case of Rhodesian Ndebele, though a decided move towards the employment of the new Zulu orthography is shown in a number of recent educational publications. No standard orthographies exist for Swazi or for Transvaal Ndebele.

[1] See Chapter II, p. 24.
[2] Later reconstituted as the Inter-University Committee for African Studies.

THE NGUNI GROUP
Phonetic and Phonological Outline

The Nguni languages employ a seven-vowel system, viz. i, e, ɛ, ɑ, ɔ, o, and u, but e and ɛ, o and ɔ respectively being but circumstantial variants of single vowel-phenomena, five vowel symbols are all that are necessary in a practical orthography.

Consonants in Nguni are of two main types, Plain Consonants and Clicks, the latter being a feature foreign to Bantu, and acquired through contact with the Bushman and Hottentot languages.

PLAIN CONSONANTS[1]

	Bilab.	Denti-lab.	Alveolar	Prepalatal	Palatal	Velar	Glottal
Explosive							
rad.						(k)	
eject.	p'		t'		c'	k'	
asp.	ph		th		ch	kh	
voic.	b mb		d nd		ɟ ɲɟ	g ŋg	
Implosive	ɓ						
Nasal							
contin.	m [mɦ]	ɱ	n		ɲ [ɲɦ]	ŋ	
syll.	m̩						
Rolled			{r}				
Lateral			l				
Fricative							
med. unv.		f	s	ʃ		x	h
med. voic.		v	z			ɣ	ɦ
lat. unv.			ɬ				
lat. voic.			ɮ				
Affricate							
med. rad.				tʃ			
med. eject.		ɱpf'	ts' nts'	tʃ' ntʃ'		kx'	
med. asp.				[tʃh]			
med. voic.		ɱbv	ndz	dʒ ndʒ			
lat. eject.			ntɬ'				
lat. voic.			ndɮ				
Semi-Vowel	((w))			j		w	

[ ] found in Xhosa only.   ( ) found in Zulu only.
{ } found in imported words only.   (( )) alternative position.

Notes on the Plain Consonants

1. Aspiration and ejection are significant features of Nguni phonology: Z. makes this distinction with explosives only (p', t', k' and ph, th, kh); X. has it also with affricates, e.g. tʃ' and tʃh. It is noteworthy that Z. uses, in addition to the aspirate and ejective, an almost radical k (slightly voiced); no orthographic distinction is made between this and the ejective, and its place is taken by the ejective in X.

2. Implosive ɓ is semantically distinct from explosive b.

3. There is a full range of nasal consonants, which appear homorganically to the consonant immediately following. When not penultimate, mu is usually contracted to syllabic m̩, and in X. is commonly so contracted even when penultimate. The denti-labial is written *m*, the prepalatal is represented by *ny* (except before consonants, when it is indicated by *n*), and the velar by *n* before k' and g. In Northern Z. dialects ŋ occurs in place of ŋg. In X.

[1] This chart has reference only to Xhosa and Zulu sounds.

THE NGUNI GROUP

ŋ occurs independently as well, and is then indicated by *ng'*. In Ndebele (of Rhodesia) ŋ and ŋg are at times phonemically distinct.

4. In X. the symbol ʃ is used for the unvoiced prepalatal fricative; in Z. this is indicated by *sh*. The radical velar fricative is indicated in X. by ɣ̣, in Z. by *h*. In Z. there is no need to distinguish it from the unvoiced glottal fricative, and the symbol *h* therefore serves both purposes. The voiced velar fricative (ɣ) occurs only in X., where it is written *gɣ̣*. In Z. both voiced and unvoiced glottal fricatives occur, the former being written *hh*. X. has only the unvoiced sound, while Sz. uses only the voiced.

5. The lateral fricatives are indicated by *hl* and *dl*; in the case of the affricates Z. orthography has *nhl* and *ndl*, while X. has *ntl* and *ndl*.

6. In the writing of the prepalatal affricates Z. and X. are very different: X. has radical *tʃ*, aspirated *tʃh*, and ejective with nasal *ntʃ*; Z. has the ejective which is written *tsh*, *ntsh*; and dialectically the radical (also written *tsh*) as a variant to *sh*. The voiced form is always written *j*.

7. X. is unique among the Nguni languages in using palatal explosives, which are indicated by *ty*, *tyh*, and *dy*: these are not found in either Z. or Sz.

8. X. further has a type of voiced aspiration with certain nasal consonants, e.g. *nyh*, *mh*, *nywh* (ɲɦ, &c.).

9. Sz. has some significant distinctions:[1]

 (a) **tsh** often takes the place of Z. and X. **th**.
 (b) **mp**, **nt**, and **ŋk** take the place of **mp'**, **nt'**, and **ŋk'**.
 (c) **t'** takes the place of **z**.
 (d) **ŋ** often takes the place of **ŋg**.
 (e) Z. and X. **v** and **z** appear in Sz., with certain speakers, as **fv** and **sz** respectively, i.e. with an unvoiced on-glide.
 (f) **tɸh** and **dβ** take the place of Z. and X. **t'** and **d** before rounded back vowels.

CLICKS[2]

	Dental	Palato-alveolar	Lateral
Radical	*c*	*q*	*x*
Rad. preceded by nasal .	(*nkc*)	(*nkq*)	(*nkx*)
Aspirated . . .	*ch*	*qh*	*xh*
Voiced	*gc*	*gq*	*gx*
Voiced preceded by nasal	*ngc*	*ngq*	*ngx*
Nasal	*nc*	*nq*	*nx*
Nasal followed by voiced glottal fricative .	[*nch*]	[*nqh*]	[*nxh*]

The above is the chart of clicks occurring in X.; in Z. those in ( ) are rare and those in [ ] are not found at all. Sz. uses mainly dental clicks, few palato-alveolars, and no laterals.

There are two phonological phenomena which require special notice in Nguni, viz. Nasalization and Palatalization.

NASALIZATION. This process of nasal assimilation occurs in Nguni in the formation of nouns in cls. 9 and 10; in Z. the following main rules (which are typical) are observed:

---

[1] In the grammatical portion of this chapter all Swazi examples quoted, unless indicated in phonetic script, will have the following simplified orthography:
  j for dʒ; *ng* for ŋ and *ŋg*; *ny* for ɲ; *tf* for tɸh; *dv* for dβ; *y* for j.
  tʃ will be retained, as in X., to distinguish from **tsh**; and ʃ will be used.

[2] Current orthography is here used; for phonetic equivalents see Chapter III, p. 36.

THE NGUNI GROUP

1. Aspirated explosives become ejective: *ph* > *mp*, *th* > *nt*, *kh* > *nk*, e.g. *uthi* (stick) > pl. *izinti*.
2. Aspirated clicks become nasal clicks: *ch* > *nc*, *qh* > *nq*, *xh* > *nx*, e.g. *incwayi* (hut-dancer) < *chwaya* (perform the hut dance).
3. Radical clicks become voiced: *c* > *ngc*, *q* > *ngq*, *x* > *ngx*, e.g. *ucezu* (slice) > pl. *izingcezu*.
4. Fricatives become affricates, unvoiced fricatives becoming ejective affricates: *f* > *mf*, *s* > *ns*, *sh* > *ntsh*, *hl* > *nhl* (X. *ntl*), e.g. *usuku* (day), > pl. *izinsuku*.
5. The bilabial implosive becomes voiced bilabial explosive, i.e. *ɓ* > *mb*, e.g. *uɓambo* (rib) > pl. *izimbambo*.
6. In rare cases *l* > *nd*, e.g. *ulimi* (tongue) > pl. *izindimi*. Generally, however, *l* is treated as *w*, *y*, and *h*, the nasal dropping away before it, e.g. the common plural of *ulimi* is *izilimi*.

PALATALIZATION. This process, due primarily to the incompatibility in Nguni of *w* with bilabial consonants, involves the substitution of a palatal (or prepalatal) sound for a bilabial (in some cases for an alveolar), and occurs (i) in the formation of verb-passives, noun-diminutives, and locatives, and (ii) in some individual noun formations, particularly in cl. 14. The changes are as follows (examples from passive):

ph > *sh* (X. *tʃh*): *ɓopha* (tie) > *ɓoshwa* (X. *ɓotʃhwa*).
b > *j*: *bubisa* (destroy) > *bujiswa*.
ɓ > *tsh* (X. *ty*): *hlaɓa* (stab) > *hlatshwa* (X. *hlatywa*).
m > *ny*: *luma* (bite) > *lunywa*.
mp > *ntsh* (X. *ntʃ*): e.g. Z. *mpampa* (flutter) > *mpantshwa*.
mb > *nj*: *ɓamba* (seize) > *ɓanjwa*.

In the case of noun-diminutives this process is extended to alveolars in Z., in which case *th*, *d*, and *nd* either remain or give place to the prepalatals *sh*, *j*, and *nj* respectively, while *t*, *nt*, and *n* always give place to *tsh*, *ntsh*, and *ny* respectively; e.g. *incwadi* (book) > *incwadana* or *incwajana*; *ikati* (cat) > *ikatshana*.

In Sz., in the case of passives **tsh** and **dz** give way to **tɸh** and **dβ** respectively; while with noun-diminutives **tsh** and **dz** become ʃ and dʒ.

Palatalization is applied in locative formation when the bilabial consonant is followed in the final syllable by *o* or *u*, e.g. *inguɓo* (blanket) > *engutsheni*; *umlomo* (mouth) > *emlonyeni*.

The words *utshani* (grass) X. *utyani*, and *utshwala* (beer) X. *utywala*, in cl. 14 are due to the prefix *uɓu-* coming before the stems *-ani* and *-ala* respectively. Similarly the word *unyana* (son), of cl. 1, was originally *umu-+-ana*; and *inja* (dog) of cl. 9 is derived from an earlier form *imbwa*.

COALESCENCE OF VOWELS occurs in possessive formation, with the conjunctive formative *na-*, and with the adverbial formatives *nga-*, *kuna-*, *njenga-*, and *nganga-* before nouns with initial vowel, e.g. *inja yomuntu*, i.e. *ya-+umuntu* (the person's dog); *induna nenkosi*, i.e. *na-+inkosi* (the captain and the chief); *ngaɓafana*, i.e. *nga-+aɓafana* (by means of the boys).

SUBSTITUTION OF *e* for an actual or implied initial vowel takes place in Sz., e.g. *neɓantu* (with the people), *ngelukhuni* (by means of firewood); cf. Z. *naɓantu*, *ngo(lu)khuni*.

ELISION OF VOWELS is of two types: (i) elision of the initial vowel of nouns after certain pronouns, e.g. *thina-ɓantu* (we people), *leso-sihlalo* (that chair)—this is always compulsory; and (ii) elision of the final vowel—optional in quick speech—e.g. *inkos' enkulu* (a big chief), *ngiɓon' umuntu* (I see a person); in current orthography this elision is not generally recorded.

STRESS in Nguni is normally on the penultimate syllable, which is also normally long; this stress moves forward with word-development, e.g. *hámba*, *hambéla*, *hambisísa*. Ultimate stress is found in a few rare instances, e.g. in contracted perfects, *siɓoné* (we saw), and certain demonstratives, *kuló* (to this one), *laphayá* (yonder). In the case of ideophones stress is typically initial.

Length is of greater significance in X. than in Z. In addition to the normal length of penultimate syllables, remote past tenses have long *a*, e.g. *saaɓona* (we saw), also demonstrative pronouns, e.g. *aaɓo* (those), *loo-mntu* (that person), nouns of cl. 2a, e.g. *ooɓawo* (our fathers), and of cl. 10, e.g. *iintonga* (sticks). In Z., where it is less frequent, its determination is left to the context.

Tone is very complicated in the Nguni languages covering a range of nine pitches with rising and falling varieties. It can be accurately indicated only by graphs or by a system of numbers.[1] In the new orthography of X. an approximation is attempted with an upper and lower upright bar to mark essential tone, e.g. *umzıi* (a rush), *umzˈi* (a homestead). The tones of these words have been more accurately recorded in Z. as *umuzi* (i.e. ⁻⁻_) and *umuzi* (i.e. ⁻\/) respectively. There are large numbers of words distinguished by tone, of which the following are examples from Z.:

iɓele (corn)　　　　　*iɓele* (breast)

inyanga (doctor)　　　*inyanga* (moon)

igugu (treasure)　　　*igugu* (cockroach)

hlanza (wash)　　　　*hlanza* (vomit)

ɓona (them)　　　　　*ɓona* (see)

lona (it)　　　　　　 *lona* (this one)

Grammatical distinctions are also achieved by tone-changes, e.g. Z.:

umuntu (person)　　　*umuntu* (it is a person)

into (thing)　　　　　*into* (things)

wahamba (he went)　　*wahamba* (thou didst go)

Grammatical Outline[2]

(1) The Noun

Comparative Prefix Table

(Class)	(Zulu)	(Xhosa)	(Swazi)
1	*um-*	*um-*	*um-, umu-*
1a	*u-*	*u-*	*u-, (u-)*
2	*aɓa-, aɓe-*	*aɓa-, aɓe-*	*(a)ɓa-*
2a	*o-*	*oo-*	*ɓo-*
3	*um-, umu-*	*um-*	*um-, umu-*
4	*imi-*	*imi-*	*imi-*
5	*i- (ili-)*	*ili-, i-*	*(i)li-*
6	*ama-*	*ama-*	*ema-*
7	*isi-*	*isi-*	*(i)si-*
8	*izi-*	*izi-*	*(i)ti-*

[1] Such as was employed in Doke's *Phonetics of the Zulu Language*.
[2] Zulu and Xhosa are drawn upon mainly throughout; certain reference is made to Swazi where significant differences have been recorded; but, as a rule, examples have not been drawn from such dialectal forms as Rhodesian or Transvaal Ndebele.

THE NGUNI GROUP

(Class)	(Zulu)	(Xhosa)	(Swazi)
9	iN-	iN-, i-	iN-
10	iziN-	iziN-, iiN-, ii-	(i)tiN-
11	u- (ulu-)	ulu-, u-	(u)lu-
14	uɓu-	uɓu-	(u)ɓu-
15	uku-	uku-	(u)ku-

N.B. Sz. prefixes are irregular in form; in cls. 2, 5, 7, 8, 10, 11, 14, and 15 there is an implied initial vowel (indicated in parentheses) which causes substitution of *e* for the *a* of *na-*, &c.

CLASSES 1 AND 2 (personal): 1. *umu-* before monosyllables in Z. and Sz., otherwise always *um-*; 2. *aɓa-* (in Sz. *ɓa-* with implied initial vowel), *aɓe-* with certain words having stem-vowel *u*, e.g. *aɓelungu* (Europeans).

    Z. *umuntu*, X. *umntu*, Sz. *umuntfu* (person).
    umfazi (woman), Sz. *umfati* (pl. *ɓafati*).
    umfana (youth), *aɓafana*.

Personal nouns derived from verbs:
    umfundi (learner < *funda*), *aɓafundi*.
    umzali (parent < *zala*), *aɓazali*.

CLASSES 1a AND 2a (proper names, relationships, personifications, and importations): Z. and X., *u-* pl. *o-*, *oo-*; Sz., prefix optional with most words in the singular, pl. *ɓo-*.

Proper names:
    uCetshwayo, uPhatho, uJojo, Sz. *Sobuza*, Z. *uNkulunkulu*, X. *uThixo* (God).

Relationships:
    Z. *uɓaɓa, oɓaɓa*; X. *uɓawo, ooɓawo*; Sz. *(u)ɓaɓe, ɓoɓaɓe* (my father).
    Z. *umame, omame*; X. *umaa, oomaa*; Sz. *(u)make, ɓomake* (my mother).
    But note: Sz. *uyihlo, unina*, &c.

Miscellaneous:
    uɓani? (who?), *oɓani?*
    X. *unomeva* (wasp).
    Z. *unogwaja*, Sz. *(u)logwaja* (hare).
    Z. *usheleni* (shilling).

Table of Concords for classes 1, 1a, and 2, 2a

	(Adj.)	(Rel.)	(Enum.)	(Poss.)	(Subj.)	(Obj.)
1 and 1a	om-	o-	mu-	wa-	u-	m-
2 and 2a	aɓa-	aɓa-	ɓa-	ɓa-	ɓa-	ɓa-

N.B. Sz. adjectival and relative concords are preceded by *l-*, e.g. *umuntfu lote* = Z. *umuntu oze*.

CLASSES 3 AND 4 (generally non-personal, trees, rivers, parts of the body, &c.): 3. *um-* (*umu-* before monosyllables in Z. and Sz.), 4. *imi-*.

    Z. *umuthi*, X. *umthi*, Sz. *umutsi* (tree); pl. *imithi*, &c.
    Z. *umuzi*, X. *umzi*, Sz. *umuti* (village); pl. *imizi*, &c.
    Z. and Sz. *umfula*, X. *umlambo* (river).
    umhlana (the back), *imihlana*.

Table of Concords for classes 3 and 4

	(Adj.)	(Rel.)	(Enum.)	(Poss.)	(Subj.)	(Obj.)
3	om-	o-	mu-	wa-	u-	wu-
4	emi-	e-	mi-	ya-	i-	yi-

N.B. In Sz. the adj. and rel. concords prefix *l-*.

THE NGUNI GROUP

CLASSES 5 AND 6 (miscellaneous, foreign acquisitions, tribal individuals): 5. *ili-, i-,* 6. *ama-* (Sz. *ema-*).

Miscellaneous:
  Z. *izwe,* X. *ilizwe,* pl. *amazwe;* Sz. *live,* pl. *emave* (country).
  Z. *itshe,* X. *ilitye,* pl. *amatye;* Sz. *litſe,* pl. *ematſe* (stone).
  Z. *ihhashi,* X. *ihaſi* (horse).

Foreign acquisitions:
  Z. *ibulukwe* (trousers) < Afr. *broek.*
  X. *ilaphu* (rag.) < Afr. *lappie.*
  X. *ivili* (wheel) < Eng. or Afr.; pl. *amavili.*

N.B. X., however, prefers cl. 9 for such acquisitions.

Tribal individuals:
  Z. *iNgisi,* X. *iNgesi* (Englishman).
  Z. *iBunu,* X. *iBulu* (Boer).
  Z. *iSwazi,* Sz. *liSwati* (Swazi).

Class 6, indicating liquids, &c.:
  Z. and X. *amanzi,* Sz. *emanti* (water).
  amafutha, Sz. *emafutsa* (fat).
  amandla (strength).

Table of Concords for classes 5 and 6

	(Adj.)	(Rel.)	(Enum.)	(Poss.)	(Subj.)	(Obj.)
5	*eli-*	*eli-*	*li-*	*la-*	*li-*	*li-*
6	*ama-*	*a-*	*ma-*	*a-*	*a-*	*wa-*

N.B. In Sz. the adj. and rel. concords prefix *l-,* e.g. *emakhosi lamaɓili* (two chiefs).

CLASSES 7 AND 8 (miscellaneous, material, groves, languages, ordinal numbers): 7. *isi-* (Sz. *si-*); 8. *izi-* (Sz. *ti-*):

Miscellaneous:
  isithupha (thumb).
  Z. *isinkwa* (bread).
  isilonda, Sz. *silondza* (sore).

Material:
  Z. *isitsha,* X. *isitya,* Sz. *sitſa* (plate).
  Z. and X. *isiɓaya,* Sz. *siɓaya,* pl. Z. and X. *iziɓaya,* Sz. *tiɓaya* (cattle-kraal).

Groves:
  isigwayi (tobacco patch).
  isikhova (banana plantation).

Languages:
  Z. *isiZulu* (Zulu).
  X. *isiXhosa* (Xhosa).
  Sz. *siSwati,* or *siNtfu* (Swazi).

Ordinal numbers:
  Z. *isiɓili,* X. *isiɓini* (the second).
  isithathu (the third).

Stems commencing in vowels:
  X. *isonka* (bread).
  Z. and X. *isandla* (hand).

Table of Concords for classes 7 and 8

			(Adj.)	(Rel.)	(Enum.)	(Poss.)	(Subj.)	(Obj.)
7	.	.	esi-	esi-	si-	sa-	si-	si-
8	.	. X.	ezi-	ezi-	zi-	za-	zi-	zi-
		Z.	eziN-	ezi-	zi-	za-	zi-	zi-
		Sz.	leti-	leti-	ti-	ta-	ti-	ti-

N.B. In Z. the adj. concord is *eziN-*, by false analogy with cl. 10, e.g. X. *izitya eziɓini* (two vessels); but Z. *izitsha ezimbili*.

CLASSES 9 AND 10 (miscellaneous and animals): 9. *iN-*, 10. *iziN-* (X. *iiN-*, Sz. *tiN-*): the prefix appears as *in-*, *im-*, *iny-*, or *i-* in the singular according to the laws of nasalization, the last only occurring in X., where no nasal consonant is found before *h* or *l* in Xhosa words, or before other consonants in words of foreign origin. Z. regularly uses *iziN-* as plural prefix, X. uses this only before monosyllables, otherwise *iiN-*. Transvaal Ndebele has sing. prefix *i-*, pl. *iN-*, e.g. *ikomo*, pl. *inkomo*.

Examples:
inkomo (beast), pl. Z. *izinkomo*, X. *iinkomo*, Sz. *tinkomo*.
Z. and X. *imbuzi*, Sz. *imbuti* (goat).
Z. *inyoni* (bird).
indlu (house).
Z. and X. *into*, Sz. *intfo* (thing), pl. Z. and X. *izinto*, Sz. *tintfo*.

Examples of X. *i-*:
ihambo (journey).
iguʃa (merino sheep) < Hottentot.
ibokwe (goat) < Afr. *bok*.
ilokwe (dress) < Afr. *rok*.

Certain words in cl. 9 take a plural from cl. 6, e.g.
Z. and X. *indoda* (man), pl. *amadoda*; Sz. *indvodza*, pl. *emadvodza*.
inkosi (chief), pl. Z. *amakhosi*, X. *iinkosi*.
Z. *insimu* (field), pl. *amasimu*; X. *intsimi*, pl. *amasimi*; Sz. *insimi*, pl. *emasimi*.

Table of Concords for classes 9 and 10

				(Adj.)	(Rel.)	(Enum.)	(Poss.)	(Subj.)	(Obj.)
9	.	.	.	eN-	e-	i-	ya-	i-	yi-
10	.	.	.	eziN-	ezi-	zi-	za-	zi-	zi-

N.B. Sz. substitutes *t* for *z* in cl. 10, and precedes adj. and rel. concords by *l-*.

CLASS 11 (miscellaneous and long objects): X. uses prefix *ulu-* before monosyllables, elsewhere long *u-*; Z. uses long *u-* with nouns throughout; Sz. uses *(u)lu-* throughout. Nouns of cl. 11 take their plural from cl. 10.

Examples:
X. *uluthi*, Z. *uthi*, Sz. *lutsi* (a stick); pl. X. and Z. *izinti*, Sz. *tintsi*.
Z. *ufudu*, X. *ufudo*, Sz. *lufutfo* (tortoise); pl. Z. *izimfudu*, X. *iimfudo*, Sz. *timfutfo*.
Z. *ulimi*, X. *ulwimi*, Sz. *lulimi* (tongue); pl. Z. *izilimi*, X. *iilwimi*, Sz. *tilimi*.

Table of Concords for class 11

(Adj.)	(Rel.)	(Enum.)	(Poss.)	(Subj.)	(Obj.)
olu-	olu-	lu-	lwa-	lu-	lu-

Sz. adj. and rel. concord *lolu-*.

CLASS 14 (collective and abstract): prefix *uɓu-*, no plural form.

Collective:
  uɓoya (wool).
  uɓuhlalu (beads).
  uɓuso (face), Sz. *ɓuso*.

Abstract:
  uɓudoda (manliness), *uɓuhle* (beauty).

Palatalization affects certain words in the class, e.g.:
  Z. *utshwala*, X. *utywala* (beer) are derived from the root *-ala*, *uɓu+-ala* becoming palatalized (*ɓ* > *tsh* in Z. and *ty* in X.).
  Z. *utshani*, X. *utyani* (grass) from root *-ani*.

N.B. In X. *uɓuhlanti* (cattle fold) takes the plural *iintlanti* (cl. 10).

Table of Concords for class 14

(Adj.)	(Rel.)	(Enum.)	(Poss.)	(Subj.)	(Obj.)
oɓu-	oɓu-	ɓu-	ɓa-	ɓu-	ɓu-

Sz. adj. and rel. concord is preceded by *l-*, i.e. *loɓu-*.

CLASS 15 (verb infinitive): *uku-*, Sz. *(u)ku-*.

  ukudla (food), Sz. *kudla*.
  ukuɓona (seeing, sight).
  ukufika (arrival).

Table of Concords for class 15

(Adj.)	(Rel.)	(Enum.)	(Poss.)	(Subj.)	(Obj.)
oku-	oku-	ku-	kwa-	ku-	ku-

Sz. adj. and rel. concord is preceded by *l-*, i.e. *loku-*, e.g. *kungahlakaniphi kwami lokukhulu* (my great lack of wisdom).

CLASSES 16, 17, AND 18 are no longer living noun-classes in Nguni, but the prefixes of cls. 16 and 17 are found as locative adverbial formatives in a number of adverbs which were originally nouns of one of these classes, e.g. Z.

  16. *pha-*: *phansi* (down).
             phandle (outside).
             phezulu (above).
  17. *ku-*: *kude* (far away).
             kuɓaɓa (to my father).
  18. Prefix is no longer found in Nguni.

Suffixes in Noun Formation

I. DIMINUTIVES are formed by suffixing *-ana*: e.g. Z. and X.

  into (thing) > *intwana* (little thing).
  imbuzi (goat) > *imbuzana* (kid).
  (*a*) *l* in a final syllable usually gives place to *dl*:
    indlela (path) > *indledlana* (little path).
  (*b*) A bilabial consonant in the final syllable is palatalized, e.g.
    Z. and X. *indaɓa* (affair) > Z. *indatshana*, X. *indatyana*.
    intambo (string) > *intanjana*.
    umlomo (mouth) > *umlonyana*.

(c) Palatalization also occurs with an alveolar consonant in the final syllable, e.g.
   Z. *inyoni* (bird) > *inyonyana*.
   Z. *isikhathi* (time) > *isikhashana* or *isikhathana*.
   Z. *incwadi* (book) > *incwajana* or *incwadana*.
(d) A feminine suffix *-azana* is found:
   Z. and X. *intombi* (girl), *intombazana* (little girl).
       inkosi (chief), *inkosazana* (chief's daughter).

II. AUGMENTATIVES and FEMININES are occasionally formed by suffixing *-kazi*, Sz. *-kati*:
   X. *ilitye*, Z. *itshe* (stone), become *ilityekazi* and *itshekazi* (boulder).
   imbuzi (goat), Sz. *imbuti* > *imbuzikazi* (ewe-goat), Sz. *imbutikati*.
   inja (dog) > *injakazi* (bitch).

(2) THE PRONOUN

(a) TABLE OF ABSOLUTE PRONOUNS

			(Z. and X.)	(Sz.)
1st pers.	s.		Z. *mina*, X. *mna*	*mine*
	pl.		*thina*	*tsine*
2nd pers.	s.		*wena*	*wena*
	pl.		*nina*	*nine*
3rd pers.	cl.	1	*yena*	*yena*
		2	*bona*	*bona*
		3	*wona*	*wona*
		4	*yona*	*yona*
		5	*lona*	*lona*
		6	*wona*	*(w)ona*
		7	*sona*	*sona*
		8	*zona*	*tona*
		9	*yona*	*yona*
		10	*zona*	*tona*
		11	*lona*	*lona*
		14	*bona*	*bona*
		15	*khona*	*kona*

These pronouns have typical ultimate *-na* assimilated to *-ne* in Sz. when there is *i* in the previous syllable, which is discarded as a rule in inflected forms, e.g. locative, *kuye*, *kubo*, Z. *kimi*, X. *kum*; instrumental, *ngawe*, *ngazo*; copulative, *yithi*, *nguwe*.

(b) DEMONSTRATIVE PRONOUNS

Nguni uses only three positions of demonstratives, and there is considerable divergence between the forms found in Z., X., and Sz.

Table of 1st Demonstrative forms

(Class)	(Zulu and Swazi)	(Xhosa)
1	*lo*	*lo*
2	*laba*	*aaba*
5	*leli*	*eli*
6	*la (lawa)*	*la*
9	*le*	*le*
10	*lezi* (Sz. *leti*)	*ezi*

Z. and Sz. forms are alike, except for phonetic interchange, e.g. *z* and *t*. X. agrees with Z. in the monosyllabic forms, but discards initial *l* in all the disyllabic forms of the 1st demonstrative.

Table of 2nd Demonstrative forms

(Class)	(Zulu)	(Swazi)	(Xhosa)
1	lowo	loyo	lowo, loo
2	laɓo	laɓo	aaɓo
5	lelo	lelo	elo
6	lawo	lawo	lawo, loo
9	leyo	leyo	leyo, loo
10	lezo	leto	ezo

As typically in Bantu, all change the final vowel of the 1st demons. to *o*, X. retains initial *l* where it occurred in the 1st demons., and in all such cases has an alternative common form *loo*.

Table of 3rd Demonstrative forms

(Class)	(Zulu)	(Swazi)	(Xhosa)
1	lowayá	loya	lowa, laa
2	laɓayá	laaɓa	aaɓaya, aaɓaa
5	leliyá	lela	eliya, elaa
6	lawayá	laawa	lawa, laa
9	leyá	leya	leya, laa
10	leziyá	leta	eziya, ezaa

Z. 3rd demons. are formed by suffixing stressed *-yá* to the 1st demons., the monosyllabic forms first assuming a second syllable, e.g. *lo* becoming *lowa*; *la*, *lawa*; and *le* alternatively *leyi* or *le* (with long vowel). Sz. forms are very irregular, cls. 11, 15, and 16, for instance, being *lolwa*, *lokwa*, and *laapha*. In X. stressed *-ya* is added to the forms of the 1st demons. which commence in vowels, while *-wa* or *-ya* is added to the monosyllabic forms. Here also alternative forms are provided by a common form *laa* for those commencing in *l*, and a suffix *-aa* in place of the final vowel of the 1st demons. forms of all others.

The general significance of the demonstrative in Nguni is: (1) this, these; (2) that, those; and (3) yonder. They may be used instead of the nouns, or in apposition before or after nouns, in the former of which cases one word-group results, e.g. Z. *laɓa*, *laɓa-ɓantu* or *aɓantu laɓa* (these people).

(c) QUANTITATIVE PRONOUNS

There are two sets of these in Nguni, viz. the simple with the roots *-nke* (all), *-dwa* (only), and the inclusive embodying the definite numerals.

For the root *-nke*, the following forms occur in Z. and X.: 1st pers. pl. *sonke* (all of us), 2nd pers. pl. *nonke* (all of you); cl. 1. *wonke*; 2. *ɓonke*; 3. *wonke*; 4. *yonke*; 5. *lonke*; 6. *onke*; 7. *sonke*; 8. *zonke*; 9. *yonke*; 10. *zonke*; 11. *lonke*; 14. *ɓonke*; 15. *konke*. Sz. has the form *ngonke* for 1st pers. s.

Similar forms are found with the root *-dwa*, Sz. *-dvwa*, but there is some divergence between Z. and X. in the forms for the 1st and 2nd persons.

	(Zulu)	(Xhosa)
1st pers. s.	ngedwa	ndedwa, ndodwa
pl.	sodwa	sedwa, sodwa
2nd pers. s.	wedwa	wodwa
pl.	nodwa	nedwa, nodwa

In the 3rd person both languages are alike, e.g. cl. 1. *yedwa*; 2. *ɓodwa*; 8. *zodwa*; &c.

The inclusive quantitative pronouns are formed with the pronominal concords prefixed to the adjectival forms, e.g. in Z.: *soɓaɓili* (both of us), *noɓathathu* (the three of you), *yomine* (all four of them, trees), *zombili* (both of them, oxen).

(d) QUALIFICATIVE PRONOUNS

In Nguni adjectives and relatives may be used pronominally without change of form, but possessives when used pronominally assume an initial vowel. This initial vowel is a secondary one, *a*, *e*, or *o* according as to whether the noun-prefix contains *a*, *i*, or *u* respectively. These possessive pronouns occur instead of their noun, or preceding it for purposes of emphasis, in which latter case they are in apposition to it.

Examples:

izinja zethu (our dogs), but *ezethu* (ours), *ezethu izinja* (ours, i.e. dogs).

(3) THE QUALIFICATIVE

(a) THE ADJECTIVE

There are very few adjectives in the Nguni languages, the following being practically a complete list for Zulu and Xhosa:

-*ɓi* (bad, ugly).
Z. -*ɓili*, X. -*ɓini* (two).
-*dala* (old).
-*de* (long, tall).
-*fuphi* (short).
Z. -*fushane*, X. -*futʃhane* (short).
-*hlanu* (five).
-*hle* (nice, good, beautiful).
-*khulu* (big, great).

Z. -*ncane*, -*ncinyane*, X. -*ncinane* (small).
Z. -*nci* (tiny).
-*ne* (four)
Z. -*ngaki?* X. -*ngaphi?* (how many?)
Z. -*ningi*, X. -*ninzi* (many).
-*nye* (some, other; in X. also = one).
Z. -*sha*, X. *tʃha* (new).
X. -*thandathu* (six).
-*thathu* (three).

The adjectival concords are formed from the noun-prefixes by preplacing the qualificative formative *a*-, e.g. cl. 1. *om*-; 2. *aɓa*-; 5. *eli*-; 6. *ama*-; 9. *eN*-; 10. *eziN*-. X. forms these concords exactly according to this rule, but Z. uses *eziN*- in cl. 8, instead of *ezi*-, by false analogy with cl. 10. It is noteworthy that Sz. preplaces *l*- to these concords throughout, e.g. *lom*-, *laɓa*-, *leli*-, &c. Examples:

umfana omkhulu (a big boy).
X. *ilifu elihle* (a beautiful cloud).
Z. *izitsha ezimbili*, X. *izitya eziɓini* (two dishes).
Sz. *tinkomo letimbili* (two cattle).

In X. when adjectives are used with nouns shorn of their initial vowel, they, too, drop the initial vowel (*i*- being substituted for *e*- in cl. 9, as in copulative formation), e.g.

Nkosi inkulu! (O great chief!).
Akukho-ɓantu ɓaninzi apha (There are not many people here).
le-mithi mide (these tall trees).

(b) THE RELATIVE

Nguni employs numerous relative stems, many of which are formed from nouns by elision of the initial vowel. These are used with direct relative concord. Examples:

-*ɓomvu* (red).
Z. -*qotho* (honest).
-*ɓuhlungu* (painful) < *uɓuhlungu* (pain).
-*manzi* (wet) < n. *amanzi* (water).

X. *ʃuʃu* (hot).
Z. -*ɓanzi* (wide).

The direct relative concords differ from the adjectival concords in omitting any nasal element in the latter; thus in Z. and X.: cl. 1. *o*-; 2. *aɓa*-; 5. *eli*-; 6. *a*-; 9. *e*-; 10. *ezi*-.

Z. *izinkomo eziɓomvu* (red cattle).
isilonda esiɓuhlungu (a painful sore).

Sz. prefixes *l-* to each of these concords.

Direct relative concords are further used in Nguni before nouns prececed by *na-*, e.g. Z. and X. *indoda enamandla* (a powerful man); and in relative clauses of subjectival relationship, e.g. Z. and X. *indoda ehambayo* (a man who travels); Sz. *umuntfu lofikile* (the person who has arrived). Relative clause construction will be discussed later.

(c) THE ENUMERATIVE

In Z. there are four monosyllabic roots in this category: *-nye* (one), *-phi?* (which?), *-ni?* (what?), and *-mbe* (different). These are used with special short concords, as follows: cl. 1. *mu-*; 2. *ɓa-*; 5. *li-*; 6. *ma-*; 9. *i-*; 10. *zi-*. In X. *-nye* only occurs as an adjectival stem, whether it means 'one' or 'other'; and X. has only three enumeratives, *-phi?*, *-ni?*, and *-mbi*. Enumeratives do not change in form whether used before or after the nouns, nor are they inflected when used predicatively. Examples:

X. *wumbi umlambo* (a different river).
X. *ɓuphi na uɓukumkani?* (which kingdom?).
Z. *izwi linye* (one word).
Z. *umuthi muni?* (what tree?).

(d) THE POSSESSIVE

There are two types of possessive in Nguni: the direct and the descriptive, the former based on pronominal or nominal stems, the latter on nominal or adverbial stems. The concords are the same in either case, with typical vowel *a*. The following is the set for Z. and X.

Cl. 1. *wa-*   2. *ɓa-*
    3. *wa-*   4. *ya-*
    5. *la-*   6. *a-*
    7. *sa-*   8. *za-* (Sz. *ta-*)
    9. *ya-*   10. *za-* (Sz. *ta-*)
    11. *lwa-*   14. *ɓa-*
    15. *kwa-*

(i) Direct possessives are divided into (*a*) those with pronominal stem, and (*b*) those comprised of concord prefixed to a substantive, e.g. noun (when coalescence takes place with the initial vowel, substitution of *e* in the case of Sz.).

List of Possessive Pronominal Stems

1st pers. s.   *-mi* (Z.), *-m* (X.)   pl. *-ithu* (Sz. *-itfu*)
2nd pers. s.   *-kho*   pl. *-inu*
3rd pers. cl. 1. *-khe*; 2. *-ɓo*; 3. *-wo*; 4. *-yo*; 5. *-lo*; 6. *-wo*; 7. *-so*; 8. *-zo* (Sz. *-to*); 9. *-yo*;
       10. *-zo* (Sz. *-to*); 11. *-lo*; 14. *-ɓo*; 15. *-kho* (Sz. *-ko*).

(a) Z. *ikhanda lakhe*, X. *intloko yakhe* (his head).
    Z. *izinkomo zami*, X. *iinkomo zam*, Sz. *tinkomo tami* (my cattle).
    uɓukhulu ɓayo (its size).
(b) With nouns of Class 1a (formative *ka-* used):
    Z. *izinkomo zikaɓaɓa* (my father's cattle).
    X. *ihaʃi likaɓawo* (my father's horse).
    Sz. *tinkomo tikaɓaɓe* (my father's cattle).
    With nouns of other classes:
    Z. *izwe lomuntu*, X. *ilizwe lomntu*, Sz. *live lemuntfu* (the person's country).

(ii) The descriptive possessive indicates some quality, characteristic, or material content of the antecedent, and not the possessor thereof; it may have either noun or adverbial base: Examples from Z.:

(a) With noun base:
  (indicating material) *indlu yotshani* (a grass hut).
  (indicating contents) *igula lamasi* (a calabash of sour-milk).
  (indicating use) *imbiza yamanzi* (a water-pot).
  (indicating features) *izwi leqiniso* (a true word).
  (indicating verbal action) *ihhashi lokugiɓela* (a riding horse).
  (indicating order) *incwadi yesithathu* (the third book).
(b) With adverbial base:
  izindaɓa zamanje (current matters).
  umkhuɓa wakhona (a local custom).

With locative adverbs with initial vowel, prelocative -*s*- intervenes, e.g. *utshani ɓasemfuleni* (river grass).

Table of Qualificative Concords

			(Adjectival)	(Relative)	(Enumerative)	(Possessive)
1st pers.	s.		—	engi- (Z.) engi- (X.)	—	—
	pl.		—	esi-	—	—
2nd pers.	s.		—	o-	—	—
	pl.		—	eni-	—	—
3rd pers.	cl.	1	om-[1]	o-[3]	mu-	wa-
		2	aɓa-	aɓa-	ɓa-	ɓa-
		3	om-	o-	mu-	wa-
		4	emi-	e-	mi-	ya-
		5	eli-	eli-	li-	la-
		6	ama-	a-	ma-	a-
		7	esi-	esi-	si-	sa-
		8	ezi-[2]	ezi-	zi-	za-
		9	eN-	e-	i-	ya-
		10	eziN-	ezi-	zi-	za-
		11	olu-	olu-	lu-	lwa-
		14	oɓu-	oɓu-	ɓu-	ɓa-[4]
		15	oku-	oku-	ku-	kwa-

(4) THE VERB

(i) THE VARIETIES OF THE VERB IN NGUNI

The four usual Bantu varieties are found:

1. The Regular disyllabic verb-stem, commencing in a consonant and ending in the vowel -*a*, e.g. *hamba* (travel), *shaya* (strike).

2. The Monosyllabic verb-stem:
   (a) Normal, e.g. *pha* (give), *dla*—X. also *tya*—(eat).
   (b) Stem with latent initial *i*- (causing a preceding *a*- to become *e*-), e.g. *za* (come), *ma* (stand).

3. The Vowel verb-stem (commencing in one of the secondary vowels *a*, *e*, or *o*), e.g. Z. *akha*, X. *aakha* (build), *enza* (do), *ona* (do wrong).

4. Derived verb-stems:

---

[1] Sz. prefixes *l* throughout, e.g. *lom-*, *laɓa-*, and substitutes *t* for *z*, e.g. *letiN-*.
[2] Z. *eziN-* as in cl. 10.
[3] Sz. prefixes *l* throughout, e.g. *lo-*, *laɓa-*, and substitutes *t* for *z*, e.g. *leti-*.
[4] Note the dropping of the *u* as *w* in incompatible with a bilabial in Nguni.

(a) Verbal derivatives, e.g. *hambela* (applied), *hambisa* (causative), &c.
(b) Ideophonic derivatives, e.g. Z. *ɓihlika* (slide apart) < *ɓihli*; X. *nyikila* (pinch) < *nyiki*.
(c) Denominative verbs, e.g. *khalipha* (be sharp) < *uɓukhali* (sharpness).

VERBAL DERIVATIVES. In Nguni the following are used regularly: Passive, Applied, Neuter, Causative, Intensive, Reciprocal, and Diminutive.

The PASSIVE is formed, as a general rule, by substituting the suffix *-wa* for the final vowel of the simple stem, e.g.
thanda (love) > *thandwa* (be loved).
ɓona (see) > *ɓonwa* (be seen).

Monosyllabic and vowel verb-stems suffix *-iwa*, e.g.
pha (give) > *phiwa* (be given).
enza (do) > *enziwa* (be done).

Verbs of which the final syllable of the stem begins with a bilabial consonant undergo palatalization, as follows:
ph > *sh* in Z., and *tʃh* in X.
ɓ > *tsh* in Z., and *ty* in X.
b > *j*.
m > *ny*.

Examples:
ɓopha (tie) > Z. *ɓoshwa*, X. *ɓotʃhwa*.
hlaɓa (stab) > Z. *hlatshwa*, X. *hlatywa*.
buba (perish) > *bujwa*.
luma (bite) > *lunywa*.

THE APPLIED is formed by the suffix *-ela*, e.g.
ɓamba (hold) > *ɓambela* (hold for)
ɓuya (return) > *ɓuyela* (return to).
lima (cultivate) > *limela* (cultivate for).

THE NEUTER is generally formed by the suffix *-eka*, but a few verbs form this species in *-akala* either instead of *-eka* or in addition to that form, e.g.
funa (want) > *funeka* (be desirable).
Z. *esaɓa* (fear) > *esaɓeka* (be formidable).
lahla (lose) > *lahleka* (be lost).
ona (spoil) > *onakala* (get spoilt).
Z. *siza* (help) > *sizeka* or *sizakala* (get help).
ɓona (see) > X. *ɓoneka* or *ɓonakala* (appear).

THE CAUSATIVE is formed by the suffix *-isa*, e.g.
ɓona (see) > *ɓonisa* (show).
ɓuya (return) > *ɓuyisa* (bring back).
seɓenza (work) > *seɓenzisa* (use).

There are contracted formations with certain verbs, the chief of which is that of final *-ala* becoming *-eza*, e.g.
fudumala (be warm) > *fudumalisa* or *fudumeza*.
khukhumala (swell up) > *khukhumalisa* or *khukhumeza*.

Note also *k* (and even *l* and *th*) becoming *s*, e.g.
vuka (wake up) > *vusa* (arouse).
suka (go away) > *susa* (send away).

thwala (carry) > *thwalisa* or *thwesa*.
ambatha (dress) > *ambathisa* or *ambesa*.

Most other seeming irregularities are due to the fact that both the original and the causative forms are ideophonic derivatives.

THE INTENSIVE is formed by suffixing *-isisa*, e.g.
beka (look) > *bekisisa* (look intently).
ɓona (see) > *ɓonisisa* (see clearly).
qonḓa (understand) > *qondisisa* (understand well).

THE RECIPROCAL is formed by suffixing *-ana*, e.g.
ɓona (see) > *ɓonana* (see one another).
siza (help) > *sizana* (help each other).

THE DIMINUTIVE is formed by a reduplication of the simple stem; e.g.
ɓona (see) > *ɓonaɓona* (see somewhat).
hamba (travel) > *hambahamba* (walk about).

In Z. monosyllabic verbs interpose the syllabic *yi*, e.g.
dla (eat) > *dlayidla* (eat a little);

and disyllabic vowel verbs interpose *y*, e.g.
akha (build) > *akhayakha*.

THE REVERSIVE only occurs sporadically in Nguni, forms existing of which no simple form is now extant, e.g. Z. *vumbulula* (uncover), *sombulula* (unwind). PERFECTIVE forms are also found occasionally, particularly in X., e.g. *ɓingelela* (sacrifice formally), cf. *ɓinga* (sacrifice); *fikelela* (reach right to), cf. *fika* (arrive).

(ii) THE CONJUGATION OF THE VERB IN NGUNI

There are two conjugations of the verb in Nguni, positive and negative.

Apart from the infinitive and imperative forms, there are five finite moods in Nguni, viz. indicative, subjunctive, participial, potential, and contingent. In addition X. is unique in employing the temporal mood.

THE INFINITIVE is formed with the prefix *uku-* (Sz. *(u)ku-*) and occurs in both positive and negative conjugations:

(Positive) (Negative)
ukuɓona (to see) *ukungaɓoni* (not to see)
ukufuna (to want) *ukungafuni* (not to want)

e.g. Sz. *kuhlakanipha kwakho* (thy wisdom); X. *ukungaseɓenzi kwam* (my not working).

THE IMPERATIVE. The plain stem of regular disyllabic and polysyllabic verbs constitutes the imperative singular, the plural being formed by substituting *-ani* for the final *-a*, e.g.

siza (help!) *sizani* (help ye!)
ɓuya (return!) *ɓuyani* (return ye!)
ɓaleka (run away!) *ɓalekani* (run ye away!)

Monosyllabic stems prefix *yi-*, except in Sz., which has a special form:

yidla (eat thou!) *yidlani* or Z. *yidlanini* (eat ye!)
yiza (come!) *yizani* (come ye!)
Sz. *phani* (give thou!) *phanini* (give ye!)
yani (go thou!) *yanini* (go ye!)

Z. has an alternative singular formed by suffixing ultimate *-na*, e.g. *dla* > *yidla* or *dlana*.

Vowel verbs prefix *y-*:
enza > *yenza* (do!), pl. *yenzani*
Z. *akha* > *yakha* (build!), pl. *yakhani*.

When an objectival concord is used with an imperative, final *-a* and *-ani* are changed to *-e* and *-eni* respectively; e.g. Z. *ngitshele* (tell me), X. *ndiɓonise* (show me), Z. *ɓasizeni* (help ye them).

The Negative of the Imperative is formed by using the deficient verb *musa* (omit), pl. *musani*, followed by the infinitive, e.g. *musa ukuhamba* (don't go!), pl. *musani ukuhamba*. Both positive and negative forms of the subjunctive mood are used imperatively for all persons and classes, the former generally preceded by *-a* or *ma-*, e.g. *mangiɓone* (let me see).

THE INDICATIVE MOOD. The three implications of the indicative mood, Simple, Progressive, and Exclusive, are found in Nguni, each being found in both positive and negative conjugations. Examples from Zulu:

Simple implication: *ngiyaɓona* (I see), *angiɓoni* (I do not see).
Progressive implication: *ngisaɓona* (I still see), *angisaɓoni* (I no longer see).
Exclusive implication: *sengiɓona* (now I see), *angikaɓoni* (I do not yet see).

The threefold distinctions of aspect are clearly exemplified in Nguni, e.g. in Zulu, past remote tenses:

Indefinite: *ngalamba* (I got hungry).
Continuous: *ngangilamba* (I was getting hungry).
Perfect: *ngangilambile* (I was hungry).

The last is confined to stative verbs.

The tense divisions, i.e. the determination of time significance, are fivefold. They are remote past, immediate past, present, immediate future, and remote future. The dividing line for the remote and immediate past tenses is between yesterday and the day before yesterday. That between the two futures is rather more vague, but generally remote future is applied to actions to take place after today. The following examples, taken from Zulu, are of the simple implication, indefinite aspect, first person singular:

	(Positive)	(Negative)
Remote past .	*ngahamba* (I travelled)	*angihambanga*
Immed. past .	*ngihambile* (I travelled)	
Present .	*ngiyahamba* (I travel)	*angihambi*
Immed. future	*ngizokuhamba* (I shall travel)	*angizukuhamba*
Remote future	*ngiyokuhamba* (I shall travel)	*angiyukuhamba*

Nguni languages have two forms of the simple present and two forms of the immediate past tense positive, a long form which may be used isolated and a short or contracted form which is more indefinite in character and is always used with an adjunct. The following are examples:

Present: *siyaɓona* (we see), but *siɓona kahle* (we see well), *siɓona umuntu* (we see a person).
Immed. past: *siɓonile* (we saw), but *siɓoné kahle* (we saw well), *siɓoné umuntu* (we saw a person).

The following lists show (*a*) the subjectival concord used (i) with present, future, and immediate past tenses positive, (ii) with remote past tenses positive, (iii) with negative tenses; (*b*) the objectival concord, indicating the definite object and immediately preceding the verb-stem in every case; (*c*) the present positive tense in full; and (*d*) the present negative tense in full. Xhosa is taken for example.

Examples of Verb Concords and Full Tenses

	Subj. concords (indic.)			Obj. concords	Pres. indic. positive	Pres. indic. negative
	Pres. fut. immed. past	Rem. past	Negative			
1st pers. s.	ndi-[1]	ndaa-[2]	ndi-[1]	ndi-[1]	ndiya-hamba[3]	andihambi
pl.	si-	saa-	si-	si-	siya-hamba	asihambi
2nd pers. s.	u-[4]	waa-[4]	ku-[5]	ku-	uya-hamba	akuhambi
pl.	ni-	naa-	ni-	ni-	niya-hamba	anihambi
3rd pers. cl. 1	u-	waa-	ka-	m-	uya-hamba	akahambi
2	ɓa-	ɓaa-	ɓa-	ɓa-	ɓaya-hamba	aɓahambi
3	u-	waa-	wu-	wu-	uya-hamba	awuhambi
4	i-	yaa-	yi-	yi-	iya-hamba	ayihambi
5	li-	laa-	li-	li-	liya-hamba	alihambi
6	a-	aa-	ka-	wa-	aya-hamba	akahambi
7	si-	saa-	si-	si-	siya-hamba	asihambi
8	zi-[6]	zaa-[7]	zi-[6]	zi-[6]	ziya-hamba	azihambi
9	i-	yaa-	yi-	yi-	iya-hamba	ayihambi
10	zi-[6]	zaa-[7]	zi-[6]	zi-[6]	ziya-hamba	azihambi
11	lu-	lwaa-	lu-	lu-	luya-hamba	aluhambi
14	ɓu-	ɓaa-	ɓu-	ɓu-	ɓuya-hamba	aɓuhambi
15	ku-	kwaa-	ku-	ku-	kuya-hamba	akuhambi

THE SUBJUNCTIVE MOOD. The present subjunctive positive is formed by changing the final vowel of the verb-stem to -e, the subjectival concords being the same as for the indicative present, except that that of cl. 1 becomes a-. The negative is formed by employing the infixed -nga- and suffixed -i, the concords being as for the positive. The following portion of the tenses (from Zulu) indicates the formation:

	(Positive)	(Negative)
1st pers. s.	ngiɓone	ngingaɓoni
pl.	siɓone	singaɓoni
2nd pers. s.	uɓone	ungaɓoni
pl.	niɓone	ningaɓoni
3rd pers. cl. 1	aɓone	angaɓoni
2	ɓaɓone	ɓangaɓoni
3	uɓone	ungaɓoni
4	iɓone	ingaɓoni

The past subjunctive is formed with auxiliary -a-, e.g. Z. ngaɓona, X. ndaɓona (and I saw), used in past consecutive construction. This tense differs from the remote past indicative in that the latter has a long a, e.g. X. ndaaɓona. The past subjunctive may be used either of remote or of immediate past time. The negative is formed by prefixing a-, e.g. Z. angaɓona (and I did not see).

The future subjunctive has strong hortative force, e.g. Z. ngiɓohamba (I must travel), with its negative form ngingaɓohambi (I must not travel).

THE POTENTIAL MOOD. In Nguni, positive and negative tenses are found in present, immediate past, and remote past time: there is no future potential. The auxiliary is infixed -nga- and the concords are as for the subjunctive. The present tenses in Zulu are as follows: positive: ngingaɓona (I can see); negative: ngingeɓone (I cannot see). Considerable difference exists between Zulu and Xhosa in the uses and applications of the auxiliaries -nga- and -nge-,

---

[1] Z. ngi- and Sz. ŋi-. [2] Z. nga- and Sz. ŋa-.
[3] Xhosa orthography separates the verb-stem in this tense from the auxiliary sections, Zulu writes ngiyahamba. [4] Low tone.
[5] Z. wu-, Sz. u- or wu-. [6] Sz. ti-. [7] Sz. ta-.

which cannot be discussed here. In Xhosa -*nga* is treated as a deficient verb in many instances. There is conditional as well as potential force in this mood.

THE CONTINGENT MOOD in Nguni languages is composed of a combination of past and future auxiliary elements, and is used to indicate what might have been (unfulfilled intention). There are various tenses in past time only, which might be represented by the Zulu:

 Immed. Past: *ɓengiyohamba* (I would have gone, if . . .).
  Neg.: *ɓengingayukuhamba.*
 Remote Past: *ngangiyohamba* (I would have gone, but . . .).
  Neg.: *ngangingayukuhamba.*

THE PARTICIPIAL MOOD. This has tenses corresponding to many in the indicative and to some in the potential and contingent moods. In Nguni it differs from indicative tenses in the subjectival concords for cls. 1, 2, and 6, which appear in Z. and X. as *e-*, *ɓe-*, and *e-* respectively. In Sz. the only difference in concord from the indicative is in cl. 1 which is *a-*. The negative formation is also considerably different, infixed *-nga-* being used. The following are the commonest participial tenses in Xhosa:

	(Positive)	(Negative)
Present	*ndihamba*	*ndingahambi*
Immed. Past . .	*ndihambile*	*ndingahambanga*
Future	*ndiya-kuhamba*	*ndingayi-kuhamba*
Remote Past . .	*ndahambayo*	

The suffix *-yo* is assumed in the Remote Past when the verb ends the sentence.

The participial mood is at the base of all relative clause construction in Nguni, the relative concord being substituted for the participial concord. The following from Zulu might be noted:

 Indic. *aɓafuni* (they do not want).
 Partic. *ɓengafuni* (they not wanting).
 Rel. *aɓangafuni* (they who do not want).

THE TEMPORAL MOOD in Xhosa is used to express an action preceding that of the main verb, e.g. *sakufika samxelela* (when we arrived, we told him); *ndakuvuka ndahamba indlela yam* (when I awoke, I went on my way). The tense is formed with infix *-aku-*, probably a contraction from *-aɓa+ku-* (of infinitive). Following is an example of the one tense in this mood:

	(Sing.)		(Plur.)
1st pers. . .	*ndakufuna*		*sakufuna*
2nd pers. .	*wakufuna*		*nakufuna*
3rd pers. cl. 1 . .	*akufuna*	cl. 2 .	*ɓakufuna*
3 . .	*wakufuna*	4 .	*yakufuna*
5 . .	*lakufuna*	6 .	*akufuna*

(iii) COMPOUND TENSES IN NGUNI

Nguni languages employ a considerable number of deficient verbs which require a verbal complement in a subordinate mood to complete them. These may be roughly divided into three types: (*a*) those followed by the subjunctive mood, (*b*) those followed by the participial mood, and (*c*) those followed by the infinitive.

 (*a*) Deficient verbs taking the subjunctive: Z. *-ɓuye* (do next), *-phinde* (do again), *-ze* (do at length), *-ke* (do sometimes), &c.; e.g. *ngike ngiɓone* (I sometimes see); *ɓaɓuye ɓakhuluma* (and then they spoke). Most of these end in *-e* in Zulu, but in *-a* in Xhosa, e.g. *uda athethe* (at length he speaks), *zosuka zimɓaleke* (on the contrary they will flee from him).

 (*b*) Deficient verbs taking the participial: Z. *-lokhu* (keep on doing), *-de* (do continually),

&c.; e.g. *ɓalokhu ɓehleka* (they always laugh); X. *-fudula* (do formerly), *-hlala* (do continually, e.g. *ndifudula ndihamba* (I used to travel).

(c) Deficient verbs taking the infinitive: Z. *-funa* (be about to do), *-sanda* (have just done), *-vama* (be wont to do), e.g. *ɓavama ukulima* (they are accustomed to plough): X. *-khova* (do just after), *-mana* (do often), e.g. *safika zakukhova ukuphuma iinkomo* (we arrived just after the cattle had gone out).

(5) THE COPULATIVE

(a) FORMATION OF COPULATIVES FROM NOUNS

The three main Nguni clusters differ considerably from one another in their rules for this formation:

(i) ZULU. Nouns commencing in the vowel *i-* lower the tone on that vowel and may preplace *y-*, e.g. *imbuzi* (goat) > *yimbuzi* (it is a goat), *isitsha* (dish) > *yisitsha* (it is a dish); nouns commencing in *a-*, *u-*, or *o-* lower the tone and may preplace *ng-*, e.g. *aɓantu* > *ngaɓantu*, *umuzi* > *ngumuzi*, *oyihlo* > *ngoyihlo*; nouns with contracted prefixes of cls. 5 and 11 take *l*, e.g. *itshe* > *litshe*, *ukhuni* > *lukhuni*.

(ii) XHOSA. The above rules are applied when a nasal is the only consonant in the nounprefix, e.g. *inkomo* > *yinkomo*, *imilambo* > *yimilambo*; *umuntu* > *ngumuntu*, *amehlo* > *ngamehlo*; also unexpectedly *aɓantu* > *ngaɓantu*. In other cases, where there is a non-nasal consonant in the prefix, the equivalent subjectival concord is used, e.g. *sisitya* (it is a dish), *ziinkomo* (they are cattle), *ɓutywala* (it is beer), *kukutya* (it is food), *lihlwempu* (it is a pauper), *zizilo* (they are beasts).

(iii) SWAZI. As a general rule no initial vowel or added prefixal element appears, except in cl. 9, and as an alternative in cl. 4, e.g.

libuɓesi silwane (the lion is an animal).
kusetʃentiswa ɓafana (to be used by boys).
intfo > *yintfo* or *intfo* (it is a thing).
mifula or *yimifula* (they are rivers).
waɓanjwa timpandze (she was caught by the roots).

(b) FORMATION OF COPULATIVES FROM PRONOUNS

With ABSOLUTE PRONOUNS Xhosa uses mainly the subjectival concords, e.g. *ndim* (it is I), *sithi* (it is we), *nguwe* (it is thou), *nini* (it is you), *nguye* (it is he), *ngaɓo* (it is they), *siso*, *lulo*, and *yiyo* (it is it); *ngu-* and *yi-* being used in cases parallel to the use of *ng-* and *y-* with nouns. Zulu uses the prefixal formative *yi-* in all cases except those of *nguwe* (2nd pers. s.) and *nguye* (3rd pers. cl. 1), e.g. *yimi, yithi, yizo, yiɓo*. Swazi recognizes two sets of forms, an 'old form' (used by the old people) and a modern one. The old form approximates to what obtains in Xhosa, the modern form is achieved by prefixing *ng-* with assimilated vowel.

	(Sing.)			(Plur.)	
	(Modern)	(Old)		(Modern)	(Old)
1st pers.	*ngimi*	—		*ngitsi*	*sitsi*
2nd pers.	*nguwe*	—		*ngini*	*nini*
3rd pers. cl. 1	*nguye*	—	cl. 2	*ngaɓo*	*ɓaɓo*
3	*nguwo*	*wuwo*	4	*ngiyo*	*yiyo*
5	*ngilo*	*lilo*	6	*ngawo*	—
7	*ngiso*	*siso*	8	*ngito*	*tito*
9	*ngiyo*	*yiyo*	10	*ngito*	*tito*
11	*ngulo*	*lulo*			
14	*nguɓo*	*ɓuɓo*			
15	*nguko*	*kuko*			

DEMONSTRATIVE PRONOUNS uniformly prefix *yi-* in Z. and X., e.g. *lezo* > *yilezo* (it is those); but *ngu-* in Sz., e.g. *ngulomlente* (it is this leg).

QUANTITATIVE PRONOUNS are not themselves inflected, but assume the inflected form from the absolute pronoun before them, e.g. *zonke* > *yizo zonke* (it is all of them).

(*c*) FORMATION OF COPULATIVES FROM ADJECTIVES

In Z. and X. the initial vowel of adjectives is elided, except in cl. 9, where *e* gives place to *i*, e.g. *umuntu omkhulu* (a big person) > *umuntu mkhulu* (the person is big); *inkosi enkulu* (a big chief) > *inkosi inkulu* (the chief is big). In Sz. the initial syllable, *l*+vowel, is elided, e.g. *sikhali lesikhulu* (the big weapon) > *sikhali sikhulu* (the weapon is big).

(*d*) OTHER FORMATIONS

Copulatives are formed with relative stems by using the ordinary subjectival concords, e.g. Z. *ngiqotho* (I am honest); *izinguɓo zimanzi* (the blankets are wet); X. *imbiza iʃuʃu* (the pot is hot). A similar formation is used with adverbs commencing in consonants, e.g. Z. *silapha* (we are here); *aɓantwana ɓaphandle* (the children are outside). If the adverb is a locative commencing in a vowel, prelocative *-s-* is inserted after the subjectival concord, e.g. Z. *ngisendlini*, X. *ndisendlwini* (I am in the house); *ɓasemseɓenzini* (they are at work).

(*e*) THE LOCATIVE DEMONSTRATIVE COPULATIVES are a feature of Nguni, lost only in the extreme Phuthi type under Sotho influence. There are examples for each of the three demonstrative positions found in Nguni, with the significance of 'here is', 'there is', 'yonder is'. The following short table illustrates the forms in Zulu:

	(1st position)	(2nd position)	(3rd position)
Cl. 1	*nangu*	*nango*	*nanguyá*
2	*nampa*	*nampo*	*nampuyá*
3	*nanku*	*nanko*	*nankuyá*
4	*nansi*	*nanso*	*nansiyá*
7	*nasi*	*naso*	*nasiyá*
11	*nantu*	*nanto*	*nantuyá*
14	*nampu*	*nampo*	*nampuyá*

X. transposes the forms for cls. 1 and 3, *naanku* being cl. 1 and *naangu* being cl. 3. X., further, uses *naaɓa* for Z. *nampa*, *naali* for Z. *nanti* (cl. 5), *naanga* for Z. *nanka* (cl. 6), with similar changes where *ɓ* or *l* occur in the noun-prefix. Other dialectal forms occur, such as *nayi* in cls. 4 and 9, *nawa* in cl. 6. Sz. diverges from Z. as follows: cl. 2. *naɓa*, cl. 4. *nanki*, cl. 5. *nali*, cl. 8. *nati* (for *nazi*), cl. 11. *nalu*, cl. 14. *naɓu*. Examples of use:

Z. *nampo aɓantu aɓagulayo* (there are the people who are sick).

nansiyá inja yakho (yonder is thy dog).

(*f*) In Nguni, the copulative, apart from its normal use in forming a plain predicate, is used as an agentive adverb, especially after passive verbs; e.g. Z. *uɓonwé yimi* (he was seen by me); *ukushaywa ngumuntu* (to be struck by a person).

(*g*) In the conjugation of copulatives, Nguni employs the auxiliary verb *-ɓa* in forming certain of the tenses, especially the indicative future, e.g. Z. *ngizoɓa-mkhulu* (I shall be big); the subjunctive, e.g. Z. *ngiɓe-mkhulu* (that I may be big); the potential, e.g. Z. *ngingaɓa-mkhulu* (I can be big); and in the infinitive and imperative forms, *ukuɓa-mkhulu* and *yiɓa-mkhulu*.

(6) THE ADVERB

(i) PRIMITIVE ADVERBS. These are comparatively few in Nguni, but note *futhi* (again, continually), X. *lee* (far off), *nini?* (when?), Z. *manje* (now), Z. *ɓelu* (of course).

(ii) NOUNS USED ADVERBIALLY: *izolo* (yesterday), *uɓusuku* (night, i.e. by night), Z. *isiminya* (truth, i.e. truly).

(iii) NOUNS MODIFIED, generally by the elision of the initial vowel: Z. *ntambama* (in the afternoon < *intambama*), X. *tanci* or *matanci* (first < *itanci*, prior time), *kuqala* (at first < *ukuqala*, to begin); and also certain shortened compounds devoid of initial vowel, e.g. Z. *mpondozankomo* (at first dawn, lit. horns of the cattle), Z. *nhliziyonye* (with one accord, lit. one heart), *ndawonye* (together, lit. one place), Z. *mhlawumbe* (maybe, lit. another day), *nyakenye* (last year).

(iv) BY USE OF ADVERBIAL FORMATIVES: in Nguni the following are used: (*a*) manner, *ka-*; (*b*) instrumental, *nga-*; (*c*) comparison, *njenga-*, *nganga-*; (*d*) conjunctive, *na-*; (*e*) contrast, *kuna-*.

(*a*) Adverbs of manner formed by prefix *ka-* from adjectival, relative, and enumerative stems:

-hle (good) > *kahle* (well).
-khulu (big) > *kakhulu* (exceedingly).
Z. *-ɓili*, X. *-ɓini* (two) > *kaɓili*, *kaɓini* (twice).
-mnandi (pleasant) > *kamnandi* (pleasantly).
Z. *-ɓuhlungu* (painful) > *kaɓuhlungu* (painfully).
Z. *-nye* (one) > *kanye* (once).

X. commonly employs the formative *kaku-*, e.g. *kakuhle* (well), *kakuɓi* (badly).

(*b*) Adverbs are formed by the instrumental *nga-* prefixed to nouns and pronouns.
Forming adverbs of manner in Z.:
ngomusa (graciously) < *umusa* (kindness).
ngamaɓomu (intentionally) < *amaɓomu* (intentions).
ngaɓo (by means of them) > *ɓona* (they).
ngokuhle (carefully) > adj. stem *-hle* (nice).
ngokunzima (with difficulty) < rel. stem *-nzima* (heavy).
ngokwami (on my own accord).
Forming adverbs of time:
X. *ngomso*, Z. *ngomuso* (tomorrow).
X. *ngoku* (now).
Z. *ngesonto* (on Sunday).
ngolwesithathu (on Wednesday).

(*c*) The two comparison formatives *njenga-* (just like) and *nganga-* (just the same size as), are basically formed from *nga-*:

Z. *njengami*, X. *nje-ngam* (like me).
Z. *njengomuntu*, X. *nje-ngomntu* (just like a person).
Z. *njengasezulwini* (just as in heaven).
Z. *ngangomntwana*, X. *nga-ngomntwana* (just the size of a child).

(*d*) Conjunctive adverbs are formed with the formative *na-*, giving the effect of 'with, together with', e.g. Z. *nomuntu*, X. *nomntu* (with a person); *nazo* (with them).
This is used in the construction equivalent to the English 'have', as in Z.:
aɓantu ɓanezindlu (the people have houses).
izilo zinezikhumba (leopards have skins).

(*e*) The contrast adverbial formative is *kuna-* and is used in Z. to express 'rather than', e.g. *ngimkhulu kunawe* (I am bigger than you). In X. the formative *ku-* is used in this construction, e.g. *ndimkhulu kuwe*.

(v) LOCATIVE ADVERBS. Of the locative noun classes, cl. 16. *pha-*, cl. 17. *ku-*, and cl. 18. *mu-*,

THE NGUNI GROUP

Nguni languages retain the formatives of only cls. 16 and 17, the locative prefix *mu-* having entirely given way to suffix-formation in these languages.

(*a*) Class 16 prefix appears as *pha-* in only a few words today which have lost any substantival significance and are used only as adverbs of place, e.g.

phakathi (inside).
Z. *phansi*, X. *phantsi* (down).
phezulu (above) < *i(li)zulu* (heaven, sky).
Z. *phesheya*, X. *pheſeya* (on the other side).

(*b*) Class 17 prefix is used as an adverbial formative of place much more frequently, e.g.
1. In words like *kude* (afar off), *kufuphi* (near).
2. In forming locatives from nouns of cls. 1a and 2a and from pronouns, e.g.
   Z. *kuβaβa*, X. *kuβawo* (to or from my father).
   X. *kooyise* (to or from their fathers).
   X. *kum*, Z. *kimi* (to me).
   kuβo (to them).
3. In forming locatives from all nouns of cls. 1 and 2 in Z. and Sz.
   Z. *kuβantu*, Sz. *kuβantfu* (to or from people), *kumfundisi* (to or from the teacher).
4. In forming locatives from nouns (mainly personal) of all classes in X. as an alternative form to that under (*c*) following, e.g.
   kuβantu (to or from people); *kwinkosi* (to the chief); *kumadoda* (among the men).

The possessive concord of cl. 17, *kwa-*, is used, generally before names of persons, to indicate 'the place belonging to', e.g. *kwaPhatho* (at Phatho's kraal); *kwamfundisi* (at the mission station).

(*c*) Class 18 locative prefix (*mu-*) is not found in Nguni, and its place seems to be taken by the suffixal formation in *-ini* or *-eni* to nouns, accompanied by change of initial vowel to *e-* (in all classes except 11, where it becomes *o-*). This type of formation is found in all classes in X. except 1a and 2a which prefix *ku-*: in Z. and Sz. cls. 1 and 2 are also excluded from this formation (see (*b*) 3, above).

The rule for choice of suffix is as follows:

Final *-a* and *-e* become *-eni*: *ukuqala* > *ekuqaleni* (in the beginning), (Z.) *izwe* > *ezweni* (in the land).
Final *-i* becomes *-ini*: X. *umkhosi* > *emkhosini* (in the army).
Final *-o* becomes *-weni*: *uβuso* > *eβusweni* (on the face).
Final *-u* becomes *-wini*: *izulu* > *ezulwini* (in the sky).

Nouns of cl. 11 usually change the initial vowel to *o*, e.g. *uthi*, *othini* (to the stick).

Certain nouns make only initial change, taking no suffix, e.g. *emnyango* (at the door), *ekhaya* (at home), X. *entloko*, Sz. *enhloko*, Z. *ekhanda* (on the head).

In the case of nouns of which the final syllable is composed of a bilabial consonant followed by the vowel *o* or *u*, palatalization takes place according to the regular rules:

ph becomes Z. *sh*, X. *tʃh*: Z. *isiβopho* (grass rope) > *esiβosheni*; X. *incopho* (pinnacle) > *encotʃheni*.
b becomes *j*: Z. *isigubu* (calabash) > *esigujini*.
β becomes Z. *tsh*, X. *ty*: Z. *inguβo* (blanket) > *engutsheni*; X. *ihloβo* (summer) > *ehlotyeni*.
m becomes *ny*: *umlomo* (mouth) > *emlonyeni*.
mp becomes Z. *ntsh*, X. *ntʃ*: Z. *uβuphompo* (shamelessness) > *eβuphontsheni*; X. *uβuhlwempu* (poverty) > *eβuhlwentʃini*.
mb becomes *nj*: X. *umlambo* (river) > *emlanjeni*.

THE NGUNI GROUP

(7) THE IDEOPHONE

In Nguni the ideophone is used almost entirely after some form of the verb *ukuthi*, with its meaning of 'to express', 'to manifest'; and when used transitively, with a definite object, an objectival concord is used with the verb *-thi*. The ideophone in these languages is subject to its own laws of stress and length, stress being typically on the initial syllable (and not penultimate as in normal grammatical forms), and all syllables being short, except in the case of monosyllabic ideophones and a few rare final prolongations.

Nguni has examples of monosyllabic, disyllabic, trisyllabic, quadrisyllabic, and even quinquesyllabic ideophones, of which the following are examples.

Monosyllabic:

X. *cho* (of picking up), *nxi* (of tying), *tsi* (of jumping up).
Z. *bu* (of beating), *mbo* (of covering over), *swi* (of fullness).
Sz. *dlo* (of jabbing), *mfi* (of fullness).

Disyllabic:

X. *jíngxe* (of amazement), *ntýwili* (of diving), *nqám* (of cutting off suddenly).
Z. *ɓáni* (of flashing), *klébu* (of redness), *dínsi* (of throwing down a heavy load).
Sz. *tfúku* (of burying in ashes), *vítsi* (of shaking out).

Trisyllabic:

X. *phúlulu* (of slipperiness), *chúnunu* (of innocence).
Z. *míkithi* (of equality), *cháphasha* (of crossing over).
Sz. *gálaja* (of jumping over), *míkitsi* (of swelling).

Quadrisyllabic:

X. *cúthalala* (of squatting listless), *hlámbululu* (of clearness).
Z. *bólokoqo* (of haemorrhage), *xhókolozi* (of jabbing in the eye).
Sz. *góɓolondvo* (of standing up), *ngwíngwiliti* (of skimming).

Of five and more syllables:

Z. *gómbolokoqo* (of turning upside-down).
X. *gólokonqhokonqho* (of falling far down).

These various types of ideophones may further be subdivided according to tone; for instance, the following tonal divisions of monosyllabic ideophones occur in Zulu:

(i) rising-falling tone: *di* (of doing nothing), *zwi* (of swinging).
(ii) low-falling tone: *be* (of blazing), *nka* (of gaping).
(iii) low-rising tone: *du* (of silence), *ngci* (of final action).
(iv) high-level tone: *ne* (of sticking tight), *nti* (of stinging).
(v) high-falling tone: *chi* (of scattering), *qwa* (of whiteness).

Examples of the use of ideophones:

X. *Ɓayithi nkxu inguɓo egazini* (They dipped the garment in the blood).
X. *Ndithé tyho eludongeni* (I hit against the wall).
Z. *Ɓeɓephethe imikhonto ithi ɓénye* (They were carrying glinting weapons).
Z. *Yangitinyela yangithi nti* (It stung me sharply).
Z. *Waɓaleka wathi hálakasha* (He rushed through the grass).
Sz. *Ngavuvuka ngatsi khúkhukhu* (I was all swollen up).
Sz. *Tahamba tatsi qháfu qháfu eludzakeni tinkomo* (The cattle walked squelching in the mud).

The ideophone is a fruitful source of verb-formation in Nguni, the most common suffixes used being -*ka* (intransitive), -*la* (transitive), and -*za* (Sz. -*ta*) or -*sa* (causative),[1] e.g. in Zulu:

dázu (of splitting apart) becoming *dazuka* (get split down), *dazula* (cleave apart).
khúmu (of coming off) becoming *khumuka* (come off), *khumula* (pull off).
bódlo (of bashing) becoming *bodloka* (get bashed), *bodloza* (bash).
bóƁo (of piercing) becoming *boƁoka* (get punctured), *boƁosa* or *boƁoza* (pierce through).

Other suffixes are also used as is shown by the following:

zwiƁa (swing) from *zwi*; *khukhumala* (swell up) from *khúkhukhu*; *chitha* (scatter) from *chi*.

(8) THE CONJUNCTIVE

As was observed in Chapter IV,[2] both true conjunctions (primitive conjunctives) and other parts of speech used as conjunctives occur in Nguni. As a whole, however, conjunctives may be divided as follows in Nguni: (i) non-influencing conjunctives, (ii) conjunctives followed by the subjunctive mood, and (iii) conjunctives followed by the participial mood.

(i) NON-INFLUENCING CONJUNCTIVES, i.e. conjunctives which do not govern the mood of a following verb:

kodwa (but), *kanti*, Sz. *kantsi* (whereas), X. *kuloko* (only that), Z. *futhi*, Sz. *futsi* (moreover), Z. *kepha* (but), e.g. Z. *Ɓanamandla amakhulu*, *futhi Ɓanemali eningi* (They have great strength, moreover they have much money); X. *Ingwe ifana nekati*, *kuloko yona inkulu* (The leopard is like the cat, only that it is larger).

(ii) CONJUNCTIVES FOLLOWED BY THE SUBJUNCTIVE MOOD

ukuƁa, Sz. *kuƁa*, and *ukuthi*, Sz. *kutsi* (in order that) when indicating purpose or intention,[3] e.g. X. *into eƁangela ukuƁa ndihlale* (the thing that causes me to stay); Z. *Wakhulumisisa ukuthi Ɓalalele* (He spoke loud in order that they should listen); *ukuze* (in order that), *hleze* (lest), X. *ngokokude* (so much that), Z. *funa* (lest), Z. *qede* (as soon as), *nce* (so that).

(iii) CONJUNCTIVES FOLLOWED BY THE PARTICIPIAL MOOD

ngokuƁa (because), e.g. *Ɓacela ukudla ngokuƁa Ɓelambile* (They asked for food because they were hungry); *nakuƁa* (although); *noko* (even if); Z. *nxa* (when, if), Z. *lapha* (when), Z. *uma* (if, when), e.g. *Uma ethanda angahamba* (If he wishes, he can go). Several of the above in X. are followed by a relative construction, e.g. *noko ndithethayo* (although I speak); *xa afikileyo* (when he arrives); *mhla wafudukayo* (when he removed his abode). This construction does not occur in Z.

(9) THE INTERJECTIVE

(*a*) RADICAL INTERJECTIONS. In Nguni striking tone variations convey a series of emotions in these, which include interjections of assent and negation.

Z. *yeƁo*, X. *ewe*, Sz. *yemu* (yes!), Z. *hhayi*, *cha* (no!).
Z. *hawu*, X. *mawo* (oh my!).
X. *heke* (well done!).
Z. *mame* (I don't care!).

(*b*) VOCATIVES. These are formed from nouns by the elision of the initial vowel, e.g. Z.

---

[1] The similarity between these and the neuter (-*eka*), applied (-*ela*), and causative (-*isa*) derivative suffixes with verbs is most noticeable.
[2] See p. 87.
[3] When stating a fact these conjunctives are followed by the indicative, e.g. X. *Undixelele ukuƁa nifikile* (He told me that you had arrived).

and X. *ɓantu*, Sz. *ɓantfu* (O people!); Z. and X. *madoda*, Sz. *madvodza* (men!); *nkosi* (O chief!); Z. *ɓaɓa*, X. *ɓawo* (father!). In the case of nouns of cl. 2a, the prefix *ɓo-* (X. *ɓoo-*) takes the place of the initial vowel, e.g. X. *ooɓawo* (our fathers) becomes *ɓooɓawo* (fathers!).

(*c*) Other parts of speech may be used interjectively; this is particularly applicable to verb imperatives, e.g. *musa*, pl. *musani* (don't! you don't say so!); *hamba* (go!).

(10) ENCLITIC AND PROCLITIC FORMATIVES

(*a*) ENCLITICS which draw the stress forward: the following are examples:

-*ke* (now, so, then), X. *Ndeza-ke* (And so I came); Z. *Ɓahambake* (So they went away).
-*ni?* (what?), *Ufunani?* (What do you want?).
-*phi?* (where?). In Z. this is a true enclitic; e.g. *Ɓavelaphi?* (Where do they come from?); but in X. it is still used as a separable adverb, e.g. *Ɓavela phi?* or *Ɓavela phina?*

(*b*) ENCLITICS which leave the stress unaltered (hyphened):

-*ɓo* (at once), e.g. *Hamba-ɓo* (Go at once!).
-*na?* (of interrogation). In X. this should be hyphened, e.g. *Uyeza-na?* (Are you coming?). In Z. this is still used as a separable adverb, e.g. *Uyeza na?*
-*nje* (just, merely), e.g. *Ɓangaɓantu-nje* (they are merely people); X. *ɓemvile-nje* (having just heard him).

(*c*) THE PROCLITIC *na-* (subject to rules of coalescence) is used conjunctively connecting substantives and adverbs, e.g.

Imvu nembuzi zifile (The sheep and the goat are dead).
Z. *umfana noyise* (the boy and his father).
izulu nomhlaɓa (heaven and earth).

Substitution of *e* takes place in Sz. *indvodza nemfati* (a man and woman).
This formative is also used adverbially indicating 'with', 'together with', as already noticed.

(11) THE NUMERALS

Z. and X. differ considerably in their expression of the numerals. In X. the first six numerals are adjectives: -*nye* (one), -*ɓini* (two), -*thathu* (three), -*ne* (four), -*hlanu* (five), and -*thandathu* (six); e.g. *umntu omnye* (one person), *izimvu ezintathu* (three sheep), *amatye amathandathu* (six stones). In Z., however, the numeral 'one' is an enumerative stem, and 'six' a noun used with relative concord; they are -*nye*, -*ɓili*, -*thathu*, -*ne*, -*hlanu*, and *isithupha* (lit. the thumb); note the parallel examples, *umuntu munye*, *izimvu ezinthathu*, and *amatshe ayisithupha*.

Higher numerals are nouns in Z., S., and Sz., e.g.

	(Zulu)	(Xhosa)	(Swazi)
7	*isikhombisa*	*isixhenxe*	*lisontfo*
8	*isishiyagalombili*	*isiɓozo*	*siphohlongo*
9	*isishiyagalolunye*	*i(li)thoɓa*	*imfiqa*
10	*i(li)shumi*	*i(li)fumi*	*lifumi*
100	*i(li)khulu*	*i(li)khulu*	*likhulu*
1,000	*inkulungwane*	*i(li)waka*	*inkulungwane*

Examples:

Seven people: Z. *aɓantu aɓayisikhombisa*, X. *aɓantu aɓasixhenxe*, Sz. *ɓantfu laɓalisontfo*.
One hundred sheep: *Izimvu ezilikhulu*.
Twenty-nine trees: Z. *Imithi engamashumi amaɓili nesishiyagalolunye*; X. *Imithi engamafumi amaɓini anethoɓa*.

(12) RELATIVE CONSTRUCTION

There are two aspects of this in Nguni, (i) the Direct Relative, and (ii) the Indirect Relative.

(i) THE DIRECT RELATIVE is used (*a*) with relative qualificative stems, e.g. Z. *umuntu oɓomvu* (a red person); (*b*) in copulative relationship, e.g. Z. *umuntu olapha* (the person who is here); and (*c*) in subjectival relationship with the relative verb. Note examples of this last, when the direct relative concord agreeing with the antecedent is used with the subordinate verb in the participial mood:

    Z. *umuntu okhulumayo*; X. *umntu othethayo* (the person who speaks).
    Z. *Aɓantu aɓangaseɓenziyo aɓayukudla* (People who do not work will not eat).
    X. *inkosi ethethe nam* (the chief who spoke to me).

It is noteworthy that in X., when the antecedent lacks an initial vowel, the ordinary indicative subjectival concord takes the place of the relative concord, e.g.

    X. *Akukho-mntu undiɓonileyo* (There is no one who has seen me); cf. Z. *Akukho-muntu ongiɓonileyo*.
    X. *eli-sela lizandla ziɓotʃhiweyo* (this thief whose hands are bound); cf. Z. *leli-sela elizandla ziɓoshiwe*.

In Sz. the relative concord begins in *l-*, e.g. *Tintfombi letihlaɓela ingoma tigidza kahle* (The girls who sing the song dance beautifully).

(ii) THE INDIRECT RELATIVE is used when the relationship between antecedent and relative predication is oblique, e.g. objectival, adverbial, &c., and is expressed by employing the indirect relative concord agreeing with the subject of the relative predicate, the antecedent being represented therewith by the objectival concord or by an adverb formed from the pronoun agreeing with the antecedent, as the case may be. Here again, in X., when the antecedent lacks an initial vowel, the indicative subjectival concord replaces the relative concord.

(*a*) Objectival relationship:
    aɓantu esiɓaɓonayo (people whom we see); X. *aaɓo-ɓantu siɓaɓonayo* (those people whom we see).
    ukudla enikuthengileyo (the food which you have bought).
    umuzi awakhayo (the kraal which he builds).

(*b*) Adverbial relationship:
    Z. *inja engalunywa yiyo* (the dog by which I was bitten).
    X. *izicaka othumele imali kuzo* (the servants to whom thou didst send money).
    X. *iinkaɓi aɓalima ngazo aɓantu* (the oxen with which the people plough); X. *Akukho-nkaɓi ɓalima ngazo* (There are no cattle with which they plough).
    Z. *itafula aɓeké phezu kwalo incwadi* (the table on top of which he put the book).

Generally speaking *-yo* is suffixed to the relative verb when it ends the sentence, in which case the full form is used if it is the perfect stem, e.g. Z. *umuntu oɓonileyo* (the person who saw), but *umuntu oɓoné kahle* (the person who saw well). In Sz. the suffix added in such a case is *-ko*, e.g. *umuntfu lohambako* (a person who travels); *letidliwako* (those which are eaten).

REFERENCES

1. *Zulu*
    W. WANGER: *Konversations-grammatik der Zulu-Sprache*, 1917.
    C. M. DOKE: *The Phonetics of the Zulu Language*, 1926.
    W. WANGER: *Scientific Zulu Grammar* (vol. i), 1927.
    C. M. DOKE: *Text-book of Zulu Grammar*, 4th ed. 1945.
    —— and B. W. VILAKAZI: *Zulu-English Dictionary*, 1948.

2. *Xhosa*

W. Bourquin: 'Adverb und adverbiale Umschreibung im Kafir' (*Zeitschrift für Kolonialsprachen* iii and iv), 1912–14.
A. Kropf: *A Kafir-English Dictionary*, 2nd ed. by R. Godfrey, 1915.
J. McLaren: *A Concise Xhosa-English Dictionary*, revised by W. G. Bennie, 1936.
—— *A Xhosa Grammar*, 3rd ed. revised by G. H. Welsh, 1936.
W. G. Bennie: *A Grammar of Xhosa for the Xhosa-Speaking*, 1939.

3. *Ngoni*

(*a*) (of Nyasaland): W. A. Elmslie: *Introductory Grammar of the Ngoni Language*, 1891.
(*b*) (of Tanganyika): C. Spiss: *Kingoni und Kisutu* (Mitteilungen des Seminars für Orientalische Sprachen), 1904.

4. *Ndebele (Rhodesian)*

J. O'Neil: *Grammar of the Sindebele Dialect of Zulu*, 1912.

5. *Ndebele (Transvaal)*

E. F. Potgieter: *Inleiding tot die Klank- en Vormleer van isiNdzundza, 'n dialek van Suid-Transvaalse Ngoeni-Ndebele* (Manuscript thesis unpublished).

6. *Swazi*

D. Ziervogel: *A Grammar of Swazi (siSwati)*, 1952.

VI

THE SOTHO GROUP

Geographical Position of the Group

The Sotho group of the South-eastern Bantu is nowhere in contact with the sea and occupies the interior lands to the west and north-west of the main Nguni area. There are three main clusters in the group, generally referred to today as Southern Sotho, Northern Sotho, and Tswana (or Western Sotho). *Southern Sotho* (S.S.) is spoken in Basutoland and portions of the Orange Free State. *Northern Sotho* (N.S.), based mainly upon the Pedi dialect, is spoken entirely within the Transvaal, and for that reason is often referred to as 'Transvaal Sotho'; there are several other contributory dialects, and to the north and east are several other Sotho dialects, such as Lovedu and Pai, the exact linguistic position of which has not yet been determined.[1] *Tswana* (T.) stretches from the Western Transvaal and Northern Cape Province and O.F.S. right through the Bechuanaland Protectorate. There are numerous dialectal forms.[1] Rolong, Tlharo, and Tlhaping have mainly been used in publications in Tswana, and until recently literary work has been mainly based on Tlhaping. In Northern Rhodesia the Lozi or Kololo language is an offshoot of Southern Sotho, which has been considerably affected by surrounding Central Bantu types. In the Kalahari area is Kgalagadi, an extreme dialectal connexion with Tswana; while in the Transvaal is Sotho-Ndebele, bearing features of both Nguni and Sotho groups. On the south-eastern borders of Basutoland is found Phuthi, which is really an Nguni type heavily influenced by Sotho. It is probable that there are about three million Sotho speakers, those speaking Southern Sotho being numerically the most important of the three main literary types. Lozi has been developed as the literary language of Barotseland, and is recognized by the Northern Rhodesian Government for official and educational purposes in the western area of that territory. Sotho speakers are to be found in large numbers in the industrial and mining areas of the Witwatersrand as well as in Pretoria and Bloemfontein.

The greatest literary development has been in Southern Sotho, *Sēsōthō sa-ha-Mōshŏèshŏè*, and vernacular writers of no mean merit have revealed their talent. In N.S. and T., as well as in S.S., the whole Bible is available, and also numerous readers for school use. There has been considerable movement towards literary unification, but achievement of this aim is still far off.

Orthography

The orthography of S.S. has been static for a considerable time; it is very far from satisfactory, but recent attempts at improvement have met with no success. In common with that of N.S. and T. this orthography is 'classically' disjunctive, a system unsuited to and absolutely incorrect for a Bantu language. In the review here given, the various elements composing each word have been gathered together by means of hyphens, so that, while showing the true words, the present orthographies are at the same time preserved. It is in the vowel representation that the greatest difficulty is presented by the orthography used in S.S. The grammarian Jacottet fully realized this and used diacritics to differentiate. The Jacottet vowel method is followed in illustrations here. S.S. symbol *o* is used to represent (i) semi-vowel *w* (J. ŏ), (ii) open *u* (J. ō), and (iii) the two varieties of mid-back vowel *o*

[1] See Chapter II.

(J. o and ò). In the same way the symbol e represents y, open i, and the two varieties of mid-forward vowel (J. ĕ, ē, e, and è). The orthographies of N.S. and T. have been dealt with in conference after conference, until today they have come very close together in form. Certain diacritics are used, there is still trouble over the vowels, and the discredited disjunctive method of word-division is still being tenaciously held. Mr. D. T. Cole has used an improved method for vowel distinction, which has been followed here in all references to T., but, as will be seen below, that can still be improved upon if only the people would be bold enough.

Phonetic and Phonological Outline

The Sotho languages employ a nine-vowel system, in which pairs of mid-forward and mid-back vowels belong to individual phonemes: orthographically, then, seven vowels are all that are necessary for a practical orthography. The following is a comparison of present methods with a suggestion for further simplification in the use of diacritics:[1]

	S.S. (official)	S.S. (Jacottet)	N.S. & T. (official)	T. (Cole)	[Proposed]
close-*i*	*i*	*i*	*i*	*i*	*î*
open-*i*	*e*	*ē*	*e*	*e*	*i*
close-*e*	*e*	*e*	*e*	*ê*	*e*
open-*e*	*e*	*è*	*ê*	*ê*	*e*
low vowel	*a*	*a*	*a*	*a*	*a*
open-*o*	*o*	*ò*	*ó*	*ó*	*o*
close-*o*	*o*	*o*	*o*	*ó*	*o*
open-*u*	*o*	*ō*	*o*	*o*	*u*
close-*u*	*u*	*u*	*u*	*u*	*û*

Note: Cole has improved on the official T. in marking both members of the mid-vowel phonemes alike and thus definitely differentiating where it is necessary.[2] However, the least-used vowels are 'close-*i*' and 'close-*u*'; if these were indicated by a diacritic there would be relatively few diacritics necessary in any page of Sotho. Such a procedure would necessitate changing present 'open-*i*' and 'open-*u*'—unfortunately written e and o today— to *i* and *u* respectively. This would be an untold advantage to Sotho writing. Further it would remove the present artificial distinction between Sotho and other Bantu languages, e.g. Nguni—*muthu* would look much more like *umuntu* than its present unfortunate form *motho* does.

The following will illustrate the sort of change that would take place:

S.S. (official) *Motho eo o lutse lefifing.*
   (Jacottet) *Mōthō eō ō lutsē lēfifing.*
   (proposed) *Muthu eu ulûtsi lifîfing.*
      (That person is sitting in the dark.)
T. (official) *Motho o utlwa ka ditsêbê, mme o bóna ka matlhó.*
   (proposed) *Muthu uûtlwa kadîtsebe, mmi ubona kamatlho.*
      (A person hears with ears and sees with eyes.)
N.S. (official) *Pele o tlo bóna legadima, moragó o kwê modumó.*
   (proposed) *Pili utlobona legadîma, murago ukwe mudumo.*
      (First you will see the lightning, and afterwards you will hear the thunder.)

[1] On this subject reference should be made to A. N. Tucker's *Sotho-Nguni Orthography and Tone-Marking*.

[2] Cole would have preferred using the symbols shown in the last column, but such changes cannot be introduced unilaterally.

Such a reform in the writing of Sotho[1] vowels, with the adoption of conjunctive word-division throughout, and the use of the semi-vowels *y* and *w* in S.S., would be of inestimable benefit to all Sotho literary development.

In Sotho, consonants may practically all be accommodated on a single chart. Clicks of one positional type do occur in S.S., but such as are found in N.S. or T. are mainly of emotional significance and may be disregarded here.

PHONETIC CHART OF SOTHO CONSONANTS[2]

	Bilab.	Denti-lab.	Alveolar	Pre-palatal	Pre-velar	Velar	Glottal	Compounds
Explosive								
eject.	p'		t'			k'		
asp.	ph		th			{[kh]}		
voic.	b		d					
Nasal								
contin.	m		n	ɲ		ŋ		
syll.	m̩		n̩	ɲ̩		ŋ̩		
Rolled								
contin.			r					
syll.			{r̩}					
Flapped			{[ɹ]}					
Lateral								
contin.			l					
syll.			l̩					
Fricative								
med. unv.	{[ɸ]}	f	s	ʃ	[ʰ]	{x}	{h}	[ɸʃ] fʃ
med. voic.	[β]	(v)	(z)	[ʒ]		[ɣ]	ɦ	[βʒ]
lat. unv.			ɬ					
Affricate								
med. eject.			ts'	tʃ'				pʃ'
med. asp.			tsh	tʃh		kxh		pʃh
med. voic.				dʒ				bʒ
lat. eject.			tɬ'					
lat. asp.			tɬh					
Semi-Vowel	((w))			j		w		

[ ] found in N.S. only.   ( ) foreign or rare sounds.
{ } found in T. only.   (( )) alternative position.

Click Consonants

S.S. uses the radical, aspirated, and nasal forms of the palato-alveolar click, represented by *q*, *qh*, and *nġ* respectively; in addition the syllabic velar nasal consonant may precede each, e.g. *nq*, *nqh*, and *'nġ*. In T. clicks (of several types) are mainly used emotionally, as in interjections.

Orthographic Representation

The consonantal chart gives the various sounds used in phonetic script. The following show how these are represented in the current orthographies.

    b and **β** are written *b* throughout.
    d and **ɹ** are *d* in N.S. and T., but *l* in S.S.
    ɲ and **ŋ** are written *ny* and *ng* respectively.
    ɸ and **f** are both written *f*.

[1] Which would then be written '*Suthu*'.
[2] This is based on Southern Sotho.

ʃ is written *sh* in S.S. and *š* in N.S. and T.
ʒ and dʒ are written *j*.
ʰh is written *h* in N.S.
x and ɣ are written *g* in T. and N.S. respectively.
ɦ is written *h* is S.S.
ɬ is written *hl*.
tsh is written thus in N.S. and T., but *tš* in S.S.
tʃ' is written *tš* in N.S. and T., but *tj* in S.S.
tʃh is written *tšh* in N.S. and T., but *ch* in S.S.
kxh is written *kg* in N.S. and T., but *kh* in S.S.
tɬ' and tɬh are written *tl* and *tlh* respectively.
j is written *y* in N.S. and T., but *e* in S.S.
w is written thus in N.S. and T., but *o* in S.S.

The compound sounds are variously represented as *fsh* and *fš*, *pj* and *pš*, *psh* and *pšh*, and *bj*.

Ejection of explosives and affricates is not indicated in current orthographies.

NOTES ON THE CONSONANTS

1. Voiced explosives are obviously a rarity. S.S. and T. use *b*, but it is pronounced very softly, and in N.S. gives way to β, the fricative. N.S. and T. write *d* for what is often a flapped consonant; the corresponding sound in S.S. is a type of 'velar-stop' explosive; in each of the languages this consonant belongs to the *l* phoneme, occurring whenever *l* is followed by the very close *i* or *u* vowels. For this reason the symbol *l* is retained for it in S.S., e.g. *bala* (read) > perf. -*balile* (phon. -**badile**). There is no voiced velar explosive (g) in Sotho, except in a few borrowings; the symbol *g* is used in N.S. and T. for the velar fricative x (or ɣ).

2. Aspiration of consonants is significant in the case of explosives and affricates. The corresponding non-aspirated forms are slightly ejective.

3. Nasals occur representative of the four positions, and each has a syllabic form; in S.S. this, when initial, is represented by an apostrophe, e.g. *'mòhò*. The doubling of the consonant, as practised when medial in S.S. (e.g. *hammòhò*), and consistently in N.S. and T. is preferable, as in *mm, nn, nny, nng*.

4. There is a full range of fricatives, though their employment is divided among the languages and various dialects.

S.S. **f** (denti-labial) is Φ (bi-labial) in N.S. and T.
v and z occur only in foreign acquisitions and ideophones.
ʒ in N.S. appears generally as dʒ in S.S. and T., though the pronunciation of the latter is very soft.
ʰh (pre-velar) occurs in N.S. usually where h is found in T., and in S.S. the usual equivalent is **f**.
x (unvoiced) in T., corresponds to ɣ (and x) in N.S. and to ɦ (voiced) in S.S. For x and ɣ the orthography uses *g*.
ɬ in N.S. and S.S. is represented by **tɬh** in T.

5. **r**, fully rolled, occurs in all three types. In S.S., under French mission influence, the rolled uvular ʀ takes its place with certain speakers. In T. syllabic r̩ occurs, e.g. *rr̩ê* (my father). Syllabic l̩ occurs in Sotho, especially in S.S., e.g. *hō-l̩la* (to cry).

6. Affricates occur in alveolar, prepalatal, and velar positions. The only voiced occurrence is of dʒ variant of ʒ. Otherwise ejective and aspirated forms of alveolar medial (**ts'**, **tsh**), alveolar lateral (**tɬ'**, **tɬh**), and prepalatal (**tʃ'**, **tʃh**) positions occur regularly. The velar aspirated affricate **kxh** is distinguished in N.S. and T. from *kh*, but in S.S. the latter is

extremely rare. It is to be noted that under nasal influence in T. and N.S. $N+h$ or $ʻh > kh$; while $N+ɦ$ (S.S.), $N+ɣ$ (N.S.), and $N+x$ (T.) in each case $> kxh$.

7. The Compounds are non-homorganic, being composed of a labial initial (bi-labial or denti-labial, explosive or fricative) followed by prepalatal fricatives, in some dialectal cases by alveolar fricatives, giving $pʃ$, $bʒ$, or $βʒ$, $ɸʃ$ or $fʃ$ with dialectal forms such as ps, $ɸs$, fs—even $ʂ$ (the 'whistling fricative'). These forms generally arise from palatalization.

8. Sotho is one of the Bantu groups of a limited area which employ lateral fricatives and affricates. It is noteworthy that no voiced forms of these, such as occur in Nguni, are found here, however.

Consonantal Phenomena in Sotho

(1) NASALIZATION. This process, called 'strengthening' by Sotho grammarians, occurs particularly in three circumstances in this group: (i) in the formation of nouns and adjectives in cls. 9 and 10; (ii) when the objectival concord of the 1st pers. s. precedes a verb-stem; and (iii) when the reflexive prefix i-[1] precedes the verb-stem. The general resultant of the influence of the homorganic nasal in Sotho is an unvoiced consonant with explosive commencement, i.e. p, t, or k; thus ejective explosives result from nasal influence upon voiced explosives, b and d (or l) and vowels (with semi-vowels); aspirated explosives result from original unvoiced fricatives s, sh ($š$), and hl as well as from h (even voiced $ɦ$). Following is a table of changes for S.S. (phonetic script):[2]

(a) Vowels and semi-vowels become: $(ŋ)k'$
(b) Voiced explosives become ejective: $b > (m)p'$
       $d, l > (n)t'$
(c) Fricatives become aspirated explosives or affricates: $f > (m)ph$
       $r > (n)th$
       $s > (n)tsh$
       $ʃ > (ɲ)tʃh$
       $ɬ > (n)tɬh$
       $ɦ > (ŋ)kxh$
(d) Voiced affricate becomes ejective: $dʒ > (ɲ)tʃ'$

The changes are the same in T., except that T. does not have initial $ɬ$, while x takes the place of S.S. $ɦ$; T. h under nasal influence becomes $(ŋ)kh$; and $dʒ$ remains unchanged.

Examples from S.S.:

(Verb-stem)	(Cl. 9 noun)	(1st pers. s. obj. cd.)	(Reflexive)
(a) Vowels and semi-vowels			
araba	karabò	hō-nkaraba	hō-ikarabèla
èma	kèmò	hō-nkèmèla	hō-ikèmèla
ŏa	..	hō-nkŏela	hō-ikŏèla
(b) Voiced explosives, &c.			
bòna	pònò	hō-mpòna	hō-ipòna
lula	tulò	hō-ntulèla	hō-itulèla
laèla	taèlò	hō-ntaèla	hō-itaèla
(c) Fricatives			
fèpa	phèpò	hō-mphèpa	hō-iphèpa
rata	thatò	hō-nthata	hō-ithata
sèba	tšèbò	hō-ntšèba	hō-itšèba

[1] Possible reasons for this cannot be discussed here.
[2] The nasal, in parentheses is omitted in certain circumstances.

(c) Fricatives (cont.)

(Verb-stem)	(Cl. 9 noun)	(1st pers. s. obj. cd.)	(Reflexive)
shapa	*chapò*	*hō-nchapa*	*hō-ichapa*
hlōpha	*tlhōphò*	*hō-ntlhōpha*	*hō-itlhōpha*
hapa	*khapò*	*hō-nkhapèla*	*hō-ikhapèla*

(d) Voiced affricate

| *ja* | *tjèò* | *hō-ntja* | *hō-itja* |

All other consonants remain unchanged.

(2) PALATALIZATION. This process, the substitution of a palatal for some other consonant, occurs in Sotho in the formation of verb passives, and of diminutives from nouns, adjectives, and relatives. The process, however, is not so regular in Sotho as it is in Nguni; the processes of velarization and alveolarization have become mingled in the same types of formation.

The following are the changes:

	S.S.	T.
(a) Labial:	p' > pʃ'	p' > tʃ'
	ph > pʃh	ph > tʃh
	b > dʒ	b > dʒ or tʃ'
	m > ɲ	m > ɲ
	f > fʃ or ʃ	f > ʃ or tʃh
(b) Alveolar:	t' > tʃ'	t' > tʃ'
	th > tʃh	..
	l > dʒ	l > dʒ (or tʃ')
	..	r > ʃ or tʃh
	n > ɲ	n > ɲ
(c) Velar:	..	x > ʃ
	ŋ > ɲ	ŋ > ɲ
(d) Glottal:	..	h > ʃ

Examples are to be found later under noun diminutives, verb passives, and in the case of T. also with certain nouns of cl. 5.

(3) ALVEOLARIZATION. By this is meant the substitution of an alveolar affricative sound for a sound of some other organic position or the transference thereto of some other alveolar sound: the resultants are (phon.) **ts'** or **tsh**. The following are the changes:

p, b, and d (or l) > ts'
ph, f, and r > tsh

In T., in addition to the above, the following also occur:

t > ts' and x > s or tsh

Examples from S.S.:

(a) Noun diminutives

 (i) Labials (with semi-vowel intrusion):
  p > ts: *sēlèpè* > *sēlètsŏana*
  ph > tš: *sēhlòpha* > *sēhlòtšŏana*
  f > tš: *mōrifi* > *mōritšŏana*

 (ii) Alveolar transference:
  l > ts: *naleli* > *naletsana*
  r > tš: *phiri* > *phitšana*

(b) Colour adjectives

  b(u) > ts: *-kŏebu* > *-kotsŏana*
  l(i, u) > ts: *-fubelu* > *-fubetsŏana*

Transference of *l* > *ts* occurs in relative and possessive concords agreeing with cls. 8 and 10, as also in the absolute and quantitative pronouns, *tsòna* and *tsohle*, for those classes. It also occurs in certain applied forms, causatives, and perfect stems of verbs. N.S. uses palatalization in some of these cases.

(4) VELARIZATION. This takes place in Sotho with nasals in certain cases where palatalization occurs in Nguni. The changes are **m** > **ŋ**, and **ɲ** > **ŋŋ**; and they occur (*a*) in verb passives, (*b*) in noun and relative diminutives, and (*c*) in nouns of cls. 1 and 3 whose stems commence in *a*- or *e*-. Examples from S.S.:

(*a*) Verb passives
 rōma (send) > *rōngŏa*
 sēnya (spoil) > *sēnngŏa*

(*b*) Diminutives
 lēlēmē (tongue) > *lēlēngŏana*
 -mōlēmò (good) > *-mōlēngŏana*

(*c*) Nouns of cls. 1 and 3
 ngŏana (child) < *mō-+-ana*
 ngŏetsi (daughter-in-law) < *mō-+-etsi*

LENGTH AND STRESS. Normally in Sotho each isolated word and the final word in each sentence has stress on the penultimate syllable accompanied by length. The length of the vowels of penultimate syllables is appreciably shortened when words are not final in the sentence. Other syllables of words in Sotho are typically short. Abnormally lengthened syllables, often final, occur for emotional purposes and are frequently found in ideophones. Ideophones, too, have a typical initial stress.

Apart from ideophones, Sotho avoids, generally, the monosyllable. For instance, in cl. 9 the nasal of the prefix does not ordinarily appear, e.g. S.S. *khomō*, *pōli*; but a syllabic nasal does appear if the stem is monosyllabic, e.g. *nku*, *ntja*, making two syllables, the nasal taking the penultimate stress. Two other methods of avoiding the monosyllable occur: (i) the employment of penultimate *ē-*, and (ii) the employment of ultimate *-na* and *-a*.

(i) Penultimate *ē-* occurs with the interrogative root *-ng*, e.g. *ēng* (what?), a noun of cl. 5. There are three instances with monosyllabic verbs when penultimate *ē-* is employed: in the present participial positive, in the past subjunctive positive, and in the imperative, e.g. S.S. *kē-ne kē-ē-ŏa*, *ba-ile ba-ē-ja*, and *ē-kha*; only certain verbs and instances are so treated.

(ii) Ultimate *-na* is found with absolute pronouns, e.g. *rōna, tsòna*.

TONE. Two tone heights are recognized in Sotho as indicating different tonemes; though individual differences and emotional conditions may vary these, it is their relative relationship that is important. Tone is both semantic and grammatical, in addition to being used to express emotion. Note, for instance, *bòna* [_-] they, and *bòna* [⁻_] see, in S.S.; or in T. *go-bua* [_-_] to speak, and *go-bua* [___] to skin; *mabêlê* [__-] sorghum, and *mabêlê* [_⁻⁻] breasts.

The grammatical and syntactical function of tone may be illustrated by the following[1] from T.:

go-tsamaya [____] to go.
tsamaya [_-_] go!
go-rêka [_-_] to buy. *dikgômo* [__-] cattle.
ke-rêka dikgômo [_⁻⁻/⁻_⁻] I buy cattle.
fa ke-rêka dikgômo [⁻/_⁻/⁻_⁻] if I buy cattle.
tsamaya, o-rêkê dikgômo [_-_/⁻⁻⁻/⁻_⁻] go and buy cattle.

[1] From Tswana MS. by D. T. Cole.

THE SOTHO GROUP
GRAMMATICAL OUTLINE

(1) THE NOUN

Comparative Prefix Table

(Class)	(S. Sotho)	(Tswana)	(N. Sotho)
1	mō-	mo-	mo-
1a	—	—	—
2	ba-	ba-	ba-
2a	bo-	bô-	bo-
3	mō-	mo-	mo-
4	mē-	me-	me-
5	lē-	le-	le-
6	ma-	ma-	ma-
7	sē-	se-	se-
8	li-	di-	di-
9	[N]-	[N]-	[N]-
10	li[N]-	di[N]-	di[N]-
11	—	lo-	—
14	bō-	bo-	bo-
15	hō-	go-	go-
16	(fa-)	(fa-)	(fa-)
17	(hō-)	(go-)	(go-)
18	(mō-)	(mo-)	(mo-)

It is only in certain T. dialects that cl. 11 persists; in S.S. and N.S. all original cl. 11 nouns have merged with cl. 5. The locative cls. 16, 17, and 18 are more operative in T. than in the other languages.

CLASSES 1 AND 2 (personal):

mōthō (person), *bathō*.[1]
mōnna (man), *banna*.
mōsali, T. *mosadi* (woman), *basali*.

Tribal names:

Mōsōthō (Sotho tribesman), *Basōthō*.
Mōtsŏana, T. *Motšwana* (Tswana tribesman), *Batsŏana*.

Personal nouns derived from verbs:

mōeti (traveller), *baeti* < *èta*.
mōruti (teacher), *baruti* < *ruta*.

While nouns derived from vowel verbs juxtapose the prefix vowel, e.g. *mōahi* (builder), certain older Bantu formations are subject to velarization, *mō*+vowel > *ngŏ*-, e.g.

-*ana*: *ngŏana*, N.S. and T. *ngwana* (child), *bana*.
-*alē*: *ngŏalē* (girl at initiation), *balē*.

The prefix *mō*- before verb-stems beginning in *b* merges the explosive element, *mm*- (written *'m* in S.S.), resulting, e.g.

'musi, T. *mmusi* (governor), *babusi* < *busa*.
'mali, T. *mmadi* (reader), *babali* < *bala*.

In T. with verbs commencing in *f*, *mo*+*f* may become *mh*, e.g. *mhênyi* or *mofênyi* (conqueror), *bafênyi* < *fênya*.

[1] Examples are given in S.S. (Jacottet orthography) unless otherwise stated.

A few nouns of cl. 1 in S.S. take the plural in cl. 6, e.g. *mōrèna* (chief) > *marèna*; *mōfumahali* (chieftainess) > *mafumahali*. In N.S. it is optional to use cl. 6 or cl. 2; in T. cl. 2 is used.

CLASSES 1a AND 2a (proper names, kinship terms, miscellaneous): no prefix in the singular, and the prefix *bo-* (*bó-*)[1] in the plural.

Proper names:
S.S. *Mōshŏèshŏè, Lērotholi, Fekisi.*
N.S. *Thulare, Sekwati.*

In older Tswana a distinction was made between the form of the proper name when used vocatively (in address) and when used as a noun (in reference):

(Vocative interjective)   (Cl. 1a noun)
   Kgama   *Kgamê*   < *kgama* (hartebeest)
   Tau   *Tawê*   < *tau* (lion)

This custom is fast dying out; but in the case of kinship terms it is still observed, e.g. *rrê* (my father), in vocative form *rra*.

Kinship terms:
S.S. *ntate*, N.S. *tatê*, T. *rrê* (my father).
S.S. *'mè*, N.S. and T. *mmê* (my mother).
S.S. *malōmè* (my maternal uncle).

Miscellaneous (including zoological terms):
mang? (who), *bomang?*
S.S. *marabè* (puff-adder).
S.S. *'mankhanē* (bat).
T. *gôpane* (monitor lizard).

The plural of nouns indicating personal names and kinship generally signifies the person and those with him, e.g. T. *bóTawê* (Tawe and his company).

Table of Concords for classes 1 and 2 (S.S.)

	(Adj.)	(Rel.)	(Enum.)	(Poss.)	(Subj.)	(Obj.)
1 .	. *e-mō-*	*ĕa-*	*ō-, mō-*	*ŏa-*	*ō-*	*mō-*
2 .	. *ba-ba-*	*ba-*	*ba-*	*ba-*	*ba-*	*ba-*

In cl. 1, T. has *yó-mo-* for adj. concord, and *yó-o-* (N.S. *yo-a-*) for relative; N.S. follows T., but has an alternative for the adj. concord the same as that of S.S. In cl. 2, T. and N.S. have *ba-ba-* for relative concord.

CLASSES 3 AND 4 (miscellaneous, mainly impersonal, trees, parts of the body, natural phenomena):

mōtsē (village), *mētsē*.
mōru (forest), *mēru*.
mōllò, T. *molelô* (fire), *mēllò*, T. *melelô*.
mōlomō, T. *molómo* (mouth), *mēlomō*.

As with cl. 1, so in cl. 3 *mō-*+stem commencing in *b* merges the explosive element, e.g. *'mala*, T. *mmala* (colour), *mēbala*.

Similarly in T. *mo-*+*f* may contract to *mh-*
mhagó or *mofagó* (journey food), *mefagó*.

In N.S. the change is to *mph-* nasalization operating.

In T. certain names of trees and plants take the regular plural in cl. 4, e.g. *morôgó* (wild spinach) > *merôgó*; but the great majority take the plural in cl. 6, e.g. *mokala* (camel-thorn) > *makala*, *mophane* > *maphane*; while some have alternative plurals, e.g. *morula* > *merula* or *marula*.

---

[1] High-toned in contradistinction to all other noun-prefixes in Sotho, which also have closer vowels.

It must be noted that *Mōlimō* (God) is in cl. 3, with the plural *mēlimō* used for 'gods'. In cl. 2 is the word *balimō*, meaning 'ancestral spirits'.

Table of Concords for classes 3 and 4 (S.S.)

	(Adj.)	(Rel.)	(Enum.)	(Poss.)	(Subj.)	(Obj.)
3	o-mō-	o-	ō-, mō-	ŏa-	ō-	ō-
4	e-mē	e-	ē-, mē-	ĕa-	ē-	ē-

T. has *ó-o-* and *é-e-* for relative concords. N.S. generally follows T.

CLASSES 5 AND 6 (miscellaneous, parts of the body, natural phenomena, tribal designations, special classes of people). In S.S. cl. 5 contains two sets of words: (a) those regularly in this class in Bantu with normal pl. in cl. 6; and (b) those derived from original Bantu cl. 11, still found in that class in T., which take their plurals alternatively in cl. 10. A few of these are similarly treated in N.S. and in some dialects of T., but T. generally employs cl. 11 as normal Bantu.

(a) Normal class 5 words:

Miscellaneous:

S.S. *leihlò*, T. *leitlhô* (eye), pl. *mahlò*, *matlhô*; *lētsatsi* (sun), pl. *matsatsi* (days), T. *malatsi*.

S.S. *lējoè*, T. *lentšwē* (stone), pl. *majŏè*, *majwē*.

Tribal individuals:

S.S. *Lēkhŏŏa*, T. *Lekgoa* (European), pl. *Makŏŏa*, *Makgoa*; *Lētèbèlè* (Ndebele tribesman), pl. *Matèbèlè*.

Special classes of people:

lēqheku (old person), *maqheku*.
lēlimō (cannibal), *malimō*.

(b) Class 5 words in S.S. (and N.S.) originally from cl. 11:

lēhōpò (N.S. *legopó*), (rib), pl. *likhōpò*, *mahōpò* (ct. T. *logopó*).
lēnaka (horn), pl. *linaka*, *manaka* (ct. T. *lonaka*).
lērakò (stone wall), pl. *lithakò* (ruins), *marakò* (walls) (ct. T. *lorakó*).

There are many such instances in S.S.

In Tswana, in the case of certain nouns, the cl. 5 prefix *le-* exerts a 'palatalizing' influence upon the initial consonant of the stem; this process is now obsolescent. Cole records the following changes: $b > ts$ or $tš(w)$; $l, d > ts$; $r > s$, tsh, $š(w)$, or $tšh(w)$; $g > š(w)$; $h > š(w)$. Examples:

letsēlē (breast), pl. *mabēlē* (though both *lebēlē* and *matsēlē* are found).
lesapó (bone) < stem *-rapó*.
lešomē (ten) < stem *-gomē*, pl. *mašomē* being more common than *magomē*.

Class 6, indicating liquids, &c.:

S.S. *mafura*, N.S. *makhura*, T. *mahura* (fat, oil).
S.S. *metsi*, N.S. *meetse*, T. *mêtse* (water).
S.S. *matla*, T. *maatla* (strength).

Table of Concords for classes 5 and 6 (S.S.)

	(Adj.)	(Rel.)	(Enum.)	(Poss.)	(Subj.)	(Obj.)
5	le-lē-	le-	lē-	la-	lē-	lē-
6	a-ma-	a-	a-, ma-	a-	a-	a-

T. has *lé-le* and *a-a-* for relative concords, and *jé-le* as a common dialectal variant in cl. 5 for both adj. and rel. concords, with *ja-* as possessive variant. N.S. generally follows T.

THE SOTHO GROUP

Classes 7 and 8 (miscellaneous, languages, characteristics, habitual actions, experts, instruments, and foreign acquisitions): cl. 7 prefix is *sē-*, that of cl. 8 *li-* (*di-* in N.S. and T.).

Miscellaneous:
S.S. *sēfate*, N.S. *sehlare*, T. *setlhare* (tree), pl. *lifate, dihlare, ditlhare.*
sēatla (hand), *liatla.*
sēèta (shoe), *lièta.*

Languages and characteristics:
Sēsōthō (Sotho language and characteristics).
T. *Setšwana* ('Tswana language and characteristics).
Sēburu (Afrikaans; Dutch customs).

Experts; persons with some habit or defect:
sēbini (expert singer) < *bina* (sing).
sēhahi (builder) < *haha* (build).
sēmumu (dumb person).
sēfofu (blind man).
sēbòta (headman).

Instruments:
sēlèpè (axe), *lilèpè.*
sēthèbè (mat), *lithèbè.*

Foreign acquisitions:
sēkolo (school), *likolo.*
sētulò (chair), *litulò.*

Table of Concords for classes 7 and 8 (S.S.)

	(Adj.)	(Rel.)	(Enum.)	(Poss.)	(Subj.)	(Obj.)
7	se-sē-	se-	sē-	sa-	sē-	sē-
8	tse-[N]-	tse-	li-	tsa-	li-	li-

Note: The introduction of nasal influence (indicated by [N]) in the adjectival concord of cl. 8 is by analogy with cl. 10; the alveolar transference of *l* or *d* to *ts* (also called 'palatalization')[1] occurs generally when an *a* would follow, e.g. in possessive or 'past' verbal concord. T. has cl. 8 adjectival concord as *tsê-diN-*, the *-di-* being at times elided; similarly T. has *tsê-di-* as relative concord of cl. 8, with *sê-se-* in cl. 7.

Classes 9 and 10 (while miscellaneous, also containing names of animals, deverbative nouns, and foreign acquisitions):

(a) Monosyllabic stems assume as prefix in cl. 9 the homorganic nasal which is syllabic, and cl. 10 superadds the prefix *li-* (T. and N.S. *di-*):

mphò (gift < *fa*, give) *limphò.*
nta (louse) *linta.*
ntja, T. *ntša* (dog) *lintja*, T. *dintša.*
nkhò, T. *nkgô* (water-pot < *kha*, draw water.)

The nasal prefix is usually retained when suffixes are added, e.g. *nthò* (thing) > *nthŏana* (small thing); but *ntlō* (house) > loc. *tlung*; and *nku* (sheep) gives diminutive *kònyana* (lamb).

(b) With noun-stems of more syllables than one, the nasal itself does not appear, but its influence is shown on the initial phone: this influence is mainly devocalizing, and generally fricative consonants become aspirates (explosive or affricative) and voiced consonants become ejectives. The following examples are taken solely from S.S.

[1] Which it actually is in N.S., where it occurs as *tš* (phon. tʃ').

$b > p; f > ph$:
  pina (song < *bina*, sing), pl. *lipina*.
  phumanò (discovery < *fumana*, find), pl. *liphumanò*.
  pōli (goat), pl. *lipōli*.

$l > t; r > th; s > t\check{s}; hl > tlh$ or remains:
  taèlò (order < *laèla*, command), *litaèlò*.
  thatò (will < *rata*, like), *lithatò*.
  tšèbò (backbiting < *sèba*, revile), *litšèbò* and *masèbò* (rumours).
  tlhalò or *hlalò* (divorce < *hlala*, divorce).

$j > tj; sh > ch$:
  tjèò (eating < *ja*, eat).
  shèbò (look < *shèba*, look).

Vowel-stems $> k; h > kh$:
  kèmò (stature < *èma*, stand).
  khapò (booty < *hapa*, capture).

The following illustrate animal names in T.:

pitse (horse, zebra)	*dipitse.*
tlóu (elephant)	*ditlóu.*
tau (lion)	*ditau.*
khudu (tortoise)	*dikhudu.*
tshêphê (springbok)	*ditshêphê.*

Many nouns in cl. 9, indicating animals, take, in addition to the cl. 10 plural, a quantitative plural in cl. 6, e.g. in S.S.:
  nku (sheep), pl. *linku*, quant. pl. *manku* (flocks of sheep).
  khomō (ox), pl. *likhomō*, quant. pl. *makhomō* (herds of cattle).

A few nouns of cl. 9 have normal plural in cl. 6, e.g. in S.S.:

ntlō (house)	*matlō.*
tšimō (field)	*masimō.*

Table of Concords for classes *9* and *10* (S.S.)

		(Adj.)	(Rel.)	(Enum.)	(Poss.)	(Subj.)	(Obj.)
9	.	e-[N]-	e-	ē-	ěa-	ē-	ē-
10	S.S.	tse-[N]-	tse-	li-	tsa-	li-	li-
	T.	tse-(di)[N]-	tse-(di)-	di-	tsa-	di-	di-
	N.S.	tše-[N]-	tše-	di-	tša-	di-	di-

CLASS 11 (miscellaneous, including long objects): In the Sotho group it is only certain forms of T. which have this as a distinctive class, with prefix *lo-* and plural in cl. 10; in S.S. and N.S. the words have merged with cl. 5 (q.v.) assuming the prefix *lē-*. Examples:

lorakô (stone wall)	*dithakô.*
loleme (tongue)	*diteme.*
lorole (dust)	*dithole.*
lobônê (lamp)	*dipônê.*
lobese (fresh milk).	
loêtô (journey < *êta*, travel), *maêtô* or *dikêtô*.	
lokwalô (book < *kwala*, write), *dikwalô*.	

Table of Concords for class *11* (T.)

		(Adj.)	(Rel.)	(Enum.)	(Poss.)	(Subj.)	(Obj.)
11	.	lô-lo-	lô-lo-	lo-	lwa-	lo-	lo-

THE SOTHO GROUP

Class 14 (abstract and collective): Most of these nouns have no plural form, but there are some 'semi-abstracts' and foreign acquisitions which take the plural in cl. 6, in the former case generally with modified or specialized meanings. Examples from S.S.:

Abstract nouns:
  bōhalē (anger), bōhlalē (wisdom).
  bōbē (evil < adj. -bē, bad).
  bōhōlō (size < adj. -hōlō, big).
  bŏrèna (chieftainship < n. mōrèna, chief).

Semi-abstract and collective nouns:
  bōsiu, T. bosigo (night), pl. masiu, T. masigo.
  bŏrŏkŏ (sleep), pl. marŏkŏ (evil dreams).
  bŏĕa (wool).
  bŏkŏ (brain).
  jŏang,[1] T. bojang, N.S. bjang (grass), pl. majŏang, majang, mabjang (varieties of grass).
  jŏala,[1] T. bojalwa, N.S. bjala (beer), pl. majŏala, majalwa, mabjala (beer parties).

Concrete nouns:
  bōhòbè (bread)   mahòbè (loaves).
  bōliba (pool)   maliba.

Nouns of locative significance:
  bōphirimèla (west).
  bōchabèla (east).
  T. Botšwana (Bechuanaland).
  T. bogwê (home of son-in-law).

Foreign acquisitions:
  bōrògò (bridge < Afr. brug), marògò.
  bōlèkè (tin can < Afr. blik), malèkè.

Table of Concords for class 14 (S.S.)

	(Adj.)	(Rel.)	(Enum.)	(Poss.)	(Subj.)	(Obj.)
14	bo-bō-	bo-	bō-	ba-	bō-	bō-

T. has jó-bo- and bó-bo- as variants for both adj. and rel. concords, N.S. using bjo-bo-. T. uses variants in the possessive, jwa- and ba-, N.S. using bja-.

Class 15 (verb infinitive): S.S. hō-, N.S. and T. go-.
  hō-ja, T. go-ja (to eat, eating).
  hō-tla, T. go-tla (to come, arrival).
  hō-bòna, T. go-bóna (to see, seeing).
  hō-sē-ratē (not to like, dislike).
  T. go-di-reka (a buying of them, i.e. dinku, sheep).

Table of Concords for class 15

	(Adj.)	(Rel.)	(Enum.)	(Poss.)	(Subj.)	(Obj.)
15. S.S.	ho-hō-	ho-	hō-	ha-	hō-	hō-
T.	mô-go-	mô-go-	go-	ga-	go-	go-
N.S.	follows the T. forms.					

Classes 16, 17, 18 (prefixes fa-, go- (S.S. hō-) and mo-). These no longer function as

---

[1] bō- + a > jŏa- by palatalization.

regular noun-prefixes in the Sotho group, but occur in various locative adverbial circumstances.[1] Locative expressions of all kinds may, however, be used substantivally as subject (or even object) of a sentence, in which case the concords for cl. 17 are employed, e.g.

T. *Kwa-nokêng go-gontlê* (At the river is beautiful).
N.S. *Godimo go-be go-tonya* (Up above it was cold).
T. *Felô fa ga-ke-go-rate* (I do not like this place).

Certain locative adverbs are found representing each of these classes, e.g.:

	(S.S.)	(T.)	(N.S.)	
16	. fatšē	fatshe	fase	(down, below)
17	. hōlimō	godimo	godimo	(above)
	hōle	golê	..	(far)
18	. mōraō	moragô	moragô	(after, behind)

The concords of these classes are the same as those for cl. 15, except in the case of adjectives and relatives which in T. and N.S. are found as follows: 16. *fa-go*; 17. *kwa-go-*; 18. *mo-go-*.

Suffixes in Noun Formation

I. NOUN DIMINUTIVES are formed by employing the suffix *-ana* or *-nyana*. The former may be reduplicated (*-anyana*) and each may have an alternative termination in *-ē* which is probably dialectal or individual; S.S. uses the reduplicated form *-anyanē*. When the suffix *-nyana* is used, it is appended to the noun without any phonetic change,[2] e.g. S.S. *thabò* (joy) > *thabònyana*; *lēseli* (light) > *lēselinyana*. The suffix *-ana* is, however, generally preferred, and then the phonetic phenomena of palatalization, alveolarization, and velarization come into play. The main rules (for S.S.) are as follows:

Rule 1: Suffix *-ana* to nouns ending in *-a*, e.g.
mōlisa (herd-boy) > *mōlisana*.
buka (book) > *bukana*.

Rule 2: Suffix *-ŏana* to nouns ending in *-u, -ō, ò*, e.g.
tau (lion) > *taŭana* (= *taŏana*).
mōthō (person) > *mōthŏana*.

Rule 3: Palatalization takes place with a number of consonants (*b, f, t, l, n, ng*), e.g.
bōhòbè (bread) > *bōhòjana*.
sēfatè (tree) > *sēfatjana*.
mabèlè (sorghum) > *mabèjana*.
lēnong (vulture) > *lēnonyanē*.

Rule 4: Alveolarization takes place with a number of consonants (*p, f, l, r*), e.g.
sēlèpè (axe) > *sēlètšŏana*.
naleli (star) > *naletsana*.
narē (buffalo) > *natšana*.

Rule 5: Velarization takes place with *m*, e.g.
khomō (ox) > *khongŏana*.

II. AUGMENTATIVES AND FEMININES are occasionally formed by suffixing *-gadi* (S.S. *-hali*) or *-adi*; e.g. in S.S.

(*a*) Feminine with nouns indicating animals:
khomō (beast) > *khomōhali* (cow).
tau (lion) > *tauhali* (lioness).

---

[1] Cf. their treatment by G. P. Lestrade in his paper; 'Locative-class Nouns and Formatives in Sotho' (*Bantu Studies*, vol. xii, pp. 35–62).

[2] For this reason, with certain speakers its use is becoming increasingly popular. In T. there is change of final *-ng* to *-nnyana*.

(b) Augmentative with nouns indicating persons and objects:
mōnna (man) > mōnnahali (big man).
lējoè (stone) > lējòèhali (huge rock).

(2) THE PRONOUN

(a) TABLE OF ABSOLUTE PRONOUNS

	(S.S.)	(T.)	(N.S.)
1st pers. s.	'na	nna	nna
pl.	rōna	rona	rena
2nd pers. s.	ŭèna	wèna	wèna (wène)
pl.	lōna	lona (nyena, lena)	lena
3rd pers. cl. 1	èèna	ènê	yèna
2	bòna	bônê	bôna
3	òòna	ônê	wôna
4	èòna	yônê	yôna
5	lòna	lônê (jônê)	lôna
6	'òna	ônê	ôna
7	sòna	šônê	sôna
8	tsòna	tšônê	tšôna
9	èòna	yônê	yôna
10	tsòna	tšônê	tšôna
11	—	lônê	—
14	bòna	jônê (bônê)	bjôna
15	hòna	gônê	gôna

In T. there are dialectal variants with final -a in place of -ê; the forms in parentheses are also dialectal variants. In S.S. 'na would more correctly be written nna, and the 2nd pers. s. form ŭèna should really be spelled òèna, but the orthographic device of using u- as subjectival concord has persisted here; also cls. 3 and 6 should both be òna; the extra syllable indicated is incorrect and the distinction artificial.

The ultimate -na or -nê, required to avoid monosyllabic words, is sometimes dropped when these pronouns are inflected prefixally, but this is not nearly so common as in Nguni.

(b) DEMONSTRATIVE PRONOUNS

T. and N.S. have the four positional types of typical Bantu, viz. (1) this, (2) that, (3) this here, and (4) that yonder. They are divided into two contrast sets, viz. (1) and (2), (3) and (4). In Sotho each may be used instead of the noun or in apposition following the noun, very rarely preceding it.

Table of Demonstratives in Tswana

(Class)	(1st position)	(2nd position)	(3rd position)	(4th position)
1	yô	yôo	yôno	yôlê
2	ba	bao	bano	balê
3	ô	ôo	ôno	ôlê
4	ê	êo	êno	êlê
5	lê (jê)	lêo (jêo)	lêno (jêno)	lêlê (jêlê)
6	a	ao	ano	alê
7	sê	sêo	sêno	sêlê
8	tsê	tsêo	tsêno	tsêlê
9	ê	êo	êno	êlê
10	tsê	tsêo	tsêno	tsêlê
11	lô	lôo	lôno	lôlê

(Class)	(1st position)	(2nd position)	(3rd position)	(4th position)
14	jó (bó)	jóo (bóo)	jóno (bóno)	jólé (bólé)
15	mó	móo	móno	mólé
16	fa	fóo (fao)	fano	falé
17	kwa	kóo	kwano	kwalé
18	mó	móo	móno	mólé

Note: An alternative to the 4th demonstrative is suffix *-la* in place of *-lé*, except where the previous syllable contains *a*. Class 17 forms all have an inherent significance of distance, even in the cases of *kwa* and *kwano*.

N.S. has alternative forms for 2nd, 3rd, and 4th positions, that for the 3rd position being remarkable for the suffix *-khwi*. The following examples illustrate N.S. demonstratives:

(Class)	(1st position)	(2nd position)		(3rd position)		(4th position)	
1	yó (y)é	yóó	yówé	yóno	yókhwi	yóla	yólé
2	ba	baó	bawé	bano	bakhwi		balé
3	(w)ó	(w)óó	(w)ówé	(w)óno	(w)ókhwi	(w)óla	(w)ólé
8	tše	tšéó	tšéwé	tšéno	tšékhwi	tšéla	tšélé
14	bjó	bjóó	bjówé	bjóno	bjókhwi	bjóla	bjólé

S.S., unlike the others above, has forms for three positions only, the 3rd position being wanting. There are, however, two forms for each position, as the following examples show:

(Class)	(1st position)		(2nd position)		(4th position)	
1	eō[1]	enŏa	eō[1]	enō	ĕanē	elŏa
2	baa	bana	baō	banō	banē	bale
3	oō	ona	oō	onō	ŏanē	ola
8	tseē	tsena	tseō	tsenō	tsanē	tsela

(c) QUANTITATIVE PRONOUNS

T. has representatives of the two simple quantitative pronouns, 'all' and 'only', as well as the definite numerals. S.S. and N.S.[2] have but representatives for 'all', viz. the stem *-hle*. T. differentiates the definite numerals from the simple quantitatives, in that the prefix of the latter is monosyllabic, that used with the former being disyllabic, the typical vowel *ó* being repeated. The following illustrates Tswana:

			-tlhé (the whole, all)	-si (only, alone)	-bédi (both)
1st pers.	s.	.	—	nósi	—
	pl.	.	rótlhé	rósi	róóbabédi
2nd pers.	s.	.	—	wési	—
	pl.	.	lótlhé	lósi	lóóbabédi
3rd pers.	cl. 1	.	—	ési	—
	2	.	bótlhé	bósi	bóóbabédi
	3	.	ótlhé	ósi	—
	4	.	yótlhé	yósi	yóómebédi
	5	.	lótlhé (jótlhé)	lósi (jósi)	—
	6	.	ótlhé	ósi	óómabédi
	7	.	šótlhé	šósi	—
	8	.	tšótlhé	tšósi	tšóópédi
	9	.	yótlhé	yósi	—
	10	.	tšótlhé	tšósi	tšóópédi
	11	.	lótlhé	lósi	—
	14	.	jótlhe (bótlhé)	jósi (bósi)	—
	15	.	gótlhé	gósi	góógobédi

[1] These differ in tone.   [2] Only occurring irregularly in N.S.

THE SOTHO GROUP

For the definite numerals, only plural forms exist. Other examples are: *róóbararo* (all three of us), *tšóónné* (all four of them), *óómatlhano* (the five of them), *yóómerataro* (all six of them). In S.S. the stem *-hle* is only used with 3rd person forms, and there is no form for cl. 1.

(d) QUALIFICATIVE PRONOUNS

In Sotho there is no formal change in qualificatives when they are used pronominally.

(3) THE QUALIFICATIVE

(a) THE ADJECTIVE

In Sotho, adjectives may be divided into two main categories, the first of which is miscellaneous, including the common adjectives and the numerals 'two' to 'five' (to 'six' in T.), and the second composed of colour terms.

List of adjectival stems in S.S. and T.:

(S.S.)	(T.)	(meaning)
-bē	-be	(bad, evil, ugly)
-beli	-bêdi	(two)
—	-bôtlana	(smaller)
-cha	-ša (-fsa, -fša)	(young, new)
-chitja	—	(round)
-hlanō	-tlhano	(five)
-hōlō	-golo	(big, large)
-kaē[1]	—	(how many?)
	-kgaraga	(thick, stout)
-khutšŏanē	-khutšhwane	(short)
-lelele	-lêlêlê (-têlêlê)	(tall, long)
	-nana	(young, fresh)
-nè	-nê	(four)
	-nêtlane	(what's-his-name)
-ngata	-ntsi	(many)
-ngŏē	-ngwe	(another)
-nyanē (-nyēnyanē)	-nnye, -nnyennyane	(small)
-rarō	-raro	(three)
	-rataro	(six)
-sēsanē	-sesane	(thin)
-tēnya	-kima	(thick)
-tlè	-ntlê	(fine, pretty)
	-tona	(big)
	-tonna	(larger)
-tōna[2]	-tonanyana	(male)
-tšēhali	-namagadi	(female)

Examples of colour adjectives from S.S.:

-*fubelu* (red)   -*kŏebu* (roan)
-*nala* (white and red)   -*sèhla* (yellow)
-*thōbōsha* (speckled)   -*tšumu* (white-faced).

There are great numbers of these, most being applicable to cattle colouring. It is noteworthy that the equivalents in Nguni are treated as relative stems, not adjectives.

Adjectival concords in Sotho contain two elements, which in T. and N.S. are the 1st

---

[1] The equivalent is a relative stem in T.
[2] In S.S. when -*tōna* and -*tōnana* are used signifying 'big', possessive (descriptive) concords are used before the noun-prefix preceding the stem.

positional demonstrative[1] followed by the noun-prefix. In S.S. the initial syllable of the demonstrative is used with the noun-prefix. It must be noted that *li-* of cls. 8 and 10 is omitted from the adjectival concord in S.S., and commonly elided in T. and N.S. By false analogy with cl. 10 the concord for cl. 8 assumes nasal influence; this is also a feature of Zulu.

The following is a list of the concords in S.S. and T.:

	(S.S.)	(T.)
Cl. 1 .	*e-mō-*	*yó-mo-*
2 .	*ba-ba-*	*ba-ba-*
3 .	*o-mō-*	*ó-mo-*
4 .	*e-mē-*	*ê-me-*
5 .	*le-lē*	*lê-le- (jê-le-)*
6 .	*a-ma-*	*a-ma-*
7 .	*se-sē-*	*sê-se-*
8 .	*tse-[N]-*	*tsê-(di)N-*
9 .	*e-[N]-*	*ê-N-*
10 .	*tse-[N]-*	*tsê-(di)N-*
11 .	—	*ló-lo-*
14 .	*bo-bō-*	*jó-bo- (bó-bo-)*
15 .	*ho-hō-*	*mó-go-*
16 .	—	*fa-go-*
17 .	—	*kwa-go- (kó-go-)*
18 .	—	*mó-go-*

The rules of nasalization, as applicable to nouns of cls. 9 and 10, operate with adjectives in cls. 8, 9, and 10.

Examples:
S.S. *pèrè e-tšŏeu* (a white horse < *-sŏeu*).
likhomō tse-mpē (miserable cattle < *-bē*).
linku tse-tharō (three sheep < *-rarō*).
T. *podi ê-kgolo* (big goat < *-golo*).
kólói ê-ntšha (new wagon < *-ša*).
dilô tsê-dingwe (other things < *-ngwe*).

In S.S. the stem *-ngŏē* (another, other) appears in its full form only in cl. 9, as *e-'ngŏē* (with syllabic nasal). In all other classes the stem is reduced to *-ng*, e.g. 1. *e-mŏng*; 2. *ba-bang*; 10. *tse-ling* (where *li* persists before the monosyllable); 15. *ho-hŏng*.

Generally throughout Sotho the diminutives of colour adjectives indicate the feminine, e.g. S.S. *khomō e-ntšō* (black beast) > *khomō e-tšŏana* (black cow); *pèrè e-kŏebu* (roan horse) > *pèrè e-kotsŏana* (roan mare).

(*b*) The Relative

Sotho employs numerous relative stems, some of which appear to be primitive, but most of them are denominative, i.e. nouns used qualificatively when preceded by the relative concord.

Examples:
(*a*) Primitive stems:
S.S. *-batsi* (wide), *-fōfō* (lukewarm), *-nòlò* (soft), *-thata* (hard).
S.S. and T. *-tala* (raw), *-khòpò*, *-kgôpô* (crooked), *-kalo*[2] (so much), *-hlala*, *-tlhaga* (wild).
T. *-kae* (how many?)

---

[1] Which, however, has lost its demonstrative function.
[2] Also used with adj. concords in S.S.

(b) Denominative stems (S.S. and T.):

-bōhalē, -bogale (sharp, fierce) = anger.
-bōhlōkō, -botlhoko (painful) = pain.
-metsi, -mêtse (wet) = water.
-mōlēmò, -molemô (good) = goodness.
-mŏnatē, monate (nice) = tastiness.

With all these, direct relative concords are used as follows:

	(S.S.)	(T.)
Cl. 1 .	ĕa-	yô-o-
2 .	ba-	ba-ba-
3 .	o-	ô-o-
4 .	e-	ê-e-
7 .	se-	sê-se-
10 .	tse-	tsê-di- (tsê-)
14 .	bo-	jô-bo- (-bô-bo).

In the T. set the forms are double as in the case of the adjectival concords, the first element being of demonstrative origin, but differ from the adjectival in that no nasal is retained, except in cls. 15 and 18.

T. has forms for the 1st and 2nd persons, e.g.

1st pers. s.   yô-ke-   pl. ba-re-
2nd pers. s.   yô-o-   pl. ba-lo- (ba-le-).

S.S., on the other hand, uses the concords for cls. 1 and 2, e.g. ŭèna ĕa-bōtsŏa (you lazy one), rōna ba-maruru (we cold ones).

Direct relative concords are also used in the formation of relative clauses of subjectival relationship, e.g. S.S. basali ba-tšèhang (women who laugh), mônna ĕa-buang (a man who is speaking); T. dikgômo tsê-di-fulang (cattle which are grazing). Relative clause construction, involving both direct and indirect relationship, will be discussed later.

(c) THE ENUMERATIVE

In Sotho, enumerative stems fall into two groups according as to whether 'strong' or 'weak' concords are used; the strong concords retain the nasal consonant in cls. 1, 3, 4, 6, and 9, weak concords dropping the nasal. The following stems occur:

(i) with strong concords: S.S. -ng, -ngŏē (one; what kind?), T. -ngwe (one; certain), -ng (what kind?).
(ii) with weak concords: S.S. -fē, T. -fe (which?); S.S. -sēlē, T. -sele, N.S. -šele (different, other); T. -pê (any, some); N.S. -tee (one).

Following are the concords in T., differing only orthographically from S.S., and in having a cl. 11 form:

(Strong)				(Weak)			
Cl. 1	mo-	2	ba-	Cl. 1	o-	2	ba-
3	mo-	4	me-	3	o-	4	e-
5	le-	6	ma-	5	le-	6	a-
7	se-	8	di-	7	se-	8	di-
9	[N]-	10	di-	9	e-	10	di-
11	lo-	14	bo-	11	lo-	14	bo-
15	go-			15	go-		

T. also uses go- to represent cls. 16, 17, and 18.

Examples:
> T. *motho mongwe* (a certain person): in S.S. participial or relative construction is used here, *mōthō a-lē mōng* or *mōthō ĕa-mōng*.
> S.S. *Kē-sēfate sēng?* (What kind of tree is it?)
> S.S. *bathō bafē?* T. *batho bafe?* (which people?)
> S.S. *jŏang bōsēlē*, T. *bojang bosele* (different grass).
> T. *felô gosele* (a different place); S.S. *hōsēlē* (elsewhere).
> T. *Ga-re-rate dinôga dipê* (We do not like any snakes).

(d) THE POSSESSIVE

There are two types of possessives in Sotho, the direct and the descriptive, the former may be based on pronominal or nominal stems, the latter on nominal or adverbial stems. In either case one set of possessive concords is used, with typical vowel *a*. The following is the set for T.:

Cl. 1	*wa-*	Cl. 2	*ba-*
3	*wa-*	4	*ya-*
5	*la(ja-)*	6	*a-*
7	*sa-*	8	*tsa-*
9	*ya-*	10	*tsa-*
11	*lwa-*	14	*jwa- (ba-)*
15	*ga-*	16, 17, 18.	*ga-*

(i) Direct possessives are divided into those with pronominal possessive stems and those formed from other pronouns or nouns.

Pronominal possessive stems are distinctive in Sotho in the singulars of the 1st and 2nd persons and in cl. 1, a distinctive form for communal possession[1] being found in the plurals of the 1st and 2nd persons and in cl. 2. Apart from these instances, the possessive concord is prefixed to the absolute pronouns. Note the following:

		(S.S.)	(N.S.)	(T.)
1st pers.	s.	*-ka*	*-ka*	*-me (-ka)*
	pl.	*-rōna [-esō]*	*-rena [-ešo]*	*-rona [-êtšho]*
2nd pers.	s.	*-haō*[2]	*-gago*[2]	*-gago*[2]
	pl.	*-lōna [enō-]*	*-lena [-eno]*	*-lona [-êno]*
3rd pers.	cl. 1	*-haē*[2]	*-gagwê*[2]	*-gagwê*[2]
	2	*-bòna [-bò]*	*-bóna [-bó]*	*-bônê [-bó]*
	3	*-òòna*	*-wóna*	*-ônê*
	4	*-ĕòna*	*-yóna*	*-yônê*
	10	*-tsòna*	*-tšóna*	*-tšônê*

Examples from S.S.:
> *khomō ĕa-ka* (my ox).
> *linku tsa-rōna* (our sheep).
> *bana besō* (children of our family).
> *linku tsa-haō lē-bòĕa ba-tsòna* (thy sheep and their wool).

Examples of the direct possessive concord with nouns in S.S.:
> *mōsali ŏa-mōrèna* (the chief's wife).
> *lĕihlò la-ngŏana* (the child's eye).
> *tjalē ĕa-'mè* (my mother's shawl).
> *linku tsa-Lērata* (Lerata's sheep); T. *dinku tsa-ga-Lerata*.

---

[1] Indicated below in brackets [ ].
[2] See discussion on word-division in note 2, p. 65.

THE SOTHO GROUP

(ii) The descriptive possessive, indicating some quality, material, or location of the substantive qualified, employs the same concords as the direct, and has either noun or adverbial base: Examples from S.S.:

With nouns:
(indicating material) *thipa ĕa-tšĕpē* (an iron knife).
(indicating contents) *pitsa ĕa-metsi* (a pot of water).
(indicating use) *ntlō ĕa-thapèlò* (house of prayer).
(indicating features) *mōnna ŏa-sēfofu* (a blind man).
(indicating order) *sēfate sa-bōrarō* (the third tree).

With adverbs of place or time:
bathō ba-teng (local people).
khomō tsa-mōreneng (cattle from the chief's place).
mōthō ŏa-pēlē (a person of olden times).

Comparative Table of Qualificative Concords in Tswana

	(Adjective)	(Relative)		(Enumerative)		(Possessive)
		(direct)	(indirect)	(strong)	(weak)	
1st pers. s.	—	yô-ke-	—	—	—	—
pl.	—	ba-re-	—	—	—	—
2nd pers. s.	—	yô-o-	—	—	—	—
pl.	—	ba-lo-	—	—	—	—
3rd pers. cl. 1	yô-mo-	yô-o-	yô-	mo-	o-	wa-
2	ba-ba-	ba-ba-	ba-	ba-	ba-	ba-
3	ô-mo-	ô-o-	ô-	mo-	o-	wa-
4	ê-me-	ê-e-	ê-	me-	e-	ya-
5	lê-le-	lê-le-	lê-	le-	le-	la-
6	a-ma-	a-a-	a-	ma-	a-	a-
7	sê-se-	sê-se-	sê-	se-	se-	sa-
8	tsê-(di)[N]-	tsê-di-	tsê-	di-	di-	tsa-
9	ê-[N]-	ê-e-	ê-	[N]-	e-	ya-
10	tsê-(di)[N]-	tsê-di-	tsê-	di-	di-	tsa-
11	lô-lo-	lô-lo-	lô-	lo-	lo-	lwa-
14	jô-bo-	jô-bo-	jô-	bo-	bo-	jwa-
15	mô-go-	mô-go-	mô-	go-	go-	ga-
16	fa-go-	fa-go-	fa-	—	—	—
17	kwa-go-	kwa-go-	kwa-	go-	go-	ga-
18	mô-go-	mô-go-	mô-	—	—	—

N.B. Variant forms are not given here.

(4) THE VERB

(i) The Varieties of the Verb in Sotho

There are the four varieties found in Bantu:

1. The Regular disyllabic verb-stem, commencing in a consonant and ending in the vowel *-a*, e.g. *rata* (love), *bitsa* (call).

2. The Monosyllabic verb-stem, divided into *i*-stems, e.g. *tla* (come), *fa* (give), and *ē*-stems, e.g. *ja* (eat), *sa* (clear).

3. The Vowel verb-stem, commencing in any one of the seven vowel phonemes, e.g. *ila*, (avoid), T. *eba* (sway), S.S. *èta*, T. *êta* (travel), S.S. *aha*, T. *aga* (build), S.S. *òtla* (strike), S.S. *ōla* (winnow), S.S. *utlŏa*, T. *utlwa* (hear).

THE SOTHO GROUP

4. Derived verb-stems:
   (a) Verbal derivatives, e.g. *ratèla* (applied), *ratisa* (causative).
   (b) Ideophonic derivatives, e.g. S.S. *qōthōla* (pinch) < *qōthō*.
   (c) Denominative verbs, e.g. S.S. *halēfa* (be angry) < *bōhalē* (anger).

VERBAL DERIVATIVES. In Sotho the following main types are used: Passive, Applied, Neuter, Causative, Reciprocal, Reversive, and Diminutive; with secondary or less-used formations for the Intensive, Perfective, Augmentative, Extensive, and Associative. [References are to S.S. unless otherwise stated.]

THE PASSIVE is formed: (a) as a general rule by suffixing *-ŏa* (T. and N.S. *-wa*), e.g. *bòna* (see) > *bònŏa* (be seen); *rata* (love) > *ratŏa* (be loved).

(b) Verbs of which the final syllable of the stem commences with one of the labial consonants *p*, *ph*, *b*, or *f* undergo palatalization, as follows:

-pa > *-pjŏa* (or *-tjŏa*): *bōpa* (mould) > *bōpjŏa* (or *bōtjŏa*).
-pha > *-pshŏa* (or *-chŏa*): *hlonēpha* (honour) > *hlonēpshŏa* (or *hlonēchŏa*).
-ba > *-jŏa* (or *-bjŏa*): *ròba* (break) > *rojŏa* (or *ròbjŏa*).
-fa > *-fshŏa* or *-shŏa*: *bòfa* (bind) > *bòfshŏa* or *bòshŏa*.

(c) When the final syllable begins in *m* or *ny* velarization takes place, as follows:

-ma > *-ngŏa*: *rōma* (send) > *rōngŏa*.
-nya > *-nngŏa*: *sēnya* (spoil) > *sēnngŏa*.

(d) Of monosyllabic verbs, ordinary *ē*-stems suffix *-ēŏa*, *ē*-stems in *-ŏa* suffix *-ōŏa*, and *i*-stems suffix *-uŏa*, e.g. *ja* > *jēŏa*, *nŏa* > *nōŏa*, *kha* > *khuŏa*.

(e) An alternate rarer passive suffix is *-uŏa* which avoids palatalizing or velarizing, e.g. *bōpa* > *bōpuŏa* or *bōpjŏa*.

THE APPLIED form, with the typical Bantu significances of 'on behalf of' and 'towards', is formed basically by the suffix *-èla*, e.g. *rèka* (buy) > *rèkèla* (buy for), *tsamaèa* (walk) > *tsamaèla* (walk towards). But in Sotho certain phonetic changes take place with particular consonants in the final syllable, as follows:

(a) Verbs ending in *-la* preceded by an open vowel, change *-la* to *-lla*, e.g. *ngòla* (write) > *ngòlla*. If *-la* is preceded by a close vowel *-èla* is suffixed, e.g. *lila* (smear) > *lilèla*.

(b) With verbs ending in *-sa*, *-tsa*, *-tsŏa*, *-ntša*, and *-nya* (except monosyllabics and, in the case of *-tsa*, polysyllabics) alveolarization takes place, *-èla* becoming *-etsa*, e.g. *khasa* (crawl) > *khasetsa*; *etsa* (do) > *etsetsa*; *bontša* (show) > *bontšetsa*; *sēnya* (damage) > *sēnyetsa*.

(c) Causative verbs with more than two syllables, ending in *-tsa*, change *-tsa* to *-letsa*, e.g. *fōkōtsa* (diminish) > *fōkōletsa*.

THE NEUTER is typically formed with the suffix *-èha*, e.g. *lahla* (throw away) > *lahlèha* (get lost); *phètha* (finish) > *phèthèha* (be complete).

A restricted number of verbs assume the suffix *-ahala* instead of *-èha*, e.g. *bòna* (see) > *bònahala* (be visible). In T. both *-ala* and *-agala* occur, e.g. *bónala*, *bónagala* (be visible), *utlwala* (be audible).

THE CAUSATIVE has the typical significances of 'cause to do' and 'help to do'.

(a) Regular formation is with the suffix *-isa*, e.g. *utlŏa* (hear) > *utlŏisa* (cause to hear); *lula* (sit) > *lulisa* (set down). Verbs ending in *-ĕa* substitute *-isa*, e.g. *bōlaĕa* (kill) > *bōlaisa* (cause to kill).

(b) Of monosyllabic verbs *i*-stems suffix *-isa*, *ē*-stems suffix *-ēsa*, e.g. *tla* (come) > *tlisa*, *ja* (eat) > *jēsa*.

(c) Verbs ending in *-nya* and disyllabic verbs in *-na* change the last syllable to *-ntša*, e.g. *benya* (glitter) > *bentša*, *bina* (sing) > *bintša*.

(d) The original Bantu causative suffix -ŷa operates in a particular way on certain Sotho consonants, particularly *l* and *n*. With certain verbs, mainly polysyllabic, final -*la*+ŷa > -*tsa*, e.g. *laèla* (order) > *laetsa*. With polysyllabic reciprocal verbs ending in -*na*, final -*na*+ŷa > -*nya*, e.g. *kòpana* (meet) > *kòpanya*.

THE RECIPROCAL is formed by suffixing -*ana*, e.g.
    bònana (see each other).
    ratana (love one another).
    latèlana (follow one another).

THE REVERSIVE is in many respects irregular in Sotho today; many reversive verbs have no extant simple forms; others, reversive in form, have no longer a reversive significance. There are signs that originally Sotho employed two sets of reversive suffixes, in each case having intransitive, transitive, and causative forms, as follows:

	(Intrans.)	(Trans.)	(Caus.)
	-ōha	-ōla	-ōsa
	-ōlōha	-ōlla	-ōlōsa

The suffix -*ōlla* appears in T. as -*olola*, and in N.S. both forms are found. Following are examples:
    bòfa (inspan) > *bofōlla* (outspan).
    tlama (bind) > *tlamōlla* (loosen), *tlamōlōha* (come untied).
    lōkōlōha (get free), *lōkōlla* (set free).
    theōha (descend), *theōla* (bring down), *theōsa* (go down).
    tla (come) > *tlōha* (go away), *tlōsa* (remove).

THE DIMINUTIVE, indicating generally a diminution of the action, but also commonly, especially in T., a repetition and thus being frequentative, is formed basically by a reduplication of the verb-stem; this is the case with disyllabic verbs, e.g.
    bòna-bòna (see somewhat).
    etsa-etsa (do a little).
    bua-bua (chatter).
    T. *raga-raga* (kick repeatedly).

Monosyllabic verbs are repeated with the vowel *ē* (in T. *a*) between them, e.g.
    ja-ē-ja (eat a little), T. *ja-a-ja*.
    nŏa-ē-nŏa (drink a little), T. *nwa-a-nwa*.

Polysyllabic verbs reduplicate the first two syllables:
    balèha > *balè-balèha* (run away a little).
    tsamaĕa > *tsama-tsamaĕa* (stroll); T. has alternative *tsamaya-tsamaya*.

There are varying rules in inflected forms, particularly in T., e.g. the perfect of *ja-a-ja* is *ja-a-jelê* or *jelê-jelê*; nasalization may affect both parts, e.g. *raga-raga* > *go-nthaga-thaga* or *go-nthaga-raga*.

Reduplication of certain derivative suffixes is a cause of intensification. Note the following:

(*a*) Reduplication of the Causative produces the INTENSIVE in -*isisa*, e.g.
    tsēba (know) > *tsēbisisa* (know very well).
    bòna (see) > *bontšisa* (see very clearly).

With some verbs the intensive is indicated merely by -*isa*, e.g.
    bōlaĕa (kill) > *bōlaisa* (kill outright).

(*b*) Reduplication of the Applied produces the PERFECTIVE in -*èlla* (T. -*êlêla*), e.g.
    òma (dry) > *òmèlla* (dry right up).
    qèta (finish) > *qètèlla* (finish completely).

Further intensification is achieved by means of the suffixes -*eletsa* (i.e. -*èlla*+*ẙa*) and -*elletsa* (i.e. -*èllèla*+*ẙa*), such forms often adding specific purpose to the action, e.g. *rōma* (send) > *rōmeletsa* and *rōmelletsa* (send a messenger by an opportunity).

(*c*) Reduplication of the simple Reversive produces the AUGMENTATIVE with suffixes -*ōlōha*, -*ōlla*, and -*ōlōsa*, the same as the fuller reversives, e.g.

phahla (remove) > *phahlōlla* (unpack extensively).
ahlama (open the mouth) > *ahlamōlōha* (come wide open), *ahlamōlla* (make wider).

Sotho employs the suffix -*aka* to indicate what is generally termed the EXTENSIVE form. This is probably not connected with the Central Bantu extensive series *aka-ala*, but rather with the 'continuous' suffix -*ga*, -*nga*, &c. Only a limited number of verbs may take this suffix, e.g.

hapa (take spoil) > *hapaka* (loot wholesale).
òtla (strike) > *òtlaka* (beat indiscriminately).

Connected with the Reciprocal is the ASSOCIATIVE form with suffix -*ahana*, indicating two or more subjects associated in action, e.g.

fina (knot) > *finahana* (shrink together).
mōma (suck) > *mōmahana* (adhere together).

(ii) THE CONJUGATION OF THE VERB IN SOTHO

There are two conjugations of the verb in Sotho, Positive and Negative, and these cover both uni-verbal and multi-verbal predicates. The latter are made up of compound tenses in the formation of which deficient verbs are used. The uni-verbal tenses, each comprising a single word, are dealt with first.

Apart from the infinitive and imperative forms, there are four finite moods used in Sotho: Indicative, Potential, Participial, and Subjunctive. For the purposes of this study Southern Sotho is used, unless otherwise specified.

THE INFINITIVE. This is formed with the prefix *hō*- (T. and N.S. *go*-), and occurs in both positive and negative conjugations:

hō-rèka (to buy); *hō-sē-rekē* (not to buy).

Future infinitives also occur, e.g. *hō-tla-rèka* (to come to buy) and *hō-ĕa-rèka* (to go to, buy), as well as a potential infinitive, e.g. *hō-ka-rèka* (to be able to buy).

Kē-batla hō-tsamaĕa (I wish to go).
hō-bònahala (visibility).
hō-nthatèla (a loving on my behalf).
hō-ithata (self-love).

THE IMPERATIVE. With verbs of more syllables than one, the positive singular is the verb-stem, the plural being formed by suffixing -*ng*:

rèka (buy!)   *rèkang* (buy ye!)
balèha (run away!)   *balèhang* (run ye away!)

With monosyllabic verbs -*a* is suffixed to the stem in the positive singular and -*ang* in the plural:

nŏa (drink) > *nŏaa* and *nŏaang*.
ja (eat) > *jaa* and *jaang*.

The verbs *rē*, *ĕa*, and *ba* assume penultimate *ē*-:

ĕa (go) > *ē-ĕa* and *ē-ĕang*.

The verb *tla* and some monosyllabic deficient verbs have special forms in -*oo*:

tla (come) > *tloo* and *tloong*.

When an objective concord is used with an imperative, final -*a* and -*ang* change to -*è* and -*eng*:
   rèka > *li-rèkè* (buy them!).
   rèkang > *li-rekeng* (buy ye them!).

The negative of the imperative is formed by prefixing *sē-* and changing final -*a* and -*ang* to -*ē* and -*ēng*:
   sē-etsē (don't do!), *sē-etsēng*.
   sē-jē (don't eat!), *sē-jēng*.

A common form is a contraction employing the deficient verb -*ka*:
   sē-ka-rèka (don't buy!), *sē-ka-rèkang*.

Commonly used is a bi-verbal form with the deficient verb -*ke*, e.g. *sē-ke ŭa-bua* (don't talk!).

THE INDICATIVE MOOD. The three implications of the indicative mood, Simple, Progressive, and Exclusive, are found in Sotho, in both positive and negative conjugations. Examples:
   Simple: *kēa-rèka* (I buy), *ha-kē-rekē* (I do not buy).
   Progressive: *kē-sa-rèka* (I still buy), *ha-kē-sa-rèka* (I no longer buy).
   Exclusive: *se-kē-rèka* < *kē-se kē-rèka*[1] (now I buy), *ha-kē-es'o-rekē* (I have not yet bought).

Distinctions of aspect are also found in Sotho, e.g. from bi-verbal forms:
   Definite: *kē-ile ka-rèka* (I bought).
   Continuous: *kē-ne kē-rèka* (I was buying).
   Perfect: *kē-ne kē-lapile* (I was hungry); this last being confined to stative verbs.

The Sotho tense division according to time is not so clear and precise as that of many other Bantu languages. There are present, past, and future tenses, and in S.S. there is a way, by using infix -*tsŏa-* of indicating an immediate past, and by using infix -*ĕa-* of indicating a relatively immediate future; but the forms are not typical of Bantu.

Paradigm of the Indicative Mood Simple Implication (Uni-verbal Tenses)

			(Positive)	(Negative)
PRESENT	(a) Indef.	. . .	*kē-rèka*	
	(b) Def.	. .	*kēa-rèka* / *kē-ĕa-rèka*	*ha-kē-rekē*
PERFECT	(a) Past	. .	*kē-rekile*	*ha-kēa-rèka*
	(b) Pres. Stative	.	*kē-lutsē*	*ha-kēa-lula*
IMMEDIATE PAST		. . .	*kē-tsŏa-rèka*	*ha-kē-ts'o-rèka*
IMMEDIATE FUTURE	(a)	. .	*kē-ĕa-rèka*	*ha-kē-ĕ'o-rèka*
	(b)	. .	*ke-il'o-rèka*	*ha-kēa-ĕa-rèka*
FUTURE	(a)	. . .	*kē-tla-rèka*	*ha-kē-tl'o-rèka*
	(b)	. . .	*kē-tlil'o-rèka*	*ha-kēa-tla-rèka*

THE POTENTIAL MOOD. Only one of the potential tenses in S.S. is uni-verbal; this, the present positive, has the characteristic infix -*ka-*, has subjectival concord of cl. 1 as *a-*, and for first person singular *kē-*+-*ka-* > *nka-*. It might be noted, however, that typical T. uses *o-* for cl. 1 subj. concord.

Examples: *Nka-ngòla Sēsōthō* (I can write Sotho).
   Ba-ka-tsamaĕa ka-labōnè (They may go on Thursday).

The negative is formed with deficient verb -*ka* (neg. form -*kē*) resulting in bi-verbal tenses, of which there are two, viz. *ha-nka-kē ka-rèka* and *nke-ke ka-rèka*, which also have the force

---
[1] This is a bi-verbal form.

of negative futures (I cannot buy, or I shall not buy). Past and future potential tenses are bi-verbal, employing the deficient verbs -*ne* and -*be* (-*tla-be*) respectively. In addition, there is a large range of other compound potential tenses with the deficient verb -*be* in the form -*ka-be*, e.g.

nka-be kē-sa-ka ka-rèka (I would not have bought).

It is noticeable that the potential mood in Sotho often has conditional significance; it mainly signifies ability or liability to act.

THE PARTICIPIAL MOOD. This mood has forms corresponding to tenses of both the indicative and potential moods. It is marked by a change of tone and, in the case of cl. 1, by a change in the subjectival concord, which is *a*-, not *ō*- as in the indicative. In the formation of the negative tenses, infixed -*sa*- takes the place of the indicative prefixed *ha*-. Tense examples:

	(Positive)	(Negative)
Present .	. *a-rèka*	*a-sa-rekē*
Perfect .	. *a-rekile*	*a-sa-rèka*
Future .	. *a-tla-rèka*	*a-sa-tl'o-rèka*

Participial tenses are used after certain conjunctives, e.g. *lēha* (although), *ha* (if, when), *hōbanē* (because); as the equivalent of the English participle in '-ing' after present, past, and future tenses, e.g. *Ō-tla a-matha* (He comes running); after a number of deficient verbs (see Groups I, IV, and V *infra*); and it is the base of relative clause construction. In regard to this last, there are relative forms of the participial, often with suffix -*ng*; e.g. *mōthō èa-rèkang* (a person who buys); *mōthō èa-tla-rèka* or *èa-tlang hō-rèka* (a person who will buy).

Examples of Verb Concords and Full Tenses (S.S.)

	Subjectival concords			Obj. concords	Pres. Indic. Neg. tense	Pres. Potent. Posit. tense
	Pres. Indic.	Past Subj.	Indic. Neg.			
1st pers. s.	*kē-*	*ka-*	*kē-*	*N-*	*ha-kē-rekē*	*nka-rèka*
pl.	*rē-*	*ra-*	*rē-*	*rē-*	*ha-rē-rekē*	*rē-ka-rèka*
2nd pers. s.	*u-*[1]	*ŭa-*	*u-*	*u-*[2]	*ha-u-rekē*	*u-ka-rèka*
pl.	*lē-*[3]	*la-*	*lē-*	*lē-*	*ha-lē-rekē*	*lē-ka-rèka*
3rd pers. cl. 1	*ō-*	*a-*	*a-*	*mō-*	*ha-a-rekē*	*a-ka-rèka*
2	*ba-*	*ba-*	*ba-*	*ba-*	*ha-ba-rekē*	*ba-ka-rèka*
3	*ō-*	*ŏa-*	*ō-*	*ō-*	*ha-ō-rekē*	*ō-ka-rèka*
4	*ē-*	*ēa-*	*ē-*	*ē-*	*ha-ē-rekē*	*ē-ka-rèka*
5	*lē-*	*la-*	*lē-*	*lē-*	*ha-lē-rekē*	*lē-ka-rèka*
6	*a-*	*a-*	*a-*	*a-*	*ha-a-rekē*	*a-ka-rèka*
7	*sē-*	*sa-*	*sē-*	*sē-*	*ha-sē-rekē*	*sē-ka-rèka*
8	*li-*[4]	*tsa-*[5]	*li-*	*li-*	*ha-li-rekē*	*li-ka-rèka*
9	*ē-*	*ēa-*	*ē-*	*ē-*	*ha-ē-rekē*	*ē-ka-rèka*
10	*li-*[4]	*tsa-*[5]	*li-*	*li-*	*ha-li-rekē*	*li-ka-rèka*
[11	*lo-*	*lwa-*	*lo-*	*lo-*	*ga-lo-rêke*	*lo-ka-rêka*]
14	*bō-*	*ba-*[6]	*bō-*	*bō-*	*ha-bō-rekē*	*bō-ka-rèka*
15	*hō-*[7]	*ha-*[7]	*hō-*	*hō-*	*ha-hō-rekē*	*hō-ka-rèka*
16, 17, 18	*hō-*[7]	*ha-*[7]	*hō-*	*hō-*	*ha-hō-rekē*	*hō-ka-rèka*

Note: The Tswana forms are given for cl. 11.

[1] Orthographically so represented in S.S., but only differing in tone from the concord of cl. 1.
[2] *go-* in T. and N.S.
[3] Usually *lo-* in T.
[4] Written *di-* in N.S. and T.
[5] *tša-* in N.S.
[6] Also *jwa-* and *ja-* in T.
[7] *go-* and *ga-* in T. and N.S.

The nasalization or 'strengthening', resultant on the use of the objectival concord of the 1st pers. s. before a verb-stem, and on the use of the reflexive prefix *i-*, has already been fully discussed (see p. 123). Reference may be made to p. 126 for an explanation of the contraction of the objectival concord of cl. 1 *mō-+-b-* to become *mm-*.

THE SUBJUNCTIVE MOOD. In Southern Sotho there are three main positive tenses of the subjunctive mood, the present-future, the perfect, and the past; to the first of these there is an equivalent negative. All three positive tenses are used in sequence construction, the present-future indicating consequential action, the perfect a type of habitual action, the past a past sequence. All three may be used as complementary predicates after certain deficient verbs. In addition the present-future is used to form 'final' clauses and hortative forms. All subjunctives have *a-* as subjectival concord for cl. 1, and past subjunctives employ the formative *-a-*, which coalesces with the subjectival concord, it being noticeable that *li-+-a-* > *tsa-* by alveolarization.

Examples:	(Pres.-fut.)	(Perfect)	(Past)
1st pers. s. . .	kē-rèkè	kē-rekē	ka-rèka
cl. 1 . .	a-rèkè	a-rekē	a-rèka
8 . .	li-rèkè	li-rekē	tsa-rèka

The negative of the present-future tense is formed with infixed *-sē-*, e.g. *kē-sē-rekē*. There are no regular negatives of the other tenses.

(iii) THE CONJUGATION OF DEFICIENT VERBS IN S.S.

There are six groupings of deficient verbs in S.S. which produce compound tenses as follows:

I. Verbs with full participial complement: these are *-se* (exclusive), *-ne* (past), and *-be* (used in subjunctive, future, and potential forms).

Kē-ne kē-rèka (I was buying).
Ba-ne ba-rē-bonē (They had seen us).
Ō-tla-be a-bua (He will be speaking).
Nka-be kē-sa-ēē Lēribè (I would not be going to Leribe).

II. Verbs with past subjunctive complement: these are *-ile* (past), *-ka* (emphatic), and *-tla* (preventive). The first of these forms the past bi-verbal tense of S.S., a common alternative to the uni-verbal tense with the perfect stem; T. does not have this, but typically uses *-nē* of I in its place.

Ō-ile a-'mata (He struck him).
Likhomō li-ile tsa-balèha (The cattle ran away).
Nkile ka-ba-bòna Gauteng (I once saw them in Johannesburg).
Ha-kēa-ka ka-rèka (I did not buy).

III. Verbs with perfect subjunctive complement: these are the habituals *-ěe*, *-be*, *-hle*, *-'ne*, and the occasional *-ke*.

Kē-ěe kē-rekē (I am wont to buy).
Rē-hle rē-jē rē-nt'o-phōmōla (We always eat first and then rest).
Ō-ne-'ne a-fielē (She was wont to sweep).
Ō-ke a-etsē hampē (He sometimes acts badly).

IV. Verbs followed by full sequence formations: there is a group of about a dozen deficient verbs which take a variety of complements (pres. particip., indicative, pres.-future subj., or past subjunctive) according to the mood and tense of the deficient verb itself. Such verbs as *-hla*, *-mpa*, *-'na*, *-bōèla*, *-phēta*, &c., are included. For instance *-hla* takes pres. particip. after pres. indic., e.g. *Kē-hla kē-ē-tla* (I come at once); indic. after perfect, e.g. *Kē-hlile kēa-tsēba* (I know indeed); pres.-fut. subj. after future indic., e.g. *Kē-tla-hle kē-tlè* (I shall come indeed); past subj. after potential, e.g. *Nka-hla ka-tsēba* (I may know indeed).

V. Verbs followed by present participial complement: these, about nine, include *-hlòla, -sala, -tsŏe*, &c.

Ō-hlòla a-ngòla (He is always writing).
Rē-tla-lala rē-mō-hōpōla (We shall think of him during the night).
Kē-setsē kē-tlile (I have already come).

It is common to use a perfect particip. after the defic. verb if that is in the perfect.

VI. Verbs followed by infinitive complement: apart from a number of borderline deficients, there are four which regularly take the infinitive, viz. *-anèla* (act merely), *-atisa* (act often), *-rata* (be on the point of doing), and *tšŏanèla* (do of necessity).

Kē-atisa hō-kula (I am often ill).
U-rata hō-tšŏarŏa (You are courting arrest).

(5) THE COPULATIVE

[The following rules apply to S.S.]

(*a*) To form copulatives from qualificatives[1] and adverbs, with all persons and classes as subject, and from substantives with 1st and 2nd person subjects, the requisite subjectival concords are prefixed to the unchanged word or word-base,[2] in the positive; while in the negative they are preceded by *ha-*:

Mōthō eō ō-mōcha (That person is young).
Kōbò ĕa-haē ē-metsi (His blanket is wet).
Ba-tlung (They are in the house).
Rē-basali (We are women).
Lē-marèna (You are chiefs).
Kē-ĕèna (I am he).
Mōthō eō ha-a-mōcha (That person is not young).
Ha-ba-hae (They are not at home).
Ha-kē-ĕèna (I am not he).

(*b*) To form copulatives from substantives with a subject in the 3rd person, the copulative formative *kē-*[3] is prefixed in the positive and *hasē-* in the negative, no subjectival concord appearing:

Kē-mōthō (It is a person).
Bathō baō kē-marèna (Those people are chiefs).
Kē-ĕèna (It is he).
Linku tseō kē-tsa-ka (Those sheep are mine).
Kē-ōfē (Which one is it?).

(*c*) To form participials of copulatives falling under section (*a*) above, the requisite subjectival concords are prefixed to the auxiliary verb *-lē* preceding the word or word-base in the positive, the auxiliary verb *-sē*[4] taking its place in the negative:

ha bathō ba-lē bahōlō (if the people are big).
lēha mōsali a-lē bōtsŏa (although the woman is lazy).
ha rē-lē tlung (when we are in the house).
lēha kē-sē mōbē (although I am not bad).
ha u-sē ĕèna (if you are not he).

---

[1] Of possessives and enumeratives the formation is from the pronominal form.
[2] Which must itself be considered copulative in function; to form the word-base from adjectives and relatives the initial syllable is elided.
[3] Of higher tone than the subjectival concord of the 1st pers. s.
[4] Not to be confused with *-sē-* in *hasē-* (neg. of *kē-*) in (*b*) above.

(d) To form participials of copulatives from substantives with a subject in the 3rd person, *ē-lē* is preplaced in the positive, and *ē-sē* in the negative:

ha liphòòfòlò tseō ē-lē lipèrè (if those animals are horses).
lēha ē-lē èèna (although it is he).
lēha linku tseō ē-sē tsa-ka (although those sheep are not mine).

(e) In one Sotho cluster, viz. Northern Sotho, are to be found LOCATIVE DEMONSTRATIVE COPULATIVES, otherwise foreign to the group, except for some sporadic examples in certain eastern types of Tswana. Forms occur corresponding to each of the four demonstrative positions, with the significance of 'here is', 'there is', &c. They are typified by the prefixal element *še-* (changed to *se-* in cl. 7 by assimilation). In the 3rd position the alternation of final *-khwi* and *-khwe* is striking, the vowels *e* and *o* in a preceding syllable taking *-e* in the final syllable. The following short table illustrates these forms:

	(1st position)	(2nd position)	(3rd position)		(4th position)
Cl. 1	šo	šoô	šono	šokhwe	šolê
2	šeba	šebaô	šebano	šebakhwi	šebalê
4	še	šeô	šeno	šekhwe	šelê
5	šele	šeleô	šeleno	šelekhwe	šelelê
7	sese	seseô	seseno	sesekhwe	seselê
10	šedi	šediô	šedino	šedikhwi	šedilê
14	šebo	šeboô	šebono	šebokhwe	šebolê

In the 4th position alternative forms are found with final *-la*, e.g. cl. 1 *šola*.

In Sotho, the copulative, apart from its normal use in forming a plain predicate, is used as an agentive adverb, especially after passive verbs, e.g. *U-tla-lōngŏa kē-ntja* (You will be bitten by the dog).

In the conjugation of copulatives the auxiliary verb *-ba* is used for mood and tense distinctions, e.g.

(Indic. future) *Kē-tla-ba mōhōlō* (I shall be big).
(Subjunctive) *hōrē a-be mōtlè* (that she might be pretty).
(Potential) *Nka-ba mōhōlō* (I may become big).

'Have' is expressed by using the conjunctive *lē-* with the copulative. In all tenses where the auxiliary *-ba* is used, *-ba* will appear before *lē-*, e.g. *hō-ba lē-ntja* (to have a dog), *Kē-tla-ba lē-ntja* (I shall have a dog). Where no auxiliary ordinarily appears with the copulative, *lē-* is preceded by the auxiliary verb *-na*, e.g. *Kē-na lē-ngŏana* (I have a child); *lēha kē-ē-na lē- ngŏana* (although I have a child). In the negative *lē-* is dropped, e.g. *Ha-kē-na ngŏana* (I have no child).

(6) THE ADVERB

[Examples are taken from S.S.]

Certain adverbs, particularly temporal adverbs, are really nouns unchanged in form but supplying adverbial function, e.g. *mōtšēarē* (in the daytime), *maōbanē* (yesterday), *bōsiu* (at night), *sēlēmŏ* (in the spring). There are very few primitive temporal adverbial stems, though *nēng?* (when?) might be cited. There are a few primitive adverbs of manner, e.g. *fèèla* (merely), *ruri* (surely).

Apart from the above, adverbs may be formed in Sotho: (i) by prefixing adverbial prefixes to other parts of speech, and (ii) by means of locative formation.

(i) USE OF ADVERBIAL PREFIXES

(a) Manner adverbs with formatives *bō-* and *ha-*:
  bō-: *bōcha* (afresh) < adj. *-cha* (new).
  butlè (carefully) < adj. *-tlè* (good); with permuted vowel.

With palatalization change (*bō-*+*a* > *jŏa-*): *jŏalo, jŏala* (thus); *jŏang?* (how?), and compare the temporal adverb *jŏalè* (now).

ha-: *hahōlō* (much), *hampē* (badly), *hantlè* (well); *hathata* (severely), *hamōlēmò* (gently); *hammòhò* (together).

(b) Instrumental adverbs with formative *ka-*:

ka-matla (with strength), *ka-majŏe* (with stones), *kahōsēlē* (differently), *ka-boomō* (on purpose).

Prefix *ka-* has also a distributive function, e.g. *ka-peli* (two by two), *ka-khŏeli* (each month).

(c) Conjunctive adverbs with formative *lē-* (T. also uses *na-* with absolute pronominal base):

kē-ĕa lē-ŭena (I go with you).
hō-tsamaĕa lē-thaba (to go along a mountain).

(d) Comparison adverbs with formatives *jŏaleka-, kaleka-, kaloka-, kanaka-,* and *kaaka-*.

(e) Agentive adverbs formed with copulative *kē-*:

Kē-shŏēle kē-tlala (I am dead of hunger).

(ii) LOCATIVE FORMATION

In Sotho there are three main methods of locative formation from nouns: (*a*) by suffixing *-ng*, (*b*) by prefixing *hō-*, and (*c*) by using the unchanged noun. Following are the rules:

(1) The suffix *-ng* or *-ēng* is attached to all nouns (except cls. 1a and 2a), certain vowel adjustments taking place:

tsēla (path) > *tsēleng*.
sēfatè (tree) > *sēfateng*.
nku (sheep) > *nkung*.
jŏang (*grass*) > *jŏanng*; T. *bojang* > *bojannyê*.

(2) All nouns of cls. 1a and 2a assume the prefix *hō-* (T. and N.S. *go-*):

ntate (my father) > *hō-ntate*; T. *rrê* > *go-rrê*.
Fekisi (Fekisi) > *hō-Fekisi*.
bo-marabè (puff-adders) > *hō-bo-marabè*.

(3) Personal nouns of all classes (other than 1a and 2a) may form their locatives either by suffix or by prefix:

ngŏana (child) > *ngŏaneng* or *hō-ngŏana*.
sēmumu (mute) > *sēmumung* or *hō-sēmumu*.

(4) Certain nouns are used as locative adverbs without any change of form. They are the following:

(*a*) Place-names (when not being the name of some common object) and cardinal points:
Kē-ĕa Lēsōthō (I go to Basutoland).
Kē-ahile Maseru (I live at Maseru).
Ba-tsŏa bōchabèla (They come from the east).

(*b*) Nouns denoting seasons, duration of time; these are temporal adverbs, already referred to.

(*c*) Certain common nouns, e.g. *mōnyakò* (doorway, at the door), *lĕŏatle* (sea, at sea), *khōtla* (at court).

(5) The possessive form of the prefix *hō-* is used to indicate 'the place belonging to'; this is *ha-* and commonly precedes nouns of cl. 1a:
   ha-Lētsiè (at Letsie's).
   Kē-ĕa ha-malōmè (I go to my uncle's place).
   ha-mōruti (at the Mission Station).

(6) In T. (and N.S.) the locatives are often preceded by one of the prefixes *fa-*, *kwa-*, and *mó-*, which define the position more exactly, e.g.:
   mó-tlung (in, inside the house).
   kwa-nokêng (at the river).
   fa-sedibêng (by the well).

Locatives are formed from pronouns by prefixing *hō-* (T. and N.S. *go-*), e.g. *Tloo hō-'na* (Come to me).

The Bantu locative cls. 16, 17, and 18 have representative adverbs with the prefixes *fa-*, *hō-* (T. *go-*) and *mō-*:

Cl. 16: S.S. *fatšē*, T. *fatshe* (on the ground, below).
   T. *felô* (a place).
Cl. 17: S.S. *hōlimō*, T. *godimo* (above).
   S.S. *hôle*, T. *golê* (far away).
Cl. 18: S.S. *mōraō*, T. *moragó* (after).
   S.S. *'mòhò*, T. *mmógó* (together).

(7) THE IDEOPHONE

In Sotho there are two constructions in which the ideophone may be used: (i) the common construction following some form of the verb S.S. *hō-rē*, N.S. and T. *go-re*, meaning 'to express', 'to manifest', in contradistinction to its meaning of 'to say'; and (ii) as intensifier or cognate descriptive following a verb or qualificative, the former very often being a derivative from the ideophone. Examples:

(i) S.S. *hō-rē kha* (to beat).
      Ō-itse bitō (He suddenly appeared).
   N.S. *Ba-re tuu* (They are quite quiet).
   T. *Pelo ya-gagwê ya-re gáro* (His heart thumped with apprehension).
(ii) S.S. *Kōbò ē-tšŏeu bjŏa* (The clothing is very white).
      Ō-qhiletsa qhíle (He is limping badly).
   T. *Di-nyêlêtse nyêlê* (They have vanished completely).

The verb *-rē*, when used with ideophones, may take a direct object, e.g. *hō-mō-rē pōtlō ka-kubu* (to hit him with a sjambok); the ideophone itself is neither transitive nor intransitive in significance; that is conveyed by the way in which *-rē* is used, e.g. *hō-rē kha* (to beat), but *hō-thŏē kha* (to be beaten); *hō-rē qéche* (to die down), but *hō-ē-rē qéche* (to finish it off).

Of the languages of the Sotho group, T. seems to use ideophones far less than S.S. or N.S., and the group as a whole uses them less than do the Nguni languages. In Sotho ideophones are subject to their own prosodic laws:

(i) They share with interjections a high degree of emotional tone, rising and falling tones, not used in ordinary grammatical speech, being found.
(ii) Stress is normally on the initial[1] (not penultimate) syllable, e.g. *bú*, *bátha*, *chálala*, *pápalala*.
(iii) While generally all syllables of ideophones are short, monosyllabic ideophones and final syllables of polysyllabics may have lengthened vowels, e.g. *hèè*, *líkaa*, *télileee*.

[1] Marked in the examples unless there is some other diacritic on the vowel concerned.

The main general division according to syllables is represented by the following examples:
Monosyllabic:
- S.S. *qi* (of arrival), *bja* (of slapping), *thō* (of reality).
- N.S. *swii* (of pitch darkness), *too* (of ice coldness).
- T. *tshe* (of fitting exactly); *gwaa* (of heavy rainfall).

Disyllabic:
- S.S. *kápe* (of spilling), *shŏdqa* (of going down), *héli* (of glancing).
- N.S. *tsérr* (of sweltering heat).
- T. *thábu* (of plunging into water), *kgóthu* (of sticks snapping).

Trisyllabic:
- S.S. *kútluku* (of pushing forward), *phúsusu* (of falling to the ground).
- N.S. *kápata* (of horse running).
- T. *pótókó* (of horse galloping), *kgólóbu* (of plunging into water).

Quadrisyllabic:
- S.S. *hláhlalala* (of being brim-full), *pélekeqe* (of thudding).
- T. *phárakgatlha* (of falling in a heap).

These various types of ideophones may be further subdivided according to tone; for instance in S.S. there are the following tonal divisions of disyllabic ideophones:

(1) (low, low) *béle* (of falling in clots), *khúru* (of galloping);
(2) (high, low) *kámō* (of breaking), *ótsi* (of slumbering);
(3) (low, high) *fáphi* (of extinguishing quickly), *lákō* (of jumping up).

Verbs are often formed from ideophones by means of suffixes, e.g. in S.S. from *réfō* (of rising up together) > intr. *refōha* (stand up together), tr. *refōla* (raise up together); from *hēlē* (of falling down) > intr. *hēlēha* (fall down), caus. *hēlētsa* (throw down). Nouns may also be formed from ideophones, e.g. *sēmètlèmètlè* (big news) < *mètlè* (of striking).

Ideophones are sometimes formed from verbs, e.g. in S.S. *kéni* (of entering) < *kèna* (enter); *kháthali* (of tiredness) < *khathala* (be tired).

Ideophones themselves are subject to suffixal inflexion for emphasis and intensity, e.g. in S.S. *chóbè* and *chóbèkè* (of entering); *ótsi* and *ótsiki* (of slumber); *phúhla* (of flopping down) and *phúhlalala* (of flopping down violently); *pótlo* (of sadness) and *pótlololo* (of deep sadness). Sometimes there is reduplication of an initial syllable, e.g. *tlèrè* and *tlètlèrè* (of redness).

(8) THE CONJUNCTIVE

Conjunctives are of varied origins in Sotho, verbal, pronominal, and adverbial, very few being primitive. They may be divided into: (i) non-influencing conjunctives, (ii) those followed by the subjunctive mood, and (iii) those followed by the participial mood. The following may be noted from S.S.:

(i) NON-INFLUENCING CONJUNCTIVES, i.e. those which do not govern the mood of the following verb:

'*mē* (and); *ēmpa, kapa* (but); *athē, kanthē* (whereas); *jŏale* (now); *fèèla* (only); e.g. *Rōna rē-ja bōhòbè, ēmpa lōna lē-ja nama* (As for us, we eat bread, but you eat meat).

(ii) CONJUNCTIVES FOLLOWED BY THE SUBJUNCTIVE MOOD:

hōba, hōbanē, hōrē (that, in order that); *hoja, hojanē* (*if*); e.g. *Kē-rata hōrē u-èè* (I want you to go); *hoja u-sē-bē ŭena* (if it had not been thou).

(iii) CONJUNCTIVES FOLLOWED BY THE PARTICIPIAL MOOD:

ha (when, if), *lēha* (although), *hōbanē* (because); e.g. *ha a-qetile hō-bua* (when he had finished speaking); *lēha ē-lē mona, lēha ē-lē manē* (whether it be here or there).

Certain conjunctives of locative origin are followed by the relative construction, basically participial, e.g. *mōhla u-khutlang Maseru* (when thou comest back from Maseru).

THE SOTHO GROUP

(9) THE INTERJECTIVE

(a) RADICAL INTERJECTIONS. Emotion plays a great part in these; among them are included the interjections of assent and negation. In S.S.:

è (yes!); S.S. *chè*, T. *nnyaa*, N.S. *aowa* (no!)
joo (of sorrow).
ichuu (of pain).
khele, eu, aō (of surprise).

(b) VOCATIVES. In S.S., nouns and pronouns may be used as vocative interjectives without any change of form, e.g. *banna!* (O men!), *Masōpha!* (O Masopha!), *ŭèna!* (O thou!), *mōnna tōǒè* (thou man!), *banna ting!* (ye men!).

In T. the vocatives of proper names and kinship terms are the basic forms, cl. 1a nouns being formed therefrom by changing the final vowel to *-ê*; e.g. *Kgama! Mafoko!* (vocatives) > *Kgamê, Mafokwê* (cl. 1a); *mma* (mother!) > *mmê* (my mother). This process is, however, tending to lapse in the case of proper names, but still operates fully with kinship terms.

(c) IMPERATIVE INTERJECTIVES

balèha! (run!), pl. *balèhang!* (run ye!)
tlōha mona! (go away from here!)

A verbal construction follows an imperative in sequence, the present-future subjunctive tense being used, e.g. *Ē-ĕa u-ba-bōlèllè litaba* (Go and tell them the news!)

(10) ENCLITIC AND PROCLITIC FORMATIVES

(i) ENCLITICS

-ng? (what?) S.S. *Ba-bòna'ng?* (What do they see?)
S.S. *-hè*, T. *-gê* or *-hê* (then, indeed).
    -ng (of relative constructions).
T.   *-tlhê* (indicating impatience or annoyance).
T.   *-wêê* (with vocatives).

(ii) PROCLITIC *lē-* is used conjunctively connecting substantives and adverbs, e.g. *ntate lē-'mè* (my father and my mother); it also signifies 'even', 'also', e.g. *Lē-ŭèna u-teng* (Thou too art present). It has already been noticed that the same formative is used adverbially indicating 'together with'.

(11) THE NUMERALS

S.S., N.S., and T. differ considerably in the distribution of the numerals among the parts of speech. In S.S. 1 is an enumerative, 2–5 are adjectives, 6–9 verbs in relative construction, and 10 a noun. In N.S. 1 is enumerative, 2–5 are adjectives, a variant 5 with 6 and 7 are verbs, while 8–10 are nouns. In T. 1 is an enumerative, 2–6 are adjectives, 7–9 verbs, and 10 a noun.

The following comparative table illustrates the forms:

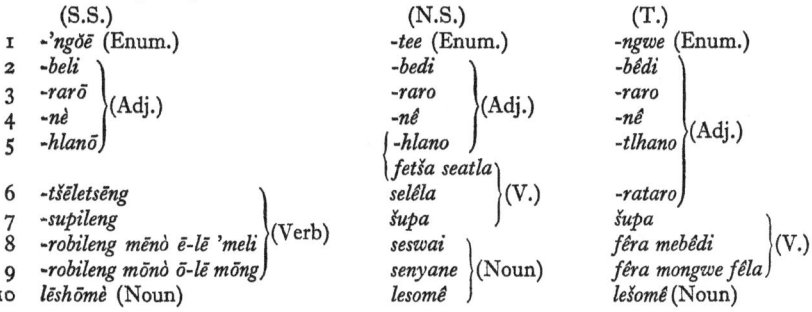

In S.S. 6 = what has crossed over (to the other hand), 7 = what has pointed, 8 = two fingers broken, 9 = one finger broken.

In N.S. the alternate 5 = finish hand, 6 = cross over, 7 = point.

In T. 6 is a reduplication of -*raro* (3), 7 = point, 8 = fold down two (fingers), 9 = fold down one (finger) only.

(12) RELATIVE CONSTRUCTION

The following outline is taken from Tswana. There are two aspects of the relative: the direct relative and the indirect relative.

(i) THE DIRECT RELATIVE is used: (*a*) with relative stems, comprising a large number of nouns and adverbs, e.g. *selêpê sê-se-bogale* (a sharp axe), *motse ô-o-gaufi* (a nearby village); and (*b*) in subjectival relationship with the relative verb, the relative concord being in agreement with the antecedent. The direct relative concords in T. (already given on p. 137) are composites, consisting of two elements, the first of which is identical in form with the first position demonstrative, the second being identical with the subjectival concord. (It is noteworthy that in this the T. forms are in striking contrast to those in S.S., which have been contracted to monosyllables.) It is clear that though the form of the demonstrative is retained, the function is no longer demonstrative: and we have here a real relative composite concord. In the relative clause the verb is basically participial and normally assumes the relative suffix -*ng* (-*go* in N.S.), which is appended to the verb-stem, or to the deficient verb-stem of compound tenses, or in the case of N.S. and S.S. to the auxiliary infixed element, if actively verbal.

Examples:

nna yô-ke-kwalang (I who am writing).
ngwana yô-o-sa-leleng (the child who does not cry).
monna yô-o-nêng a-tšoma ditau (the man who was hunting lions).
S.S. *mōthō ĕa-tla-rèka* or *ĕa-tlang hō-rèka* (a person who will buy).

(ii) THE INDIRECT RELATIVE is used when the relationship of the relative clause to the antecedent is oblique, being either objectival, possessive, or adverbial. In T. the indirect relative concord is identical in form with the demonstrative of the first position, though no longer carrying demonstrative function; it is therefore a monosyllabic form, but it must be observed that the antecedent is also indicated by an objectival concord or possessive or adverbial representative, as the case may be.

Examples:

(*a*) Objectival relationship:

dikgômo tsê-re-di-rêkilêng (cattle which we have bought).
golô mô-ke-go-ratang (a place which I like).
monna yô-batho ba-mo-nyatsang (the man whom the people despise).

(*b*) Subjectival Possessive relationship:

monna yô-dikgômo tsa-gagwê di-timêtseng (the man whose cattle have got lost).
basadi ba-bana ba-bônê ba-bantlê (women whose children are beautiful).

(*c*) Adverbial relationship:

batho ba-ke-buang le-bônê (people with whom I am speaking—conjunctive).
thipa ê-nama e-segwang ka-yônê (the knife with which the meat is cut—instrumental).
motse ô-re-nnang mô-go-ônê (the village in which we live—locative).
ntlo ê-ba-êmeng fa-go-yônê (the house by which they are standing—locative).

REFERENCES

General

K. ENDEMANN: *Versuch einer Grammatik des Sotho*, 1876.
—— *Wörterbuch der Sotho-Sprache*, 1911.
A. N. TUCKER: *Comparative Phonetics of the Suto-Chuana Group of Bantu Languages*, n.d.
G. P. LESTRADE: 'Locative-class Nouns and Formatives in Sotho' (*Bantu Studies*, vol. xii, 1938).
A. N. TUCKER: 'Sotho-Nguni Orthography and Tone-marking' (*Bulletin of School of Oriental and African Studies*, vol. xiii, 1949).

Southern Sotho

A. MABILLE and H. DIETERLEN: *Southern Sotho-English Dictionary*, rev. by R. A. Paroz, 1950.
A. CASALIS: *English-Sesuto Vocabulary*, 5th ed. 1925.
E. JACOTTET: *Practical Method to Learn Sesuto*, with additions by H. E. Jankie, 1936.
—— *A Grammar of the Sesuto Language*, ed. C. M. Doke, 1927.
B. I. C. VAN EEDEN: *Inleiding tot die Studie van Suid-Sotho*, 1941.
R. A. PAROZ: *Elements of Southern Sotho*, 1946.

Tswana

J. T. BROWN: *Secwana Dictionary*, 2nd ed. 1910.
W. CRISP: *Notes towards a Secoana Grammar*, 5th ed. 1924.
A. J. WOOKEY: *Secwana Grammar with Exercises*, 2nd ed. 1921.
D. JONES and S. T. PLAATJE: *A Sechuana Reader*, 1916.
—— *The Tones of Sechuana Nouns* (Memo. VI of International Institute of African Languages and Cultures, 1929).
G. P. LESTRADE: *A Practical Orthography for Tswana*, 1937.
D. T. COLE: *Introduction to Tswana Grammar* (in the press).

Northern Sotho

G. P. LESTRADE: *The Practical Orthography of Transvaal Sotho*, 1930.
T. M. H. ENDEMANN: *Handleiding by die aanleer van Transvaal-Sotho (Sepedi)*, 1939.
D. ZIERVOGEL: *Noordsotho-Leerboek*, 1949.
T. J. KRIEL: *The New Sesotho-English Dictionary*, 1950.

VII

VENDA

Geographical Position of the Venda-speaking Peoples

LINGUISTICALLY the Venda share features both with the Shona group to the north of them and with the Sotho, particularly the Pedi of Northern Sotho, who live to the south of them. The language today, however, definitely constitutes a group of the South-eastern Bantu, quite distinct from these others. The people inhabit the Northern Transvaal, from beyond Pietersburg to the Limpopo River, and are found in scattered communities in Southern Rhodesia beyond the Limpopo. Their neighbours to the east and south-east are the Tsonga, to the south and south-west the Lovedu and Tlokwa Sotho-speakers, to the north the Karanga of the Shona group. Venda has less dialectal division than most South-eastern Bantu groups, but literary work in the language is based on the Phani and Tavhatsindi dialects. Venda owes much to the missionary brothers T. and P. Schwellnus for its literary development. The whole Bible was translated into Venda by Dr. P. Schwellnus, and there is a dictionary of the language, but there is definite need for the publication of a real grammar.

Orthography

Venda orthography is based on the Lepsius system, and certain diacritics are used to distinguish, more particularly, the dental from alveolar consonants. The language is written in an ultra-disjunctive form of word-division. In order to bring this present study into relationship with the other languages of Southern Africa, a system of hyphening the components of the true words is employed in this chapter as in those dealing with Sotho and Tsonga. No alteration is otherwise made to the current orthography.

Phonetics and Phonology

Venda, typical of South-eastern Bantu, employs a seven-vowel system, with three basic vowels a, i, and u, and two varieties each of mid-forward and mid-back vowels, e and ɛ, o and ɔ, respectively; but as these latter are but circumstantial variants of single phonemes, the five vowel symbols, *i, e, a, o, u*, are all that are necessary in a practical orthography.

PHONETIC CHART OF CONSONANTS

	Bilab.	Denti-lab.	Dental	Alveolar	Retro-flex	Labio-alveolar	Pre-palatal	Velar	Glottal
EXPLOSIVE eject.	p'		t̪'	t'				k'	
asp.	ph		t̪h	th				kh	
voic.	b mb		d̪ n̪d̪	d nd				g ŋg	
NASAL contin.	m		n̪	n			ɲ	ŋ	
syll.	m̩		n̪̩	n̩			ɲ̩	ŋ̩	
ROLLED				r					
LATERAL			l̪		ɭ				
FRICATIVE unv.	ɸ	f		s		ṣ	ʃ	x	
voic.	β	v		z		ẓ	ʒ	ɣ(w)	ɦ

	Bilab.	Denti-lab.	Dental	Alveolar	Retro-flex	Labio-alveolar	Pre-palatal	Velar	Glottal
AFFRICATE eject. asp. voic.		ɸf' ɸfh ɓv mɓv		ts' tsh dz ndz		tṣ' tṣh dẓ ndẓ	tʃ' tʃh dʒ ndʒ		
SEMI-VOWEL	(w)						j	w	

In addition to the above, there are the following compound forms in Venda:

		Palatalized (alveolar)	Velarized (labial)
EXPLOSIVE:	eject. asp. voic.	tj' — dj ndj	px' pxh bɣ mbɣ
NASAL:	contin. syll.	— —	mŋ m̱ŋ̱

(a) ORTHOGRAPHIC REPRESENTATION

The preceding chart gives the various sounds used in phonetic script. The current orthography differs from this in the following respects.

The aspiration of affricates is not distinguished.

Φ is written *fh*.
β is written *vh*.
ɸf' and ɸfh are written *pf*.
ɓv and mɓv are written *bv* and *mbv* respectively.
ṇḍ and ṇ are written *nḍ* and *ṇṇ* respectively.
ts' and tsh are both written *ts*.
ḷ is written *l*.
ṣ is written *sw*.
ẓ is written *zw*.
tṣ' and tṣh are both written *tsw*.
dẓ and ndẓ are written *dzw* and *ndzw* respectively.
ɲ is written *ny*, and ɲ̱ is written *nny*.
ʃ is written *sh*.
ʒ is written *zh*.
tʃ' and tʃh are both written *tsh*.
dʒ is written *dzh*.
ndʒ is written *nzh*.
j is written *y*.
ŋg is written *ng*.
ŋ is written *ṅ*, and ŋ̱ is written *ṅṅ*.
ɣ is written *h*.
ɦ is written *h*.
tj' is written *ty*.
dj and ndj are written *dy* and *ndy* respectively.
px' is written *pw*, and pxh is written *phw*.
bɣ and mbɣ are written *bw* and *mbw* respectively.
mŋ is written *mw* (or *ṅw*, variant).
m̱ŋ̱ is written *mmw*.

(b) NOTES ON THE CONSONANTS

1. Aspiration and ejection of explosive and affricative consonants are significant features of Venda phonology, though the current orthography takes note of aspiration only in the case of the explosives. The consonants affected are p, ṱ, t, k, px, ɸf, ts, tṣ, and tʃ. Voiced forms of both explosive and affricative consonants occur in full range, and are also found in association with a homorganic nasal preceding them.

2. It is typical of Venda that dental and alveolar explosives are phonemically distinct, the former being distinguished by a diacritic beneath; thus there are ṱ, ḓ, ṋ in distinction from t, d, n. Dental lateral ḽ is also distinguished from ḷ, which in this case is not alveolar but retroflex. This retroflex lateral is a flapped lateral, for which current orthography uses the plain symbol *l*.

3. Venda has a full range of fricative consonants, both voiced and unvoiced. The bilabial fricatives Φ and β (written *fh* and *vh* respectively) are phonemically distinct; the former occurs in the Sotho group also; the latter is much more widely used in Bantu languages. In the pronunciation of the labio-alveolar fricatives, lip-rounding is prominent and the enunciation is accompanied by a hissing. These 'whistling fricatives', as they are commonly called, occur also in Shona and Tsonga, though the whistling note is rarely heard in Venda. The common orthography uses the digraphs *sw* and *zw* with no inconvenience, for, unlike in Shona, *s* and *z* when accompanied by *w* tend to permute into ṣ and ẓ.

4. There are four sets of affricates in Venda. Unlike Shona the denti-labial, commonly written *pf* and *bv*, are fully homorganic, i.e. the explosive element is also denti-labial, viz. ȹ and ȸ; in Shona the explosive element in the corresponding affricates is bilabial.

5. In the current orthography, while the velar unvoiced fricative is written *x*, the voiced form, occurring always with lip-rounding as ɣ(w), is not distinguished from the glottal fricative ɦ, both being written *h*. The glottal fricative is typically voiced, though it is sometimes heard unvoiced when initial.

6. The velarized consonants, slightly reminiscent of the phenomenon in Shona, are very limited in Venda, being confined to bilabials. The forms px, pxh, bɣ, and mŋ are written *pw, phw, bw,* and *mw* respectively; though the last usually appears in alternative form as ŋw, written *ṅw*. Reference may be made to Shona for a discussion of velarized consonants.

7. Venda is remarkable for its large range of consonants, some of which have variant pronunciations. As noted above, velarization of consonants is but slight; there are no clicks in the language, no implosives, and no lateral fricatives. It tends more towards the Shona type than towards that of Nguni or Sotho; but is unique among these languages in its differentiation of dental from alveolar consonants.

There are three consonantal phenomena in Venda which require special notice, viz. Nasalization (with another process acting in the reverse way), Velarization, and Vocalization.

NASALIZATION occurs in Venda in the formation of nouns in cls. 9 and 10, with adjectives in agreement therewith, and when the objectival concord of the 1st pers. s. precedes the verb-stem; in addition, it reveals itself with certain word stems. In the case of the objectival concord, and in cls. 9 and 10, when the stem is monosyllabic or the consonant voiced, the nasal consonant is retained (in syllabic form), otherwise the nasal itself drops, and only the succeeding consonant (often permuted) remains. The following are the rules observed:

(i) The equivalents or the primitive Bantu explosives, *fh, r, h, vh,* and *l*, become explosive, i.e. *ph, th, kh, mb,* and *nd*; while ḽ becomes *ndy*; e.g. *fhura* (cheat) > *phura* (deception); *lulimi* (tongue) > pl. *ndimi*; ḽa (eat) > *ndya-mbila* (mamba, lit. dassie-eater).

(ii) Fricatives become affricates, the unvoiced being aspirated, and the voiced preplacing the nasal, i.e. *f, s, sw, sh* become *pf(h), ts(h), tsw(h), tsh(h)*[1]; *v, z, zw, zh* become *mbv, ndz, ndzw, n(d)zh*; e.g. *lufayo* (family resemblance) > pl. *pf(h)ayo*; *luvalo* (diaphragm) > pl. *mbvalo*.

(iii) Denasalized sounds regain their nasalization, the unvoiced being aspirated and the voiced preplacing the nasal, i.e. *p, ṭ, t, k,* become *ph, ṭh, th, kh*; *b, ḍ, d, g* become *mb, nḍ, nd, ng*; similarly with the affricates *pf > pf(h)*, &c., and *bv > mbv*, &c. Examples: *lupenyo* (lightning) > pl. *phenyo*; *lutanga* (reed) > pl. *thanga*; *lubonda* (club) > pl. *mbonda*.

(iv) Vowel-stems generally preplace *ny*-, though some, probably of earlier origin, preplace *ṇ*, e.g. *ita* (do) > *nyito* (deed); *luambo* (language) > pl. *nyambo*; while *ṇari* (buffalo), *ṇotshi* (bee) come from the stems -*ari* and -*otshi* (or -*utshi*) respectively.

Associated with nasalization is a reverse process, denasalization, which occurs particularly when nouns of cls. 9 and 10 are used in cl. 20 with the diminutive prefix *ku-*. Here aspiration (if occurring) disappears, as does any nasal consonant. Examples:

ph > p: phaha (wild cat) > *kupaha* (small wild cat).
pf(h) > pf: pf(h)ene (baboon) > *kupfene* (small baboon).
mb > b: mbudzi (goat) > *kubudzi* (small goat).
nḍ > ḍ: nḍou (elephant) > *kuḍou* (small elephant).
mbg > bg: mmbga (dog) > *kubga* (small dog).

VELARIZATION. For this, reference may be made to the relevant section for Shona. In Venda, velarization occurs particularly in passive formation with stems having bilabial consonants in the final syllable. The changes are as follows:

fh > xw; vh > hw (phon. **ɣw**); *m > mw* (phon. **mŋ**) or *ṅw* (phon. **ŋw**); *ph > phw* (phon. **pxh**); *p > pw* (phon. **px'**); *b > bw* (phon. **bɣ**); *mb > mbw* (phon. **mbɣ**).

Examples: *vhofha* (tie) > pass. *vhoxwa*; *luma* (bite) > pass. *luṅwa* or *lumwa* (phon. **lumŋa**). Glottal *h* is similarly affected, becoming *hw* (phon. **ɣw**).

VOCALIZATION. This process of 'voicing', occurring in the formation of nouns of cl. 5, is more regularly carried out in Shona, to which reference may be made. In Venda the formations are very irregular, and only a certain proportion of the mutations are 'voicings', others being a substitution of fricative or affricative sounds for the stem initial. Such as the following are found: *fh > f* or *b*; *r > sh, d,* or *dz*; *h > f, v* or *s*; *vh > v* or *b*; *l > d* or *dz*; *p > b*; *t > d*; *ṭ > ḍ*; *k > g*, &c. As with Shona, the most regular changes occur with the explosives, *p, ṭ, t,* and *k* becoming voiced; with fricatives and affricates the process is irregular.

Examples: *bako* (cave), pl. *mapako*; *dope* (mud), pl. *matope*; *ḍaka* (bush), pl. *maṭaka*; *gumbu* (big calabash), pl. *makumbu*.

In each case the unaffected stem consonant is shown in the plural, the voiced consonant of the singular indicating the action of the suppressed prefix *ḷi-*.

ELISION AND COALESCENCE OF VOWELS. As Venda employs no initial vowel in the noun-prefixes, elision of vowels is not found, and only traces of coalescence are to be discovered in the deficient or auxiliary elements with the verb, where the coalescence of a final -*a* with the infinitive prefix *u*- results in *o*, e.g. *edza+u-* > -*dzo-*; *kona+u-* > -*kono-*; *bva+u-* > -*bvou-*; *ita+u-* > -*to-*.

STRESS AND LENGTH. It is generally agreed that the penultimate syllable of Venda words is of longer duration than the others, and this is especially true of the final word in a sentence. There is, however, difference of opinion upon the position of stress in the words; Meinhof and Westphal believe the stress to be generally upon the root syllable (which is often penultimate), though it seems to fall on the prefix of monosyllabic stems, showing a tendency towards penultimate position as a feature.

[1] The *h* in these affricates is unfortunately not indicated in the current orthography.

TONE. There are two main tones in Venda, one relatively higher than the other. v. Warmelo records[1] three tones, high, low, and falling from high to low. He states regarding the last: 'Though there is every reason to believe that the falling high-low tone is one of secondary origin, I do not find that one could dispense with distinguishing it from high or low.' This difficult subject cannot be discussed here, though Westphal goes into it in considerable detail in his manuscript, and uses a system of tone-marking throughout.

As in most Bantu languages, tone may be the sole differentiator in Venda between words semantically distinct. A few examples are here given:

vhònea (be visible): *vhonea* (illuminate).
tshèla (arrive late): *tshelà* (forage for fruit).
phangà (travel under difficulties): *phanga* (desert); *phàngà* (knives).
fulà (pick fruit; remove pot from fire; graze): *fùla* (twitch; work iron).

GRAMMATICAL OUTLINE

(1) THE NOUN

Prefix Table

Cl.	(Singular)		(Plural)
1	mu-	2	vha-
1a	—	2a	vho-
3	mu-	4	mi-
5	[ḽi]-	6	ma-
7	tshi-	8	zwi-
9	[N]-	10	dzi[N]- (and 6 rare)
11	lu-		(10, and rarely 6 and 14)
14	vhu-		(rare 6)
15	u-		
20	ku-		(8)
21	ḓi-		(6 superimposed)

CLASSES 1 AND 2 (personal):
muthu (person), pl. *vhathu*.
munna (man, male person), *vhanna*.
musidzana (girl), *vhasidzana*.

One noun (< B. *mu-ana*) undergoes velarization of the prefix in the singular, viz. *ṅwana* (child), pl. *vhana*.

Personal nouns derived from verbs:
mubiki (cook) < *bika*, *vhabiki*.
mutshimbili (traveller) < *tshimbila*, *vhatshimbili*.

CLASSES 1a AND 2a (proper names, relationship terms, animal personifications, &c.): No prefix in the singular, and plural prefix *vho-*.

Proper names:
Tshivhasa, Makhado, Marole.

Relationship terms:
khotsi (father), *vhokhotsi*.
mme (mother), *vhomme*.
makhulu (grandparent), *vhomakhulu*.

The possessive relation has to be added as a suffix in Venda, e.g. *khotsi-anga* (my father), *khotsi-ashu* (our father), &c.

[1] *Tshivenḓa-English Dictionary*, p. 13.

Animal terms are sometimes personified in this class, as *ndau* (lion), *vhondau*; which, however, is commonly treated in cl. 9. The interrogative *nnyi* (who?) is also a noun of cl. 1a.

The plurals of these nouns, while they may indicate ordinary plurality, also convey sometimes a collectivity, e.g. *vhomme* (mother and those with her), sometimes an honorific significance, e.g. *Vhotshivhasa*.

Table of Concords for classes 1 (1a) and 2 (2a)

	(Adj.)	(Rel.)	(Enum.)	(Poss.)	(Subj.)	(Obj.)
1 and 1a.	*mu-*	*a-*	*mu-, u-*	*wa-*	*u-*	*mu-*
2 and 2a.	*vha-*	*vha-*	*vha-*	*vha-*	*vha-*	*vha-*

CLASSES 3 AND 4 (miscellaneous, trees, rivers, parts of the body, natural phenomena):

muri (tree), *miri*.
muvhuyu (baobab), *mivhuyu*.
mulayo (law), *milayo*.
muḍi (village), *miḍi*.
mulomo (mouth), *milomo*.
munwe (finger), *minwe*.
mulambo (river), *milambo*.
mulilo (fire), *mililo*.

Alternative velarized prefixes are generally used in cl. 3 with vowel-stems:

mwedzi or *ṅwedzi* (moon).
mwaha or *ṅwaha* (year).

The plurals of such forms are superimposed, e.g. *miṅwedzi*, *miṅwaha*.

Table of Concords for classes 3 and 4

	(Adj.)	(Rel.)	(Enum.)	(Poss.)	(Subj.)	(Obj.)
3	*mu-*	*u-*	*u-*	*wa-*	*u-*	*u-*
4	*mi-*	*i-*	*i-*	*ya-*	*i-*	*i-*

CLASSES 5 AND 6 (miscellaneous, augmentative, sometimes pejorative; suggestion of things in pairs, certain parts of the body and fruits; cl. 6 pluralia tantum). In cl. 5 of Venda, changes due to 'vocalization' take place, but they are not so regular as in Shona, and seem to have become very confused with certain other processes. The position is roughly as follows:

(a) With monosyllabic stems *ḽi-* is prefixed in the singular:

-*ṋo* > *ḽiṋo* (tooth), *maṋo*.
-*ṱo* > *ḽiṱo* (eye), *maṱo*.
-*la* > *ḽila* (intestine), *mala*.

Prefix *ḽi-* is even found with a disyllabic stem, e.g. *ḽivhadzi* (scar), *mavhadzi*.

(b) With vowel-stems, various voiced consonants, e.g. *g*, *dz*, *zh* are prefixed in the singular, and *ma-* superimposed in the plural, e.g. -*anda* > *dzanda* (bundle of withies), *madzanda*.

(c) Nouns whose stems commence in unvoiced explosive consonants (*p*, *ṱ*, *t*, or *k*) have the initial consonant voiced in the singular (*b*, *ḍ*, *d*, *g*):

-*panga* > *banga* (knife), *mapanga*.
-*tope* > *dope* (mud), *matope*.
-*kumba* > *gumba* (egg), *makumba*.

Stems with voiced initials are generally unchanged, e.g. *gona* (knee), *magona* < stem -*gona*.

(d) There are frequent examples of *r* > *sh* (e.g. *shamba* (wild orange), *maramba*), and *vh* > *v* (e.g. *vudzi* (hair), *mavhudzi*), while odd cases of *fh* > *f*, and *h* > *f* (e.g. *fumi* (ten), *mahumi*) occur, as well as other spasmodic irregularities.

(e) Augmentatives and tribal names are sometimes formed by the use of the prefix *ḽi-*, when the stem initials are already voiced, e.g. *l̗iGula* (Indian), *maGula*; *l̗in̩oni*[1] (large bird), *man̩oni*.

CLASS 6, in addition to acting as the normal plural of cl. 5, forms the plural to a few words of cls. 9, 14, and 21, e.g.

Cl. 9: *khosi* (chief), *mahosi*.
14: *vhuluvha* (flower), *maluvha*.
21: *d̗ithu* (huge thing), *mad̗ithu*.

As pluralia tantum, cl. 6 in Venda has typical Bantu usage, with such examples as *mad̗i* (water), *mafhi* (milk), *mapfura* (oil).

Table of Concords for classes 5 and 6

	(Adj.)	(Rel.)	(Enum.)	(Poss.)	(Subj.)	(Obj.)
5 . . .	*l̗i-*	*l̗i-*	*l̗i-*	*l̗a-*	*l̗i-*	*l̗i-*
6 . . .	*ma-*	*a-*	*a-*	*a-*	*a-*	*a-*

CLASSES 7 AND 8 (miscellaneous, material, customs, languages and diminutive, sometimes derogatory). Class 8 is also used as plural to cl. 20.

tshithu (thing), *zwithu*.
tshienda (shoe), *zwienda*.
tshiVend̗a (Venda language, customs, &c.).
tshid̗i (small village), *zwid̗i* (cf. *mud̗i*, village).

Impersonal nouns derived from verbs:

tshigayo (grindstone) < *gaya* (grind).
tshipengo (madness) < *penga* (be mad).

Table of Concords for classes 7 and 8

	(Adj.)	(Rel.)	(Enum.)	(Poss.)	(Subj.)	(Obj.)
7 . . .	*tshi-*	*tshi-*	*tshi-*	*tsha-*	*tshi-*	*tshi-*
8 . . .	*zwi-*	*zwi-*	*zwi-*	*zwa-*	*zwi-*	*zwi-*

CLASSES 9 AND 10 (miscellaneous, animals). The prefix in each of these classes is indicated by nasal influence, the additional prefix *dzi-* of cl. 10 being generally omitted, and only indicated in the concord. For rules of nasal influence see 'Nasalization'; briefly stated, the homorganic nasal appears with voiced explosives; unvoiced explosives appear aspirated without a preceding nasal; monosyllabic stems assume a syllabic nasal.

nngu (sheep), pl. *dzinngu* or *nngu*.
nnd̗u (house), pl. *dzinnd̗u* or *nnd̗u*.
khuhu (fowl).   *mbudzi* (goat).
nd̗evhe (ear).   *thavha* (mountain).
mbvula (rain).   *mvbuvhu* (hippopotamus).
ṅanga (witch-doctor).

The prefix of cl. 6 is used to form the plural of certain words in cl. 9, e.g.

khosi (chief), pl. *mahosi*.
tshimu (garden), pl. *masimu*.

With some words the cl. 6 prefix indicates a quantitative plural, e.g.

tshika (dirt), *mashika* (quantity of dirt).
n̩owa (snake), *dzin̩owa* (snakes), *man̩owa* (snakes, as a class of creatures).

---

[1] The word *tshin̩oni* (bird) in cl. 7, is probably a diminutive formation from obsolete original *n̩oni*, in which case the use of *l̗i-* would really be pre-prefixal here.

Generally the plural is indicated merely by the concord, e.g. *Mbudzi yanga yolala* (My goat is asleep); *Mbudzi dzanga dzolala* (My goats are asleep).

Table of Concords for classes 9 and 10

	(Adj.)	(Rel.)	(Enum.)	(Poss.)	(Subj.)	(Obj.)
9.	(N)-	i-	i-	ya-	i-	i-
10.	(N)-	dzi-	dzi-	dza-	dzi-	dzi-

CLASS 11 (miscellaneous, long objects, abstract formations from verbs, languages). Most nouns in this class have plurals in cl. 10 by nasalization, e.g.

lufhanga (knife), *(dzi)phanga*.
luvhabvu (rib), *mbabvu*.
lufo (ladle), *mmpfo*.
lufu (death), *mmpfu*.
luimbo (song), *nyimbo*.
luhuni (piece of firewood), *khuni*.
lulimi (tongue), *ndimi*.

Certain nouns in this class have plurals in cl. 14, though these plurals are often collective, e.g.

lunyunyu (mosquito), *vhunyunyu*.
lukumbe (climbing plant), *vhukumbe*.

Some abstracts derived from verbs become concrete, with plural formation in cl. 6, e.g.

lupfumo (wealth), *mapfumo* (riches).

Generally, abstracts from verbs have no plural equivalent, e.g.

lutendo (faith) < *tenda*.

Table of Concords for class 11

	(Adj.)	(Rel.)	(Enum.)	(Poss.)	(Subj.)	(Obj.)
11.	lu-	lu-	lu-	lwa-	lu-	lu-

CLASS 14 (mainly abstract, and collective; a few concrete names are included and these take plural in cl. 6):

(a) Concrete nouns:
vhura (bow), *mavhura*.
vhunamelo (ladder).
vhurala (platform).

It is evident that cl. 14 originally contained many concrete nouns, *vide* Lamba, and that the locative, collective, and abstract formations were of later development; the plural is sometimes by super-addition.

(b) Nouns indicating place:
vhudzulo (dwelling-place), pl. *madzulo*.
vhuhadzi (home of woman's husband), *vhuhwe* (wife's home).
vhukovhela (west), *vhulelo* (eating place).

Certain of these are deverbative nouns.

(c) Collective nouns:
vhulungu (bead, beads), pl. *malungu*.
vhuluvhi (brain).
halwa (beer), pl. *mahalwa*.
hatsi (grass), pl. *mahatsi*.

Where the plural is used with these it is quantitative, e.g. *mahatsi*, much grass, heaps of grass.

(*d*) Abstract nouns (no plural):
   vhuṭali (wisdom), *vhutsila* (skill), *vhutshilo* (life).
   vhuhosi (chieftainship) < *khosi* (chief).
   vhukonani (friendship) < *khonani* (friend).
   vhuvhi (evil) < adj. *-vhi* (evil).
   vhuhulu (size) < adj. *-hulu* (large).

(*e*) Class 14 is sometimes used as a plural (often collective) to certain nouns in cl. 11, q.v.

In this class certain original Bantu stems commencing in *a-* cause *vhu-*+*a-* to become *ha-*, e.g.
   halwa (beer) < *vhu-*+*-alwa*.
   hatsi (grass) < *vhu-*+*-atsi*.
   hana (childhood) < *vhu-*+*-ana*.

Compare this process with velarization in Shona and palatalization in Nguni. Other vowel-stems merely juxtapose, e.g. *vhuada* (impurity), *vhuambi* (oratory).

Table of Concords for class 14

	(Adj.)	(Rel.)	(Enum.)	(Poss.)	(Subj.)	(Obj.)
14. . .	vhu-	vhu-	vhu-	ha-	vhu-[1]	vhu-[2]

CLASS 15 (verb infinitive, used as verbal noun):[3]
   u-fa (to die, dying, death).
   u-imba (singing).
   u-ḷa (to eat, eating).
   u-tshimbila (to walk, journeying).

Negative infinitives are also used as nouns:
   u-saḓa (non-arrival).

Example of use:
   u-fa hawe (his death).

Table of Concords for class 15

	(Adj.)	(Rel.)	(Enum.)	(Poss.)	(Subj.)	(Obj.)
15. . .	hu-	hu-	hu-	ha-	hu-	hu-

CLASSES 16, 17, 18 (prefixes *fha-*, *hu-*, and *mu-*). These hardly function as noun classes any longer in Venda. They are mainly used as locative adverbs. Any locative formation, however, may still be used substantively as subject of a sentence, in which case the concords used throughout are those for cl. 17, which in Venda are the same as those for cl. 15; e.g.
   Thavhani hu-na vhathu (On the mountain are people).
This might equally be rendered: *Hu-na vhathu thavhani* (There are people on the mountain); and from this arises the 'indefinite locative' construction with concord *hu-*.

Actual Venda words commencing in *fha-*, *hu-*, and *mu-* are typically adverbs, such as *fhasi* (below), *hugede* (somewhere), *huṅwe* (elsewhere), *murahu* (behind); there are very few of them, and though such a word as *hukhethwa* (holy place) and such a concord as *hayani hanga* (at my home) have been recorded, these classes are almost confined in representation to the 'pronominal' forms such as the demonstratives, e.g. *fhala* (there), *fhano* (here), *hula* (there), &c.

CLASS 20. Diminutive in Venda, though generally augmentative where it occurs in other Bantu languages. By using the prefixes, *ku-* in singular and *zwi-* (of cl. 8) in the plural,

---
[1] Present tense form is *vhu-*, past tense *ho-*, dependent *ha-*.
[2] An alternative form *hu-* occurs.
[3] Current orthography writes the infinitive prefix as a separate word from the verb-stem.

VENDA

diminutives are formed from other nouns. Note that cls. 7 (*tshi-*) and 8 also have a diminutive function.

kuṋoni (small bird), pl. *zwiṋoni* (< *tshiṋoni*).
kwana (little child), pl. *zwana* (< *ṅwana*).
kuḓi (small village), pl. *zwiḓi* (< *muḓi*).

Note: The suffix *-ana* (*-ane* or *-nyana*) is sometimes used in association with the diminutive prefix of cls. 7 and 20 (pl. 8), e.g.

pfeṋe (baboon) > *tshipfeṋana* (little baboon).
khali (pot) > *khalana* (small pot), and *kukalana* (very small pot).

Sometimes no special diminutive prefix is used, e.g. *mvuvhelo* (water jar) > *mvuvhelwana* (small water jar); *tshidongo* or *ndongwana* (small earthenware dish); *thavha* (mountain) > *thavhana* (hill).

Table of Concords for class 20

	(Adj.)	(Rel.)	(Enum.)	(Poss.)	(Subj.)	(Obj.)
20.	ku-	ku-	ku-	kwa-	ku-	ku-

CLASS 21. Augmentative, expressive of very big objects. The prefix of this class is *ḓi-*, but for concord purposes it has merged with cl. 5; for the plural, cl. 6 prefix is superimposed.

ḓithu (monstrosity), pl. *maḓithu* (< *tshithu*).
ḓikolomo (huge beast), pl. *maḓikolomo* (< *kholomo*).

Example of use:

Ḓikolomo ḽanga iḽo ḽiafula (That huge ox of mine is grazing).

(2) THE PRONOUN

(*a*) TABLE OF ABSOLUTE PRONOUNS

1st pers. s.   *nṋe*   pl. *riṋe*
2nd pers. s.   *iwe*   pl. *inwi*
3rd pers. cl. 1. *ene*; 2. *vhone*; 3. *wone*; 4. *yone*; 5. *ḽone*; 6. *one*; 7. *tshone*; 8. *zwone*; 9. *yone*; 10. *dzone*; 11. *lwone*; 14. *hone*; 15. *hone*; [17. *hone*]; 20. *kwone*.

The typical form of the absolute pronoun in Venda is found from cl. 2 onwards, viz. the pronominal concord (in *-o*) and ultimate *-ne*. It is remarkable that the 1st pers. forms employ ultimate *-ṋe* (dental *n*), while the 2nd pers. forms are quite distinct, following the pattern of Shona with penultimate *i-*. Class 1, as everywhere, is distinctive in form. Note that the forms for the 1st pers. s. and pl. and the 2nd pers. pl. have a high tone on the final syllable; all the other forms have the high tone on the first syllable.

In addition to their mere pronominal use, these pronouns in Venda are generally emphatic:

Nṋe a-thi-zwi-vhoni, fhedzi ene u-a-zwi-vhona (*I* do not see it, but *he* does).
Inwi ni-bva ngafhi? (Where do *you* come from?).
zwithu zwone (the very things).

(*b*) TABLE OF DEMONSTRATIVE PRONOUNS

Venda has four positional sets of demonstrative pronouns, comprising two sets of contrast pairs, as in Shona; e.g. 1st position 'this, these'; 2nd position 'that, those'; 3rd position 'this here, these here', pointed at or indicated; 4th position 'that yonder, those yonder', pointed at or indicated.

(Class)	(1st position)	(2nd position)	(3rd position)	(4th position)
1	*uyu*	*uyo*	*uno*	*uḽa*
2	*avha*	*avho*	*vhano*	*vhaḽa*
3[1]	*uyu*	*uyo*	*uno*	*uḽa*
4	*iyi*	*iyo*	*ino*	*iḽa*
5	*iḽi*	*iḽo*	*ḽino*	*ḽiḽa*
6	*aya*	*ayo*	*ano*	*aḽa*
7	*itshi*	*itsho*	*tshino*	*tshiḽa*
8	*izwi*	*izwo*	*zwino*	*zwiḽa*
9	*iyi*	*iyo*	*ino*	*iḽa*
10	*idzi*	*idzo*	*dzino*	*dziḽa*
11	*ulu*	*ulwo*	*luno*	*luḽa*
14	*uvhu*	*uvho*	*vhuno*	*vhuḽa*
15	*uhu*	*uho*	*huno*	*huḽa*
16	*afha*	*afho*	*fhano*	*fhaḽa*
17[2]	*uhu*	*uho*	*huno*	*huḽa*
18	—	—	*muno*[3]	—
20	*uku*	*uko*	*kuno*	*kuḽa*

N.B. Cl. 21 as for cl. 5. The tones of these primary demonstratives are uniformly low.

In Venda, as in Shona, each positional type of demonstrative has four degrees of emphasis. Though the interpretation and use of these emphatic forms vary somewhat from speaker to speaker, roughly they signify as follows:

1st degree: 'this, that'; 2nd degree: 'this one, that one'; 3rd degree: 'this very one, that very one'; 4th degree: 'this self-same one, that self-same one'.

Examples of 1st position

(Class)	(1st degree)	(2nd degree)	(3rd degree)	(4th degree)
1	*uyu*	*hoyu*	*onoyu*	*onohoyu*
2	*avha*	*havha*	*vhenevha*	*vhenehavha*
5	*iḽi*	*heḽi*	*ḽeneḽi*	*ḽeneheḽi*
10	*idzi*	*hedzi*	*dzenedzi*	*dzenehedzi*

Examples of 4th position

1	*uḽa*	*houḽaa*	*onouḽa*	*onohouḽaa*
2	*vhaḽa*	*havhaḽaa*	*vhenevhaḽa*	*vhenehavhaḽaa*
5	*ḽiḽa*	*heḽiḽaa*	*ḽeneḽiḽa*	*ḽeneheḽiḽaa*
10	*dziḽa*	*hedziḽaa*	*dzenedziḽa*	*dzenehedziḽaa*

The basic forms of the four positions are typical Bantu, 1st position having like vowels on either side of the prefix consonant (with semi-vowels in nasal prefix cases), 2nd position having typical *-o* suffixed to 1st position form, 3rd and 4th positions formed with class prefix before *-no* and *-la* stems respectively. These closely resemble Shona and Central Bantu.

Rules for the formation of the emphatic forms are as follows:

The 2nd degree is formed from the first by prefixing *ha-*, which coalesces with the initial vowel in the 1st and 2nd positions and with an implied initial in the 3rd and 4th positions. In the case of the 4th position the final vowel is doubled.

The 3rd degree is formed from the first by prefixing *-ene-* (when penult. vowel is *a* or *i*) and *-ono-* (when penult. vowel is *o*) preceded by the prefix consonant, elision of initial vowels of the 1st degree taking place with 1st and 2nd position forms.

[1] As for cl. 1, except in the emphatic forms.
[2] As for cl. 15 throughout.
[3] Mbedzi dialect.

The 4th degree is formed from the second by the same prefixal forms as occur in the 3rd degree.

The forms listed for the locative classes 16, 17, and 18 are adverbs of place, no longer being used as pronouns in Venda. The meanings are 'here, there, right here, yonder', respectively for the four positions. The only example of this in cl. 18 is with the word *muno* found in the Mbedzi dialect as synonymous with *fhano*.

In Venda, as in Shona and Nguni, the demonstrative may be used after the noun, before the noun (when a single word-group results), or alone, instead of the noun. Examples:

Munna uyu ndi-muLemba (This man is a Lemba).
Avha-vhathu ndi-vhasadzi (These people are women).
Izwi ndi-zwihuru fhedzi izwo ndi-zwiṭuku (These are big ones but those are small ones).

(c) QUANTITATIVE PRONOUNS

Only one of these, rt. *-ṭhe*, is found in Venda, but it has two significations: (a) when used in apposition to the noun, it signifies 'all', 'the whole'; (b) when used with a participial copulative concord, it signifies 'being alone, being by oneself'.

Table of forms

			(a)	(b)
1st pers.	s.		—	ndindoṭhe
	pl.		roṭhe	riroṭhe
2nd pers.	s.		—	uwoṭhe
	pl.		noṭhe	ninoṭhe
3rd pers.	cl. 1		woṭhe	eeṭhe
	2		vhoṭhe	vhevhoṭhe
	3		woṭhe	uwoṭhe
	4		yoṭhe	iyoṭhe
	5		ḽoṭhe	ḽiḽoṭhe
	6		oṭhe	eoṭhe
	7		tshoṭhe	tshitshoṭhe
	8		zwoṭhe	zwizwoṭhe
	9		yoṭhe	iyoṭhe
	10		dzoṭhe	dzidzoṭhe
	11		lwoṭhe	lulwoṭhe
	14		hoṭhe	huhoṭhe
	15		hoṭhe	huhoṭhe
	20		kwoṭhe	kukwoṭhe

Examples:
Vhathu vhoṭhe vho-vha vhe-hone (All the people were present).
Ndo-vhona vhanna vhe-vhoṭhe (I saw the men by themselves).
Kholomo dzashu dzo-fa dzoṭhe (All our cattle are dead).
duvha ḽoṭhe (the whole day).
zwithu zwi-zwoṭhe (the things alone).

(d) QUALIFICATIVE PRONOUNS

In Venda there is no formal change in qualificatives when they are used pronominally.

(e) RELATIVE PRONOUNS

Venda is unique in possessing this type of pronoun, used in introducing relative clauses; it is not found in the other groups of Southern Bantu languages.

Table of Relative Pronouns

	1st pers. s.	*ndine*	pl.	*rine*
	2nd pers. s.	*une*	pl.	*nine*
	3rd pers. cl. 1	*ane*	cl. 2	*vhane*
	3	*une*	4	*ine*
	5	*line*	6	*ane*
	7	*tshine*	8	*zwine*
	9	*ine*	10	*dzine*
	11	*lune*	14	*hune*
	15	*hune*	20	*kune*

The formation of these relative pronouns is built up on the relative concord and ultimate *-ne* (as with the absolute pronouns of the 3rd person). The final syllable throughout bears a high tone.

Note (i): Common alternatives in the 1st and 2nd persons are sing. *ane*, pl. *vhane* of the 3rd person.

Note (ii): In past tense construction the relative assumes a contracted form as follows:
1st pers. s. *nde*, pl. *re*; 2nd pers. s. *we*, pl. *ne*.
3rd pers. cl. 1. *we*; 2. *vhe*; 3. *we*; 4. *ye*; 5. *le*; 6. *e*; 7. *tshe*; 8. *zwe*; 9. *ye*; 10. *dze*; 11. *lwe*; 14. *he*; 15. *he*; 20. *kwe*.

Examples:
Vhathu vhane vha-tshimbila fhala . . . (People who walk yonder . . .).
Vhathu vhe nda-vha-vhona . . . (People whom I saw . . .).

[Relative Construction as a whole is treated later.]

(3) THE QUALIFICATIVE

(*a*) THE ADJECTIVE

In form the adjective is the same as the noun in Venda, consisting of stem and prefix, e.g. *mu-thu mu-lapfu* (tall person), *vha-thu vha-lapfu* (tall people). The adjectival stem, however, differs from that of the noun in that it may take concord with each of the noun classes and the concord in cl. 15 is *hu-*, not *u-* as the noun-prefix. [For this, see the discussion on the adjective in the chapter on Shona.][1]

The following is a fairly full list of ordinary adjectives in Venda, with examples of the forms they assume when in agreement with nouns of cls. 2, 7, and 9/10:

(Stem)	(Meaning)	(Cl. 2)	(Cl. 7)	(Cls. 9/10)
-denya	thick	vhadenya	tshidenya	ndenya
-hulu	big	vhahulu	tshihulu	khulu
-hulwane	important	vhahulwane	tshihulwane	khulwane
-khwivhilu	red	vhakhwivhilu	tshikhwivhilu	khwivhilu
-lala	old	vhalala	tshilala	ndala
-lapfu	long	vhalapfu	tshilapfu	ndapfu
-ngafha	as big as this	vhangafha	tshingafha	ngafha
-ngafhani?	how big?	vhangafhani	tshingafhani	ngafhani
-ngafho	as big as that	vhangafho	tshingafho	ngafho
-ngana?	how many?	vhangana	—	ngana
-nzani?	what sort?	vhanzani	tshinzani	nzani
-nzhi	many	vhanzhi	tshinzhi	nnzhi
-na	four	vhana	—	nna
-nu	wet	vhanu	tshinu	nnu

[1] Chapter IX, p. 217.

-ṅwe	some, other	vhaṅwe	tshiṅwe	nṅwe
-pfufhi	short	vhapfufhi	tshipfufhi	pfufhi
-raru	three	vhararu	—	tharu
-rema	black	vharema	tshirema	thema
-sekene	thin	vhasekene	tshisekene	tsekene or tsekhene
-seṱha	yellow	vhaseṱha	tshiseṱha	tseṱha
-swa	young, new	vhaswa	tshiswa	nntswa
-tete	soft	vhatete	tshitete	thethe
-thihi	one	—	tshithihi	nthihi
-tshena	white	vhatshena	tshitshena	tshena
-tswu	black	vhatswu	tshitswu	nntswu
-tswuku	red	vhatswuku	tshitswuku	tswuku
-ṱanu	five	vhaṱanu	—	ṱhanu
-ṱuku	small	vhaṱuku	tshiṱuku	ṱhuku
-vhi	bad	vhavhi	tshivhi	mmbi
-vhili	two	vhavhili	—	mbili
-vhisi	green, raw	vhavhisi	tshivhisi	mbisi
-vhuya	good-natured	vhavhuya	tshivhuya	mbuya

In addition, terms indicating cattle colours and markings are adjectives in Venda. The term to indicate the female, the cow, in each case assumes the suffix *-ana*. The following are a few examples given in cls. 9 and 10, in which these adjectives are generally found:

dala (white with small black spots), *dalana*.
godzwa (white with small brown spots), *godzwana*.
phaswa (black with white belly), *phaswana*
nnkhwe (black with white stripe on back), *khwana*.

This use is similar to what occurs in the Sotho group.

Examples of adjectival use:

Mufumbu mutshena u-a-ḽiwa (The white bran is being eaten).
Zwivhanda zwivhi zwo-vhulaha dzimbudzi (The evil beasts killed the goats).
Ḽiluvha ḽitswuku ḽi-a-nukha (The red flower is smelling).
Nnḓu khulu i-a-fhaṱiwa (The big house is being built).
kwana kuṱuku (a very small child); *ḓithu ḽihulu* (huge monster;) *u-lwa huvhi* (evil fighting).

(*b*) THE RELATIVE

As in Shona, there are no primitive relative stems in Venda, but relative concords are used in the formation of relative clauses, as an alternative to the more usual construction employing relative pronouns. In Venda the relative concord differs from the subjectival concord in the cl. 1 form only. In this class the indicative subjectival concord is *u-*; the relative concord is *a-*. As the whole subject will be treated under Relative Construction later, only a few examples are given here:

muthu a-itaho (the person who does).
vhathu vha-do-itaho (the people who will do).

Modification of the concord takes place in the past tenses, e.g.

muthu o-itaho (the man who did).
vhathu vho-faho (dead people).

(*c*) THE ENUMERATIVE

In Venda there are three enumerative roots, one monosyllabic: *-ṋe* (self), and two disyllabic: *-fhio?* (which?) and *-sili* (different). These assume weak prefixes in all cases, except with the cl. 1 form of the root *-ṋe*. Following is the table:

	(-ṇe)	(-fhio)	(-sili)
Cl. 1	muṇe	ufhio	usili
2	vhaṇe	vhafhio	vhasili
3	uṇe	ufhio	ụsili
4	iṇe	ifhio	isili
5	ḽiṇe	ḽifhio	ḽisili
7	tshiṇe	tshifhio	tshisili
14	vhuṇe	vhufhio	vhusili

Note: *muṇe* (cl. 1) has, as a substantive, the meaning of 'master'; as an enumerative the root indicates 'self', when it is generally used following the absolute pronoun, e.g. *ṇowa yone iṇe* (the snake itself), *Vha-a-ya vhone vhaṇe* (They go themselves). The root *-fhio* is interrogative meaning 'which one', e.g. *miri ifhio?* (which trees?); it is often used repeated, when it signifies 'whichever', 'everyone', e.g. *ḍuvha ḽifhio na-ḽifhio* (whatever day).

Weak enumerative concords have the same form in Venda as subjectival concords.

(*d*) THE POSSESSIVE

The two types of possessive, direct and descriptive, occur in Venda, the former with pronominal and nominal base, the latter with nominal and adverbial base.

The direct possessives may be divided into (i) those used with possessive pronominal stem, and (ii) those formed from nouns (and pronouns) by prefixing the possessive concord.

The possessive concord in Venda is typical of Bantu, being formed with basic *-a*, e.g. *wa-*, *vha-*, *zwa-*, &c.

List of Possessive Pronominal Stems

1st pers. s.   *-nga*   pl.   *-shu*
2nd pers. s.   *-u*   pl.   *-ṇu*
3rd pers. cl. 1. *-we*; 2. *-vho*; 3. *-wo*; 4. *-yo*; 5. *-ḽo*; 6. *-o*; 7. *-tsho*; 8. *-zwo*; 9. *-yo*; 10. *-dzo*; 11. *-lwo*; 14. *-ho*; 15. *-ho*; 20. *-kwo*.

Examples of use:
  danga ḽashu (our cattle kraal).
  mbudzi dzawe (his goats).
  mmbwa na-zwiḽiwa zwayo (the dog and its food).

Direct possessive with noun-stem:
  mbudzi dza-munna (the man's goats).
  nnḍu ya-khotsi (my father's house).

Following are some of the uses of the descriptive possessive in Venda:
(*a*) With noun base:
  (i) indicating quality, type, &c.:
    musadzi wa-vhuthu (kind woman).
    munna wa-maanda (strong man).
    maivha a-thavha (mountain pigeon).
    phukha ya-nduna (male animal).
  (ii) indicating material:
    nnkho dza-matombo (stone jars).
    mufumbu wa-mavhele (maize bran).
  (iii) indicating contents:
    khali ya-halwa (pot of beer).
  (iv) indicating order:
    ṅwana wa-vhuṭanu (the fifth child).

(b) With adverbial base:
>*tshisima tsha-tsini* (a nearby spring).
>*munna wa-Tshitandani* (a man from Tshitandani).
>*vhathu vha-kale* (people of old).

Table of Qualificative Concords

			(Adjectival)	(Relative)	(Enumerative)	(Possessive)
1st pers.	s.		—	*ndi-*	—	—
	pl.		—	*ri-*	—	—
2nd pers.	s.		—	*U-*[1]	—	—
	pl.		—	*ni-*	—	—
3rd pers.	cl. 1		*mu-*	*a-*	*mu-, u*	*wa-*
	2		*vha-*	*vha-*	*vha-*	*vha-*
	3		*mu-*	*u-*	*u-*	*wa-*
	4		*mi-*	*i-*	*i-*	*ya-*
	5		*ḽi-*	*ḽi-*	*ḽi-*	*ḽa-*
	6		*ma-*	*a-*	*a-*	*a-*
	7		*tshi-*	*tshi-*	*tshi-*	*tsha-*
	8		*zwi-*	*zwi-*	*zwi-*	*zwa-*
	9		[*N-*]	*i-*	*i-*	*ya-*
	10		[*N*]-	*dzi-*	*dzi-*	*dza-*
	11		*lu-*	*lu-*	*lu-*	*lwa-*
	14		*vhu-*	*vhu-*	*vhu-*	*ha-*
	15		*hu-*	*hu-*	*hu-*	*ha-*
	20		*ku-*	*ku-*	*ku-*	*kwa-*

(4) THE VERB

(i) THE VARIETIES OF THE VERB IN VENDA

There are the four varieties found in Bantu:
(a) The Regular disyllabic verb-stem, ending in the vowel *-a*, e.g. *ṱoḓa* (seek), *vhona* (see).
(b) The Monosyllabic verb-stem, e.g. *fa* (die), *la* (eat).
(c) The Vowel verb-stem, e.g. *ita* (do), *enda* (travel).
(d) Derived verb-stems: (1) Verbal derivatives, e.g. *vhonana* (reciprocal), *vhonisa* (causative), &c.; (2) Ideophonic derivatives, e.g. *takula* (lift) < *táku* (of getting up); and (3) Denominative verbs, e.g. *pfufhifha* (be short) < *-pfufhi*.

VERBAL DERIVATIVES. In Venda there is a good range of these, the most regularly used being the Passive, Applied, Neuter, Causative, Intensive, Reciprocal, and Reversive.

THE PASSIVE is formed by the suffix *-wa*, e.g. *funa* (love) > *funwa* (be loved), *renda* (praise) > *rendwa* (be praised). A common alternative is to suffix *-iwa*, e.g. *funiwa* (be loved), *vakasha* (visit) > *vakashiwa*. Monosyllabic verb-stems always suffix *-iwa*, e.g. *pfa* (hear) > *pfiwa* (be heard); *ka* (pick) > *kiwa* (be picked).

When a labial consonant occurs in the final syllable of the simple stem, either velarization occurs with suffix *-wa* or else *-iwa* is suffixed with no consonantal change.

fh > *x*	*vhofha* (tie) > *vhoxwa* or *vhofhiwa*.
vh > *h*	*ḓivha* (know) > *ḓihwa* or *ḓivhiwa*.
p > *px*	*napa* (switch) > *napxa* or *napiwa*.
ph > *phx*	*khopha* (break off cob) > *khophxa* or *khophiwa*.
b > *bg*	*beba* (beget) > *bebga* or *bebiwa*.
m > *ṅw*	*lima* (hoe) > *liṅwa* or *limiwa*.
h > *hw*	*vhulaha* (kill) > *vhulahwa* or *vhulahiwa*.

[1] The capital is used to distinguish low-toned *u-* of 2nd pers. s. from the cl. 3 form.

The *h* of the combination *hw* is voiced. When *s* and *z* are followed by *w*, the alveolar gives place to the labialized equivalent, thus: *liswa* (phon. ḻi:ṣa, be herded), *vhudzwa* (phon. βu:dʐa, be informed). The defective verb *-ri* (say) > *-pfi* (be said).

THE APPLIED is formed by the suffix *-ela*:
  ita (do) > *itela* (do for).
  gidima (run) > *gidimela* (run towards).
  vhofha (tie) > *vhofhela* (tie for).
  ṭoḓa (seek) > *ṭoḓela* (seek for).

Verbs in Venda which formerly contained a *k* before the final *-a* (e.g. *sea* < orig. *seka, *vuwa* < orig. *vuka) assume *-tshela* in the applied form, e.g.
  sea (laugh) > *setshela* (laugh for).
  vuwa (wake up) > *vutshela* (wake up for).

THE NEUTER is formed by the suffix *-ea* (originally **-eka*):
  ita (do) > *itea* (be feasible).
  vula (open) > *vulea* (come open).
  vhumba (mould) > *vhumbea* (be mouldable).

Certain verbs prefer the suffix *-ala*, e.g.
  pfa (hear) > *pfea* or *pfala* (be audible).
  vhona (see) > *vhonala* (be visible).

THE CAUSATIVE, indicating 'cause to do', 'help to do', is formed, as a general rule, by means of the suffix *-isa*:
  ṭoḓa (seek) > *ṭoḓisa* (cause to seek).
  fara (hold) > *farisa* (assist).
  vhona (see) > *vhonisa* (show).

From the original Bantu suffix **-ŷa* are more contracted forms, e.g.
  -na > *-nya*: *ṭangana* (meet) > *ṭanganya* (join).
  -la > *-dza*: *huvhala* (get hurt) > *huvhadza* (hurt); *fhola* (get well) > *fhodza* (cure).
  orig. **-ka*, now *-wa* > *-sa*: *vuwa* (wake up) > *vusa* (waken); *ṭuwa* (go away) > *ṭusa* (send away).

Alternatives with *-isa* are also found, e.g. *hula* (grow) > *hulisa* or *hudza*; *ṭuwa* > *ṭuwisa* or *ṭusa*.

Further, certain irregular causatives occur, e.g. *fura* (be satiated) > *fusha* (satiate); *nwa* (drink) > *nwisa* or *nusa* (give to drink); *hwala* (carry) > *hwalisa* or *hwesa* (help up a load); *shuwa* (be startled) > *shusha* (scare away); *ambara* (dress oneself) > *ambadza* (dress another); *ṭhaphuwa* (come to abrupt end) > *ṭhaphudza* (bring to abrupt end).

THE INTENSIVE is formed by suffixing *-esa* (and *-esesa*):
  pfa (hear) > *pfesa* (hear well), *pfesesa* (hear very well).
  ita (do) > *itesa* (act with a will).

Some of these verbs indicate excessive action, e.g. *ḻa* (eat) > *ḻesa* (over-eat).

THE RECIPROCAL is formed by suffixing *-ana*:
  ṭoḓa (seek) > *ṭoḓana* (seek one another).
  vhona (see) > *vhonana* (see each other).
  ṋea (give) > *ṋeana* (give to one another).

THE REVERSIVE. The intransitive form has suffixes *-uwa*, *-uluwa*, *-owa*, *-olowa*, and the transitive form *-ula*, *-ulula*, *-ola*, *-olola*; the suffixes with vowel *o* are used with verb-stems having vowel *o*:

shela (pour into < orig. *sha) > *shuluwa* (get spilt), *shulula* (pour out).
tupuwa (become uprooted), *tupula* (uproot).
ṱoma (prick into) > *ṱomowa* (become extracted), *ṱomola* (extract).
vhofha (bind) > *vhofholowa* (come undone), *vhofholola* (untie).

REDUPLICATED SUFFIXES generally express an intensity of action in Bantu, and this is true to a certain extent in Venda; nevertheless the applied reduplication *-elela* has the special significance of the 'perfective', e.g. *itelela* (do completely), and the reversive reduplication *-ulula*, &c., has the special repetitive significance, e.g. *lima* (plough) > *limulula* (replough).

REDUPLICATION OF THE VERB-STEM occurs indicating a diminishing and repetition of the action, e.g. *ṱoḓa-ṱoḓa* (seek here and there).

Other less active forms are:
STATIVE-POSITIONAL in *-ama*, e.g. *gwadama* (kneel), *kombama* (be crooked); *dzumba* (hide)>*dzumbama* (be in hiding).
CONTACTIVE in *-ara*, e.g. *ambara* (dress oneself), *fara* (hold).

(ii) THE CONJUGATION OF THE VERB IN VENDA

There are two conjugations of the verb in Venda, Positive and Negative.

Apart from the infinitive and imperative forms, there are five finite moods in Venda, viz. Indicative, Subjunctive, Potential, Participial, and Dependent.

THE INFINITIVE is formed with the prefix *u-*, and occurs in both positive and negative conjugations:

     (Positive)   (Negative)
     u-vhona (to see) *u-sa-vhona* (not to see)
     u-gidima (to run) *u-sa-gidima* (not to run)

e.g. *Ndi-ṱo-ḓa u-ḽa* (I want to eat); *u-tshimbila ha-khosi* (the chief's journeying).

THE IMPERATIVE. The plain stem of the verb constitutes the imperative singular of verbs of more than one syllable, the plural being formed by suffixing *-ni* thereto.[1]

 vhona (see!), *vhonani*.
 fhumula (keep quiet!), *fhumulani*.
 ita (do!), *itani*.

Monosyllabic stems prefix *i-*:
 ima (stand!), *imani*.

When an objectival concord is used with an imperative, final *-a* and *-ani* are changed to *-e* and *-eni* respectively; e.g. *mu-vhidze* (call him!), *mu-vhidzeni*.

The Negative of the Imperative is formed by using the verb *litsha* (leave off) followed by the infinitive, e.g. *litshani u-levha* (don't tease!).

More commonly the negative of a subjunctive tense with infixed *-songo-* is used, e.g. *ni-songo-ya thavhani* (don't go to the mountain).

THE INDICATIVE MOOD. There are only traces of the three implications of the indicative mood, Simple, Progressive, and Exclusive, in Venda: the progressive in the negative (the positive being indicated by a compound tense), and the exclusive only in the negative, and that indicated by a compound tense.

Examples:
 Simple Implication: *ndi-a-vhona* (I see)
        a-thi-vhoni (I do not see).

---

[1] It must be observed, however, that the use of the simple stem form to anyone but one's own children is considered rudely familiar. To persons of lower rank the plural form in *-ni* is used; while to strangers, equals, and superiors subjunctive forms are used, e.g. *kha-vha-ḓe* (please come; lit. let them come!).

172   VENDA

Progressive Implication: [*ndi-ḓo-vhuya nda-vhona* (I still see)]
a-thi-tsha-vhoni (I no longer see).
Exclusive Implication: [*a-thi-athu u-vhona* (I do not yet see)].

Distinctions of aspect are not as clear in Venda as in some Bantu languages, but, as in Shona, the perfect aspect of stative verbs is clear.

Paradigm of the Basic Tenses of the Indicative Mood

	(Positive)	(Negative)
Past	*ndo-vhona* (I saw)	*a-tho-ngo-vhona* (I did not see)
Pres. perf. of stative verbs	*ndo-neta* (I am tired)	*a-tho-ngo-neta* (I am not tired)
Present . . .	*ndi-vhona* / *ndi-a-vhona* (I see)	*a-thi-vhoni* (I do not see)
Future . . .	*ndi-ḓo-vhona* (I shall see)	*a-thi-nga-vhoni*[1] (I shall not see)

Venda does not distinguish between more immediate and more remote times for either past or future.

Venda has two forms of the simple present tense. The longer form, with formative *-a-* is used when no word follows the predicate. If it is used when a word follows the predicate, it emphasizes that word, e.g.

ndi-vhona zwavhuḓi (I see clearly).
ndi-vhona muthu (I see a person).
ndi-a-mu-vhona (I see him).
ndi-a-vhona (I see).
ndi-a-vhona muthu (I *do* see the person).

	Subj. concords. (indic.)			Obj. concords	Pres. Indic. positive	Pres. Indic. negative
	Pres. Fut.	Past	Neg.			
1st pers. s. .	*ndi-*	*ndo-*	*thi-*[2]	N-	*ndi-a-vhona*	*a-thi-vhoni*
pl. .	*ri-*	*ro-*	*ri-*	*ri-*	*ri-a-vhona*	*a-ri-vhoni*
2nd pers. s. .	*U-*	*wo-*	*u-*	*U-*	*U-a-vhona*	*a-U-vhoni*
pl. .	*ni-*	*no-*	*ni-*	*ni-*	*ni-a-vhona*	*a-ni-vhoni*
3rd pers. cl. 1	*u-*	*o-*	*a-*[3]	*mu-*	*u-a-vhona*	*ha-vhoni*
2	*vha-*	*vho-*	*vha-*	*vha-*	*vha-a-vhona*	*a-vha-vhoni*
3	*u-*	*wo-*	*u-*	*u-*	*u-a-vhona*	*a-u-vhoni*
4	*i-*	*yo-*	*i-*	*i-*	*i-a-vhona*	*a-i-vhoni*
5	*ḽi-*	*ḽo-*	*ḽi-*	*ḽi-*	*ḽi-a-vhona*	*a-ḽi-vhoni*
6	*a-*	*o-*	*a-*[3]	*a-*	*a-a-vhona*	*ha-vhoni*
7	*tshi-*	*tsho-*	*tshi-*	*tshi-*	*tshi-a-vhona*	*a-tshi-vhoni*
8	*zwi-*	*zwo-*	*zwi-*	*zwi-*	*zwi-a-vhona*	*a-zwi-vhoni*
9	*i-*	*yo-*	*i-*	*i-*	*i-a-vhona*	*a-i-vhoni*
10	*dzi-*	*dzo-*	*dzi-*	*dzi-*	*dzi-a-vhona*	*a-dzi-vhoni*
11	*lu-*	*lwo-*	*lu-*	*lu-*	*lu-a-vhona*	*a-lu-vhoni*
14	*vhu-*	*ho-*	*vhu-*	*vhu-*	*vhu-a-vhona*	*a-vhu-vhoni*
15	*hu-*	*ho-*	*hu-*	*hu-*	*hu-a-vhona*	*a-hu-vhoni*
20	*ku-*	*kwo-*	*ku-*	*ku-*	*ku-a-vhona*	*a-ku-vhoni*

Various compound tenses are achieved by using the verb *-vha* (become) in present, past, and future forms, followed by participial complements, e.g.

ndo-vha ndi-tshi-vhona (I was seeing).
ndo-vha ndo-vhona (I had seen).

[1] Also potential negative.
[2] Note that prefix *a-* + *ndi-* > *athi-* in 1st pers. s.
[3] Note that the negative prefix in all classes other than 1 and 6 is *a-*; in cls. 1 and 6 prefix and concord appear as *ha-*.

ndo-vha ndi-thi-ḓo-vhona[1] (I was going to see).
ndi-ḓo-vha ndi-tshi-vhona (I will be seeing).
ndi-ḓo-vha ndo-vhona (I will have seen).

The lists on p. 172 show: (*a*) the subjectival concord used, (i) with present and future tenses positive, (ii) with past tenses positive, (iii) with negative tenses; (*b*) the objectival concord, indicating the object and immediately preceding the verb-stem in every case; (*c*) the present positive tense in full; and (*d*) the present negative tense in full.

THE SUBJUNCTIVE MOOD. The present or present-future subjunctive is formed by changing the final vowel of the verb-stem to -*e*, the subjectival concords being the same as for the indicative present, except that that of cl. 1 becomes *a*-. In the negative the auxiliary -*sa*- is infixed.

The following portion of the tenses indicates the formation:

			(Positive)	(Negative)
1st pers.	s.		*ndi-vhone*	*ndi-sa-vhone*
	pl.		*ri-vhone*	*ri-sa-vhone*
2nd pers.	s.		*U-vhone*	*U-sa-vhone*
	pl.		*ni-vhone*	*ni-sa-vhone*
3rd pers.	cl. 1		*a-vhone*	*a-sa-vhone*
		2	*vha-vhone*	*vha-sa-vhone*
		3	*u-vhone*	*u-sa-vhone*
		4	*i-vhone*	*i-sa-vhone*

The present subjunctive is used:

(*a*) After certain conjunctives indicating purpose; e.g. *Vha-ṱoḓa uri re-ṱuwe* (They want us to go).
(*b*) In permissive interrogation; e.g. *Ndi-dzule?* (Am I to sit down?).
(*c*) As a polite imperative after *kha-*; e.g. *Kha-tshi-vhuye* (Let it return).
(*d*) In a sequence of tenses following a true imperative, e.g. *Vhuyani ni-lime* (Come back and plough).

THE POTENTIAL MOOD. In Venda the potential mood has a present positive tense, and shares, for the negative, that of the future indicative. Each of these has, as its characteristic, the infix -*nga*- and the use of the subjectival concord *a*- for cl. 1.

Examples:

		(Positive)	(Negative)
1st pers. s.		*ndi-nga-vhona*	*a-thi-nga-vhoni*
3rd pers. cl. 1		*a-nga-vhona*	*ha-nga-vhoni*
	2	*vha-nga-vhona*	*a-vha-nga-vhoni*

The force of this mood in Venda tends more to the conditional than the pure potential, and the translation of *ndi-nga-vhona* is rather 'I may see', 'I could see', 'I might see' than 'I can see'.

THE PARTICIPIAL MOOD. This mood is used in the formation of certain relative clauses in Venda, with the ordinary participial sense of the English participle, and after certain conjunctives. The tenses employing infixed -*tshi*- are not used in relative constructions, and for that reason a 'relative' has been unnecessarily postulated. Participial forms of potential tenses occur, but the usual parallel is with the indicative. It is in the negative that the participial is noticeably distinct, the infixes -*sa*- and -*songo*- being used. Cl. 1 subjectival concord is -*a*.

The following is a paradigm of the simple tenses of the participial mood:

[1] Such forms are treated as contingent mood in Nguni.

	(Positive)	(Negative)
Past	ndo-vhona	ndi-songo-vhona
Present	ndi-vhona / ndi-tshi-vhona	ndi-sa-vhoni
Future	ndi-no-ḓo-vhona / ndi-tshi-ḓo-vhona	ndi-sa-ḓo-vhona

Examples of the use of the participial mood:

(a) in relative construction: *muthu a-tshimbilaho* (the person who walks).
(b) with participial sense: *O-ṱuwa a-tshi-ri-sema* (He went away scolding us).
(c) after conjunctives: *arali ndi-tshi-mu-vhona* (if I see him).

THE DEPENDENT MOOD. This non-committal term has been chosen to designate certain tenses in Venda admittedly very difficult to classify. E. Westphal treats them as constituting a 'consecutive mood', but it is difficult to reconcile that term with the use in the relative construction. Every instance of the use of these tenses is definitely in subordinate construction, hence the use of the term 'dependent'.

The feature of the dependent mood is the use of the auxiliary *-a-*, e.g. in the positive: *nda-vhona, ra-vhona*, &c., with cl. 1 as *a-vhona*. The negative has, in addition, infixed *-sa-* and final *-e*, e.g. *nda-sa-vhone*. The main usages of the dependent mood are as follows:

(i) After certain deficient verbs, e.g. *Ndo-vhuya nda-mu-vhona* (I once saw him).

(ii) In consecutive construction: (a) present, e.g. *Ndi-a-shuma nda-la* (I work and then eat); (b) past, *Ndo-ya tsimuni nda-wana mavhele o-oma* (I went to the garden (and) found the mealies dry). This use is similar to that of the past subjunctive in Nguni.

(iii) With participial forms, particularly in conditional construction, e.g. (*Arali*) *nda-mu-vhona ndi-ḓo-mu-vhudza* (If I should see him, I will tell him).

(iv) In the relative construction, when relative pronouns are employed, e.g. *mbavhala ye ya-i-vhona* (the bushbuck which he (cl. 9) saw); *vhe vha-dzula* (they who lived); *vhe vha-sa-dzule* (they who did not live).[1]

(iii) COMPOUND TENSES IN VENDA

Compound tenses of various types are formed with the aid of deficient verbs. These may in Venda be divided mainly into three types as follows:

(a) Deficient verbs followed by the infinitive, in which case the final vowel *-a* of the verb usually coalesces with the infinitive prefix *u-* to form *o*. The following are a few examples:

-*tou-* or *-to-* (< *ita*, do) expressing emphasis, e.g. *Ndo-tou-shuma* (I have indeed worked).
-*ṱolo-*: do always.
-*dzo-* (< *edza*, try): try to do, e.g. *Mmpheni ndi-dzo-vhona* (Give me and let me try to see).
-*kono-* (< *kona*, be able): may do, e.g. *Iḽani ni-kono-shuma* (Eat so that you may work).
-*bvou-* (< *bva*, come from): have just done, e.g. *Vha-bvou-ḽa* (They have just finished eating).

(b) Deficient verbs followed by the dependent mood:

-*vhuya*, once (in negative, 'never'), e.g. *Ndo-vhuya nda-mu-vhona* (I once saw him); *A-thongo-vhuya nda-mu-vhona* (I have never seen him).
-*dovha*, do again, e.g. *Ndo-dovha nda-rwiwa* (I was beaten again).
-*shuma*, do well.

(c) Deficient verbs followed by the participial:

---

[1] The ordinary negative ends in *-e*, even in the relative construction, but the negative participial ends in *-a*. In its consecutive use, a potential form is found, e.g. *nda-nga-vha-vhudza* (... and should I happen to tell them).

-*vha*, in the formation of continuous tenses, e.g. *Ndo-vha ndi-tshi-vhona* (I was seeing).
-*ṭwa*, keep on, e.g. *U-ṭwa u-tshi-nndina* (He keeps on worrying me).

(*d*) In addition the defective and deficient verb -*ri* has a wide idiomatic use in Venda.

(5) THE COPULATIVE

(i) THE FORMATION OF COPULATIVES FROM NOUNS

1st and 2nd persons use the subjectival concord, e.g.
ndi-muthu (I am a person).
ri-vhathu (we are people).

In the 3rd person the immutable copulative formative *ndi-* is prefixed, e.g.
ndi-miri (they are trees).
Ntsundeni ndi-musadzi (Ntsundeni is a woman).

(ii) FROM PRONOUNS

The general rule is to prefix the copulative formative *ndi-* to the pronoun, e.g.
ndi-ene (it is he).
ndi-havhano (it is these).

Qualificatives are not directly inflected to form copulatives, but pronouns formed from them are so used, e.g. *Vhathu ndi-vhapfufhi* (The people are short ones); *Ndi-dzanga* (They are mine); also with 1st or 2nd pers. subjectival concords, *Ri-vhapfufhi* (We are short ones).

(iii) FROM ADVERBS

The subjectival concord is prefixed to the adverb in all three persons, and in indefinite formation the copulative formative *ndi-* is prefixed.

(*a*) *u-kule* (he is far); *ri-fhano* (we are here); *dzi-fhano* (they are here).
(*b*) *ndi-fhano* (it is here, that . . .); *ndi-masiari* (it is afternoon).

(iv) LOCATIVE DEMONSTRATIVE COPULATIVES

Venda has forms for each demonstrative position, formed by means of a prefixed *kha-* modified by assimilation to *khe-* and *kho-*, and signifying 'here is', 'there is', &c. The following short table illustrates these forms:

	(1st position)	(2nd position)	(3rd position)	(4th position)
Cl. 1	*khoyu*	*khoyo*	*khouno*	*khouḽa*
2	*khevha*	*khevho*	*khevhano*	*khevhaḽa*
4	*kheyi*	*kheyo*	*kheino*	*kheiḽa*
5	*kheḽi*	*kheḽo*	*kheḽino*	*kheḽiḽa*
7	*khetshi*	*khetsho*	*khetshino*	*khetshiḽa*
11	*kholu*	*kholo*	*kholuno*	*kholuḽa*
14	*khovhu*	*khovho*	*khovhuno*	*khovhuḽa*

A variant to the 4th position ends in -*ḽaa*, e.g. *khouḽaa* (yonder he is). A dialectal variant is found with *nga-* (*nge-* and *ngo-*) in place of *kha-*, e.g. *ngoyu*, *ngeḽi*, &c. A third form in *asi-* (and *asu-*) has special implications, sometimes being used of moving objects, e.g. *asiyi* (cl. 9) 'here it is, take it'. These forms appear as *asuyu* (cl. 1), *asivha*, (cl. 2), *asiḽi* (cl. 5), &c.

In the conjugation of the copulatives, the auxiliary verb -*vha* is used in past and future tenses, e.g.

(Present)   *ndi-ṅanga* (I am a doctor).
(Past)   *ndo-vha ndi-ṅanga* (I was a doctor).
(Future)   *ndi-ḓo-vha ndi-ṅanga* (I shall be a doctor).

(6) THE ADVERB

Apart from a certain number of nouns indicating time, such as *madekwe* (last night), *vhusiku* (night), *ṅwedzi* (month), which are also used as temporal adverbs, in Venda adverbs are formed from other parts of speech by means of adverbial prefixal (or suffixal) formatives. These may be briefly listed as (i) Conjunctive, (ii) Instrumental, (iii) Manner, (iv) Comparison, (v) Locative, and (vi) Temporal.

(i) THE CONJUNCTIVE FORMATIVE

This formative, *na-*, indicates 'together with', e.g. *Ndo-zwi-vhea na-thundu* (I put them with the goods). Certain idiomatic forms are found with *na-*, e.g. *na-zwino* (truly), *na-musi* (even though).

(ii) THE INSTRUMENTAL FORMATIVE

The formative *nga-* indicates: (*a*) by means of (true instrument), (*b*) by (agent), and (*c*) concerning.

(*a*) *u-fhira nga-bere* (to pass on horseback); *u-rwa nga-tombo* (to strike with a stone).
(*b*) *u-liwa nga-mapfeṇe* (to be eaten by baboons).
(*c*) *u-amba nga-kholomo* (to talk about cattle).

Certain formations have become regularly used, e.g. *nga-vhuya* (slowly), *nga-maanḍa* (exceedingly).

(iii) THE MANNER FORMATIVE

This is *zwi-* (of cl. 8) prefixed to qualificatives; e.g. *zwituku* (slightly); or in possessive form, e.g. *zwavhuḍi* (nicely).

(iv) THE COMPARISON FORMATIVE

The formative *sa-* indicates 'like', e.g. *U-tshimbila sa-mbava* (He walks like a thief); *sa-vhathu* (like people).

(v) LOCATIVE FORMATIVES

Apart from the remnant of noun class prefixes 16, 17, and 18, noticed when dealing with the noun classes, Venda uses the locative suffix *-ni*; the prefixes *ha-*, *kha-*, *vhu-*; and a modifying prefix *nga-*.

(*a*) The suffix *-ni*: This is the regular formative for locatives from nouns, e.g.
miri (trees) > *mirini* (in, from, at the trees).
Ndi-bva mulamboni (I come from the river).
Zwi-mbudzini (They are on the goat).

Certain nouns of locative import do not suffix *-ni*, e.g. *musanda* (at the head-kraal), *ngomu* (inside), *seli* (beyond); and place-names, e.g. *Makonde, Venḍa* (in Vendaland).

(*b*) *ha-* is prefixed to nouns of cls. 1a and 2a, especially when the place owned is indicated, e.g. *ha-khotsi* (to my father; at my father's place); *ha-Tshivhasa* (in Tshivhasa's country). This prefix is similarly used with possessive pronominal stems, e.g. *hanga* (at my place), *haṇu* (at your place).

(*c*) *kha-* is prefixed to pronouns, e.g. *kha-nṇe* (to me), *kha-vhone* (to them). This prefix used with nouns makes a more definite form than that by suffix, e.g. *mbavani* (where the thief is), but *kha-mbava* (on the thief's person); *bugini* (in a book), but *kha-bugu* (in the book).

(*d*) Class 14 prefix *vhu-* is used to indicate places or countries, e.g. *vhuMbedzi* (in the Mbedzi country), *vhukovhela* (in the west), *vhuambelo* (place of refuge).

(*e*) The prefix *nga-* is used to modify or make indefinite locative forms, e.g.
thungo yafhasi (the lower side), *ngathungo yafhasi* (towards the lower side).
fhasi (on the ground), *ngafhasi* underneath).

(vi) Temporal Formatives

The instrumental formative is used with temporal nouns, e.g. *nga-ḍuvha* (on the day), *nga-musumbuluwo* (on Monday). In addition, the prefixes *ka-*, *lu-*, and *zwi-* are used:

(*a*) *ka-* prefixed to qualificatives, e.g. *ka-nzhi* (often), *ka-vhili* (twice).
(*b*) *lu-* prefixed to qualificatives, e.g. *lu-nzhi* (often), *lu-ngana ?* (how many times ?).
(*c*) *zwi-* occurs in a few formations, e.g. *zwino* (now), *zwenezwo* (forthwith).

(7) THE IDEOPHONE

In Venda, ideophones are commonly used after the verb *-ri* (which may be submerged in the subjectival concord, e.g. *vhe'*, from *vha+ri*), or its passive form *-pfi*. The preceding verb often appears as *-tou'*, which is believed to be a contraction of *ita+u-ri* (lit. do-to-manifest). Following are examples classified according to the number of syllables:

Monosyllabic:

pha (of fullness): *Mudavhini ho-tou' vhathu pha* (The plain was teeming with people).
thwee (of coldness of water).
duu (of dead silence).

Disyllabic:

gávhi (of snatching): *a-ri gávhi* (he snatched).
dúgu (of flaming up): *dúgu-dúgu*.
búdu (of a resounding blow): *Ndo-mu-budula nda-tou'mu búdu* (I hit him a resounding blow).
kúmbvu (of small stone falling into water).
nyéke-nyéke (of shimmering of heat).

Trisyllabic:

ṭódzidzi (of peeping out).
ṭháṭhara-ṭháṭhara (of staggering).

Quadrisyllabic:

pílivhili (of redness): *O-tou' pílivhili* (He was red).

The ideophones in Venda have a greater tone range than the non-emotional words. Normally the stress is on the initial syllable, and long vowels are rare except in final positions.

Verbs and nouns are formed from ideophones in Venda, and the following examples of verb-formation might be noted:

táku (of getting up) > intr. *takuwa* (get up), tr. *takula* (lift), caus. *takusa* (cause to get up).
nyámbu (of switching) > tr. *nyambudza* (hit with a switch).
gídi-gídi (of running) > intr. *gidima* (run).

(8) THE CONJUNCTIVE

There are not many conjunctives in Venda. The following might be noted:

fhedzi (but): *Ndi-na-mushumo fhedzi ndi-ḍo-ḍa* (I am busy, but I will come).
ngahezwo, zwenezwo (therefore): *Ndi-khou-lwala; ngahezwo ndi-ḍo-ya ṅangani* (I am ill; therefore I will go to the doctor).
zwino (now; whereupon).
izwi, izwo (but).
huno (but).
uri followed by indicative, that; followed by subjunctive, so that): *Ndi-a-zwi-ḍivha uri ha-nga-ḍoḍa* (I know that he will not come); *Ndo-mu-vhudza uri a-tuwe* (I told him that he should go).

kana . . . kana (whether . . . or).
arali (if, when), followed by participial mood: *Arali ni-tshi-ya musanda, ni-mbudze* (If— or when—you go to the head-kraal, tell me).
musi (when).
naho (although).

(9) THE INTERJECTIVE

(i) RADICAL INTERJECTIONS, of which Venda has many, and in which emotion is expressed by tone and length:

hai, m'm, aiwa-vho (no!)
ee, ĩĩ, 'm (yes!)
ahee (look out!)
'm-hm (serves you right!)
o-hoo (shame on you!)

(ii) VOCATIVES. There is no inflexion (formal or tonal) to form vocative interjectives from nouns, e.g. *fhumulani vhakomana!* (keep quiet, boys!). *Hee* is often prefixed when using titles, e.g. *hee-vhakoma!* (headman!); *hee-vhoSiaba!* (Siaba!).

To 2nd person absolute pronouns, however, *di-* is prefixed, e.g. *iwe* (you, sg.) > *diwe!*

(iii) VERB-IMPERATIVES, already treated, function as interjectives.

(10) ENCLITIC AND PROCLITIC FORMATIVES

(i) ENCLITICS.
-ni? (what?) *O-vhulaha-ni?* (What did he kill?)
-ḓe? (what sort?) *Ndi-zwithu-ḓe izwi?* (What sort of things are these?)
-fhi? (where?) *Vho-ya-fhi?* (Where did they go?).

(ii) THE PROCLITIC *na-*. This is used conjunctivally, joining substantives and adverbs, e.g.
mbudzi na-kholomo (goats and cattle).
Khosi na-gota vha-a-pfana (The king and the councillor agree).
haṋu na-havho (at your place and their place).

This formative has already been considered as an adverbial conjunctive formative.

(11) THE NUMERALS

In Venda the numeral system is strictly quinary, the first five numerals being adjectives; six to nine are compounded forms, 'five and one', 'five and two', &c.; ten is a noun.

1. *-thihi*: *muthu muthihi* (one person).
2. *-vhili*: *vhanna vhavhili* (two men).
3. *-raru*: *thonga tharu* (three sticks).
4. *-ṋa*: *maṱambi maṋa* (four herds).
5. *-ṱanu*: *zwithu zwiṱanu* (five things).
6. *miṅwaha miṱanu-na-muthihi* (six years).
7. *madzuvha maṱanu-na-mavhili* (seven days).
8. *vhathu vhaṱanu-na-vhararu* (eight people).
9. *mbohwana ṱhanu-na-ṋṋa* (nine bullocks).
10. *fumi*: *vhanna vha-fumi* or *vha-na-fumi* (a possessive construction).

(12) RELATIVE CONSTRUCTION

(i) THE DIRECT RELATIVE, used when the antecedent is in subjectival relationship to the relative predicate, may be expressed in Venda in one of three ways:

(a) With participial concord and suffix *-ho*, e.g.
  muthu a-tshimbilaho fhano (the person who walks here).
  fhethu hu-fanelaho (a suitable place).
(b) With participial concord and infix *-no-*, e.g.
  muthu a-no-tshimbila fhano (the person who walks here).
  khosi i-no-vhusa shango ḻavho (the chief who governs their country).
(c) With the relative pronoun followed by the predicate in the dependent mood, e.g.
  muthu ane a-tshimbila fhano (the person who walks here).
  zwithu zwine zwa-takadza (the things which are pleasing).

(ii) THE INDIRECT RELATIVE, used when the antecedent is in some oblique relationship to the relative predicate, is expressed in Venda by the use of the relative pronouns and the dependent mood:

(a) Objectival relationship:
  munna we nda-mu-vhona (the man whom I saw).
  ṅwana ane a-khou-mu-rwa (the child he is beating).
  mbavhala ye ra-i-vhona (the bushbuck which we saw).

(b) Adverbial relationship:
  (conjunctive): *muthu ane ra-amba nae* (the person with whom we are speaking).
  (instrumental): *thonga ine vha-mu-rwa ngayo* (the stick with which they beat him);
    mukoma ane vha-amba ngae (the headman concerning whom they speak).
  (locative): *kha-*, *ha-*, and *hu-* used: *munna we a-ya khae* (the man to whom he went);
    vhoSiaba vhane ndo-ya havho (Siaba to whose place I went); *thavhani hune ra-ya hone* (the mountain to which we go).
  (comparison): *khonani dzine a-amba sa-dzone* (the friends like whom he speaks).

REFERENCES

CARL MEINHOF: 'Das Tṣi-venḓa' (*Zeitschrift der Morgenländischen Gesellschaft*, lv. Heft iv, 1901).
N. J. V. WARMELO: *Tshivenḓa–English Dictionary*, 1937.
E. WESTPHAL: *A Scientific Analysis of the Phonetics, Morphology and Syntax of the Venḓa Language* [unpublished MS. 1946].

VIII

THE TSONGA GROUP

Geographical Position of the Group

This has been well described by the late H. A. Junod in the introduction to his *Grammaire Ronga*, published in 1896. The home of the Tsonga, or as they are commonly called 'Shangaan', peoples is in the Mozambique district of Portuguese East Africa. There they stretch from the borders of Zululand in the south to the great Sabi River in the north, where their neighbours are groups of the Eastern Ndau section of the Shona. In the north-west a section of the Tsonga is found in Southern Rhodesia abutting on the Karanga and Venda. In the west they are found across the border in the Northern and North-eastern Transvaal in considerable numbers in the Zoutpansberg, Lydenburg, and Waterberg districts.

The term Tsonga (Tg.) has now been accepted generally as a term of reference for the whole group, which has three important literary sections: the Ronga (Ro.) in the south, around Lourenço Marques and bordering on the Zulu and the Swazi; the Tonga (To.) in the centre and west, the principal form of which in the Transvaal is called Gwamba; and the Tswa (Ts.) in the north, in the hinterland of Inhambane, a form closely allied to the wide-flung Hlengwe. There are various smaller dialects with special peculiarities, such as the Jonga, Bila, Ngwalungu, &c., which have contributed to one or other of the literary forms now used. The total number of Tsonga speakers must today be over one and a quarter million. The complete Bible has been translated into each of the three literary forms, and grammatical studies have been contributed on each, those on Ronga and Tonga by the late H. A. Junod, and that on Tswa by J. A. Persson. Tsonga has been considerably influenced by Zulu, especially in vocabulary, through which have been carried even click sounds, e.g. *qala* (begin), though these are definitely still considered foreign to Tsonga.

Orthography

Tsonga presents several features which have caused trouble to orthographists, and changes have been made from time to time: Ro. and To. have today a common orthography to a great extent, due to the work of the Swiss Mission; that of Ts. differs in certain particulars, and is the work of missionaries of the Methodist Episcopal Mission. The Swiss missionaries used the Lepsius system with the symbols $š$ and $ž$ (palatal fricatives), $ŝ$ and $ẑ^1$ ('whistling' fricatives), $ṅ$ (velar nasal), $ṭ$, $ḍ$, and $ṛ$ ('cerebrals'), $ṽ^2$ (bilabial voiced fricative). The orthography used by Persson for Tswa, while retaining $ŝ$, $ẑ$, and $ṅ$, uses b for the fricative and $\underline{b}$ for the explosive bilabial, the Portuguese x in place of $š$, and the symbol c for $tš$ of the others.

All forms of written Tsonga use disjunctive word-division. In the present treatment hyphens are used to connect up the elements of the real words; otherwise the orthographies represented in the Bible translations are followed, except that of the Tswa Bible where a strange system of italicized letters is used.

Phonetics and Phonology

Tsonga employs a seven-vowel system, with the three basic vowels **a**, **i**, and **u**, and two varieties each of the mid-forward and mid-back vowels, **e** and **ɛ**, **ɔ** and **o**, the higher qualities

[1] Not provided for by Lepsius.

[2] $ṽ$ is not a Lepsius symbol; it is used in To.; in Ro. the symbol b is used for both fricative and explosive sounds.

occurring, as in Nguni, when a close vowel, i or u, is in the succeeding syllable. There are thus five phonemes only, represented by the usual five symbols.

PHONETIC CHART OF TSONGA CONSONANTS

	Bilab.	Denti-lab.	Alveolar	Retro-flex	Labio-alveolar	Pre-palatal	Palatal	Velar	Glottal
EXPLOSIVE									
eject.	p'		t'	[t̪']			{c'}	k'	
asp.	ph		th	[t̪h]			{ch}	kh	
voic.	b[bɦ]		d	[ɖ]			{ɟ}	g(gɦ)	
	mb		nd	ɳɖ			ɲɟ	ŋg	
NASAL	m		n	[ɳ]		ɲ		ŋ	
	mɦ		nɦ					ŋɦ	
ROLLED			r	[ɽ]					
LATERAL			l						
FRICATIVE									
med. unv.		f	s		ʂ	ʃ			h
med. voic.	β	(v)	z		ʐ	ʒ			(ɦ)
lat. unv.			ɬ						
lat. voic.			ɮ						
AFFRICATE									
med. eject.	pf'		ts'		tʂ'(pʂ')	tʃ'			
med. asp.			tsh		tʂh				
med. voic.	bv		dz		(bʐ)	dʒ			
lat. eject.			tɬ'					(kɬ')	
lat. asp.			tɬh					(kɬh)	
SEMI-VOWEL	((w))					j		w	

( ) found in Ts. only.   { } found in To. only.
[ ] found in Ro. only.   (( )) alternative position.

(a) ORTHOGRAPHIC REPRESENTATION

The preceding chart gives the various sounds used in phonetic script. The current orthographies differ from this as follows:

ɦ is written *h*.
b is written *b* in Ts.
β is written *b* in Ts. and Ro., *v̌* in To.
ɬ is written *hl*.
ɮ is written *dl*.
tɬ' and tɬh are written *tl* and *tlh* in To. and Ro.
t̪', t̪h, ɖ, and ɽ are written *ṭ*, *ṭh*, *ḍ*, and *ṛ* in Ro.
c', ch, and ɟ are written *ṭ*, *ṭh*, and *ḍ* in To.
ɳ (homorganic) is written *n*.
ʂ and ʐ are written *š* and *ž* respectively.
ʃ and ʒ are written *š* and *ž* in To. and Ro., and *x* and *zh* in Ts.
tʃ' is written *tš* in Ro. and To. and *c* in Ts.
dʒ occurs sometimes as *dž*, at others as *dj* or *ḍ*.
j is written *y*.
ŋ is written *ṅ*.
kɬ' is written *kl* in Ts.

(b) NOTES ON THE CONSONANTS

1. Aspiration is a significant feature with unvoiced explosives, and occurs to a certain extent with unvoiced affricates. Ejection is not very marked. Especially noticeable is the use

of the 'voiced-ɦ' in association with the nasals **m**, **n**, and **ŋ**, giving **mɦ**, **nɦ**, and **ŋɦ**, reminiscent of what occurs in Shona. The voiced glottal fricative, **ɦ**, occurs in Ts. in such a word as **fiwe:ti** (moon), and is associated with **g** as in **ŋgɦɑ:lɑ** (lion). In Ro. a strange transposition of **ɦ** from **nɦ** gives **bɦ** in *bhanu* (people), cf. To. βanɦu.

2. Ro. is unique in its regular use of retroflex or 'cerebral' explosives, orthographically indicated by *ṭ*, *ṭh*, and *ḍ*. The equivalents in To. are prepalatal explosives **c'**, **ch**, and **ɟ**. These were represented by the symbols *tj* and *dj*; but the latest orthography of the Bible uses the same symbols *ṭ* and *ḍ* as for the Ro. Corresponding to these Ts. often uses the affricates *ts* and *dz*. The following are the series in the orthography of the grammars:

	(Ro.)	(To.)	(Ts.)
(to) break	*ṭhoba*	*tjoṿa*	*tsoba*
1st pers. s. concd.	*nḍi-*	*ndji-*	*nzi-*
(to) kindle	*ṭibela*	*tjiṿela*	*dzibela*

But simple *ḍ* of Ro. is usually *r* in both To. and Ts., e.g.

| (to) weep | *ḍila* | *rila* | *rila* |

3. Tsonga is well represented by fricative consonants, having the typical Southern and Central Bantu bilabial voiced fricative **β**, and voiced and unvoiced forms of the alveolar, labio-alveolar, and prepalatal fricatives. Ts. is the only one of the languages to use **v** (dentilabial) apart from the affricative combination **bv**; Ts. is also alone in using the voiced glottal **ɦ**, apart from nasal or other combination. The 'whistling' fricatives, **ṣ** and **ẓ**, are typical of Tsonga, as well as their affricative counterparts **tṣ'** and perhaps **dẓ**, though Ts. seems to favour a labial rather than an alveolar commencement, using **pṣ'** and **bẓ** respectively.

4. Affricates occur commonly in Tsonga, but it must be observed that the labial series, **pf'** and **bv**, is only semi-homorganic, as occurs in Shona, the explosive element being bilabial and the fricative denti-labial.

5. Tsonga shares with Nguni and Sotho lateral fricatives, **ɬ** and **ɮ**, and lateral affricates, **tɬ'** and **tɬh**. Ts. differs from the other dialects in that the first element of the affricates is velar and not alveolar; this has the effect of retracting the position of the accompanying fricative.

6. Tsonga has a very wide range of consonantal combinations with a velar glide, the semi-vowel **w**, Ro. recording *gw*, *hw*, *kw*, *lw*, *nw*, *ṅw*, *ṛw*, *šw*, *tw*, *ṭw*, *dlw*, *tlw*, *hlw*, *nhw*, *ṇhw*, *ṭhw*, *khw*, *tlhw*. There are also certain combinations with the palatal glide, the semi-vowel **j**, Ro. again recording *ty*, *ḍy*, *ṭhy*, *py*, and *by*. It is noticeable that, in the case of bilabials, there is usually a modification of the glide, Ts. having a tendency to transform these into the labio-alveolar fricatives, viz. **pṣ** and **bẓ** respectively.

7. As has been observed, clicks have been introduced into Tsonga from Zulu contact; in some cases they are taken over unchanged, e.g. Ro. *qala* (begin); but in other cases some alteration has taken place, e.g. Ts. *qama* (ram) < *inqama*, Ro. *nxa* (no!) < *qha* or *cha*.

Of consonantal phenomena, the one to be noted in Tsonga is that of NASALIZATION. There are two instances of this, and each is governed by separate rules:

(i) In cl. 3 of nouns (and slightly in cl. 1) the prefix *mu-* has a nasalizing effect, as follows:

mu- + explosive consonant > N^1+consonant, resulting in *nt*, *mp*, *nk*, *nd*, *mb*.

mu- + fricative consonant > consonant only, nouns commencing in *s*, *f*, *hl*; though in To. and Ro. the homorganic nasal often accompanies the fricative, giving *ns*, *nhl*.

mu- + *ṿ* > *mb*.   *mu-* + *r* > *nḍ* (Ts. *nz-*).

mu- + *l* > *n*.

(ii) In cls. 9 and 10 of nouns the rules of nasalization go farther back, and are obviously of much earlier formation, as follows:

[1] N = homorganic nasal.

(a) The homorganic nasal may be prefixed to all consonants in Ro. and To., but in Ts. it is omitted before unvoiced fricatives and *v*; thus are found *mp*, *mf* (Ts. *f*), *nt*, *nd̰*, *nṭ*, *ndl*, *ntl*, *nhl*, (Ts. *hl*), *ns* (Ts. *s*), *nš* (Ts. *x*), *nk*, *ng*; and Ts. *v*.

(b) Original Bantu *p*, *t*, and *k* become *mh*, *nh*, and *h* respectively, as in Shona; the *h* being voiced (phon. **fi**).

(c) *v̌* (or *b*) > *mb*.
   l > *nd̰* (Ts. *nẓ*).

(d) Vowel-stems assume *ny-* or *ň*.

Instead of coalescence of vowels, Tsonga employs SUBSTITUTION OF *I* in certain cases where the vowel *a* comes into contact with a noun or other part of speech (e.g. pronoun, locative adverb) in which there is, actually or implicit, an initial vowel, proclitic *a-* in Ro. and Ts., proclitic *e-* in To. There are two instances in which substitution of *i* takes place:

(i) With the conjunctive formative or proclitic *na-* (= and), which becomes *ni-*, e.g.
   na-tatana (< *tatana*, cl. 1a with no initial vowel).
   ni-v̌anhu (< *e-v̌anhu* (To.), *a-banhu* (Ts.) cl. 2).
   ni-hosi (< *a-hosi*, cl. 9).

(ii) With the instrumental formative *ha-*, which becomes *hi-*, e.g.
   ha-manana (<*manana*, cl. 1a with no initial vowel).
   hi-nsati (< *a-nsati*, cl. 1).

STRESS AND LENGTH. Stress is normally on the penultimate syllable of each word, and that syllable is long. In the case of locative adverbs or imperative plurals, when the suffix is contracted by elision of the final vowel in quick speech, the stress remains unchanged and is still penultimate since the final consonant has become syllabic; thus, *fambán* < *fambáni*, *misabén* < *misabéni*. Ultimate stress does occur in the 3rd position demonstratives, e.g. *labayá*. Stress is typically on the initial syllable of ideophones.

TONE is significant in Tsonga, as in other Bantu languages. While Junod referred to it, and Persson gave examples of pairs of words distinguished by tone, research and recording on this feature have yet to be published in the group.[1]

GRAMMATICAL OUTLINE

(1) THE NOUN

Comparative Prefix Table

(Class)	(Ronga)	(Tonga)	(Tswa)
1	*mu-*	*mu-*	*mu-*
1a	—	—	—
2	*ba-*	*v̌a-*	*ba-*
2a	*ba-*	*v̌a-*	*ba-*
3	*mu-*	*mu-*	*mu-*
4	*mi-*	*mi-*	*mi-*
5	[*di-*]	[*ri-*]	[*gi-*]
6	*ma-*	*ma-*	*ma-*
7	*ši-*	*ši-*	*xi-*
8	*ši-*	*ši-*	*ẑi-*
9	*yi[N]-*	*yi[N]-*	*yi[N]-*
10	*ti[N]-*	*ti[N]-*	*ti[N]-*
11	*li-*	*ri-*	*li-*
14	*bu-*	*v̌u-*	*wu-*
15	*ku-*	*ku-*	*ku-*

[1] Cf. Endemann's unpublished thesis: *Die Intonasie van Tsonga*.

The differences between the three sets here given are mainly orthographic, e.g. *b* and *v̌* indicating the same sound, also *s* and *x*. There are, however, striking concord differences in cl. 5, and Tswa differs from the others in cl. 8 and in the treatment of cls. 9 and 10.

Tsonga employs an initial vowel, *e-* in To. and *a-* in Ro. and Ts., which has been almost entirely discarded in the written form. It is probable that this practice is seriously affecting its persistence in the spoken languages. The rules of its use are much akin to those of the initial vowel in Nguni, but it is used sometimes even with locatives. It is not found with nouns of cl. 1a, or with axiomatic negatives; it drops in vocative formation and after certain formatives; but it exerts an influence upon the conjunctive formative *na-* and the instrumental formative *ha-*, substitution of *i* taking place, and those appearing as *ni-* and *hi-* respectively.[1]

CLASSES 1 AND 2 (personal). The prefix in cl. 1 is *mu-* and in its plural (cl. 2) *v̌a-* (written in Ro. and Ts. as *ba-*). Examples:

munhu (person), pl. To. *v̌anhu*, Ts. *banhu*.

[Note that Ro. uses a peculiar form for this, viz. *mhunu*, pl. *bhanu*, in which the aspiration has been transferred from the stem to the prefix.]

mulungu (European).
muyeni (stranger).

Personal nouns derived from verbs:

mufambi (traveller) < *famba*, *v̌afambi*.
mutiri (worker) < *tira*, *v̌atiri*.

Vowel-stems have a velarized prefix in cl. 1:

ṅwana (child) < *-ana*, *v̌ana* [Ts. *ṅwanana*, *banana*].
Ro. *ṅwinyi* (master) < *-inyi*, *benyi* (in which coalescence of *ba*+*i* > *be* has taken place).

A few nouns of cl. 1 have prefix *wa-*, with *v̌av̌a-* in the plural (cl. 2); these are originally pronouns of possessive origin:

Ts. *wanuna* (man), *babanuna*.
Ts. *wasati* (woman), *babasati*; To. *wansati*, *v̌av̌asati*.

In Ro. certain contractions and nasal assimilations of the prefix *mu-* take place with polysyllabic stems, e.g. *nsati* (woman), *basati*; *nkata* (spouse), *bakata*; *nala* (enemy), *balala*; from *mu-sati*, *mu-kata*, and *mu-lala* respectively. This is a more regular feature in cl. 3 throughout Tsonga.

CLASSES 1*a* AND 2*a* (proper names, relationship terms, animals). No prefix in the singular, and *v̌a-* or *ba-* in the plural.

Proper names:

Matolo,   *v̌aMatolo*.
Mbata,   *v̌aMbata*.

Relationship terms:

tatana (my father), pl. *v̌atatana*; Ts. *dadani*, *badadani*.
mamana (my mother), pl. *v̌amamana*; Ts. *mamani*, *bamamani*.
Ts. *raru* (your, his father) *bararu*.
sati (wife), pl. *v̌asati*.

Miscellaneous:

Ts. *mani?* (who?), *bamani?* To. *mane?*
Ro. *mangulwe* (species of antelope), *bamangulwe*.
Ts. *nyakološe* (lizard), *banyakološe*.

[1] See H. L. Bishop: 'On the Use of the "Proclitic *a*" in Šironga', *Bantu Studies*, vol. ii.

Ordinary animal names are personified by using the prefix ṅwa-, e.g. Ṅwavundla (Mr. Hare) < vundla; Ts. Ṅwafutsu (Mr. Tortoise).

Table of Concords for classes 1 (1a) and 2 (2a)

	(Adj.)	(Rel.)	(Enum.)	(Poss.)	(Subj.)	(Obj.)
1 and 1a	lwe'mu-, lo'n- Ts. mu-	a- Ro. lw'a-	mu-, u-	wa-	u-, o-, a-	ṅwi-, mu-
2 and 2a	la'v̌a-, Ts. ba-	v̌a-, Ro. la'ba-	v̌a-	v̌a-	v̌a-	v̌a-

CLASSES 3 AND 4 (non-personal, trees, parts of the body, natural phenomena). The prefix mu- of cl. 3 is used with monosyllabic stems; rarely with polysyllabic.

muti (village), *miti*.
muri (tree, medicine), *miri*.
muzwa (thorn), *mizwa*.
Ts. *mukwana* (knife), *mikwana*.

With nouns of polysyllabic stems the prefix *mu-* of this class generally gives way to a nasal homorganic to the initial consonant, e.g.

ntiro (work), *mitiro*.
nkonzo (foot), *mikonzo*.
Ts. *nanzu* (debt), *milanzu*.
Ro. *mhaṇḍu* (fruit), *mihaṇḍu*.
nhlana (back), *mihlana*.

In certain cases, particularly in Ro., the prefix *mi-* of cl. 4 is superimposed on the cl. 3 form, e.g.

Ro. *ntuṛu* (handkerchief), *mintuṛu*
mpimu (measure), *mimpimu*.
Ts. *mbingano* (boundary), *mimbingano*.

The nasal effects illustrated in cl. 3 (and to a lesser degree in cl. 1) may be summarized as follows:

mu- + explosive consonant > N+consonant.
mu- + fricative consonant > consonant only.[1]
mu- + v̌ > mb.   mu- + r > nḍ (Ts. nz).
mu- + l > n.

[The nasal permutations applicable to cls. 9 and 10, where N+p, N+t, N+k > mh, nh, and h respectively, do not apply here.]

Table of Concords for classes 3 and 4

	(Adj.)	(Rel.)	(Enum.)	(Poss.)	(Subj.)	(Obj.)
3	lo'wu-, Ts. mu-	wu-, Ro. lo-	mu-, wu-	wa-	wu-	wu-
4	le'mi- Ts. mi-	yi-, Ro. le'mi-	mi-, yi-	ya-	yi-	yi-, mi-

CLASSES 5 AND 6 (miscellaneous, including fruits):

(a) With monosyllabic stems the prefixes *ti-* and *ṛi-* (*ḍi-*, *ri-* variants) are found in the singular, and *ma-* in the plural (sometimes super-added), e.g.

ṛibye, *ḍibye*, *ribye* (stone), pl. *maṛibye* or *mabye*.
To. Ro. *ṛito*, *ḍito*, *rito* (speech), pl. *maṛito* or *mato*.
tihlo (eye), pl. *mahlo* (Ro. *mahlu*).

---

[1] This varies within the group, cf. Ro. *nsati*, *nhlana*, but Ts. *sati*, *hlana*.

(b) With vowel-stems, the singular prefixes *t*-, and coalescence may occur in the plural, e.g.
Ts. *tanza*, To. Ro. *tanḍa* (egg), pl. *manza*, *manḍa*.
Ts. *tino* (st. -*ino*, tooth), pl. *meno*; To. *tino*, pl. *mino* (i.e. *ma+ino*, *a*- elided); Ro. *tinyo*, pl. *menyo*.

(c) Polysyllabic stems show no prefix in cl. 5:

tiba (lake), *matiba*.
tiko (country), *matiko*.
bito (name), *mabito*.
Ts. *haxi* (horse), *mahaxi*.
To. *khombo* (accident), *makhombo*.
Ts. *gambo*, Ro. *dambu*, To. *dyambu* (sun), pl. *ma*-.

(d) Certain nouns are found in cl. 6 (i.e. in the plural) only; e.g. *mati* (water), *mafura* (fat), Ts. *malanga* (understanding).

In the concords used with cl. 5 there is considerable variation between the dialects.

Table of Concords for classes 5 and 6

		(Adj.)	(Rel.)	(Enum.)	(Poss.)	(Subj.)	(Obj.)
5.	Ro.	le'ḍi-	le'ḍi-	ḍi-	ḍa-	ḍi-	ḍi-
	To.	le'ri-	ri-	ri-	ra-	ri-	ri-
	Ts.	gi-	gi-	gi-	ga-	gi-	gi-
6.		la'ma-, Ts. ma-	ma-, Ro. la'ma-	ma-, wa-	ya-	ma-	ma-, a-, ya-

[Jonga dialect features *ri*- and Bila dialect *li*- in cl. 5.]

CLASSES 7 AND 8 (miscellaneous, concrete, instrument, personal agent, language, and characteristics). Cl. 7 prefix is *ši*- (written *xi*- in Ts.), and the prefix of cl. 8 is *ši*- in Ro. and To., and *ẑi*- in Ts.

šilo, Ts. *xilo* (thing), pl. *šilo*, Ts. *ẑilo*.
Ts. *xivimbo* (cork) < *vimba* (stop up).
To. *šihlamariso* (miracle) < *hlamarisa* (astonish).
Ts. *xifambi* (traveller) < *famba* (travel).
šiRonga (Ronga language).
xiTswa (Tswa language).

Table of Concords for classes 7 and 8

		(Adj.)	(Rel.)	(Enum.)	(Poss.)	(Subj.)	(Obj.)
7.	Ro. To.	le'ši-	ši-, Ro. le'ši-	ši-	ša-	ši-	ši-
	Ts.	xi-	xi-	xi-	xa-	xi-	xi-
8.	Ro. To.	le'ši-	ši-, Ro. le'ši-	ši-	ša-	ši-	ši-
	Ts.	ẑi-	ẑi-	ẑi-	ẑa-	ẑi-	ẑi-

CLASSES 9 AND 10 (miscellaneous, animals). Words in these classes have the initial subject to nasal influence, while monosyllabic stems assume the prefix *yi*- in addition. The plurals, in cl. 10, superimpose the prefix *ti*-

yingwe (leopard), *tiyingwe*.
yindlu (hut), *tiyindlu*.
ndlebe (ear), *tindlebe*.
nhloko (Ts. *hloko*, head), *tinhloko* (Ts. *tihloko*).
nduna (officer), *tinduna*.
mbyana (dog), *timbyana*.

Rules of formation

(i) The homorganic nasal is prefixed to all consonants in Ro. and To., but in Ts. it is omitted before unvoiced fricatives and *v*, and sometimes before other consonants.

Ts. *sinya* (tree), *tisinya*.
Ts. *yivu* (sheep), *tiyivu*.

(ii) Original *p*, *t*, and *k* become *mh*, *nh*, and *h* respectively:

p > *mh*: *mhisi* (hyena), *mhongo* (he-goat).
t > *nh*: *nhamu* (neck), *nhonga* (walking-stick).
k > *h*: *homu* (ox), *huku* (fowl).

(iii) *v̆* > *mb*, e.g. *mboni* (witness) < *v̆ona* (see).
l > *ṇḍ*, e.g. *ṇḍuv̆o* (tax), cf. *luv̆isa* (tax).

But *l* > *nz* in Ts., e.g. *nzowolo* ('lobolo') < *lowola* (pass over cattle at marriage).

(iv) Vowel-stems assume *ny-* or *ṅ-*, e.g.

nyoka (snake), *ṅanga* (doctor).

Table of Concords for classes 9 and 10

	(Adj.)	(Rel.)	(Enum.)	(Poss.)	(Subj.)	(Obj.)
9	*le'yi-*, Ts. *yi-*	*yi-*, Ro. *le'yi-*	*yi-*	*ya-*	*yi-*	*yi-*
10	*le'ti-*, Ts. *ti-*	*ti-*, Ro. *le-ti-*	*ti-*	*ta-*	*ti-*	*ti-*

CLASS 11 (miscellaneous, long objects, abstracts of verbal origin). The singular prefix is *li-* (*ri-* in To.) and the plural is in cl. 10 with prefix *ti[N]-*, but in Ts. the nasal influence in the plural is omitted.

Ro. *lišaka*, Ts. *lixaka* (tribe), pl. Ro. *tinšaka*, Ts. *tixaka*.
To. *rifa*, Ts. *lifa* (crack), pl. To. *timfa*, Ts. *tifa*.
lipapa (wing), pl. *timpapa* (Ts. *tipapa*).
Ro. *likambu* (branch), pl. *tinkambu* or *tihambu*.
To. *riv̆ala*, Ts. *libala* (plain), pl. To. *timbala*, Ts. *tibala*.

Ts. has the one word *lufu* (death) in cl. 11 with prefix *lu-* of original Bantu; in To. the equivalent is *rifu* (cl. 5) with plural *mafu*.

Certain words in cl. 11 take no plural, e.g. To. *rifumu* (riches), *rifambo* (wandering), *rihati* (lightning), *riraṇḍu* (love) Ts. *liranzo*.

Table of Concords for class 11

		(Adj.)	(Rel.)	(Enum.)	(Poss.)	(Subj.)	(Obj.)
11.	Ro.	*lo'li-* or *le-ḍi-*	*lo'li-* or *le-ḍi-*	*li-*, *ḍi-*	*la-*, *ḍa-*	*li-*, *ḍi-*	*li-*, *ḍi-*
	To.	*le'ri-*	*le'ri-*	*ri-*	*ra-*	*ri-*	*ri-*
	Ts.	*li-*	*li-*	*li-*	*la-*	*li-*	*li-*

CLASS 14 (mainly abstract, but with certain nouns indicating collectivity or liquids, and traces of concrete nouns). The prefix appears as To. *v̆u-*, Ro. *bu-*, Ts. *wu-*; certain non-abstract nouns have plurals in cl. 6 with prefix *ma-*.

(i) Abstract nouns:

Ts. *wukulu*, To. *v̆ukulu* (greatness).
Ts. *wuhosi*, Ro. *buhosi* (chieftainship).
Ts. *wuxinji* (mercy).
To. *v̆urena* (bravery).

(ii) Collectives, liquids:

Ts. *wusokoti* (small ants); Ts. *wulombe*, To. *v̆ulombe*, Ro. *bulombe* (honey);
Ts. *wuluba* (cotton); To. *v̆usura* (palm wine); To. *v̆usiku*, Ts. *wusiku* (night).

Ro. *bongwe* (brain), pl. *mabongwe*.
Ro. *bulongo* (manure), pl. *malongo*.

(iii) Indicating place or country:

Buronga (Ronga country).
Ro. *buša* (the east).
Ts. *wutsamo* (place), pl. *matsamo*.
Ro. *Buthwa* (Zululand).

(iv) When the stem of the noun commences in a vowel, the prefix *ŭu-* becomes *by-*, e.g.

byanyi (grass, st. *-anyi*), pl. *mabyanyi*.
byato (boat, st. *-ato*), pl. *mabyato*.
byala (beer, st. *-ala*), pl. *mabyala*.
To. *byako* (dwelling-house < v. *aka*, build) pl. *mabyako*.

Table of Concords for class 14

		(Adj.)	(Rel.)	(Enum.)	(Poss.)	(Subj.)	(Obj.)
14	Ro. To. .	*le'byi-*	*le'byi-*	*byi-*	*bya-*	*byi-*	*byi-*
	Ts. .	*wu-*	*gi-*	*gi-*	*ga-*	*gi-*	*gi-*

CLASS 15 (verb-infinitive):

ku-suka (departure), *ku-lwa* (fighting), *ku-fa* (death).

Negative forms are also used, e.g. Ts. *ku-nga-tibi* (ignorance).

Table of Concords for class 15

		(Adj.)	(Rel.)	(Enum.)	(Poss.)	(Subj.)	(Obj.)
15	.	*lo'ku-, ku-*	*lo'ku-, ku-*	*ku-*	*ka-*	*ku-*	*ku-*

Ex. *ku-hela ka-ku-lwa ka-V̌angoni* (the end of the fighting of the Zulus).

CLASSES 16, 17, AND 18 (prefixes: *ha-*, *ku-*, and *mu-*) are no longer living noun classes in Tsonga, but reveal themselves in certain adverbs of place, e.g.

ha-: *laha* (here); *hansi*, Ts. *lahasi* (below);
henhla, Ts. *hehla* (above); *handle*, Ts. *lahandle* (outside).
ku-: *kule* (far away); *kusuhi*, Ts. *kusuhani* (near).
mu-: *lomu* (in here).

Suffixes in Noun Formation

I. DIMINUTIVES are formed by suffixing *-ana* or *-nyana*, the former taking the place of the final vowel, the latter being added to the final vowel. Extra diminution is achieved by reduplicating the suffix *-ana*, which becomes *-anyana*.

mhisi (hyena) > *mhisana* (*mhisanyana*), *mhisinyana*.

When employing the suffix *-ana* (or *-anyana*) the following must be observed:

(i) With final vowel *-o* or *-u*, *-wana* is used:[1]

tiko (country) > *tikwana*.
mulungu (white man) > *mulungwana*.

(ii) Certain consonants in the final syllable of the noun cause either velarization or palatalization to occur as follows:

m (followed by *o* or *u*) > *ṅw*: *homu* (ox) > *hoṅwana*.

b and *w* (followed by *o* or *u*) > *by*: *rumbu* (stomach) > *rumbyana*; *vuwu* (hippopotamus) > *vubyana*.

r and *l* (when not followed by *o* or *u*) > *g*: *mafura* (fat) > *mafugana*; *ndlela* (path) > *ndlegana*.

n (when not followed by *o* or *u*) > *ny*: *mufana* (boy) > *mufanyana*.

[1] Examples are taken from Ts., where the rules seem to be most fully observed.

II. FEMININES of a few nouns indicating living beings are formed by suffixing *-ati* or *-kati*, but these are not regular today. Note in Ro. *tatana* (father) and *ṛaṛakati* (father's sister) < obs. *ṛaṛa*; *ndlopfu* (elephant) and *hulukati* (female elephant).

(2) THE PRONOUN

(*a*) TABLE OF ABSOLUTE PRONOUNS

			(To.)	(Ro.)	(Ts.)
1st pers.	s.	.	mina	mine	mina
	pl.	.	hina	hine	hina
2nd pers.	s.	.	wena	wene	wena
	pl.	.	ṅwina	ṅwine	ṅwina
3rd pers.	cl.	1.	yena	yene	yena
		2.	ʋona	bone	bona
		3.	wona	wone	wona
		4.	yona	yone	yona
		5.	rona	ḍone	gona
		6.	wona	wone	wona
		7.	šona	šone	xona
		8.	žona	žone	žona
		9.	yona	yone	yona
		10.	tona	tone	tona
		11.	rona	lone, ḍone	lona
		14.	byona	byone	gona
		15.	kona	kone	kona

As in Nguni, these pronouns have typical ultimate *-na* (*-ne* in Ro.); in Ro. and To., in quick speech, the ultimate syllable may be elided when the pronoun is inflected, e.g. Ro. *hi-mine* or *hi-mi* (it is I); *ka-we* or *ka-wene* (to you); in Ts., however, the use of the full form is practically universal, e.g. *hi-tona* (by them), *na-žona* (with them).

(*b*) DEMONSTRATIVE PRONOUNS

Three positions of demonstratives are used in Tsonga, and there are in addition certain modifications for time distance and emphasis. The 1st position (this) has the typical vowel of the class prefix, the 2nd position (that) has final *-o*, and the 3rd position (yonder) has final stressed *-ya*; each demonstrative has a prefixal *la-*, as is typical in Nguni, coalescing with the prefix vowel. The 'time distance' form, indicating 'long ago', is formed by suffixing to the 3rd demonstrative *-ni* (in Ts.), *-n* (in Ro.), and *-ne* or *-n* (in To.).

Demonstratives may be used instead of the nouns, or in apposition before or after them, in the former of which cases one word group results, e.g. Ts. *leti*, *leti-tihomu* or *tihomu leti* (these cattle).

The following table represents the forms in Tswa, with alternatives in the other dialects noted:

(Class)	(1st position)	(2nd position)	(3rd position)
1	loyi[1]	loye[2]	gaya[3]
2	laba	labo	labaya
3	lowu	lowo	lowuya
4	leyi	leyo	leyiya
5	legi[4]	lego	legiya
6	lawa	lawo	lawaya
7	lexi[5]	lexo	lexiya
8	leži[6]	levo	leživa

9	*leyi*	*leyo*	*leyiya*
10	*leti*	*leto*	*letiya*
11	*leli*⁷	*lelo*	*leliya*
14	*legi*⁸	*lego*	*legiya*
15	*loku*	*loko*	*lokuya*

Notes: (1) Ro. *lweyi*. (2) Ro. *lweyo*. (3) Ro. *lwaya*; To. *luya* (or *riya*, *ḍiya*). (4) Instead of *g*, Ro. has *ḍ* throughout, and To. *r*. (5) Ro. and To. *š* for *x* throughout. (6) Ro. and To. *ś* for *ź* throughout. (7) Instead of *l*, Ro. has *ḍ* throughout, and To. *r*. (8) Ro. and To. *by* for *g* throughout.

A modification of the 3rd position form indicates something pertaining to long ago, e.g. Ts. *mahungu lawayani* (those matters of long ago); *gayani*, *leliyani*, &c. To. *lav̌ayane*, *leyiyane*, *lebyiyan*, &c. Ro. *labayan*, *lowuyan*, &c.

Emphatic demonstratives, indicating 'the same', 'the very', are formed in Ts. from the 1st and 2nd position forms by prefixing a type of possessive prefix, e.g. *yaloyi* (or *ywaloyi*), *balaba*, *xalexi* (or *xwalexi*), *taleto* (or *twaleto*). In To. and Ro. these appear as *toleti*, *yoloyi*, *yoloye*, &c., and are extended to the 3rd position, e.g. *toletiya*, *yoluyan*, *kolokuyan*, &c.

(*c*) Quantitative Pronouns

These occur in Ts., but not in Ro. or To. There are two stems: *-nkle* (the whole, all) and *-ce* (only), the latter occurring in Jonga as *-še*. The quantitative concord generally has typical *-o-*, e.g. cl. 2. *boce*, *bonkle*; cl. 7. *xoce*, *xonkle*; 1st pers. s. is *nzoce* (I alone); for 2nd pers. s. and pl. and cl. 1, the vowel is *-e-*, e.g. *wece*, *nwece*, *yece* (Jo. *yeše*).

In place of the quantitative stem *-nkle*, Ro. and To. use an obsolete noun **hiku* with possessive suffixes, e.g. *hikwenu* (all of us), *hikwav̌o* (all of them); this is used appositionally to the noun, e.g. *šikomu hikwašu* (all the pickaxes).

(*d*) Qualificative Pronouns

In Tsonga there is no formal change in qualificatives when they are used pronominally.

(3) THE QUALIFICATIVE

(*a*) The Adjective

In Tsonga there are very few true adjectives indeed; Ro. seems to use eight, To. seven, and Ts. only four. The following is the list:

To. Ro. and Ts.	*-nene* (good)
To and Ro.	*-kulu* and *-khulukumba* (big)
	-ṭongo (small)
	-ntŝha (new); enumerative in Ts.
	-tomi (healthy)
	-v̌isi (raw); *-mbisi* in To. and Ts.
To.	*-ṭanana* (small)
Ro.	*-mhanti* (green, not dry)
	-fani (bad)
Ts.	*-nyingi* (many); enumerative in To. and Ro.
	-tsongwani (small, few).

Two sets of concords are used: To. and Ro. use the 1st demonstrative before the adjective which assumes the noun-prefix,¹ a contraction generally occurring; thus in cl. 4 *leyi mi-* > *le'mi*, and so on. While such forms are found in Ts., the usual form is that of noun-prefix only. Following is a table of concords:

¹ This is modified in cls. 3 and 14.

THE TSONGA GROUP

	(To. and Ro.)	(Ts.)
Cl. 1	lo'n-; lwe'mu-	mu-
2	la'ǎa-	ba-
3	lo'wu-	mu-
4	le'mi-	mi-
5	le'ri-; le'ḍi-	gi-
6	la'ma-	ma-
7	le'ši-	xi-
8	le'ŝi-	ŝi-
9	le'yi-	yi-
10	le'ti-	ti-
11	le'ri-; lo'li-, le-ḍi-	li-
14	le'byi-	wu-
15	lo'ku-	ku-

Examples: Ro. *mutiri lwe'munene* (the good workman);
   byala le'byintŝha (new beer).
To. *muri lo'wukulu* (a big tree);
   munhu lo'nkulu (a big person).
Ts. *hosi yinene* (a good chief);
   tiyivu titsongwani (few sheep).

In Ts. the equivalents of the other Tsonga adjectives are used with a possessive construction; some of them are -*hombe* (large), -*tsi* (nice), -*haba* (false), &c.

Examples: *haxi ga-hombe* (a big horse), *nhanyana wa-tsi* (a beautiful girl).

(*b*) The Relative

There are no primitive relative stems in Tsonga, but relative concords are used in the formation of relative clauses with verbs. The relative construction as a whole will be discussed later, but here it must be observed that a significant relative suffix Ts. -*ko*, To. and Ro. -*ka*, is added to the relative predicate; and while the relative concord corresponds to the subjectival concord, except in cl. 1, almost without exception the 1st demonstrative pronoun is used immediately before it, contractions regularly taking place in Ro. and To. The following is a list of the forms:

Cl. 1. *a-; lw'a-*   2. *ǎa-; la'ǎa-*
3. *wu-; lo-*   4. *yi-; le'mi-*
5. *ri-, gi-; le'ḍi-*   6. *ma-; la'ma-*
7. *ši-, xi-; le'ši-*   8. *ŝi-, ẑi-; le'ŝi-*
9. *yi-; le'yi-*   10. *ti-; le'ti-*
11. *li-; lo'li-, le'ḍi-, le'ri-*   14. *gi-; le'byi-*
15. *ku-; lo'ku-*

Examples:
Ts.   *a-khumba gi-fambako* (the pig which walks).
Ts.   *hosi le'yi-wonako* (the chief who sees).
To. Ro.   *tihomu leti ti-dyaka* (cattle which eat).
Ro.   *mhunu lweyi a-fambaka*, or *lwe a-* or *lw'a-* (the person who walks).

(*c*) The Enumerative

There are several enumerative roots in Tsonga, which includes in this category the first three numerals. Ts. treats the root -*ŝa* (new) among the enumeratives; its equivalent in Ro. and To. is an adjective. To. and Ro. treat -*nyingi* (adjective in Ts.) as an enumerative. The full list is as follows:

To. Ro. and Ts. -ṅwe (one).
-mbiri (two); -ϑiri also in To. and Ro.
-nharu (three); -raru also in To. and Ro.
To. and Ro. -ṅwana, -ṅwanyana (other); Ts. -ṅwani.
-mbe (different).
-ni? or -ini? (what?)
-nyingi (many).
-ngani (To. some; Ro. how many?)
Ts. -ša (new).
-hi? or -ihi? (which?)

The enumerative concords are as follows:

Cl. 1. mu-, u-   2. ϑa-
3. mu-, wu-   4. mi-, yi-
5. ḍi-; ri-; gi-   6. ma-, wa-
7. ši-; xi-   8. ši-; ži-
9. yi-   10. ti-
11. ḍi-; ri-; li-   14. byi-; gi-
15. ku-

Cls. 1, 3, 4, and 6 have strong and weak alternative concords; the weak concords being u-, wu-, yi-, and wa- respectively. The enumeratives -mbe, -ni?, and -hi? take weak concords, the others strong, except -ṅwana and -ṅwanyana which take weak concords in cls. 1 and 3, and may take either in cl. 4.

Examples:
Ts. khumba giṅwe (one pig).
muti muša (a new village).
Ro. makwenu wini? (which brother of yours?)
munhu muṅwe (one person).
To. šibye šiṅwana (another pot).

In Ts., for 'what', an immutable form muni? is used, e.g. mahungu muni? (what is the matter?).

(d) THE POSSESSIVE

Two types of possessive, direct and descriptive, are used in Tsonga, the former with pronominal and nominal base, the latter with nominal and adverbial base.

The possessives with pronominal stem resemble the forms used in Sotho rather than those in Nguni. The possessive concord may be prefixed to unchanged absolute pronouns throughout, but an alternative with possessive pronominal stems is found in the 1st and 2nd pers. and in cls. 1 and 2. The possessive concord in Tsonga is typical of Bantu, being formed with basic -a, e.g. ϑa-, ša-, ša-, &c.

List of Pronominal stems

1st pers. s.	. -nga	-mina	pl.	-iru	-hina
2nd pers. s.	. -ku, Ts. -ko	-wena	pl.	-inu	-ṅwina
3rd pers. cl. 1 .	. -kwe	-yena	2.	To. -ϑo, Ro. -bu, Ts. -bye	-ϑona
3 . .		-wona	4.		-yona
5 . .		-rona, Ts. -gona	6.		-wona

and so on for the other classes, using the absolute pronouns, Ro. forms differing somewhat, e.g. -wone, -ḍone, &c. In Ro. and To. the short forms are quite commonly found; in Ts., however, this is the case for cls. 1 and 2, but in the 1st pers. -nga is only used in endearment,

and all the forms for 1st and 2nd pers. are found enclitically with relationship terms. Examples from Tswa:
 dada wanga! (oh daddy!)
 makweru (my, our sister).
 ntiro wa-mina (my work).
 yindlu yabye (their house).
 a-ximanga ni-masi ya-xona (the cat and its milk).

Direct possessive with noun-stem:
 Ts. *ṅwanana wa-dadani* (my father's child).
  ndlwini ya-hosi (to the chief's house).
 To. *ʋurena bya-nyimpi* (the bravery of the army).
  śikomo śa-ʋasati (the hoes of the women).

Examples of the use of the descriptive possessive in Tsonga:
(a) With noun base:
 To. *ribye ra-ku-sila* (a stone for grinding).
  ku-hela ka-ku-lwa (the end of the fighting).
 Ts. *tindlu ta-maribye* (stone houses).
  banhu ba-ntamo (strong people).
  nyama ya-mhuti (duiker meat).
  xibya xa-xiketse (an iron dish).

Forms with the infinitive, cl. 15 base are very common in Tsonga, e.g. in Ts.:
 hosi ya-kululama (a righteous chief).
 tiyivu ta-kuseseka (good sheep).

In rapid speech, contractions with the infinitive take place:
 haxi go-pśuka (a red horse < *ga-ku-pśuka*).
 xibya xo-eta (a deep dish).
 śilo śo-biha (evil things).

(b) With probable adjectival base, in Ts.:
 haxi ga-hombe (a big horse).
 munhu wa-ntima (a black man).
 phongolo wa-panga (an empty barrel).

(c) With adverbial base; examples in Ts.:
 śihari źa-kale (old animals).
 banhu ba-lomo congweni (river people).
 hosi ya-ka-Yingwani (a Yingwani chief).

Table of Qualificative Concords

	(Adjectival)		(Relative)		(Enumerative)		(Possessive)
	(To.)	(Ts.)	(Ro.)	(Ts.)	(Strong)	(Weak)	
1st pers. s.	—	—	lweyi nḍi-	nzi-	—	—	—
pl.	—	—	lweyi u-	hi-	—	—	—
2nd pers. s.	—	—	laba hi- la'hi-	u-	—	—	—
pl.	—	—	laba mi- la'mi- ṅwi mi-	mu-	—	—	—
3rd pers. cl. 1	lo'n-	mu-	lw'a-	a-	mu-	u-	wa-
2	la'ʋa-	ba-	la'ʋa-	ba-	ʋa-		ʋa-
3	lo'wu-	mu-	lo-	wu-	mu-	wu-	wa-
4	le'mi-	mi-	le'mi-	yi-	mi-	yi-	ya-
5	le'ri-	gi-	le'ḍi-	gi-	ḍi-, ri-, gi-		ḍa-, ṛa-, ga-
6	la'ma-	ma-	la'ma-	ma-	ma-	wa-	ya-

	(Adjectival)		(Relative)		(Enumerative)		(Possessive)
	(To.)	(Ts.)	(Ro.)	(Ts.)	(Strong)	(Weak)	
7.	le'ši-	xi-	le'ši-	xi-	ši-, xi-		ša-, xa-
8.	le'ŝi-	ŝi-	le'ŝi-	ŝi-	ŝi-, ŝi-		ŝa-, ŝa-
9.	le'yi-	yi-	le'yi-	yi-		yi-	ya-
10.	le'ti-	ti-	le'ti-	ti-	ti-		ta-
11.	le'ri-	li-	le'ḍi-	li-	ḍi-, ri-, li-		ḍa-, ra-, la-
14.	le'byi-	wu-	le'byi-	gi-	byi-, gi-		bya-, ga-
15.	lo'ku-	ku-	lo'ku-	ku-	ku-		ka-

(4) THE VERB

(i) THE VARIETIES OF THE VERB IN TSONGA

There are the four varieties found in Bantu:

(a) The Regular disyllabic verb-stem, commencing in a consonant and ending in the vowel -a, e.g. *luka* (weave), *v̌ona* (see).

(b) The Monosyllabic verb-stem, e.g. *pfa* (come out), *ha* (give).

(c) The Vowel verb-stem, e.g. *oma* (dry), *aka* (build).

(d) Derived verb-stems: (1) Verbal derivatives, e.g. *tirela* (applied), *tirisa* (causative), &c.; (2) Deideophonic verbs, e.g. Ts. *kwezima* (sparkle) < *kwéze-kwéze*, *cikela* (arrive) < *cīke*; (3) Denominative verbs, e.g. *loloha* (be lazy) < *lolo* (lazy person).

VERBAL DERIVATIVES. In Tsonga the following are used regularly: Passive, Applied, Neuter, Causative, Intensive, Reciprocal, Diminutive, and, to a less regular extent, the Reversive.

THE PASSIVE is formed, as a general rule, by substituting the suffix *-iwa* for the final vowel of the simple stem, e.g. *v̌ona* (see) > *v̌oniwa* (be seen); *dya* (eat) > *dyiwa*, Ts. *ga* > *giwa*; *kuma* (find) > *kumiwa* (be found).

In Ts. verbs ending in *-ba* > *-byiwa* in the passive, e.g. *laba* (seek) > *labyiwa*.

In Ro. a rarer alternative suffix is *-wa*, e.g. *pfuna* (help) > *pfuniwa* or *pfunwa*. This leads to changes of velarization or palatalization (as in locative formation); *-ma* > *-ṅwa* and *-ba* > *-bywa*, e.g. *kuma* (find) > *kumiwa* or *kuṅwa*. This shorter suffix occurs in Ts. with the passives of derivative forms, e.g. *wonela* (look out for) > *wonelwa*.

THE APPLIED is formed by the suffix *-ela*, and has in Tsonga the typical Bantu significances:
 tira (work) > *tirela* (work for).
 Ts. *vuka* (rise) > *vukela* (rise against).
 dyoha (sin) > *dyohela* (sin against).
 haha (fly) > *hahela* (fly towards).

THE NEUTER is formed by the suffix *-eka*, e.g. Ts. *ranza* (love) > *ranzeka* (be lovable); *tira* (work) > *tireka* (get done; be workable); *kuma* (find) > *kumeka* (occur).

In To. and Ts. a few words form the neuter with suffix *-akala*, e.g.
 v̌ona (see) > *v̌onakala* (be visible), Ro. *v̌oneka*.
 To. *twa*, Ts. *zwa* (hear) > *twakala*, *zwakala* (be audible).

This suffix does not occur in Ro.

THE CAUSATIVE is formed, as a general rule, by suffixing *-isa*, e.g.
 v̌ona (see) > *v̌onisa* (show).
 Ts. *ga* (eat) > *gisa* (feed).
 Ts. *klela* (return) > *klelisa* (send back).
 tiv̌a (know) > *tiv̌isa* (inform).

Verbs ending in *-ana* change *-ana* to *-anyisa*, e.g.
 Ts. *komana* (be short) > *komanyisa* (shorten).

Many verbs ending in *-ka* and *-la* change that ending to *-ša* and *-ta* respectively:
>longoloka* (follow in line) > *longološa* (arrange in line).
rivala (forget) > *rivata* (cause to forget).

Ts. has certain irregular forms, e.g. *-ama* > *-ameta* as in *lulama* (be straight) > *lulameta* (straighten); and forms reminiscent of Nguni, e.g. *ambala* (dress oneself) > *ambexa* (dress another), *rwala* (carry a load) > *rwexa* (help a load up).

The causative, in addition to the basic notion of 'cause to do', also indicates 'help to do', and (as in Nguni) 'to do like', e.g. To. *Va-akisa ši-šošo* (They build in that way); Ts. *Ba-holobisa ku-kwa-timbyana* (They fight like dogs).

THE INTENSIVE is formed generally by the suffix *-isisa*, though some verbs take *-isa*, particularly (in Ts.) causatives ending in *-ta*.

(a) *komba* (show) > *kombisisa* (show clearly).
vona (see) > *vonisisa* (see clearly).
pima (measure) > *pimisisa* (measure exactly).

(b) To. *vula* (say) > *vurisa*[1] (say well).
Ts. *mbheta* (finish) > *mbhetisa* (destroy utterly).

Further types of intensive are formed by a reduplication of the applied suffix, as *-elela*, *-etela*, e.g.
rola (pick up) > *rolelela* (pick up extensively).
faya (break) > *fayetela* (smash up).

THE RECIPROCAL is formed by suffixing *-ana*, e.g. *vonana* (see one another); *dlayana* (kill each other). Monosyllabic stems suffix *-anana*, e.g.
ba (beat) > *banana* (beat each other).
Ts. *zwa* (hear) > *zwanana* (hear each other).

THE REVERSIVE is not a living derivative formation today in Tsonga; few simple stems exist alongside the reversives. Note the following with suffix *-ula*:
pakela (load), *pakula* (unload).
kuleka (tie), *kulula* (untie).
landa (follow), *landula* (come back; deny).

THE DIMINUTIVE of the verb is expressed by a reduplication of the stem or of the first two syllables of the stem, e.g.
famba (walk) > *famba-famba* (stroll).
khomana (catch one another) > *khoma-khomana* (play at catches).

To. and Ro., however, have a diminutive form of the verb with the diminutive suffix *-anyana*, e.g.
tala (be abundant) > *talanyana* (be fairly numerous).
leši hi-fambanyaniki tolo (since we travelled somewhat yesterday).

An extreme diminutive is formed by a combination of both methods, e.g. *va-tira-tiranyana* (they pottered about a bit).

(ii) THE CONJUGATION OF THE VERB IN TSONGA

There are two conjugations of the verb in Tsonga: Positive and Negative.

Apart from the infinitive and imperative forms there are four finite moods in Tsonga, viz. Indicative, Subjunctive, Potential, and Participial.

THE INFINITIVE is formed with the prefix *ku-* and occurs in both positive and negative conjugations:

---

[1] Note change of *l* > *r* due to following vowel *-i*; similarly in the passive *vula* > *vuriwa*.

	(Positive)	(Negative)
	ku-famba (to walk)	*ku-nga-fambi* (not to walk)
	ku-v̌ona (to see)	*ku-nga-v̌oni* (not to see)

e.g. Ts. *Kuyimbelela ka-wena ku-sasekile* (Your singing is good). The infinitive is also used:
(a) (emphatically): Ts. *A-ku-wona nza-wona* (I certainly see).
(b) (consecutively): Ts. *A-banana ba-lo-hlakana ni-ku-hleka* ('The children played and laughed).

THE IMPERATIVE. The plain stem of the verb constitutes the imperative singular of verbs of more than one syllable, the plural being formed by suffixing *-an*[1] (To. and Ro.) or *-ani* (Ts.):

Ts. *engena* (enter!), pl. *engenani*.
maha lexi (do this!), pl. *mahani lexi*.
To. and Ro. *v̌ona* (see!), pl. *v̌onan* (see ye!).

Monosyllabic verbs suffix 'ultimate *-na*', e.g.
nwana (drink! < *nwa*), pl. *nwanan, nwanani*.
Ts. *gana* (eat! < *ga*), pl. *ganani*.

When an objectival concord is used with an imperative, final *-a* and *-ani* (*-an*) are changed to *-e* and *-eni* (*-en*) respectively, e.g.
Ts. *mu-tsike* (leave him!), pl. *mu-tsikeni*.
To. *hi-hakele* (pay us!), pl. *hi-hakelen*.

In Ro. this change is confined to the singular, e.g.
tibone (take care!), pl. *tibonan*, where *ti-* is objectival reflexive prefix.

There is no true negative of the imperative in Tsonga, recourse being had to the negative of the subjunctive to fill this need, e.g. Ts. *u-nga-woni*, Ro. *u-nga-bone* (do not see!).

THE INDICATIVE MOOD. There are only traces of the three implications of the indicative mood, Simple, Progressive, and Exclusive in Tsonga, a positive and negative progressive and a negative exclusive being found in addition to the simple forms.

The progressive is indicated by infix *-ha-*, the exclusive by the deficient verb *-se*. Examples:

Progressive (positive):
Ro. *Nḓa-ha-v̌ona* (I still see).
Ts. *Wa-ha-caba ku-fa* (He still fears death).

Progressive (negative):
Ro. *A-nḓa-ha-v̌oni* (I no longer see).

Exclusive (negative):
Ts. *A-nga-se ku-wuya*; To. *A-nga-si-v̌uya* (He has not yet come back).

Distinctions of aspect, definite and indefinite, the perfect, and what Junod terms 'the descriptive' are of regular occurrence in Tsonga.

Paradigm of the Basic Tenses of the Indicative Mood, Positive

	(Ro. and To.)	(Ts.)
Rem. Past	*nḓa-v̌onile* (I saw)	—
Imm. Past	*nḓi-v̌onile* (I have seen)	*nzi-wonile*
Perfect	*nḓi-tḥamile* (I am seated)	*nzi-tsamile*
Present (indef.)	*nḓi-v̌ona* (I see)	*nzi-wona*
Present (def. and contin.)	*nḓa-v̌ona* (I am seeing)	*nza-wona*
Future	*nḓi-ta-v̌ona* (I shall see)	*nzi-ta-wona*
Future (emphatic)	*nḓa-ta-v̌ona* (I shall see)	—

[1] With syllabic *n*.

Ro. has additional tenses, past, present, and future, which Junod labels 'descriptif', viz. *nḍe-ku-bona*, *nḍo-bona* (contracted from *nḍi-ku-bona*), and *nḍi-ta-ku-bona*; in which the infix *-ku-* is used. The immediate past tense is used of an action which has happened on the day of speaking, the remote of actions before that. The present perfect is the same in form as the immediate past, but is used with stative verbs. The two present tenses differ in function, as do their equivalents in Nguni.[1] It is usual, especially when the verb is not final in a sentence, to contract the perfect stem, thus *nḍi-v̌oni* for *nḍi-v̌onile*.

Paradigm of the Basic Tenses of the Indicative Mood, Negative

	(Ro. and To.)	(Ts.)
Rem. Past	⎱ *a-nḍi-v̌onanga(e)*	⎰ *(nzi-lo-kala ku-wona)*
Imm. Past	⎰	⎱ *a-nzi-wonangi*
Perfect	*a-nḍi-thamanga(e)*	*a-nzi-tsamangi*
Present	*a-nḍi-v̌oni*	*a-nzi-woni*
Future	⎰ *nḍi-nga-ka nḍi-nga-v̌oni* ⎱ *a-nḍi-nga-v̌one(i)*	*nzi-nga-ta-wona*

Certain more complicated tenses are formed in Ro. and To. by means of the conjunctive *a* (Ro. *afa*) followed by the participial mood, e.g.

(a) Past Continuous: *a nḍi-v̌ona* (I was seeing); neg. *a nḍi-nga-v̌oni*.
(b) Pluperfect: *a nḍi-v̌onile* (I had seen); neg. *a nḍi-nga-v̌onange*.
(c) Contingent: *a nḍi-ta-v̌ona* (I would see); neg. *a nḍi-nga-ti-v̌ona*.

The equivalent tenses in Ts. are strikingly different:

(a) *nzi-wa-wona*; neg. *nzi-wa-nga-woni*.
(b) *nzi-wa-wonile*; neg. *nzi-wa-nga-wonangi*.
(c) *nzi-wa-ta-wona*; neg. *nga-nzi-nga-wonangi*.

A commonly used compound tense, employing the deficient verb *-v̌a* followed by the participial mood, and labelled by Junod and Persson as 'future perfect' is as follows:

To. *nḍi-ta-v̌a nḍi-v̌onile* (I shall have seen); neg. *nḍi-nga-ka nḍi-nga-v̌i nḍi-v̌onile*.
Ts. *nzi-ta-ba nzi-wonile*; neg. *nzi-nga-ta-ba nzi-wonile*.

		Subj. concords. (Indic.)				Obj. concords	Pres. Indic. positive	Pres. Indic. negative
		Simple	+-*a*-	+-*ku*-	Neg.			
1st pers.	s.	*nḍi-*	*nḍa-*	*nḍo-*	*nḍi-*	*nḍi-*	*nḍi-bona*	*a-nḍi-boni*
	pl.	*hi-*	*ha-*	*ho-*	*hi-*	*hi-*	*hi-bona*	*a-hi-boni*
2nd pers.	s.	*u-*	*wa-*	*wo-*	*u-*, *ku-*	*ku-*	*u-bona*	*a-u-boni*
	pl.	*mi-*, *ṅwi-*	*ma-*, *ṅwa-*	*mo-*, *ṅwo-*	*mi-*, *ṅwi-*	*mi-*, *ṅwi-*	*mi-bona*	*a-mi-boni*
3rd pers. cl.	1	*a-*[2]	*a-*, *wa-*, *awa-*, *iwa-*	*o-*	*nga-*, *ka-*	*mu-*	*a-bona*	*a-nga-boni*
	2	*ba-*	*ba-*	*bo-*	*ba-*	*ba-*	*ba-bona*	*a-ba-boni*
	3	*u-*, *wu-*	*wa-*	*wo-*	*wu-*	*wu-*	*u-bona*	*a-wu-boni*
	4	*mi-*	*ma-*	*mo-*	*mi-*	*yi-*, *mi-*	*mi-bona*	*a-mi-boni*
	5	*ḍi-*	*ḍa-*	*ḍo-*	*ḍi-*	*ḍi-*	*ḍi-bona*	*a-ḍi-boni*
	6	*ma-*	*ma-*	*mo-*	*ma-*	*ma-*	*ma-bona*	*a-ma-boni*
	7	*ši-*	*ša-*	*šo-*	*ši-*	*ši-*	*ši-bona*	*a-ši-boni*
	8	*ši-*	*ša-*	*šo-*	*ši-*	*ši-*	*ši-bona*	*a-ši-boni*
	9	*i-*, *yi-*	*ya-*	*yo-*	*yi-*	*yi-*	*i-bona*	*a-yi-boni*
	10	*ti-*	*ta-*	*to-*	*ti-*	*ti-*	*ti-bona*	*a-ti-boni*
	11	*li-*, *ḍi-*	*la-*, *ḍa-*	*lo-*, *ḍo-*	*li- ḍi-*	*li-*, *ḍi-*	*li-bona*	*a-li-boni*
	14	*byi-*	*bya-*	*byo-*	*byi-*	*byi-*	*byi-bona*	*a-byi-boni*
	15	*ku-*	*ka-*	*ko-*	*ku-*	*ku-*	*ku-bona*	*a-ku-boni*

[1] Cf. Chapter V, p. 107.
[2] In Ts. concord is *i-*; in To. it is *u-* or *a-*, *u-* here having a higher tone than that of the 2nd pers. s.

The above lists show, for Ro.: (*a*) the subjectival concord used (i) in its simple form, (ii) compounded with auxiliary -*a*-, (iii) contracted with auxil. -*ku*-, (iv) in the negative conjugation; (*b*) the objectival concord; (*c*) the indefinite present tense in full; and (*d*) the present negative tense in full.

THE SUBJUNCTIVE MOOD. This is not so clearly formed in Tsonga as in most Bantu languages. In Jonga dialect it seems to be regular, e.g. *nḓi-fambe* (that I travel) in the positive. In Ro. this is only found in the hortative form with the prefix *a*-, e.g. *a-nḓi-fambe* (let me travel). There is, however, a regular negative in Ro., e.g. *nḓi-nga-fambe* (that I do not travel), as well as the hortative, *a-nḓi-nga-fambe*. Ts. has the negative subjunctive (used imperatively in the 2nd pers.), e.g. *u-nga-susi* (don't remove), *nzi-nga-fambi* (that I do not travel).

Ts. has the following positive tense, used in consecutive construction:

1st pers. s.	*nzi-famba*	pl.	*hi-famba*
2nd pers. s.	*u-famba*	pl.	*mu-famba*
3rd pers. cl. 1	*a-famba*	2	*ba-famba*

It is noteworthy that the concord for cl. 1 is *a*-, not *i*-, which suggests either participial or subjunctive for this tense. The fact that it accompanies past as well as future tenses leans towards participial function; against this, however, is the fact of its use in Ro. paralleled with a true subjunctive in Jonga. The -*a* ending seems to be taking the place of the -*e* ending in Tsonga. Note the following examples:

Ts. *I-lo-teka kopo, a-yi-daya* (He took the cup and broke it).

U-ta-mu-wona lomo, u-mu-tibisa hi-mhaka leyi (You will see him there and tell him about this matter).

Compare the following subjunctive use in Ro.:

Nḓi-kombela u-nḓi-fambisa, u-nḓi-twela busiwana (I beg that you conduct me and have pity on me;)

which appears in Jonga as:

Nḓi-kombela u-nḓi-fambise, u-nḓi-twele busiwana.

Ro. and To. differentiate between a dual implication and a plural in the subjunctive, e.g.

a-hi-fambe (let us go, we two—dual).

a-hi-famben (let us go, we many—plural).

THE POTENTIAL MOOD. In Tsonga the potential mood has a present tense positive and negative; each has the characteristic infix -*nga*-, and the negative is made by changing final -*a* of the stem to -*i*. The concord for cl. 1 is *a*- (even in Ts.). Examples:

	(Positive)	(Negative)
Ro.	*nḓi-nga-v̌ona* (I can see)	*nḓi-nga-v̌oni*
Ts.	*a-nga-ranza* (he can love)	*a-nga-ranzi*.

The tense has both potential and conditional signification, with the idea of 'may' as well as of 'can'.

THE PARTICIPIAL MOOD. This mood is used as the basis of relative construction, but it is not necessary to postulate a 'Relative Conjugation' as do the Tsonga grammar writers. Typical of the mood is the use of *a*- as subjectival concord in cl. 1, and, especially when used relatively, the suffixing of -*ka*, -*ko*, or some modification, to the stem or to the auxiliary if verbal, e.g. Ts. *loyi a-ranzako* (he who loves); Ro. *mine nḓi-boniki* (I who have seen); *mine nḓi-taka-bona* (I who will see). The participial mood is used after certain conjunctives, e.g. Ro. *leši* (since), *leši u-nḓi-holobelaka* (since you scold me); Ts. *nga* (past conditional indication), *nga nzi-ranzile* (I might have loved), *nga nzi-nga-ranzangi* (I might not have loved). The participial appears in many compound verb forms, e.g. Ro. *nḓi-nga-ka nḓi-nga-boni* (I will not see).

The following are the usual participial tenses in Ro.

	(Positive)	(Negative)
Remote Past	ndi-nga-bona	
Imm. Past	ndi-bonile (rel.) ndi-boni(ki)	ndi-nga-bonanga(kiki)
Present	ndi-bona(ka)	ndi-nga-boni(kiki)
Future	ndi-ta(ka)-bona	ndi-nga-ti(ki)-bona
Potential	ndi-nga-bona(ka)	ndi-nga-boni(kiki)

(iii) COMPOUND TENSES IN TSONGA

Compound tenses of various types are formed with the aid of a limited number of deficient verbs, which fall into two groups: those which take a participial complement, and those followed by the infinitive.

(a) Deficient verbs followed by the participial:

Ro. and To.   -ko (do at length): v̌a-ko v̌a-fa (until they die).
               -kari (be in process): V̌a-ri-kari v̌a-ta (They are coming).
               -tama (do continually).
               -tlhela (do again).
               -buya (do consequently).
Ts.   -ba: zin-ta-ba nzi-ranzile (I shall have loved).
       -nga: nzi-wa-ta-nga nzi-ranzile (I should have loved).

(b) Deficient verbs followed by the infinitive:

Ts.   -kala (omit to do): Nzi-lo-kala ku-ranza (I did not love).
Ro.   -dyula (be on the point of): A-dyula ku-fa (He is on the point of death).

(5) THE COPULATIVE

(i) THE FORMATION OF COPULATIVES FROM NOUNS AND ADJECTIVES

1st and 2nd pers. use the subjectival concords before the noun-stem or adjective:

ndi-ṅwana (I am a child), Hi-v̌ana (We are children).

In the 3rd pers. the copulative formative i- is used in the positive and a-hi- in the negative:

Miri leyi i-yikulu (These trees are big).
Munhu loyi i-Mungoni (This person is a Zulu).
A-hi-muri lo'wukulu (It is not a big tree).
Munhu loyi a-hi-nkulu (This person is not big).

(ii) FROM PRONOUNS

The prefix i- or hi- is used before absolute and demonstrative pronouns; a-hi- is the negative:

Ndlela hi-leyi (The road is this one).
hi-yena (it is he); a-hi-yena (it is not he).

(iii) FROM ADVERBS

The subjectival concord is prefixed to the adverb in all three persons, and in the indefinite formation the copulative formative hi- is prefixed:

(a) v̌a-kule (they are far away).
     ši-hikwaku (they are everywhere).
(b) hi-lomu ... (it is in here that ...).

In some of the Tsonga dialects the prefix *i-* exerts a nasalizing influence, becoming *N-*, e.g.

    To. *n'tikulu* (they are big).
    Ts. *himani?* (who is it?), but plur. *mbamani?* (who are they?)
    To. *V̌anhu lav̌a m'banene* (These people are good).

The copulative verbs *-li* (*-ri*) and *-v̌a* are used as auxiliaries in the conjugation of copulatives.

The verb *-li* appears in all participial forms, e.g.
    Ro. *loko ba-li bakulu* (if they are big).
          la'ba-nga-liki bakulu (these who are not big—relative).

The verb *-ba* is used in past and future tenses of the indicative, in the imperative, infinitive, subjunctive, potential, &c., e.g. in Ro.
    ku-ba nkulu (to be big).
    bana nkulu (be big).
    nḍi-ta-ba nkulu (I shall be big).
    nḍi-bile nkulu (I was big).
    ŝa-ḍyuleka nḍi-ba nkulu (I ought to be big—subjunctive).

(6) THE ADVERB

Tsonga employs a certain number of adverbs of time, place, and manner, which are largely substantives of one kind or another, or of primitive locative origin. The following examples from Ts. may be noted:

(*a*) Time: *makunu* (now), *ẑaleẑi* (just now), *kale* (long ago), *atolo* (yesterday), *manziko* (tomorrow), *ṅwakani* (next year).

(*b*) Place: Examples from original *ha-*, *ku-*, and *mu-* were given on p. 188; to these may be added *anzako* and *lenzako* (behind a near object, and a far object), *xibaḫa* (on the left), *xinene* (on the right).

(*c*) Manner: *futsi* (truly), *leŝo* (like that), *kwatsi* (nicely), *mahala* (in vain), *nguvu* (very).

Apart from such, in Tsonga, adverbs are formed from other parts of speech by means of various adverbial formatives, mainly prefixal, viz. conjunctive, instrumental, agentive, temporal, and locative.

(i) THE CONJUNCTIVE FORMATIVE

This formative, *na-*, indicates 'together with', and is found before nouns of cl. 1a, pronouns, and in axiomatic negatives; where, however, there is possibility of an initial vowel, in Tsonga *a-* or *e-*[1], substitution of *i* takes place, and *na-* appears as *ni-*[2]; examples from To.

(*a*) *na-tatana* (with my father).
    na-Ritav̌i (with Ritavi).
    famba na-yena (go with him).
    a-nḍi na-mali (I have no money—axiomatic negative).
(*b*) *famba ni-hosi* (go with the chief).
    famba ni-ṅwana (go with a child).

(ii) THE INSTRUMENTAL FORMATIVE

This formative, *ha-*, indicates 'by means of', with a secondary significance of 'concerning', and is found before nouns of cl. 1a, pronouns, and in axiomatic negatives; where, however, there is possibility of an initial vowel, substitution of *i* takes place, and *ha-* appears as *hi-*; examples from Ro.:

[1] See p. 184.
[2] In Tswa the rules with respect to pronouns are somewhat different from those in To. and Ro.

(a) *famba ha-ndlela-yimbe* (go by another road).
ha-manana (because of my mother).
(b) *hi-ndlela* (by road).
hi-nsati (because of a wife).
hi-ku-biha (badly).
hi-ku-nana (slowly).
hi-milenge (by foot, on foot).

There are some exceptional forms, e.g. *ha-čomu* (on purpose), *ha-hombe* (slowly).

(iii) THE AGENTIVE FORMATIVE

This is none other than *hi-*, the copulative formative:
   To. *Makweru u-dlayiwe hi-yingwe* (My brother has been killed by a leopard).
   Ro. *A-ndi-hluliwanga hi-yene* (I was not overcome by him).

(iv) THE TEMPORAL FORMATIVE

The prefix *ka-* is used with qualificative stems, e.g.
   Ts. *kambe* (again), *kanyingi* (often), *kanwe* (once), *kararu* (three times).
   Ro. more commonly uses the prefix *ku-*, e.g.
      kubiri or *kabiri* (twice)
      kungani? or *kangani?* (how many times?)

(v) THE LOCATIVE FORMATION

Apart from the remnants of noun class prefixes 16, 17, and 18 already referred to, locative adverbs are regularly formed from substantives, according to the following rules:

(a) Ordinary nouns, in place of the final vowel, suffix as follows: *-a,'-e* > *-en(i)*; *-i* > *-in(i)*; *-o* > *-wen(i)*; *-u* > *-win(i)*; the final *i* of the locative suffix is often omitted in quick speech, especially in Ro. and To.; the final *n* is then syllabic. Examples from Ro.

   misaba (the earth) > *misaben* (or *misabeni*).
   ntiṛo (work) > *ntiṛwen* (or *ntiṛweni*).
   Ts. *banhu* (people) > *banhwini*.

(b) If the final syllable of the noun contains *m* or *b* (*v̌*) followed by *o* or *u*, phonetic change takes place, *ṅw-* and *by-* resulting, e.g. in Ro.

   nomo (mouth) > *noṅwen*.
   nkhubu (feast) > *nkhubyin*.
   mombo (face) > *mombyen*.

(c) Certain words assume no suffix, e.g. *kaya* (home; at home); *mananga* (desert; in the desert).

(d) Nouns of cl. 1a prefix *ku-* in Ro., e.g. *ku-makweṛu* (to my brother); and for the locative indicating 'the place of' the possessive form *-ka-* is used, e.g. *ka-makweṛu* (to my brother's place), *ka-Tembe* (to Tembe's village). Both To. and Ts. have lost the use of *ku-* and employ *ka-*, even when the locative indicates 'to, from, &c., the person', e.g. Ts. *nziya ka-Mbata* (I go to Mbata).

Pronouns are similarly treated, prefixing *ku-* in Ro., but *ka-* in To. and Ts., e.g.
   Ro. *Tanani ku-mine* (Come unto me).
   To. *Tanani ka-mina*.
   Ts. *Ngonani ka-mina*.

In Ts. the possessive implication in the prefix *ka-* is still felt in that 'to him' is expressed either by *ka-yena* or *kakwe*, using the pronominal possessive stem.

(e) Before certain names of places Ts. prefixes *le-*, which is probably the equivalent of Nguni *e-*, e.g. *famba le-Pembe* (go to Pembe).

(f) Compound locatives are formed with old Bantu prefix forms followed by a concord *ka-* or *na-(ni-)*, e.g. in Ro. *hansi ka-* (beneath); *handle ka-* (outside); *nḍen ka-* (inside); *makaṛi ka-* (between); *kule na-* (far from); *kusuhi na-* (near).

(7) THE IDEOPHONE

In Tsonga the ideophone is used in association with three monosyllabic verbs, *-ku, -li,* and *-ti,* each of which has basically the significance of 'say' in addition to this ideophonic significance of 'demonstrate'. According to Bishop,[1] the verb *-ku* is by far the most frequently used, *-li* and *-ti* being confined to certain types of monosyllabic ideophones. The verb *-li* is connected with the auxiliary meaning 'to be', the verb *-ti* is the one found in Nguni, Sotho, Shona, and Venda. Examples from Ro.

Monosyllabic:
dzuu (of redness), *ku-ku dzuu* (to be red).
ṭwee (of falling).
baa (of whiteness), *Maṛibye ma-li baa* (The stones are pure white).
mphu (of darkness), *ku-ti mphu* (to be dark).

Disyllabic:
pfótlo (of sound of eating), *Ba-ku pfótlo* (They are eating noisily).
dlúnyu (of nakedness), *A-ku dlúnyu* (He is naked).
hingi (of passing quickly).

Trisyllabic:
pshúlulu (of straightness, freedom).
títiti (of freshness, coolness).

Quadrisyllabic:
góboḍolo (of sitting sadly).
húmelelo (of sudden appearance).

In Ts., in addition to the verbs *-ku* and *-ti* (*-te*), are *-lo* and *-su*, e.g.
Nzi-lo jíri-jíri (I hesitated).
U-ta-su hútsetse (You will be lost).

Verbs and nouns are formed from ideophones in Tsonga, e.g.
dzuu (of redness) > *dzuka* (be red).
pháti-pháti (of brilliance) > *phatima* (be brilliant).
šwee (of clearness) > *šweta* (noun of cl. 5; clearness of water).

Ideophones may also be formed from verbs, e.g.
húmelelo (of sudden appearance) < *humelela* (appear suddenly).
wólolo ko (of standing erect) < *wololoka* (stand on end).

(8) THE CONJUNCTIVE

Among the conjunctives, the following might be noted from To.:
(i) Uninfluencing conjunctives:
kutani, and then.
kambe, but.
loko, when, if: *loko hi-ya kaya* (when we go home).

---

[1] H. L. Bishop, 'The Descriptive Complement in the ŠiRonga Language', *The South African Journal of Science*, vol. xix.

THE TSONGA GROUP

hikuɓa, because.

leŝaku, in order that: *Nḍi-ku-byela leŝaku u-ya* (I tell you that you go); here the tense is used subjunctivally (see p. 198).

kumbe, perhaps.

(ii) Conjunctives followed by the participial mood:

leŝi, since: *Leŝi u-kumeke mali, hakela* (Since you have money, pay.)

laha . . . kona, where: *laha u-yaka kona* (where you go).

(9) THE INTERJECTIVE

(i) RADICAL INTERJECTIONS, e.g. in Ro.

yo! (alas!)
ehe! (oh my!)
mawaku! (if only!).

(ii) VOCATIVES. Nouns may be used in the vocative without inflexion, except that they may not then assume the initial vowel (*a-* or *e-*):

Ts. *Engenani bafana!* (Come in, boys!)
lolo nzi-wena! (you lazy beggar!)
we hosi! (you chief!).

(iii) VERB IMPERATIVES function as interjectives.

(10) ENCLITIC AND PROCLITIC FORMATIVES

(i) ENCLITICS. These seem to be less used in Tsonga than in the other Southern Bantu languages. The following may be noted:

To. *-ka, -ke* (so, then): *famba-ka!* (go then!), *hi-yini-ke?* (what is it then?).

Ts. *-wu* (also): *ba-ta-wonawu* (they will see too).

(ii) PROCLITIC *na-*. This is used conjunctivally joining substantives and adverbs; before nouns which would assume the initial vowel (Ts. and Ro. *a-*, To. *e-*), this proclitic becomes *ni-*, by substitution of *i*:

tatana ni-ṅwana (father and son).
ṅwana na-tatana (son and father).
ni-hosi (and the chief).
hina na-ɓona (we and they).

(11) THE NUMERALS

In Tsonga the numeral system is strictly quinary, the first three numerals being enumeratives, 4, 5, and 10 nouns, and the numbers 6 to 9 being compounded, 5+1, 5+2, &c. Examples from To.:

1. *-ṅwe: munhu uṅwe* (one person).
2. *-ɓiri, -mbiri: ɓanhu ɓambiri* (two people).
3. *-raru, -nharu: ɓanhu ɓararu* (three people).
4. *mune* (cl. 3): *ɓanhu ɓa-mune* or *mune wa-ɓanhu* (four people).
5. *ntlhanu* (cl. 3): *tihomu ta-ntlhanu* (five cattle).
6. *ŝilo ŝa-ntlhanu na-ŝiṅwe* (six things).
7. *ŝilo ŝa-ntlhanu na-ŝiɓiri* (seven things).
8. *timbuti ta-ntlhanu na-tiraru* (eight goats).
9. *timbuti ta-ntlhanu na-mune* (nine goats).
10. *khume* (cl. 5): *khume ra-miti* or *miti ya-khume* (ten villages).

(12) RELATIVE CONSTRUCTION

(i) THE DIRECT RELATIVE, used when the antecedent is in subjectival relationship to the relative predicate, is formed generally by using the 1st position demonstrative, followed by the relative predicate in participial form, closed by the suffix *-ka* or *-ko-*, e.g.

Ro. To. *tihomu leti ti-fambaka* (cattle which eat).

In certain classes, demonstrative and subjectival concord coalesce, e.g.

Ro. *nḏau le'yi-lebyaka* (a lion which is savage).
mhunu lw'a-fambaka (a person who travels).
To. *munhu loyi a-fambaka* (a person who travels).
Ts. *laba ba-nga-giko* (these who do not eat).
a-khumba gi-fambako (the pig which travels).

From the last example it is seen that Ts. very commonly omits the demonstrative pronoun.

(ii) THE INDIRECT RELATIVE, used when the antecedent is in some oblique relationship to the relative predicate, is expressed similarly, but with the antecedent indicated 'pronominally' with the predicate:

(*a*) Objectival relationship (antecedent indicated by objectival concord, in addition to the demonstrative):

Ts. *nanza legi nzi-gi-ranzako* (the servant whom I love).
To. *tihomu leti hi-ti-risaka* (the cattle which we herd).
Ro. *siku leḏi ba-hi-bekeliki ḏone* (the day which they arranged for us).

(*b*) Adverbial relationship (antecedent indicated by an adverb formed from its pronoun, in addition to the demonstrative):

Ts. *a-xitiri lexi nzi-tirako naxo* (the worker with whom I labour).
To. *ndlela leyi hi-sukeke ha-yona* (the road by which we started).
ṋwana loyi ṽa-boheke ṽakulu ṽa-yena (the child whose parents they arrested).

REFERENCES

H. A. JUNOD: *Grammaire Ronga*, 1896.
P. BERTHOUD: *Éléments de Grammaire Ronga*, 1920.
C. W. CHATELAIN: *Pocket Dictionary: Thonga (Shangaan)-English, English-Thonga (Shangaan)*, 1907.
H. A. JUNOD: *Elementary Grammar of the Thonga-Shangaan Language*, 1907.
W. EISELEN: 'Nasalverbindungen im Thonga' (*Festschrift Meinhof*, pp. 256–62), 1927.
A. A. JAQUES: *Tsonga Lectures* (cyclostyled, n.d.).
—— 'Shangana-Tsonga Ideophones and their Tones' (*Bantu Studies*, vol. xv, pp. 205–44, 1941).
J. A. PERSSON: *Outlines of Tswa Grammar*, 1932.
—— *An English-Tswa Dictionary*, 1928.
H. L. BISHOP: 'The "Descriptive Complement" in the ŠiṚonga language, compared with that in SeSotho and Zulu' (*The South African Journal of Science*, vol. xix).
—— 'On the Use of the "Proclitic *a*" in Šironga' (*Bantu Studies*, vol. ii).
T. M. H. ENDEMANN: MS. thesis, *Die Intonasie van Tsonga* (unpublished).

IX

THE SHONA GROUP

Geographical Position of the Shona-speaking Peoples

The Shona group is linguistically a buffer between the South-eastern zone, the Central zone, and a section of the Eastern zone of Bantu languages, the Sena group. A century and a half ago the Shona group occupied almost the whole of what is now Southern Rhodesia, between the Zambesi and the Limpopo Rivers, and sections of the present Portuguese territory to the east. Over a hundred years ago, however, the irruption of Mzilikazi and his Zulu impis drove a wedge between the main Shona speakers and their western section, and Matabeleland was occupied by Ndebele Zulu speakers. Today there are six clusters of the Shona group: (1) the *Korekore* (Ko., Northern Shona), stretching in a broad belt south of the Zambesi from longitude 28° almost to 33°—these include the Tavara, Shangwe, Gova, and Budya; (2) the *Zezuru* (Ze., Central Shona), radiating from the vicinity of Salisbury, and comprising eleven dialects; (3) the *Karanga* (Kr., Southern Shona), radiating from Fort Victoria, and including such dialects as Duma, Jena, Mhari, Govera, and Nyubi; (4) the *Manyika* (Ma., North-eastern Shona), centring in Umtali and including Hungwe, Teve, and eleven other dialects; (5) the *Ndau* (Nd., South-eastern Shona), in Melsetter and Mozambique, including Garwe, Danda, and Shanga; and (6) the *Kalanga* (Kl., Western Shona) from Plumtree to Wankie, including Nyai, Nambzya, Rozwi, and Lilima. Today the total number of Shona speakers considerably exceeds a million.

For many years literary work had been carried on in five of the six clusters by various missionary societies. The whole New Testament had been translated and printed in Karanga, Zezuru (then called Chishona), Manyika (misnamed Chiswina), and Ndau, while the Gospels and Acts had been issued in Kalanga. In Korekore no literary work has ever been attempted. In 1929 a survey of the linguistic position in Southern Rhodesia was undertaken, resulting in the acceptance of a new unified orthography and proposals for unification over most of the area. Western Shona was excluded from this unification owing to too great a divergence from the other clusters. Since that time numerous publications have appeared in Union Shona; these include a complete translation of the Bible.

Unification and Orthography

The unification decided upon involved the adoption of conjunctive word-division and of certain special symbols; *ɓ* and *ɗ* (implosive) were necessary in addition to *b* and *d* (explosive), *v* (bilabial fricative) in addition to *v* (denti-labial), *ṣ* and *ẓ* (whistling fricatives) in addition to *s* and *z*; *sh* and *zh* were retained for the palatal fricatives, but *c* was adopted instead of the hitherto-used *ch*; the symbol *ŋ* was adopted for the velar nasal. In addition, the digraphs *ty* and *dy* were adopted for certain compound sounds which occur with great variation in the various clusters and dialects. The symbols *x*, *g*, and *ŋ* were agreed upon to mark velarization where that was necessary.

It was further decided that the unified grammar be standardized on the basis of Karanga and Zezuru, while for vocabulary purposes words from Zezuru, Karanga, Manyika, and Ndau be drawn upon, the introduction of words from other dialects being discouraged.

THE SHONA GROUP
PHONETICS AND PHONOLOGY

Shona shares with several of the Central Bantu languages a five-vowel system, two front (**i, e**), two back (**u, o**), and one low vowel (**a**). Vowels are commonly juxtaposed constituting separate syllables, as in *taura* (speak), *bgaira* (wink), each being of three syllables.

Consonants in Shona are divided into two main types, Plain Consonants and Velarized Consonants, the velarization of consonants being a characteristic feature of Shona. They are listed in the following tables:

CHART OF PLAIN CONSONANTS FOR KARANGA AND ZEZURU

	Bilab.	Dentilab.	Dental and Alveolar	Labio-alveolar	Pre-palatal	Velar	Glottal
EXPLOSIVE unv.	p		t			k	
voic.	b mb		d nd		–	g ŋg	
IMPLOSIVE	ɓ		ɗ				
NASAL	m mɦ		n nɦ		ɲ	ŋ	
ROLLED			r				
FLAPPED LATERAL unv.			(lç)				
voic.			l (lj)				
FRICATIVE unv.		f	s	ş	ʃ		
voic.	(β) mv	v	z nz	ʐ nʐ	ʒ		ɦ
AFFRICATE unvoic.		pf	ts	tş	tʃ		
voic.		bv	dz	dʐ	dʒ ndʒ		
SEMI-VOWEL		[β̆]			j	w	

[ ] in Zezuru only.   ( ) in Karanga only.

CHART OF VELARIZED CONSONANTS FOR KARANGA AND ZEZURU

	Plain velarization		Velarization with semi-vowel			Plain semi-vowel	
	Bilab.	Pre-palatal	Dental and alveolar	Labio-alveolar	Pre-palatal	Velar	Glottal
EXPLOSIVE unv.	[pk]		[tkw]			kw	
voic.	(px) [bg] (bɣ)		dɣw			gw	
NASAL	mŋ	[ɲŋ]	[nŋw]		[ɲŋw]	ŋw	
ROLLED			rɣw				
FRICATIVE unv.			[skw]	[şkw]	[ʃkw]	(xw)	
voic.			zɣw	(şxw) ʐɣw	(ʃxw) ʒɣw		ɦw
AFFRICATE unv.		[tʃk]	[tskw]		[tʃkw]		
voic.		[dʒg]	dzɣw		[dʒɣw]		
SEMI-VOWEL							

[ ] in Zezuru only.   ( ) in Karanga only.

THE SHONA GROUP

NOTES ON THE CONSONANTS

1. The homorganic nasal consonant is combined only with voiced consonants, e.g. **mb, nd, ŋg** (explosives), **mv, nz, nʒ** (fricatives).

2. Implosive **ɓ** and **ɗ** are significantly distinct from **b** and **d**, e.g. **bara** (write) and **ɓara** (give birth) in Ma., or **dededza** (toddle) and **ɗeɗedza** (bite) in Ze. Western Shona does not use implosives.

3. The rolled consonant, **r**, is common throughout the main Shona dialects, though in some Western and some Eastern Shona dialects **l** takes its place, e.g. general Shona **gara** (sit), but Shanga (Eastern) and Kl. **gala**. In Kr., Ko., and Ma. there is a subsidiary member of the **r**-phoneme, viz. the flapped lateral **l**, which commonly appears before front vowels, but does not need to be distinguished in writing.

4. Kr. uses the bilabial fricative, β, phonemically distinct from **v**, e.g βanhu (people). This sound is also found in parts of the Nd. and Ko. area. In Ma. its place is taken by **w**, e.g. **wanfiu**, while in Ze. and sections of the Nd. and Ko. a denti-labial semi-vowel takes its place.

5. All the dialects employ the labio-alveolar fricatives ş and ʒ, commonly called 'whistling fricatives'. In the pronunciation of these there is lip-rounding and tongue-flattening to such an extent that considerable hissing (rather than whistling) accompanies the articulation. Since the sounds **sw** and **zw** also occur in the language, it was necessary to use special symbols for ş and ʒ, e.g. *iʒi* (these), *izwi* (word), *şika* (arrive). There are also affricates, **tş** and **dʒ**, as well as the nasal compound **nʒ**.

6. Practically all the dialects use the voiced glottal fricative, approximating to the Afrikaans pronunciation of *h* in *hand* (fiant), in contrast to the English pronunciation (hænd). This fricative is also found in combination with **m** and **n**. Note the following in the new orthography where the symbol *ɦ* is used: *huku* (fowl), *mhuka* (animal), *nhasi* (today).

7. One of the most curious phenomena of inter-dialectal sound-change in Shona is that connected with the words for 'eat' and 'fear'. With bewildering difference one finds for the former **kudʒga, kulja, kurja, kurga, kudja, kuɦa, kudʒa**, &c., and for the latter **kutʃka, kultça, kutça, kutʃa, kuɬa**, &c. For unification it was decided to write *kudya* and *kutya* respectively, with the liberty of local dialectal interpretation in pronunciation.

There are three consonantal phenomena in Shona which require special notice, viz. Nasalization, Velarization, and Vocalization.

NASALIZATION occurs in Shona in the formation of nouns and adjectives of cls. 9 and 10, where the following main rules are observed:

(1) Unvoiced explosives: $p > mh$, $t > nh$, $k > h$, e.g. *mhuka huru* (big animal) < *-puka* + *-kuru*.

(2) Implosives: $ɓ > mb$, $ɗ > nd$, e.g. *mbato* (pincers) < *ɓata* (grasp).

(3) Rolled consonant: $r > nd$, e.g. *ndimi* (tongues), pl. of *rurimi*.

(4) Nasals and unvoiced affricates and fricatives remain unchanged, though the last on rare occasions give way to affricates.

(5) Voiced fricatives preplace the homorganic nasal, resulting in *mv* and *nz*, *v* becoming *mb*, and *zh* appearing in Kr. where Ze. has *nz*. Examples: *mvura* (water), *nzira* (path—Kr. *zhira*), *mboni* (pupil of eye) < *vona* (see).

There are variant rules for some of the extreme dialects, especially in Nd. and Kr., but space does not allow of discussion of these here.

VELARIZATION. This is a phonetic phenomenon brought about by an abnormal raising of the back of the tongue towards the soft palate instead of the usual slight raising effected in pronouncing the velar semi-vowel **w**. This abnormal raising (involving the intrusion of a velar consonantal sound) may take the place of the semi-vowel or, in certain cases, precede it. There are varying degrees of velarization according to dialect: Ze. favours explosive velarization, e.g. **pka, bga, mŋa**; Kr. and Nd. fricative velarization, e.g. **pxa, bɣa, mŋa**; while velarization tends to diminish sharply in Ma. and Ko., practically disappearing in the Northern types of the latter, e.g. **pwa, bwa, mwa**.

Reference to the consonantal chart will show examples of three types of velarization: (1) plain velarization (instead of the semi-vowel) is found with bilabials (**px, bɣ, mŋ**), and in Ze. with prepalatals (**ɲŋ, tʃk, dʒg**); (2) velarization with the semi-vowels occurs with dental, alveolar, and prepalatal sounds (e.g. **tkw, skw, ʐgw**); (3) while the plain semi-vowel occurs with velar and glottal sounds (**kw, gw, ŋw, ɦw**).

The most common occurrence of velarization is in passive formation, e.g. *rapa* (cure) > *rapka* or *rapxa*; *tava* (stretch) > *tabga*; *ɓata* (hold) > *ɓatwa* (phon. *ɓatxwa*); *rega* (leave off) > *regwa*. Other common words in which velarization occurs are *imbga* (dog) also appearing as *imbɣa, mbɣa, imbwa*, &c., *mɲana* (child), *ibge* (stone), *mɲoto* (fire), *mɲari* (deity), *vuswa* (phon. βusxwa, grass).

VOCALIZATION. This is a process of voicing or the substitution of a voiced for an unvoiced consonant. In Shona it occurs in nouns and adjectives of cl. 5, where a voicing of the initial consonant of the stem takes the place of the prefix *ri*-, which, however, occurs with all concords other than the adjectival. The main changes are **p > ɓ, t > ɗ, k > g**, a regular formation with unvoiced explosives, e.g. *-padza* > *ɓadza* (hoe), pl. *mapadza*; *-tope* > *ɗope* (mud), pl. *matope*; *-kore* > *gore* (cloud), pl. *makore*; less regular changes take place with affricates, e.g. *-cena* > *jena* (i.e. phon. **tʃ > dʒ**, white), *-tsuku* > *dzuku* (red), but *pfumo* (spear), *tsiru* (heifer) are unchanged; while fricatives are not influenced by vocalization.

COALESCENCE OF VOWELS occurs in possessive formation and with *na*- and *sa*- before nouns which have a latent initial vowel, e.g. *nehuku* < (*i*)*huku* (fowl), *nomunhu* < (*u*)*munhu* (person), *mɲana weshumba* (the lion's child) < (*i*)*shumba*. In Kr. particularly, this process is carried farther, and coalescence is normal after verbs ending in the vowel *-a*, e.g. *ndinoɗo-munhu* (I like a person) for *ndinoɗa*+(*u*)*munhu*; *vanorise-mbudzi* (they are herding goats). In these cases the resultant is a single word-group.

In Ma., in possessive and similar constructions, substitution of *e* takes place instead of coalescence, e.g. *nemunhu* (with a person), *kashiri kemupxere* (the child's little bird), *ŋgemutsa* (kindly).

PENULTIMATE *i*. Apart from Kr. and a few minor dialects, monosyllabic words are not favoured in Shona, and quite commonly disyllabic words are formed from monosyllabic stems by prefixing a penultimate *i*. This is so with imperatives of monosyllabic verb-stems, *ipa* (give!), *iɗa* (love!); in cl. 1a, *ishe* (chief), pl. *vashe*; in Kr. *she*; with nouns and adjectives of cls. 5, 9, and 10, *ibge* (stone), *iŋgwe* (leopard), *idza* (new), where Kr. has *bge, ŋgwe*, &c. All pronouns of the 3rd pers. have penultimate *i*, e.g. *iye, idzo* forming *naye, sadzo*, &c. (though *naiye* occurs emphatically).

STRESS is normally on the penultimate syllable in Shona, e.g. *muko'mana* (boy), *ndinova'vona* (I see them). Where it has been stated to be otherwise, e.g. *ta'kura* regarded as '*takura* (carry), it is generally that a high tone on an unstressed syllable has misled the recorder.

LENGTH of vowels has no significant function in Shona, there being a marked distinction from the regular penultimate length of the Nguni languages. Syllables are all normally short in Shona, and this imparts to the language a somewhat staccato pronunciation.

In regard to TONE, Shona is like the Central Bantu languages with three level tones in normal speech. Of these three tones only two are really significant, i.e. high and low tone. The sentence is thus characterized by peaks of tone. There are numerous examples of semantic tone in words, for instance in Zezuru:

ìshe (nest of rats)   *ishè* (chief)
ɗorò (rice garden)   *ɗòro* (beer)
ɓata (grasp)   *ɓàta* (duck)

kaná (little child)   kána (if)
mbíra (coney)   mbira (hand-piano).

There is considerable change in the intonation of words from dialect to dialect, as for example ɓáta (Ko.), ɓata (Ze.) for 'grasp'.

In the extra-normal phonetics of interjection and ideophone the intonation is considerably more varied, with rising and falling tones, very much as in the ordinary intonation of Nguni, for instance *kuti bu*: ⁻⁻\ (to blaze up); *heya* -⁻ (very well then), *he: ya*: -\ (I have heard all you say).

Grammatical Outline

(1) The Noun

Prefix Table

(Singular)		(Plural)	
Class 1	(u)mu-	Class 2	(a)va-
1a	—	2a	va-
3	(u)mu-	4	(i)mi-
5	(i)[ri-]	6	(a)ma-
7	(i)ci-	8	(i)zi-
9	(i)[N-]	10	(i)[N-]
11	(u)ru-	10 and 6	
13	(a)ka-	12	(u)tu-
14	(u)vu-		
15	(u)ku-		
16	pa-		
17	ku-		
18	mu-		
19	(i)ṣi-		
21	(i)zi-		

N.B. In all classes except 1a, 2a, 16, 17, and 18, there is an implied initial vowel (indicated in parentheses) which causes coalescences in certain circumstances.

CLASSES 1 AND 2 (personal)

munhu (person)	vanhu
muruŋgu (European)	varuŋgu
mukomana (boy)	vakomana
mukadzi (wife)	vakadzi.

Vowel-stems have velarized prefix in cl. 1:

mŋana (child) < -ana, vana.
mŋene (owner) < -ene, vene.

Personal nouns derived from verbs:

muɓiki (cook) < ɓika, vaɓiki.
mufambi (traveller) < famba, vafambi.

CLASSES 1a AND 2a (proper names, relationship terms, animal personifications, &c.):
Proper names:

Ŋgoshi	vaŊgoshi
Mŋari (deity)	vaMŋari
Mambo (king)	vaMambo.

Relationship terms:

ɓaɓa¹ (father)   vaɓaɓa
tenzi (master)   vatenzi
ishe or she² (chief)   vashe
mai or amai³ (mother)   vamai or vadzimai
hanʒadzi (brother)   vahanʒadzi.

Animals:

maŋgoyi (cat)   vamaŋgoyi
kundoro (mole-rat)   vakundoro.

Ordinary animal names may be personified, e.g. *Ruŋgano rwaTsuro naBveni* (The Story of Hare and Baboon) instead of *Ruŋgano rwetsuro nebveni* (the Story of a hare and a baboon).

Plurals in these classes are generally honorific, e.g. *vaŊgoshi* (Mr. Ngoshi).

Table of Concords for classes 1(1a) and 2(2a)

	(Adj.)	(Rel.)	(Enum.)	(Poss.)	(Subj.)	(Obj.)
1 and 1a	mu-	u-	mu-, u-	wa-	u-, a-	mu-
2 and 2a	va-	va-	va-	va-	va-	va-

CLASSES 3 AND 4 (non-personal, trees, natural phenomena, &c.):

muti (tree), *miti*
mukuyu (fig), *mikuyu*
mufaro (joy) < *fara*, *mifaro*
musha (village), *misha*
munda (garden), *minda*
musoro (head), *misoro*.

Natural phenomena do not change the noun-prefix to form plurals, but plural concords are assumed, e.g.

mŋedzi (moon), *mŋedzi mizhinji* (many months).
mŋeya (spirit), *mŋeya yose* (every spirit).
moto or *mŋoto* (fire).

Velarized prefixes are used in cl. 3 with vowel-stems, e.g. *mŋenje* (torch) < *-enje*; *mŋise* (tail) < *-ise*.

Table of Concords for classes 3 and 4

	(Adj.)	(Rel.)	(Enum.)	(Poss.)	(Subj.)	(Obj.)
3	mu-	u-	mu-, u-	wa-	u-	u-
4	mi-	i-	mi-, i-	ya-	i-	i-

CLASSES 5 AND 6 (miscellaneous and augmentative):[4]

(a) With monosyllabic stems penultimate *i* is used in the singular in most dialects, but omitted in Kr.:

ibge, Kr. *bge* (stone), *mabge*.
igo, Kr. *go* (wasp), *mago*.

---

[1] Kr. also uses *ɓambo*. An alternative plural is *vadziɓaɓa*, while a plural *madziɓaɓa* (in cl. 6) is used to indicate 'ancestors', though this latter is the regular plural in Kr. Unlike their use in Nguni (and many other Bantu groups) *ɓaɓa* and *ɓambo* in Shona are not confined to 1st pers. possession, and the forms *ɓaɓa waŋgu* (my father), *ɓaɓa wako* (thy father), and so on are used. The same applies to *mai*, e.g. *mai wake* (her mother).

[2] The penultimate *i* is used in dialects other than Kr.

[3] *Amai* is the usual form in Ze., where it is used with plural concords, e.g. *Amai vaŋgu* (my mother); in Kr. the usual plural is *madzimai*.

[4] For a detailed statement regarding the forms in cl. 5, cf. Doke, *A Comparative Study in Shona Phonetics*, pp. 125–31.

(b) With vowel-stems, z- is prefixed in the singular (cf. cl. 21):
 -iso > ziso (eye), meso, maziso.
 -ino > zino (tooth), meno, mazino.
 -ano > zano (counsel), mano, mazano.

(c) Nouns, whose stems commence in unvoiced explosive consonants (p, t, or k), have that initial consonant voiced in the singular (ɓ, ɗ or g):
 -padza > ɓadza (hoe), mapadza.
 -taŋga > ɗaŋga (cattle-kraal), mataŋga.
 -kore > gore (cloud), makore.

If the initial of the stem is already voiced, no prefixal influence is felt in the singular:
 -ɓasa > ɓasa (work), maɓasa.

Vocalization is not so regular with initial affricates:
 jembere (old hag), *macembere*.
 pfumo (spear), *mapfumo*.

With fricatives there is no vocalization.

(d) Certain nouns are found in cl. 6 (i.e. in the plural) only, e.g. *mafuta* (fat), *masikati* (noon), *madziya* (hot season).

Table of Concords for classes 5 and 6

	(Adj.)	(Rel.)	(Enum.)	(Poss.)	(Subj.)	(Obj.)
5	.(vocalizn.)	ri-	ri-	ra-	ri-	ri-
6	ma-	a-	ma-, a-	a-	a-	a-

Ex. *Biza raŋgu guru rinodya* (My big horse is eating).
 Mabiza aŋgu makuru anodya (My big horses are eating).

CLASSES 7 AND 8 (miscellaneous, material, language):[1]
 cinhu (thing), *zinhu*.
 cigunwe (toe), *zigunwe*.
 ciŋgwa (bread), *ziŋgwa*.
 ciKaraŋga (Karaŋga language).

Elision of *i* of prefix takes place before vowel-stems:
 coto (fire-place), *zoto*.
 curu (ant-hill), *zuru*.

Impersonal nouns derived from verbs:
 cigaro (seat) < *gara* (sit), *zigaro*.
 cipo (gift) < *pa* (give), *zipo*.

This class also indicates half-grown animals or things, e.g. *mukomana* (boy) > *cikomana* (half-grown boy), *zikomana*; *mɲana* (child) > *cana* (toddler), *zana*.

Table of Concords for classes 7 and 8

	(Adj.)	(Rel.)	(Enum).	(Poss.)	(Subj.)	(Obj.)
7	ci-	ci-	ci-	ca-	ci-	ci-
8	zi-	zi-	zi-	za-	zi-	zi-

CLASSES 9 AND 10 (miscellaneous, animals). Prefix in each class indicated merely by nasal influence (singular and plural of the noun being the same):[2]

---
[1] The prefix of cl. 7 is *shi-* in the Karombe dialect of Ma.
[2] For a detailed statement of the forms of the prefix in these classes, cf. Doke, *A Comparative Study in Shona Phonetics*, pp. 62–71.

huku (fowl) < *-kuku*.
mhepo (wind) < *-pepo*.
nhaŋga (pumpkin) < *-taŋga*.
mbereko (carrying-skin) < *ɓereka* (carry).
mbezo (adze) < *veza* (work wood).
ndima (garden plot) < *rima* (plough).
nyuci (honey) < *-uci*.
ŋombe (cattle) < *-ombe*.
nzira, zhira[1] (path).
nzou, zhou[1] (elephant).
mvuvu (hippopotamus).
mvura (water, rain).

Normally no nasal influence is found on an initial fricative consonant:

fuŋgo (thought) < *fuŋga* (think).
simba (genet).
shiri (bird).
ṣovi (courtier).

In Ze., however, *s* sometimes becomes *ts* in these classes:

tsono (needle) < *sona* (sew).
tsungo (perseverance) < *suŋga* (persevere).

The monosyllabic stem *-mba* appears as *imba* (house; Ma. *umba*) plural *dzimba*.

Table of Concords for classes 9 and 10

	(Adj.)	(Rel.)	(Enum.)	(Poss.)	(Subj.)	(Obj.)
9	(N-)[2]	*i-*	*i-*	*ya-*	*i-*	*i-*
10	(N-)	*dzi-*	*dzi-*	*dza-*	*dzi-*	*dzi-*

Examples:

Iyi-huku yake nhema inodya (This black fowl of his is eating).
Idzi-huku dzake nhema dzinodya (These black fowls of his are eating).

CLASS 11 (miscellaneous, long objects)

Those taking cl. 6 plural:

ruvoko (arm), *mavoko*.
rutadzo (fault), *matadzo*.
rukodzi (hawk), *makodzi*.

Those taking cl. 10 plural:

rudzi (tribe), *ndudzi*.
rukuni (firewood), *huni*.
rumbo (song), *dzimbo*.

Some take both plurals, cl. 6 generally indicating the quantitative plural:

rutsaŋga (reed), *tsaŋga, matsaŋga*.
ruware (flat rock), *ŋgware, maware*.

Nouns formed from verbs, with no change for plural:

runako (goodness) < *naka* (be good).
rudo (love) < *ɗa* (love).
rufu (death) < *fa* (die).

---

[1] The latter in each of these cases is found in Kr.
[2] *N-* indicates nasalization.

THE SHONA GROUP

Table of Concords for class 11

	(Adj.)	(Rel.)	(Enum.)	(Poss.)	(Subj.)	(Obj.)
11	ru-	ru-	ru-	rwa-	ru-	ru-

CLASSES 12 AND 13 (diminutive)

(a) Prefixed to word-stem only (with nouns of cls. 1a, 2a, 5, and 11):
ishe (chief) > *kashe* (small chief).
vadaŋgwe (first-born) > *tudaŋgwe* (small first-born children).
badza (hoe) > *kapadza* (small hoe).
rurimi (tongue) > *karimi* (small tongue).

(b) Preprefixed to complete word (with nouns of cls. 3, 4, 9, and 10):
muti (tree) > *kamuti* (small tree).
misha (villages) > *tumisha* (small villages).
hanẓadzi (brother) > *kahanẓadzi, tuhanẓadzi*.
imbga[1] (dog) > *kambga, tumbga*.

(c) Alternative formations (with nouns of cls. 1, 2, 6, 7, and 8):
munhu (person) > *kanhu* or *kamunhu*.
vana (children) > *twana* or *tuvana*.
mapadza (hoes) > *tupadza* or *tumapadza*.
mabge (stones) > *tubge* or *tumabge*.
cigaro (seat) > *kagaro* or *kacigaro*.
ẓinhu (things) > *tunhu* or *tuẓinhu*.

Table of Concords for classes 12 and 13

	(Adj.)	(Rel.)	(Enum.)	(Poss.)	(Subj.)	(Obj.)
12	tu-	tu-	tu-	twa-	tu-	tu-
13	ka-	ka-	ka-	ka-	ka-	ka-

Note 1. Some dialects of Shona use cl. 14 as plural to cl. 13, e.g.

(a) Ko., *ka-, hu-*:
kana (little child), *hwana* or *twana*.
kambudzi (little goat), *humbudzi* or *tumbudzi*.

(b) Nd., *ka-, hu-*:
kamundhu (inferior person), *humundhu*.
kapxere (little boy), *hupxere*.

Note 2. In Kr. the diminutive is generally formed by suffixing *-ana*, e.g. *mbudzi* (goat) > *mbudzana* (kid); or by double diminutive in *-anana*, e.g. *mbga* (dog) > *mbganana* (puppy). Both prefix and suffix are sometimes found, e.g. *kambudzana* (little kid).

Note 3. In the Mhari dialect of Kr., cls. 19 and 14 are used for the diminutive.

CLASS 14 (mainly abstract, but containing a few concrete nouns). Prefix *(u)vu-* in Kr., *u-* in Ze., *wu-* in Ma., *hu-* in Nd.

(1) Abstract (no plural):
vukomana (boyhood) < *mukomana* (boy).
vuroyi (witchcraft) < *muroyi* (witch).
vukuru (greatness) < *-kuru* (big).
vunyoro (mildness) < *-nyoro* (soft).

(2) Concrete and collective (rare pl. in cl. 6):
vuta, utati (bow), pl. *mavuta*.
uṣaṣi (net).

[1] The *i-* here is merely penultimate and not a prefix.

vuswa (grass).
vupenyu (life).
vuci (honey).

(3) Vowel-stems: *vu-* > *bg-*, *u-* or *hu-* > *hw-*.
bgabga or *hwahwa* (beer).
bgana or *hwana* (childhood).

(4) As plural to cl. 13 in Ko. and Nd.

Table of Concords for class 14

	(Adj.)	(Rel.)	(Enum.)	(Poss.)	(Subj.)	(Obj.)
14 . . .	*vu-*	*vu-*	*vu-*	*bga-*	*vu-*	*vu-*

Dialectal variants substitute *u-*, *hu-* for *vu-*; and *wa-*, *hwa-* for *bga-*.

CLASS 15 (verb-infinitive):
kuvuya (coming).
kufa (death).
kuṣika (arrival).

Table of Concords for class 15

	(Adj.)	(Rel.)	(Enum.)	(Poss.)	(Subj.)	(Obj.)
15 . . .	*ku-*	*ku-*	*ku-*	*kwa-*	*ku-*	*ku-*

CLASSES 16, 17, AND 18 (locative classes): 16. *pa-* indicates position (by, on, &c.); 17. *ku-* indicates direction (to, towards, from, at); 18. *mu-* indicates interior or encircling (in, into, out of, round). These are preprefixes, being added to nouns already having a prefix.

16. *pakati* (in the middle).
pasi pomuti (beneath the tree).
Pamberi paŋgu pakaipa kwaẓo (In front of me it is truly bad).
panzimbo pa- (instead of).
pamusoro pa- (on the top of).

17. *kunze* (outside).
kumusha kwaŋgu (to my village).
Kumba kwedu kwose kwakanaka (Everywhere around our house is beautiful).

18. *mukati* (inside).
Mumba menyu huru munemoto here? (Is there a fire in your big house?)
Mumba maŋgu munopisa (In my house it is hot).

Table of Concords for classes 16, 17, and 18

	(Adj.)	(Rel.)	(Enum.)	(Poss.)	(Subj.)	(Obj.)
16 . . .	*pa-*	*pa-*	*pa-*	*pa-*	*pa-*	*pa-*
17 . . .	*ku-*	*ku-*	*ku-*	*kwa-*	*ku-*	*ku-*
18 . . .	*mu-*	*mu-*	*mu-*	*ma-*	*mu-*	*mu-*

CLASS 19 (diminutive in Mhari dialect of Kr.): (*i*)*ṣi-*, using cl. 14 as pl. These take the place of cls. 13 and 12.

ṣana (little child), *bgana*.
ṣiŋguruve (little pig), *vuŋguruve*.
ṣimbudzi (little goat), *vumbudzi*.

Table of Concords for class 19

	(Adj.)	(Rel.)	(Enum.)	(Poss.)	(Subj.)	(Obj.)
19 . . .	*ṣi-*	*ṣi-*	*ṣi-*	*ṣa-*	*ṣi-*	*ṣi-*

CLASS 21 (augmentative); preprefix *zi-* to nouns, with concords as for cl. 5:
ziɓere (big hyena).
zinzara (big claw).

In Shona the significances of the class prefixes are clearer than in most Bantu languages, e.g.

(1) Augmentative: cls. 5 and 21 (pl. 6).
(2) Diminutive: cl. 13 (pl. 12 or 14).
(3) Derogatory (half-sized): cl. 7 (pl. 8).
(4) Long-shaped: cl. 11 (pl. 10).
(5) Monstrous: cl. 3 (pl. 4).
(6) Abstract: cl. 14.

Note the following as examples:

(a) **cembere* (cl. 9, old woman).
   mucembere (cl. 1, old woman, more personal).
   cicembere (cl. 7, tottering old woman).
   iembere, zijembere (cl. 5 and 21, old hag, insulting).
   muzijembere (cl. 3, old hag, most insulting).
   rucembere (cl. 11, tall, frail old woman, disrespectful).
   kacembere (cl. 13, little old woman).
   vucembere (cl. 14, old womanhood).

(b) **iɓge* (cl. 5, rock, stone).
   ciɓge (cl. 7, medium-sized boulder).
   ziɓge (cl. 21, huge rock).
   kaɓge (cl. 13, pebble).
   ruɓge (cl. 11, long-shaped stone, used for throwing).

There is always a normal form, which may be in any one of the classes. In the above examples the normal forms are marked with an asterisk. Two other examples will illustrate this: (i) From the stem *-komo* we have the following series in decreasing order of magnitude: *zigomo* (cl. 21, large hill), **gomo* (cl. 5, hill, normal form), *cikomo* (cl. 7, smallish hill), and *kakomo* (cl. 13, little hill). (ii) From the stem *-pumi* we have the following series in decreasing order of magnitude: *ziɓumi* (cl. 21, huge wild-dog), *ɓumi* (cl. 5, big wild-dog), **mhumi* (cl. 9, wild-dog, normal form), *cipumi* or *cimhumi* (cl. 7, half-grown wild-dog), *kapumi* or *kamhumi* (cl. 13, little wild-dog). From these examples it is seen that prefixes are sometimes substituted, sometimes super-added.

(2) THE PRONOUN

(a) TABLE OF ABSOLUTE PRONOUNS

1st pers. s. . . *ini*   pl. *isu.*
2nd pers. s. . . *iwe*   pl. *imi* (*imɲi*).
3rd pers. cl. 1. . *iye*; 2. *ivo*; 3. *iwo*; 4. *iyo*; 5. *iro*; 6. *iwo*; 7. *ico*; 8. *izo*; 9. *iyo*; 10. *idzo*; 11. *irwo*; 12. *itwo*; 13. *iko*; 14. *iɓgo* (*iwo*); 15. *iko*; 16. *ipo*; 17. *iko*; 18. *imo*; 19. *iṣo*.

Note 1. The initial vowel in all cases of the 3rd pers. is penultimate *i*: in the 1st and 2nd pers. it is part of the stem, and causes coalescence, e.g. *neni, nesu,* but *naye, navo,* &c.

Note 2. A dialectal variant to *imi* (2nd pers. pl.) is *imɲi* found in Ma. and Kr. Examples:
Vakadzi vacatirakidza ivo (The women will show *them*—children—to us).
Ndakamupa ico (I gave *it* to him).
Endai mutore muti iwo musasa (Go and fetch a tree, and that a *musasa*).

(b) TABLE OF DEMONSTRATIVE PRONOUNS

(Class)	(1st position)	(2nd position)	(3rd position)	(4th position)
1	*uyu*	*uyo*	*uno*	*uya*
2	*ava*	*avo*	*vano*	*vaya*
3	*uyu*	*uyo*	*uno*	*uya*
4	*iyi*	*iyo*	*ino*	*iya*
5	*iri*	*iro*	*rino*	*riya*
6[1]	*aya*	*ayo*	*ano*	*aya*
7	*ici*	*ico*	*cino*	*ciya*
8	*izi*	*izo*	*zino*	*ziya*
9	*iyi*	*iyo*	*ino*	*iya*
10	*idzi*	*idzo*	*dzino*	*dziya*
11	*urwu*	*urwo*	*rwuno*	*rwuya*
12	*utwu*	*utwo*	*twuno*	*twuya*
13	*aka*	*ako*	*kano*	*kaya*
14[2]	*ubgu*	*ubgo*	*bguno*	*bguya*
15	*uku*	*uko*	*kuno*	*kuya*
16	*apa*	*apo*	*pano*	*paya*
17	*uku*	*uko*	*kuno*	*kuya*
18	*umu*	*umo*	*muno*	*muya*
19	*işi*	*işo*	*şino*	*şiya*

Note 1. More emphatic reduplicated forms of these are found, e.g. *iyeyu, ivava*; *iyeyo, ivavo*, &c.; and after *na-* even triplications, e.g. *nerwurwurwu, nedzedzedzo, newuyuyu*, &c.

Note 2. In Shona the 1st and 2nd demonstratives constitute contrast pairs, 'this' and 'that', e.g. *vupfu ubgu* (this meal), *ɓaŋga iro* (that knife); the 3rd and 4th demonstratives also constitute contrast pairs, 'this here' and 'that yonder', e.g. *imba ino* (this house here), *ŋombe iya* (yonder ox).

Examples:
gomo irero (that hill).
cino (this very thing).
mabiza ayo (those horses).
uyu-munhu (this person).
idzo-mombe (those cattle).

N.B. *Uyu munhu, izdo mombe*, when separate words, indicate that the noun is copulative, and mean 'this is a person', 'those are cattle', respectively.

(c) QUANTITATIVE PRONOUNS

There are two of these in Shona, viz. *-se* (all) and *-ga* (only):

Table of forms

1st pers.	s.	(*ndose*)	*ndoga*
	pl.	*tose*	*toga*
2nd pers.	s.	(*wose*)	*woga*
	pl.	*mose*	*moga*
3rd pers. cl.	1	*wose*	*oga, woga*
	2	*vose*	*voga*
	3	*wose*	*woga*
	4	*yose*	*yoga*
	5	*rose*	*roga*

[1] Kr. has *awa* and *awo* for 1st and 2nd positions.
[2] Ze. has *uwu* (*uhwu*), *uwo* (*uhwo*), *uno* (*huno*), *uya* (*huya*).

6	. ose	oga
7	. cose	coga
8	. ʒose	ʒoga
9	. yose	yoga
10	. dzose	dzoga
11	. rwose	rwoga
12	. twose	twoga
13	. kose	koga
14	. bgose	bgoga
15	. kwose	kwoga
16	. pose	poga
17	. kwose	kwoga
18	. mose	moga
19	. ṣose	ṣoga

Note 1. Alternative forms are found for all these sets, substituting the vowel *e* for *o*, e.g. *ndega*, *ega*, *dzese*, *vese*, &c.; the *e-* form always occurs in Ma.

Note 2. The two forms in brackets are very rarely used.

Note 3. In cl. 14 Ze. uses *wose* and *woga*.

Note 4. To make a numeral definite the stem *-se* is used with it, e.g. *imbga mbiri dzese* (both dogs), *ʒigaro ʒitatu ʒese* (all three chairs).

(*d*) QUALIFICATIVE PRONOUNS

In Shona there is no formal change in qualificatives when they are used pronominally.

(3) THE QUALIFICATIVE

(*a*) THE ADJECTIVE

In Shona it is somewhat difficult to distinguish the adjective from the noun. In form adjectival concords are the same as noun prefixes, but it may be observed that there are no adjectives corresponding to cl. 1a of nouns, and that apart from this the adjectives may have forms to correspond to every class of nouns. No noun-stem can be treated in that way: although one noun-stem may take the prefixes of several different classes, it cannot do so of them all. Noun-stems further undergo change of meaning from class to class, e.g. *munhu* and *cinhu*, but adjectives merely undergo change of reference, as some noun is invariably expressed in the case of the adjective.

But perhaps the most certain test to decide the difference lies in the fact that the locative prefixes (cls. 16, 17, and 18), which are preprefixes and are added to the full noun with its prefix, appear merely as concords added directly to the adjectival stem, e.g. *pacigaro pakuru* (on the big seat).

The following is a fairly full list of adjectives in Shona, with examples of the forms they assume in cls. 5, 7, and 10:

(Stem)	(Meaning)	(Cl. 5)	(Cl. 7)	(Cl. 10)
-cena	white	jena	cicena	cena
-ɖiki	small	ɖiki	ciɖiki	ndiki, ɖiki
-ɖuku	small	ɖuku	ciɖuku	nduku, ɖuku
-kobvu	thick	gobvu	cikobvu	hobvu
-kukutu	hard	gukutu	cikukutu	hukutu
-kuru	big	guru	cikuru	huru
-mbishi	raw	mbishi	cimbishi	mbishi
-na	four	—	—	ina
-nomŋe	seven	—	—	nomŋe

(Stem)	(Meaning)	(Cl. 5)	(Cl. 7)	(Cl. 10)
-nyoro	soft	nyoro	cinyoro	nyoro
-ŋgani?	how many?	—	—	ŋgani
-pami	wide	ɓami	cipami	mhami
-penyu	living	ɓenyu	cipenyu	mhenyu
-pfumbamŋe	nine	—	—	pfumbamŋe
-pfumbu	greyish	bvumbu	cipfumbu	pfumbu
-pfupi	short	pfupi	cipfupi	pfupi
-refu	long	refu	cirefu	ndefu, refu
-sere	eight	—	—	tsere, sere
-shanu	five	—	—	shanu
-sharu	old	sharu	cisharu	sharu
-shoma	few	—	—	shoma
-shora	yellow	shora	cishora	shora
-tanhatu	six	—	—	nhanhatu
-tatu	three	—	—	nhatu
-tema	black	ɖema	citema	nhema
-tete	thin	ɖete	citete	nhete
-tsa	new	idza	citsa	itsa
-tsuku	red	dzuku	citsuku	tsuku
-viri	two	—	—	mbiri
-zhinji	many	—	—	zhinji

Examples:

mukomana murefu (a tall boy).
zigaro zitsa (new chairs).
Wairwara mazuva mazhinji (He was ill for many days).
vanhu vakuru (big people); used pronominally (i.e. as a qualificative pronoun) *vakuru* means 'ancestors', 'elders'.

Note: Shona also uses occasionally a possessive construction with the pronouns formed from adjectives, e.g. *munhu mukuru* or *munhu womukuru*; *miti mikuru* or *miti yemikuru*, a construction similar to that in Nyanja. In each case the possessive construction has a modified meaning, viz. 'a truly great person', 'a really big tree'.

(b) THE RELATIVE

There are no primitive relative stems in Shona, but relative concords are used: (a) before nouns preceded by *na-*, and (b) in forming relative clauses with verbs. In the verbal construction two tenses of the participial mood are generally used, the present and the stative perfect. Some verbs are preferably used with the one, others preferably with the other; nevertheless both forms are possible with one and the same verb, e.g. *munhu wakanaka* (a good person, i.e. one who has become good), *munhu unonaka* (a person who is becoming good).

(a) With conjunctive adverbs formed from nouns

munhu unesimba, Ze. *anesimba* (a man with strength, a strong man).
vana vanenyota (thirsty children).
huku dzinenzara (hungry fowls).
imbga inamafuta (a fat dog).

(b) Verbal relatives

(i) Present:

imba inoyera (a sacred house).

ɓaŋga rinopinza (a sharp knife).
mvura inopisa (hot water).

(ii) Perfect:
ɗonƶo rakanaka (a nice stick).
mukomana wakaipa (a bad boy).
mhuru yakakora (a fat calf).

(iii) Present or perfect alternatives:
cinhu cinotana or cakatana (a hard thing).
ƶinhu ƶinorema or ƶakarema (difficult things).

Note 1. Further discussion of relative construction will be dealt with later.
Note 2. The difference between the qualificative and the predicative use is generally determined by context and intonation, e.g. *Munhu wakanaka* (The person is good); *Munhu wakanaka unoşika* (The good person is arriving).

(c) THE ENUMERATIVE

There are two enumerative roots in Shona, each monosyllabic, viz. *-mɲe* 'one' (when used after the noun), 'other' (when used before the noun), and *-pi?* 'which?'; the latter always assumes the shorter form of concord, while the former has alternatives according to dialect. Examples:

ɓaŋga rimɲe (one knife).
ŋombe imɲe (one ox).
munhu mumɲe (one person).
mamɲe mabiza (other horses).
dzimɲe mbudzi (other goats).
murume upi? (which man?)
ɓadza ripi? (which hoe?)

Note 1. In Ze. the adverb *cete* (only) generally follows the numeral *-mɲe*, e.g. *rusero rumɲe cete* (one winnowing basket); in Kr. the quantitative pronoun *-ga* (only) is similarly used, e.g. *mɲana mumɲe woga* (one child); in Ma. *-mɲe* is generally used alone.

Note 2: Enumerative concords differ from adjectival concords in that *ri-* is used instead of vocalization in cl. 5, *i-* and *dzi-* instead of nasalization in cls. 9 and 10, while *mu-*, *mi-*, and *ma-* are alternatively reduced to *u-*, *i-*, and *a-* (except in cl. 18, which may only appear as *mu-*).

(d) THE POSSESSIVE

Two types of possessive, direct and descriptive, are used in Shona, the former with pronominal and nominal base, the latter with nominal, adverbial, and relative base.

Direct possessives are of two kinds: (i) those with pronominal possessive stem, and (ii) those composed of concord prefixed to a noun or pronoun, in the case of a noun base coalescence taking place with an implied initial vowel.

List of Possessive Pronominal Stems

1st pers. s. . . -ŋgu   pl. -iɗu[1]
2nd pers. s. . . -ko   pl. -inyu[1]
3rd pers. . . cl. 1 -ke (-kwe); 2. -vo; 3. -wo; 4. -yo; 5. -ro; 6. -wo; 7. -co; 8. -ƶo;
9. -yo; 10. -dzo; 11. -rwo; 12. -two; 13. -ko; 14. -bgo (-wo);
15. -ko; 16. -po; 17. -ko; 18. -mo; 19. -şo

Possessive concords are regularly formed with the basic *-a*, e.g. *wa-*, *ra-*, *dza-*, &c.

[1] Old Manyika used *-su* and *-nu* respectively, e.g. *Tiŋgoenda hasu*, We are going home.

Examples:
  (i) *ɓaŋga rake* (his knife).
      ŋombe dzedu (our cattle).
      vukuru bgaco (the size of it).
  (ii) *ɓaŋga romunhu* (the person's knife).
       ŋombe dzashe (the chief's cattle).
       vana vavaya (the children of yonder ones).

Descriptive possessives are of three kinds: (i) those with noun base indicating some quality, content, characteristic, or order, (ii) those with adverbial base indicating some position or locality, and (iii) those with verbal base indicating indirect relative relationship.
Examples:
  (i) *imba yamabge* (a stone house).
      hari dzemvura (water pots).
      ziŋgwa zokudya (loaves for eating).
      mŋana wokutaŋga (the first child).
  (ii) *vanhu vapamberi* (the people in front).
       mitovo yazino (present customs).
  (iii) *ŋombe dzandakavona* (the cattle which I saw).

Note: This last type of possessive construction will be discussed later.

Table of Qualificative Concords

		(Adjectival)	(Relative)	(Enumerative)	(Possessive)
1st pers.	s.	—	*ndi-*	—	—
	pl.	—	*ti-*	—	—
2nd pers.	s.	—	*u-*	—	—
	pl.	—	*mu-*	—	—
3rd pers. cl.	1	*mu-*	*u-*, *a-*	*mu-*, *u-*	*wa-*
	2	*va-*	*va-*	*va-*	*va-*
	3	*mu-*	*u-*	*mu-*, *u-*	*wa-*
	4	*mi-*	*i-*	*mi-*, *i-*	*ya-*
	5	(voiced)	*ri-*	*ri-*	*ra-*
	6	*ma-*	*a-*	*ma-*, *a-*	*a-*
	7	*ci-*	*ci-*	*ci-*	*ca-*
	8	*zi-*	*zi-*	*zi-*	*za-*
	9	(*N-*)	*i-*	*i-*	*ya-*
	10	(*N-*)	*dzi-*	*dzi-*	*dza-*
	11	*ru-*	*ru-*	*ru-*	*rwa-*
	12	*tu-*	*tu-*	*tu-*	*twa-*
	13	*ka-*	*ka-*	*ka-*	*ka-*
	14[1]	*vu-*	*vu-*	*vu-*	*bga-*
	15	*ku-*	*ku-*	*ku-*	*kwa-*
	16	*pa-*	*pa-*	*pa-*	*pa-*
	17	*ku-*	*ku-*	*ku-*	*kwa-*
	18	*mu-*	*mu-*	*mu-*	*ma-*
	19	*ṣi-*	*ṣi-*	*ṣi-*	*ṣa-*

[1] Dialectal alternatives for *vu-* are *u-* and *hu-*, for *bga-* are *wa-* and *hwa-*.

(4) THE VERB

(i) THE VARIETIES OF THE VERB IN SHONA

There are the four varieties found in Bantu:
  (a) The Regular disyllabic verb-stem, ending in the vowel -a, e.g. *famba* (walk), *rova* (strike).
  (b) The Monosyllabic verb-stem, e.g. *ɗa* (love), *dya* (eat).
  (c) The Vowel verb-stem, e.g. *enda* (travel), *ita* (do).
  (d) Derived verb-stems: (1) Verbal derivatives, e.g. *fambira* (applied), *fambisa* (causative), &c.; (2) Ideophonic derivatives, e.g. *susuvara* (sit hunched up) < *súsuva*, *tabvuka* (bounce) < *tabvu*; and (3) Denominative Verbs, e.g. *fupisa* (shorten) < *-fupi*.

VERBAL DERIVATIVES. In Shona the following are used regularly: Passive, Applied, Neuter, Causative, Intensive, Reciprocal, and Reversive.

THE PASSIVE is formed, as a general rule, by substituting the suffix *-wa* for the final vowel of the simple stem, e.g. *suŋga* (bind) > *suŋgwa* (be bound); *ɓata* (hold) > *ɓatwa*, Kr. sometimes *ɓaxwa* (be held).

Monosyllabic verb-stems substitute *-iwa* for the final vowel, e.g. *nwa* (drink) > *nwiwa* (be drunk); *ɗa* (love) > *ɗiwa* (be loved).

There are also certain special formations, such as *-ti* (say) > *-nzi* (be said); *-ɗaro* (do thus) > *-nzarwo* (be done thus).

THE APPLIED is formed by the suffix *-ira* when the stem-vowel of the verb is primary, i.e. *a*, *i*, or *u*, and by *-era* when the stem-vowel is secondary, i.e. *e* or *o*, e.g.
  ɓata (catch) > *ɓatira* (catch for).
  ɓika (cook) > *ɓikira* (cook for).
  ruma (bite) > *rumira* (bite for).
  rega (omit) > *regera* (omit for).
  dzoka (return) > *dzokera* (return towards).

THE NEUTER is formed by the suffix *-ika* when the stem-vowel of the verb is primary, and by *-eka* when the stem-vowel is secondary, e.g.
  rasa or *rasha* (lose) > *rasika* or *rashika* (get lost).
  bvisa (remove) > *bvisika* (get removed).
  punza (break, tr.) > *punzika* (break, intr.).
  rega (omit) > *regeka* (be omitted).
  vona (see) > *voneka* (be visible).

THE CAUSATIVE is formed as a general rule by suffixing *-isa* if the stem-vowel of the verb is primary, and *-esa* if the stem-vowel is secondary, e.g.
  famba (walk) > *fambisa* (cause to walk).
  ṣika (arrive) > *ṣikisa* (bring).
  kura (grow) > *kurisa* (cause to grow).
  rega (omit) > *regesa* (cause to omit).
  vona (see) > *vonesa* (show).

There are many seemingly irregular methods of forming the causative, among which the following are the chief:

Verbs ending in *-ra* have alternative contracted forms by substituting *-dza* for *-ra*, e.g. *pera* (come to an end) > *peresa*, *pedza* (bring to an end); *zara* (be full) > *zarisa*, *zadza* (fill).

Certain intransitive verbs ending in *-nda* have alternative contracted forms by substituting *-nza* for *-nda*, e.g. *pinda* (enter) > *pindisa*, *pinza* (bring in); *wonda* (be thin) > *wondesa*, *wonza* (make thin).

Intransitive verbs ending in *-ka*, and some ending in *-ta* have alternative contracted forms by substituting *-tsa* for the final syllable, e.g.

seka (laugh) > *sekesa, setsa* (make laugh); *naka* (be good) > *nakisa, natsa* (make good); *neta* (be tired) > *netesa, netsa* (weary, annoy).

THE INTENSIVE is formed according to the general rule for the causative, by suffixing either *-isa* or *-esa*, e.g. *taura* (speak) > *taurisa* (speak up); *vona* (see) > *vonesa* (see clearly).

There is no contraction of suffix with the intensive. When a word has two forms for the causative, the contracted is the form more often used with causative meaning, and the full form with intensive meaning, e.g. *naka* (be good), *nakisa* (be very good), *natsa* (make good); though *nakisa* also means 'make good'.

There is a further intensified form in *-isisa* and *-esesa*, e.g. *gara* (sit down) > *garisisa* (sit right down).

THE RECIPROCAL is formed by suffixing *-ana*, e.g. *d'a* (love)>*d'ana* (love one another); *taurira* (talk to) > *taurirana* (chat).

THE REVERSIVE is formed by suffixing *-ura* if the stem-vowel of the verb is *a, e, i*, or *u*, and *-ora* if the stem-vowel is *o*; e.g. *suŋga* (bind) > *suŋgura*[1] (untie), *mona* (wind) > *monora*[1] (unwind). This form is subject, however, to many irregularities with such suffixes as *-unura* —*tuta* (load) > *tutunura* (unload)— *-urura*, &c.; and in many cases the reversive form corresponds to an applied and not a simple form, e.g. *funira* (cover) > *funura* (uncover).

The intransitive reversive is formed in *-uka*.

(ii) THE CONJUGATION OF THE VERB IN SHONA

There are two conjugations of the verb in Shona, positive and negative. Apart from the infinitive and imperative forms, there are four finite moods in Shona, viz. indicative, subjunctive, potential, and participial.

THE INFINITIVE is formed with the prefix *ku-*, and occurs in positive and negative conjugations:

(Positive) (Negative)
kuvuya (to come) *kusavuya* (not to come)
kugara (to sit) *kusagara* (not to sit)
kuvona kwaŋgu (my seeing)

THE IMPERATIVE. Of disyllabic and polysyllabic verbs the simple stem forms the singular of the imperative, the plural being formed by substituting *-ai* (or *-ayi*) for final *-a*, e.g. *gara* (sit!), *garai* (sit ye!); *batisisa* (grip tightly!) *batisisai* (grip ye tightly!).

Monosyllabic stems prefix the vowel *i-*, e.g. *id'a* (love!), *id'ai* (love ye!); *idya* (eat!), *idyai* (eat ye!).

An immediate imperative is formed by prefixing *ci-*, e.g. *cienda* (go at once!), pl. *ciendai*.

The negative of the imperative is formed by using the deficient verb *rega* (pl. *regai*, omit, leave off) followed by the infinitive, e.g. *rega kugara* (don't sit down!), pl. *regai kugara*.

When an objectival verb concord is used with an imperative, the final *-a* and *-ai* are changed to *-e* and *-ei* respectively, e.g. *ndinzwe* (hear me!), *tipei* (give ye us!).

Both positive and negative forms of the subjunctive mood are used imperatively for all persons and classes.

THE INDICATIVE MOOD. The three implications of the indicative mood, Simple, Progressive, and Exclusive, are found in Shona, though the last is confined to the negative conjugation, and then only occurs as a compound tense.

Simple Implication: *ndinotora* (I take), *handitori* (I do not take).
Progressive Implication: *ndicatora* (I am still taking), *handicatori* (I no longer take).
Exclusive Implication: *handisati ndatora*[2] (I do not yet take).

[1] More commonly heard as *sunuŋgura* and *monyorora*.
[2] Kr. *handizati ndatora*.

THE SHONA GROUP

Distinctions of aspect are not as clear in Shona as in some Bantu languages, but the perfect aspect with stative verbs is distinguished.

Paradigm of the Simple Tenses of the Indicative Mood

	(Positive)	(Negative)
Remote Past	*ndakatora* (I took)	{ *handinakutora* / *handizakatora* } (I did not take)
Immed. Past	*ndatora* (I took)	
Present[1]	*ndinotora* (I take)	*handitori*[2] (I am not taking)
Pres. Stative	*ndigere* (I am sitting)	*handigere* (I am not sitting)
Immed. Future	*ndicatora* (I shall take)	*handiŋgatori*[3] (I shall not take)
Remote Future	{ *ndicazotora* / *ndinozotora* } (I shall take)	*handizotori*[3] (I shall not take)

The following lists show (*a*) the subjectival concord used (i) with present and future tenses positive, (ii) with past tenses positive, (iii) with negative tenses; (*b*) the objectival concord, indicating the object and immediately preceding the verb-stem in every case; (*c*) the present positive tense in full; and (*d*) the present negative tense in full.

Examples of Verb-Concords and Full Tenses

	Subj. concords (indic.)			Obj. concords	Pres. Indic. positive	Pres. Indic. negative
	Pres. Fut.	Past	Neg.			
1st pers. s.	*ndi-*	*nda-*	*ndi-*	*ndi-*	*ndinotora*	*handitori*
pl.	*ti-*	*ta-*	*ti-*	*ti-*	*tinotora*	*hatitori*
2nd pers. s.	*u-*	*wa-*	*u-*	*ku-*	*unotora*	*hautori*
pl.	*mu-*	*ma-*	*mu-*	*ku...(y)i*[4] *mu...(y)i*	*munotora*	*hamutori*
3rd pers. cl. 1	*u-*[5]	*wa-*	*a-*	*mu-*	*unotora*	*haatori*
2	*va-*	*va-*	*va-*	*va-*	*vanotora*	*havatori*
3	*u-*	*wa-*	*u-*	*u-*	*unotora*	*hautori*
4	*i-*	*ya-*	*i-*	*i-*	*inotora*	*haitori*
5	*ri-*	*ra-*	*ri-*	*ri-*	*rinotora*	*haritori*
6	*a-*	*a-*	*a-*	*a-*	*anotora*	*haatori*
7	*ci-*	*ca-*	*ci-*	*ci-*	*cinotora*	*hacitori*
8	*zi-*	*za-*	*zi-*	*zi-*	*zinotora*	*hazitori*
9	*i-*	*ya-*	*i-*	*i-*	*inotora*	*haitori*
10	*dzi-*	*dza-*	*dzi-*	*dzi-*	*dzinotora*	*hadzitori*
11	*ru-*	*rwa-*	*ru-*	*ru-*	*runotora*	*harutori*
12	*tu-*	*twa-*	*tu-*	*tu-*	*tunotora*	*hatutori*
13	*ka-*	*ka-*	*ka-*	*ka-*	*kanotora*	*hakatori*
14	*vu-* / *v-*	*bga-* / *wa-*	*vu-* / *u-*	*vu-* / *u-*	*vunotora* / *unotora*	*havutori* / *hautori*
15	*ku-*	*kwa-*	*ku-*	*ku-*	*kunotora*	*hakutori*
16	*pa-*	*pa-*	*pa-*	*pa-*	*panotora*	*hapatori*
17	*ku-*	*kwa-*	*ku-*	*ku-*	*kunotora*	*hakutori*
18	*mu-*	*ma-*	*mu-*	*mu-*	*munotora*	*hamutori*
19	*ṣi-*	*ṣa-*	*ṣi-*	*ṣi-*	*ṣinotora*	*haṣitori*

---

[1] Ze. distinguishes between present habitual *ndinotora* (I take), and present continuous *ndiri kutora* (I am taking), a compound tense, this latter having a negative *handiri kutora*.

[2] Ze. has final -*e* in the negative, e.g. *handitore*.

[3] There is considerable variance in these futures, there occurring *handicatori* (Ze. *handicatora*), *handicazotori* (Ze. *handicazotora*), &c.

[4] The form of the objectival concord of the 2nd pers. pl. varies considerably with the dialects, appearing alternatively as *ku...i* (*ku...yi*) or *mu...i*; e.g. *tinokuvonayi* (we see you), or *tinomuvonai*. In Ma. always and generally in Kr. this concord is *mu-*, e.g. *tinomuvona*.

[5] In Ze. this appears as *a-*. The general difference between the 2nd pers. s. and the 1st cl. of the 3rd

THE SUBJUNCTIVE MOOD. The present subjunctive is formed by changing the final -a of the simple stem to -e, the subjectival concords being the same as those used in the indicative, except that that of cl. 1 is invariably a-. In the negative the auxiliary -sa- is infixed. The following portion of the tenses indicates the formation.

		(Positive)	(Negative)
1st pers.	s.	nditore	ndisatore[1]
	pl.	titore	tisatore
2nd pers.	s.	utore	usatore
	pl.	mutore	musatore
3rd pers. cl.	1.	atore	asatore
	2.	vatore	vasatore
	3.	utore	usatore
	4.	itore	isatore

In addition to its use after certain conjunctives indicating purpose, the subjunctive in Shona is used imperatively, and in a sequence of tenses following a true imperative, e.g. *endai mutore* (go ye and take). It is also used in permissive interrogation, e.g. *ndipinde?* (am I to enter?).

There are also future subjunctive tenses, e.g. *ndigotora* (that I may take).

Another form of the negative subjunctive is made with the deficient verb *rega*, e.g. *ndirege kutora* (that I take not).

THE POTENTIAL MOOD. Forms occur in the potential mood for both present and future time, with concords as for the subjunctive.

Present Potential:

Positive: *ndiŋgatora*[2] (I can take).

Negative: *handiŋgatori*[2] (I cannot take).

Note: This negative is the same as the negative of the future indicative.

THE PARTICIPIAL MOOD. This mood is used in the formation of relative clauses, and also in ordinary participial construction. The following is a paradigm of the simple tenses of the participial mood:

	(Positive)		(Negative)
Remote Past	ndakatora	} ndikatora	ndisakatora (ndikasatora)
Immediate Past	ndatora		
Present	ndinotora		ndisiŋgatori
	ndicitora		
Future	ndicatora		ndisiŋgazotori

The tenses represented by *ndicitora* and *ndisiŋgatori* are used in circumstances akin to the English participle.

In relative construction, when the antecedent is the subject of the subordinate verb, the tenses of the participial mood are employed with relative concords, e.g. *munhu unotora* (the person who takes), *vanhu vasiŋgavoni* (people who do not see), &c. When, however, the antecedent is not the subject of the subordinate verb, a possessive construction is used, in which the possessive concord agreeing with the antecedent is used with the tenses of the participial mood, in which case the cl. 1 concord, if employed, appears as *a*-, e.g. *ŋgoro yaanofamba nayo* (the wagon with which he travels).

pers. is in the tone, e.g. *unotora* (low tone on *u*), 'thou takest', and *unotora* (high tone on *u*) 'he takes' (cl. 1) and 'it takes' (cls. 2 and 14 (*b*)).

[1] In Kr. this is *ndisatora*, &c.
[2] In Ze. these are *ndiŋgatore* and *handiŋgatore* respectively.

(iii) COMPOUND TENSES IN SHONA

Compound tenses of various types are formed with the aid of deficient verbs, which are of two types:

(a) Monosyllabic verbs, mainly defective, e.g.:

-ri, used in forming a present tense, e.g. ndiri kutora (I am taking), making this tense distinct from the simple present ndinotora, which may be used also of the habitual action, 'I take'.

-ŋga, used in forming past continuous tenses, e.g. ndaŋga ndicitora (I was taking). In this case the deficient verb is followed by a participial mood tense. Notice also such tenses as ndakaŋga ndakatora, ndaŋga ndicatora, &c.

-ti, used in certain compound negative tenses, e.g. handizati ndatora (I did not take).

(b) Deficient verbs ending in -o, being a contraction of -a + -ku of the infinitive. The result is that these deficient verbs appear to be followed by the simple stem of the verb, e.g.

-karo- (do almost), ndakaro-punzika (I nearly fell).

-ṣiko- (do immediately), acigondoṣiko-tema mapaŋgo (he then goes and immediately sets about cutting poles).

-iṣo- (do intensely), ẓakaiṣo-naka (they are awfully nice.)

There are many more of these, including such verbs as -diso-, -fano-, -swero-, -garo-, -natso-, -pingo-, -ziviro-, &c.; and a large number of monosyllabic forms such as -ndo-, -to-, -do-, -ŋgo-, -mbo-, -go-, &c.[1]

(5) THE COPULATIVE

(i) FORMATION OF COPULATIVES FROM NOUNS

A raising of the tone on the noun-prefix is the usual inflexion for forming a copulative therefrom, e.g. cigaro (seat) > cígaro (it is a seat); munhu (person) > mùnhu (it is a person).

With nouns of cl. 1a the prefixal formative ndi- is used, e.g. ndiƁaƁa (it is father), ndiŊgoshi (it is Ngoshi).

Nouns of cls. 5, 9, and 10, having as a rule no prefix expressed as a syllable, are inflected by prefixing i-, e.g.

ŋombe (cattle) > iŋombe (they are cattle).
Ɓaŋga (knife) > iƁaŋga (it is a knife).
ibge, bge (stone) > ibge (it is a stone).
shumba (lion) > ishumba (it is a lion).

(ii) FORMATION OF COPULATIVES FROM ABSOLUTE PRONOUNS

These are formed by prefixing the formative ndi-, e.g. ndini (it is I), ndisu (it is we), ndiwe (it is thou), ndimi (it is you), ndiye, ndivo, ndiwo, ndico, ndidzo, &c.

In the negative such tense forms as the following are found: handisirini (it is not I); hadzisiridzo (they are not they); hatisati tiri hanẓadzi dzako (we are not your sisters).

(iii) FORMATION OF COPULATIVES FROM DEMONSTRATIVE PRONOUNS

From demonstrative pronouns, copulatives are formed by prefixing nda-, nde-, or ndo- according as the vowel of the demonstrative is a, i, or u, e.g. ndoyu (it is this, cl. 1); ndavano (it is these here, cl. 2); ndeiri (it is this, cl. 5); ndedziya (it is those yonder, cl. 10). There is, however, a fair amount of latitude in the choice of vowel, for such forms as ndevano, ndetuno, are often heard, especially in Ma. where substitution of e replaces coalescence.

There is no special inflexion of quantitative pronouns to form copulatives, but the pronoun in that case is preceded by the copulative formed from the absolute pronoun corresponding, e.g. ndini ndoga (it is I alone); ndidzo dzose (it is all of them).

[1] For details regarding these, see Marconnès, *A Grammar of Central Karanga*, pp. 145–51.

(iv) FORMATION OF COPULATIVES FROM ADJECTIVES

The rules in this case are similar to those for the formation from nouns:
munhu murefu (a tall person) > *munhu mùrefu* (the person is tall).
ŋombe tṣuku (a red beast) > *ŋombe itṣuku* (the beast is red).
ɓaŋga ɗete (a thin knife) > *ɓaŋga iɗete* (the knife is thin).

(v) FORMATION OF COPULATIVES FROM POSSESSIVES

The inflexion is similar to that for demonstratives, e.g. *ndewaŋgu* or *ndowaŋgu* (it is mine, cl. 3); *ndeveɗu* or *ndaveɗu* (they are ours, cl. 2); *ndeẓake* (they are his, cl. 8).

(vi) The auxiliary *-ri* is brought into use when no substantival subject is expressed, and in past tenses, e.g. *tiri vanhu* (we are people); *munhu uyu waŋga ari muvezi* (this person was a carpenter).

The auxiliary *-va* (otherwise a monosyllabic verb meaning 'become') is used in forming, amongst others, the subjunctive mood, e.g. *ŋgavave vakuru* (let them become great).

(6) THE ADVERB

At times it is difficult in Shona to distinguish the adverb from the noun. Certain nouns are used adverbially, e.g. *masikati* (at noon), *vusiku* (at night), *maŋgwana* (tomorrow), *nhasi* (today). In addition, locatives of cls. 16, 17, and 18 may be used either as nouns or as adverbs. Hence most adverbs in Shona are formed from other parts of speech by means of adverbial prefixal formatives. These are principally the following: (i) instrumental and conjunctive formative, *na-*, (ii) manner formatives, *ka-*, *ẓi-*; (iii) comparison formative, *sa-*; (iv) locative formatives, *pa-*, *ku-*, *mu-*.

(i) THE INSTRUMENTAL AND CONJUNCTIVE FORMATIVE

The adverbial formative *na-* in Shona has two main significances:

(*a*) As a conjunctive formative signifying 'together with' (see also under 'Conjunctive'), e.g. *Mukomana wavuya nehanẓadzi yake* (The boy came with his sister).

(*b*) As an instrumental formative signifying 'by', 'by means of', 'by reason of'. (Note that in Ma. and Ndau dialects *na-* is replaced by *ŋga-* when instrumental.) In some cases the resulting adverb seems to be one of manner. Examples: *kurova netṣimbo* (to beat with a stick); *kufa nenẓara* (to die of hunger); *kutaura neciZezuru* (to speak in the Zezuru dialect); *nokucimbidza* (quickly); *nesimba* (strongly).

This formative may be placed before nouns, when it will appear as *na-*, *ne-*, or *no-* according to whether there is an implied initial vowel, and to whether that vowel is *a*, *i*, or *u*. It may similarly be placed before the absolute pronouns, when coalescence with the initial *i-* takes place with the 1st and 2nd persons, but elision of the *i-* with all classes of the 3rd person when not emphatic, e.g. *neni*, *nesu*, *newe*, *nemi*, but *naye*, *navo*, *naco*, *nadzo*, &c.

(ii) THE MANNER FORMATIVES

Adverbs are formed from certain adjectival stems by prefixing *ka-*, e.g. *kamŋe* (once); *kaviri* (twice); *kazhinji* (often); *kashoma* (rarely).

Other adverbs are formed by using the cl. 8 concord, either relatively or adjectivally, e.g. *ẓikuru* (much, greatly); *ẓakanaka* (well); *ẓakaipa* (badly).

(iii) THE COMPARISON FORMATIVE

The adverbial formative *sa-* is prefixed to indicate 'as', 'like', e.g. *saɓaɓa* (like father); *somunhu* (like a person); *saye* (like him); *seni* (like me). This formative undergoes changes from *sa-* to *se-* or *so-*, in the same way as the formative *na-*.

(iv) THE LOCATIVE FORMATIVES (cf. noun cls. 16, 17, and 18)

pa- indicating 'at, on, under', generally of rest at: *pamusha* (at the village); *pamusoro* (on the top, on the head).

ku- indicating generally motion to and from a relatively distant place: *kugomo* (to the mountain); *kumusha* (from the village).

mu- indicating 'in, inside, out from, round': *mumiti* (among the trees); *mumuromo* (in the mouth).

pana-, *kuna-*, and *muna-* are the prefixal forms used before (*a*) nouns of cl. 1a, e.g. *kunaɓaɓa* (to father); and (*b*) pronouns, e.g. *kunaye* (to him).

pa-, *kwa-*, and *ma-* are the prefixal (possessive) forms used to indicate 'the place of', with proper names, e.g. *kwaGutu* (to Gutu's village); *paCinamora* (at Chinamora's place).

Place-names which are not taken from the names of persons are used without inflexion as locative adverbs in Shona, e.g. *Ŋombe dzinoenda Harare* (The cattle are going to Salisbury); *Hwai dzinobva Cishawasha* (The sheep come from Chishawasha).

(7) THE IDEOPHONE

Monosyllabic, disyllabic, and trisyllabic ideophones are quite commonly found in Shona.
Monosyllabic:

ɓù (of biting the finger): *Wakanditi ɓù munwe waŋgu* (He gave my finger a bite).
dì (of quick walk): *Ari kufamba kuti dì dì dì* (He is walking fast).
bu̧ (of blazing up).
du̧ (of snapping).
da̧ (of stretching).
si̧:: (of darkness).

Disyllabic:

gumi gumi gumi (of gait of chameleon).
baru (of tearing): *Ndakariti jira baru* (I tore the cloth).
undu (of moulting): *Huku yakanzi undu minheŋga* (The fowl had its feathers plucked out).

Trisyllabic:

cácaca (of heavy rain).
zùŋguze zùŋguze (of restless motion).
pápata (of galloping).
férere (of sound of flute).

Note 1. Abnormal length, gliding tones, and unusual phonetic phenomena are found, particularly with the monosyllabic forms.

Note 2. Shona uses the verb *kuti* (passive *kunzi*) in sentence construction with ideophones.

Note 3. Verbs and nouns are formed from ideophones in Shona; note the following examples of verb-formation by suffix:

-*ka* (intr.): *tabvu* > *tabvuka* (bounce); *undu* > *unduka* (moult, come out); *do* > *doka* (be downcast); *ridiɓu* > *ridiɓuka* (run with shambling gait, as baboon); *bvaru* > *bvaruka* (get torn).

-*ra* (tr.): *tabvura* (make bounce); *undura* (pluck out), *bvarura* (tear).

-*dza* (caus.): *nyŋa nyŋa* (of dog running) > *nyŋanyŋadza* (amble along); *nyere nyere* > *nyeredza* (tickle); *di* > *dinidza* (smack).

-*ma* (stat.): *tayi* > *tayima* (glitter).

(8) THE CONJUNCTIVE

There are not many conjunctives in Shona. The following might be noted:

asi, also *bva* in Kr., (but): *Wakaridza mhere, asi hapana wakauya* (He called for help, but nobody came).

nokuti or *ẓa* (because): *Ʋakashaiwa ẓiyo nokuti mvura haina kuna* (They had no corn because the rain didn't come).

kana (if, when; in Ma., although): *Kana vasika, vabvunze* (If they have come, ask them); *kana acid'a, kana asiŋgad'i* (whether he likes it or not).

nyaŋgwe, in Ze. *kunyaŋge* (although): *nyaŋgwe akapika* (although he swore to it).

kuti (that, in order that) followed by the subjunctive mood: *Wakavaudza kuti acazodzoka gore rinotevera* (He told them that he would return the following year); *Ndakamukumbira kuti avaregere* (I asked him to forgive them).

(9) THE INTERJECTIVE

(i) RADICAL INTERJECTIONS. Shona has many, in which varying emotions are expressed and tone plays a large part. Note the following:

hoŋo, huŋgu, heya (yes!).
kwete, 6od'o, ṣa (no!).
maiwe (expressing astonishment).
yowe (expressing pain or sorrow).

(ii) VOCATIVES. There is no inflexion of nouns to express the vocative in Shona, but nouns may become vocative interjectives syntactically; note:

Ndinokud'a, Ngoshi! (I want you, Ngoshi!).
Tarirayi, vakomana! (Look, boys!).
Chaŋgamire! (My great Lord!).

(iii) VERB IMPERATIVES. Apart from ordinary imperatives, which have already been noticed, note such forms as *kwaziwa* (pl. *kwaziwayi*) the greeting 'good-day' (Ma., *kwaiwa*); *hekani* (thank you, just so!).

(10) ENCLITIC AND PROCLITIC FORMATIVES

(i) ENCLITICS which draw the stress forward:

Ma. *-ẓe* (again): *Ʋuyaẓe* (Come again).
-pi? (where?): *Wabvepi?* (Where do you come from?).

(ii) ENCLITICS which do not draw the stress forward (hyphened):

-vo, not an enclitic in Kr. [(1) also, (2) please]: *Ʋamŋe-vo vanoẓiita* (Others, too, do it); *Unoɓud'a-vo?* (Are you well also?); *Ndipe-vo* (Please give it to me).
-ko (interrogative): *Ʋanod'eyi-ko?* (What do they want?).

Also used as a separate adverb initially: *Ko waiteyi?* (Whatever have you done?).

The locative enclitics: *-po, -ko, -mo*: *Takava-po* (We were there); *Ndakaenda-ko* (I went there); *Wabva-mo* (He came outside).

(iii) The PROCLITIC *na-* (subject to rules of coalescence): This is used conjunctivally connecting substantives and adverbs, e.g. *Bobo naGutu vauya* (Bobo and Gutu have come); *mabiza neŋombe nehwai* (horses and cattle and sheep); *pano napaya* (here and yonder). This formative is also used adverbially indicating: (*a*) together with, e.g. *Ndakauya naye* (I came with him); and (*b*) instrument, e.g. *kuceka neɓaŋga* (to cut with a knife).

(11) THE NUMERALS

(i) The following are used in counting without the naming of the object:

1 *poshi* (Kr. *motsi*: Ma. *posi* or *potsi*); 2 *piri*; 3 *tatu*; 4 *cina* (Kr. *cinna*); 5 *shanu*; 6 *tanhatu*; 7 *cinomŋe*; 8 *rusere*; 9 *pfumbamŋe*; 10 *gumi*.

(ii) The following are used in counting with the name of the object:

1 *-mŋe* (enumerative stem), e.g. *ɓanga rimŋe* (one knife). 2–9 are adjectives: 2 *-viri*;

THE SHONA GROUP

3 *-tatu*; 4 *-na* (Kr. *-nna*; Ma. *-roŋgomuna*); 5 *-shanu*; 6 *-tanhatu*; 7 *-nomŋe*; 8 *-sere*; 9 *-pfumbamŋe*; e.g. *mabiza manomŋe* (seven horses), *ẓinhu ẓina* (four things).

10 *gumi* (pl. *makumi*), noun of cl. 5, used followed by a possessive construction, e.g. *gumi ramabiza* (ten horses), *makumi matatu eŋombe* (thirty cattle).

(12) RELATIVE CONSTRUCTION

This may be divided into the two aspects of (i) Direct Relative, and (ii) Indirect Relative.

(i) THE DIRECT RELATIVE construction is used when the antecedent is in subjectival relationship to the relative predicate. In this the relative concord[1] precedes the relative predicate, which is in the participial mood. Examples:

munhu ari pano (the person who is here).
ɓaŋga rakanaka (a lovely knife).
Ndinoďa kuiteŋga shiri inoimba ẓakanaka (I want to buy a bird that sings nicely).
Mŋana usiŋgacemi haakuri (A child who does not cry does not grow).

(ii) THE INDIRECT RELATIVE, in which the relationship between antecedent and relative predication is oblique, e.g. objectival, adverbial, &c., is expressed in one of two ways: (*a*) by the employment of possessive construction, and (*b*) by the use of demonstrative pronouns, this latter being the construction in Ma. In each case the basis of the relative predicate is participial.

(*a*) Use of descriptive possessive construction:

Objectival relationship:

Ɓaŋga rawakarasha raŋga riri raŋgu (The knife which you lost was mine).
Twana twavanoďaidza turi mumunda (The little children whom they are calling are in the garden).
mŋana wausiŋgaďi (the child whom you do not like).

Locative relationship:

Uuya neswanda maakaisa vupfu (Bring the basket in which she put the meal).
pamusha pausiŋgavati (the village at which you do not sleep).

Instrumental and Conjunctive relationship:

Ɓadza randinoɓata naro (the hoe with which I work).
vupfu bgaanoɓika sadza rake nabgo (the meal with which she cooks her porridge).

(*b*) Use of demonstrative pronouns:

Objectival relationship:

Muti uyo varume vakautema waŋga wakareɓa (The tree which the men cut down was tall).
Cigaro ico murume usiŋgaciďi ciri panze (The chair which the man does not want is outside).

Subjectival-possessive relationship:

Musikana uyo mai vake vakafa uri pano (The girl whose mother died is here).
vupfu ubgo mŋene wabgo asiŋgavuteŋgisi (the meal whose owner does not sell it).

Objectival- or adverbial-possessive relationship:

Muruŋgu uyo ŋgoro yake wakavuya nayo wakaṣika (The white man with whose wagon he came has arrived).

---

[1] The relative concord is the same as the subjectival concord; in cl. 1 *a-* and *u-* are used in either case according to dialect.

(iii) There is also an elliptical construction of the relative shared by Shona with the Central Bantu languages, in which the concord for the object is substituted for that of the subject, and the possessive concord omitted entirely:

ɓaŋga rakarasha mukomana (the knife the boy lost).
cinhu cinoďa mŋana (the thing the child wants).

REFERENCES

[H. Buck]: *A Dictionary with Notes on the Grammar of the Mashona Language commonly called Chiswina* [this is Manyika dialect], 1911.
E. Biehler: *English-Chiswina Dictionary with an Outline Chiswina Grammar* [this is Zezuru dialect], 3rd ed. 1927.
C. S. Louw: *A Manual of the Chikaranga Language*, 1915.
[A. J. Orner]: *Chindau-English and English-Chindau Vocabulary with Grammatical Notes*, 1915.
J. P. Dysart: *Chindau Lessons* [cyclostyled, n.d.].
C. M. Doke: *A Comparative Study in Shona Phonetics*, 1931.
F. Marconnès: *A Grammar of Central Karanga*, 1931.
B. H. Barnes: *A Vocabulary of the Dialects of Mashonaland*, 1932.
J. O'Neil: *A Shona Grammar, Zezuru Dialect*, 1935.

APPENDIX I

CHOPI TABLES

CHOPI is the most important member of the Inhambane Group of the South-eastern Bantu zone. Other dialects are Lenge (influenced by Tsonga) and Tonga (giTonga, which has considerable Portuguese influence on vocabulary). Little linguistic work had been done in these languages. For Chopi we have: H. P. Junod, *Éléments de grammaire tchopi* (Sociedade de Geografia de Lisboa, pp. 42, 1933); and for Lenge: Bishop Smyth and John Matthews, *A Short Grammar of the Shilenge Language* (*Xilenge*) (S.P.C.K., pp. 44, 1902). A short phonological and grammatical study of Tonga was published by N. J. v. Warmelo in the *Zeitschrift für Eingeborenen-sprachen* (vol. xxii, pp. 16–46), entitled 'Das Gitonga'.

VOWELS. Chopi has a five-vowel system, **i, e, ɑ, o,** and **u**.[1]

CONSONANTAL CHART

	Bilabial	Denti-labial	Alveolar	Prepalatal	Velar	Glottal
EXPLOSIVE eject. asp. voic.	p' ph b mb		t' th d nd		k' kh g ŋg	
IMPLOSIVE	ɓ		ɗ			
NASAL contin. syll.	m mɦ m̩		n	ɲ	ŋ	
ROLLED LATERAL			r l			
FRICATIVE unv. voic.	β	f	s z			h
AFFRICATE eject. voic.	pf' bv	mbv	ts' dz ndz	tʃ' dʒ ɲdʒ		
SEMI-VOWEL	(w)			j	w	

Notes:
1. **d** is rarely found apart from **nd**.
2. Lenge uses ʃ, not commonly found in Chopi.
3. Palatalized forms, e.g. **dj, pj, gj, hj, mbj**, &c., occur.
4. Velarized forms, e.g. **lw, kw, rw, mbw, pjw**, &c., occur.
5. The heterorganic combination **ps**, which is found, is probably a development from the labio-alveolar affricate **pʂ**.
6. Absence of lateral fricatives is noteworthy.

Regarding GRAMMATICAL FEATURES, the locative is formed by suffix, as also the noun diminutive. In relative formation the suffix **-ku** is used.

VOCABULARY features often point to Central Bantu.

[1] In these appendixes all examples are given in phonetic script.

CONCORD TABLES

	N.P.	A.C.	R.C.[1]	E.C.	P.C.	S.C.	O.C.	Q.P.[2]
1st pers. s.	—	—	ni-	—	—	ni-	ni-	no-
pl.	—	—	hi-	—	—	hi-	hi-	ho-
2nd pers. s.	—	—	u-	—	—	u-	k'u-	we-
pl.	—	—	mi-, (mu-)	—	—	mi-, (mu-)	mi-	mo-
3rd pers. cl. 1	m-, (N-)[3]	wam-	a-	wu-, wi-, ji-	wa-	a-	m-	je-
1a	—							
2	βa-	βaβa-	βa-	βa-	βa-	βa-	βa-	βo-
2a	βa-							
3	m-, (N-)[3]	wawu-	wu-	mu-, wu-	wa-	wu-	wu-	wo-
4	mi-	jaji-, jami-	ji-	mi-, ji-	ja-	ji-, (i-)	ji-	jo-
5	ɗi-	ɗaɗi-	ɗi-	ɗi-	ɗa-	ɗi-	ɗi-	ɗo-
6	ma-	ama-	a-	ma-, wa-	a-	ma-	ma-	o-
7	tʃ'i-	tʃ'atʃ'i-	tʃ'i-	tʃ'i-	tʃ'a-	tʃ'i-	tʃ'i-	tʃ'o-
8	ts'i-[4]	ts'ats'i-	ts'i-	ts'i-	ts'-a	ts'i-	ts'i-	ts'o-
9	(i)N-	jaji-	ji-	ji-	ja-	ji-, (i-)	ji-	jo-
10	t'iN-[5]	t'at'i-	t'i-	t'i-	t'a-	t'i-	t'i-	t'o-
11	li-	lali-	li-	li-	la-	li-	li-	lo-
14	βu-[6]	βaβu-	βu-	βu-	βa-[7]	βu-	βu-	βo-
15	k'u-	k'ak'u-, k'wak'u-	k'u-	k'u-	k'a-	k'u-	k'u-	k'o-

Notes: Some Lenge alternatives are in parentheses.
[1] Relative Concord is preceded by the 1st position demonstrative in relative construction.
[2] Quantitative roots are -ts'e (all) and -ka (only).
[3] Lenge and Tonga usually have N- (iN-) as prefix of these classes, where N = homorganic nasal before initial consonant of the stem.
[4] Variant forms throughout use s for ts', e.g. si-, sa-, &c.
[5] There are variant forms with ts' for t'.
[6] There are variant forms with w for β.
[7] Variant vwa-.

PRONOMINAL TABLES

	Absolute pronoun	Demonstrative pronouns				Poss. stem
		1st position	2nd position	3rd position	4th position	
1st pers. s.	ani, mina	—	—	—	—	-ŋgu
pl.	athu, hina	—	—	—	—	-thu
2nd pers. s.	awe, wena	—	—	—	—	-k'u
pl.	anu, mwina	—	—	—	—	-nu
3rd pers. cl. 1	ene, jena	awu	(ajo)	awua	awule	-k'we
2	awe, βona	aβa	(aβo)	aβaa	aβale	-we
3	(a)wu, wona	awu	(awo)	wua	awule	-wona
4	(a)ji, jona	aji	ejo	jija	ajile	-jona
5	(a)ɗi, ɗona	aɗi	eɗo	ɗija	aɗile	-ɗona
6	hawa, ona	hawa	(awo)	waja	awale	-ona
7	(a)tʃ'i, tʃ'ona	atʃ'i	etʃ'o	tʃ'ija	atʃ'ile	-tʃ'ona
8	(a)ts'i, ts'ona	ats'i	ets'o	ts'ija	ats'ile	-ts'ona
9	(a)ji, jona	aji	ejo	jija	ajile	-jona
10	(a)ti, tona	ati	eto	tija	atile	-tona
11	(a)li, lona	ali	elo	lija	alile	-lona

PRONOMINAL TABLES (cont.)

	Absolute pronoun	Demonstrative pronouns				Poss. stem
		1st position	2nd position	3rd position	4th position	
3rd pers. cl. 14	(a)βu, βona	aβu	—	βua	aβule	-βona
15	(a)k'u, k'ona	ak'u	—	k'uwa	ak'ule	-k'ona
16	— —	aha	—	hawa	ahale	—
17	(a)k'u, k'ona	ak'u	—	k'uwa	ak'ule	—
18	— —	amu	—	mua	amule	—

Notes
1. Absolute pronouns have alternative forms.
2. There is a great number of dialectal variants with the demonstratives; further distances of the 4th position are found, such as atʃ'ileja, &c. There is great irregularity with the 2nd position forms, which correspond to Bantu forms with suffix -no; some have not been identified.

NUMERALS

1. -mwe
2. -ɓidʼi } (enumeratives)
3. -raru
4. mune
5. mtʃ'anu
6. mtʃ'anu ni-( )mwe
7. mtʃ'anu ni-( )ɓidʼi } (nouns)
8. mtʃ'anu ni-( )raru
9. mtʃ'anu nimune
10. dʼigume

( ) = enumerative concord required.

The COPULATIVE FORMATIVE is either ŋgu- or i-.

APPENDIX II

PHUTHI TABLES

PHUTHI is an extreme type of Nguni of the Tekeza cluster with strong Sotho influence. It is spoken in the East Griqualand district of the Cape Province and over the border in Southern Basutoland. Apart from a brief article by W. Bourquin, information on this dialect is to be obtained from the monograph by G. I. M. Mzamane entitled *A Concise Treatise on Phuthi, with special reference to its Relationship with Nguni and Sotho* (Fort Hare Papers, vol. i, no. 4, 1949).

VOWELS. Seven phonemes as in Sotho, represented by ɩ, i, e, a, o, u, ʉ; e and o each having an open and a close variety, ɛ, e and ɔ, o respectively; only the phoneme representative is given in the tables.

CHART OF PLAIN CONSONANTS

	Bilabial	Denti-labial	Alveolar	Pre-palatal	Velar	Glottal	Compound
EXPLOSIVE							
eject.	p'		t'		k'		
asp.	ph		th		kh		
voic.	b		d	ɉ*	g		
IMPLOSIVE	ɓ		(ɗ)				
NASAL							
contin.	m		n	ɲ	ŋ		
syll.	m̩		n̩				
asp.				ɲɦ			
ROLLED			r				
LATERAL							
contin.			l				
syll.			l̩				
FRICATIVE							
med. unv.		f	s	ʃ	x	h	
med. voic.		v	z	ʒ	ɣ		
lat. unv.			ɬ				
AFFRICATE							
med. unv.			ts	tʃ			
med. asp.			tsh	tʃh	kxh		tfh
med. voic.			dz	dʒ			dv
lat. unv.			tɬ				
lat. voic.			dɮ				
SEMI-VOWEL	(w)			j	w		

* Palatal, rather than prepalatal.

Note: The unvoiced affricates are probably ejective.

Regarding ɗ, Mzamane describes it as 'soft-*d*', semi-implosive, not as distinctly implosive as in Shona, and almost the same sound 'as represented by Tucker' as ɺ (the flapped member of the l phoneme).

PHUTHI TABLES

CLICK CONSONANTS

	Dental	Palato-alveolar	Lateral
Radical	ʇ	C	ʖ
Aspirated	ʇh	Ch	ʖh
Voiced	ʇg	Cg	ʖg
Nasal	ʇŋ	Cŋ	ʖŋ
Nasal-asp.	ʇŋɦ	Cŋɦ	ʖŋɦ

CONCORD TABLES

		N.P.	A.C.	R.C.	E.C.	P.C.	S.C.	O.C.	Q.P.
1st pers.	s.	—	—	—	—	—	gi-	gi-	go-, ge-
	pl.	—	—	—	—	—	si-	si-	so-
2nd pers.	s.	—	—	—	—	—	u-	ku-	wo-, we-
	p.	—	—	—	—	—	li-	li-	lo-
3rd pers. cl.	1	mu-	lomu-	lo-	mu-, u-	wa-	u-(a-)	mu-	wo-, ye-
	1a	—							
	2	eɓa-	laɓa-	laɓa-	ɓa-	ɓa-	ɓa-	ɓa-	ɓo-
	2a	ɓo-							
	3	mu-	lomu-	lo-	mu-, wu-	wa-	u-	wu-	wo-
	4	mi-	lemi-	le-	mi-, ji-	ja-	i-	ji-	jo-
	5	li-	leli-	leli-	li-	la-	li-	li-	lo-
	6	ema-	lama-	la-	ma-, a-	a-	a-	wa-	wo-
	7	si-	lesi-	lesi-	si-	sa-	si-	si-	so-
	8	ti-	leti-	leti-	ti-	ta-	ti-	ti-	to-
	9	i[N]-	le[N]-	le-	i-	ja-	i-	ji-	jo-
	10	ti[N]-	leti[N]-	leti-	ti-	ta-	ti-	ti-	to-
	11	lu-	lolu-	lolu-	lu-	la-	lu-	lu-	lo-
	14	ɓu-	loɓu-	loɓu-	ɓu-	ɓa-	ɓu-	ɓu-	ɓo-
	15	ku-	loku-	loku-	ku-	kwa-	ku-	ku-	ko-

Note: Possessive concord undergoes substitution of e before nouns other than cls. 1a and 2a, e.g. **mili:go jemo:ja** (temptations of the soul).

PRONOMINAL TABLES

		Absolute pronouns	Demonstrative pronouns			Poss. stem
			1st position	2nd position	4th position	
1st pers.	s.	mine, mina	—	—	—	-mi
	pl.	tshine, tshina	—	—	—	-thfu
2nd pers.	s.	wena	—	—	—	-kho
	pl.	line, lina	—	—	—	-inu
3rd pers. cl.	1	jena	lo(na)	lowo	lowaa	-khe
	2	ɓona	laɓa	laɓo	laɓaa	-ɓo
	3	wona	lo(na)	lowo	lowaa	-wo
	4	jona	le(na)	lejo	lejaa	-jo
	5	lona	leli	lelo	lelaa	-lo
	6	wona	la(na)	lawo	lawaa	-wo
	7	sona	lesi	leso	lesaa	-so
	8	tona	leti	leto	letaa	-to
	9	jona	le(na)	lejo	lejaa	-jo
	10	tona	leti	leto	letaa	-to
	11	lona	lolu	lolo	lolaa	-lo
	14	ɓona	loɓu	loɓo	loɓaa	-ɓo
	15	kona	loku	loko	lokwaa	-ko

NUMERALS

1. **-ne**
2. **-ɓini**
3. **-tshathfu** } (adjectives)
4. **-ne**
5. **-ɬanu**
6. **-jeȽgele** (crossed over)
7. **-subije** (pointed)
8. **-phulije minwana lemiɓini** } (verbs)
9. **-phulije munwana lomuɲe**
10. **-liʃumi** (noun)

APPENDIX III

NGONI TABLES[1]

THERE are two types of Ngoni, offshoots from Zulu. That in Nyasaland shows very little divergence from the parent language; on this W. A. Elmslie wrote an *Introductory Grammar of the Ngoni Language, as spoken in West Nyasaland* in 1891. But the other type, that spoken in the present Tanganyika Territory, while retaining typical Zulu vocabulary and morphology, particularly that of the verb, has acquired much from Eastern Bantu, including the diminutive classes 12 and 13 and a full concordial use of the three locative classes 16, 17, and 18. The assumption of the prefix-suffix form of objectival concord for the 2nd pers. pl. is also striking. In regard to phonetics, our information is insufficient upon which to base conclusions; but it is probable that there has been a considerable simplification.

The information given here has been gleaned from the article 'Kingoni und Kisutu' contributed by C. Spiss to the *Mitteilungen des Seminars für Orientalische Sprachen* in 1904.

VOWELS. Five vowel phonemes are used, i, e, a, o, and u; and it is not known whether the mid-vowels e and o have two varieties each or not.

CONSONANTAL CHART

	Bilabial	Dentilabial	Alveolar	Pre-palatal	Velar	Glottal
EXPLOSIVE						
unv.	p		t		k	
voic.	b mb		d nd		g ŋg	
NASAL						
contin.	m		n	ɲ	ŋ	
syll.	m̩		n̩			
ROLLED			r			
LATERAL			l			
FRICATIVE						
med. unv.		f	s	ʃ		h
med. voic.		v ɱv	z nz			
lat. unv.			ɬ			
lat. voic.			ɮ nɮ			
AFFRICATE						
unv.				tʃ		
voic.				dʒ ndʒ		
SEMI-VOWEL	(w)			j	w	

Notes. There is insufficient information upon the sounds of Tanganyika Ngoni. It seems that implosive ɓ has been dropped. We do not know whether there is still distinction between ejective and aspirated explosives and affricates; nor is it known whether fricatives when preceded by the homorganic nasal become affricates or remain fricatives.

ONE CLICK of Zulu only, the palato-alveolar ꞓ, as in ꞓina (be strong), has been preserved; in Nyasaland Ngoni all three click types persist.

---
[1] These deal with the Tanganyika Ngoni dialect.

NGONI TABLES

CONCORD TABLES

	N.P.	A.C.	R.C.[1]	E.C.	P.C.	S.C.	O.C.	O.P.[2]
1st pers. s.	—	—	ni-, ndi-	—	—	ŋgi-, ndi-	ŋgi-, ndi-	nde-, ne-, no-
pl.	—	—	ti-	—	—	ti-	ti-	te-, to-
2nd pers. s.	—	—	u-	—	—	u-	ku-	we-, wo-
pl.	—	—	mu-	—	—	mu-	wa--ni	mwe-, mo-
3rd pers. cl. 1	mu-, m̥-	mu-, m̥	u-, a-	a-	wa-	u-	m̥-	je-, jo-
1a	—							
2	wa-	wa-	wa-	wa-	wa-	wa-	wa-	wo-
2a	wa-							
3	mu-, m̥-	mu-, m̥-	u-	u-	wa-	u-	u-	we-, wo-
4	mi-	mi-	i-	i-	ja-	i-	i-	je-, jo-
5	li-	li-	li-	li-	lja-	li-	li-	lje-, ljo-
6	ma-	ma-	ga-	ga-	ga-	ga-	ga-	ge-, go-
7	ki-[3]	ki-	ki-	ki-	tʃa-	ki-	ki-	tʃe-, tʃo-
8	vi-[4]	vi-	vi-	vi-	vja-	vi-	vi-	vje-, vjo-
9	(i)N-	i-	i-	i-	ja-	i-	i-	je-, jo-
10	ziN-	zi-	zi-	zi-	za-	zi-	zi-	ze-, zo-
11	lu-	lu-	lu-	lu-	lwa-	lu-	lu-	lwe-, lo-
12	tu-	tu-	tu-	tu-	twa-	tu-	tu-	twe-
13	ka-	ka-	ka-	ka-	ka-	ka-	ka-	ke-, ko-
14	u-	u-	u-	u-	wa-	u-	u-	we-, wo-
15	ku-	ku-	ku-	ku-	kwa-	ku-	ku-	ko-
16	pa-	pa-	pa-	pa-	pa-	pa-	pa-	pe-, po-
17	ku-	ku-	ku-	ku-	kwa-	ku-	ku-	ko-
18	mu-	mu-	mu-	(mu-)	mwa-	mu-	mu-	mwe, mo-

Notes: Nyasa Ngoni uses the initial vowel with the N.P. as does Zulu; Tanganyika dialect has lost the initial vowel.

[1] There is some uncertainty regarding the relative concords: in cl. 1, u- seems to be used with relative stems, a- with the relative clause construction.

[2] Of the quantitative pronouns, -dwa (only) takes e or o forms, but -ŋke (all) takes only o forms.

[3] Nyasa Ngoni has itʃi-.

[4] Nyasa Ngoni has alternates ivi-, izi-.

PRONOMINAL TABLES

	Absolute pronoun	Demonstrative pronouns			Poss. stem
		1st position	2nd position	4th position	
1st pers. s.	miɲne	—	—	—	-mi
pl.	tini	—	—	—	-itu
2nd pers. s.	wena	—	—	—	-ko
pl.	nina, mwena	—	—	—	-inu
3rd pers. cl. 1	jena	loju	lojani	loja	-ke
2	wona	lawa	lawajani	lawajá	-o
3	wona	lou	lojani	loja	-wo
4	jona	lei	leijani	leijá	-jo
5	lona	leli	lelijani	lelijá	-lo
6	gona	laga	lagajani	lagajá	-go
7	tʃona	leki	letʃijani	lekijá	-tʃo
8	vjona	levi	levijani	levijá	-vjo
9	jona	lei	leijani	leijá	-jo
10	zona	lezi	lezijani	lezijá	-zo
11	lona	lolu	lolujani	lolujá	-lo
12	tona	lutu	lutujani	lutujá	-to
13	kona	laka	lakajani	lakajá	-ko

PRONOMINAL TABLES (cont.)

	Absolute pronoun	Demonstrative pronouns			Poss. stem
		1st position	2nd position	4th position	
3rd pers. cl. 14	wona	lou	lojani	loja	-wo
15	kona	loku	lokujani	lokujá	-ko
16	pona	lapa	lapajani	lapajá	-po
17	kona	loku	lokujani	lokujá	-ko
18	mona	lomu	lomujani	lomujá	-mo

Note: Alternative to the use of the possessive stems is the use of the full absolute pronoun, e.g. **wami** or **wamiɲne, wetu** or **watini**, &c.

NUMERALS

1. **-mozi, -ɲe** ⎫
2. **-wili** ⎪
3. **-tatu** ⎪
4. **-ṇne** ⎪
5. **-ɬano** ⎬ (adjectives)
6. **-ɬano na-( )mozi** ⎪
7. **-ɬano na-( )wili** ⎪
8. **-ɬano na-( )tatu** ⎪
9. **-ɬano na-( )ṇne** ⎭
10. **itʃumi** (noun)

( ) = adjectival concord required.

Though adjectival concords seem generally to be used with the basic numerals, enumerative concords are also found, e.g. **matʃumi mawili** or **gawili**.

APPENDIX IV

LOZI TABLES

Lozi, or Kololo, is the language of Barotseland in the western portion of Northern Rhodesia towards the upper reaches of the Zambesi River. It belongs to the Sotho group, having its origin in Southern Sotho. Lozi has, however, undergone considerable influence from local members of the Central and West-central Bantu zones, particularly from Luyi. While, to a large extent, Sotho vocabulary and many grammatical forms persist, there are today considerable divergencies from the parent stock which show themselves in phonetics and grammar.

The vowels are reduced to five phonemes (as in Nguni and in many Central Bantu languages). The consonants have been simplified: lateral fricatives have been dropped and there is a big reduction of affricates. In the noun classes Lozi has retained 11, and has acquired the diminutives 12 and 13 as well as 19; retaining at the same time the diminutive suffixes -ana and -ɲana. Locative is by suffix as in S. Sotho.

For Lozi we have three little books published by A. Jalla in 1917: *Elementary Grammar of the Sikololo Language*, *English-Sikololo Dictionary*, and *Sikololo-English Dictionary*; also S. Colyer's little book on *Sikololo* (1914). I have used M. Gluckman's paper, 'Prefix Concordance in Lozi' (*African Studies*, 1942) in preparing these Tables.

VOWELS: i, e (ɛ), a, o (ɔ), u.

CONSONANTAL CHART

	Bilabial	Dentilabial	Alveolar	Pre-palatal	Velar	Glottal
EXPLOSIVE unv.[1]	p		t		k	
voic.	b mb		d[2] nd		ŋg	
NASAL contin.	m		n		ŋ	
syll.	m̩		n̩	ɲ̩	ŋ̩	
ROLLED			(r)[3]			
LATERAL			l			
FRICATIVE unv.		f	s	ʃ		h
voic.	(β)[4]		z			
AFFRICATE unv.				tʃ		
voic.				dʒ		
SEMI-VOWEL	(w)			j	w	

Notes:

[1] The unvoiced explosives are slightly aspirated.

[2] This is a permutation of l when followed by i or u (orthography: li, lu); many speakers seem to make no change, using l in all circumstances.

[3] Rarely used.

[4] The b is very soft, and often appears as β.

LOZI TABLES

CONCORD TABLES

	N.P.	A.C.	R.C.	E.C.	P.C.	S.C.	O.C.	Q.P.
1st pers. s.	—	—	*	—	—	ndi-, ni-	ni-	—
pl.	—	—	*	—	—	lu-	lu-	*
2nd pers. s.	—	—	*	—	—	u-	ku-	—
pl.	—	—	*	—	—	mu-	mi-	*
3rd pers. cl. 1	mu-	jomu-	ja-	mu-, u-	wa-	u-, (a-)	mu-	—
1a	—							
2	ba-	baba-	baba-	ba-	ba-	ba-	ba-	bo-
2a	bo-							
3	mu-	omu-	o-	mu-, u-	wa-	u-	u-	o-
4	mi-	jemi-	je-	mi-, i-	ja-	i-	i-	jo-
5	li-	leli-	leli-	li-	la-	li-	li-	lo-
6	ma-	ama-	a-	ma-, a-	a-	a-	a-	o-
7	si-	sesi-	sesi-	si-	sa-	si-	si-	so-
8	li-	ze-	ze-	li-	za-	li-	li-	zo-
9	N-	je-	je-	i-	ja-	i-	i-	jo-
10	liN-	ze-	ze-	li-	za-	li-	li-	zo-
11	lu-	lolu-	lolu-	lu-	lwa-	lu-	lu-	lo-
12	tu-	totu-	totu-	tu-	twa-	tu-	tu-	to-
13	ka-	kaka-	kaka-	ka-	ka-	ka-	ka-	ko-
14	bu-	bobu-	bobu-	bu-	bwa-	bu-	bu-	bo-
15	ku-	koku-	koku-	ku-	kwa-	ku-	ku-	ko
19	bi-	bjebi-	bjebi-	bi-	bja-	bi-	bi-	-bjo

* Indicates forms not recorded.

Notes:
1. The locative prefixes, cls. 16 (fa-), 17 (ku-, kwa) and 18 (mwa-) are used as adverbial formatives.
2. In addition to the si-li class (7–8), Lozi has a pejorative class si-bi (7–19) indicating 'contempt, thickness, dumpiness' (Jalla).

PRONOMINAL TABLES

	Absolute pronoun	Demonstrative pronouns				Poss. stem
		1st position	2nd position	3rd position	4th position	
1st pers. s.	ŋna	—	—	—	—	-ka
pl.	luna	—	—	—	—	-luna (-isu)
2nd pers. s.	wena	—	—	—	—	-hao
pl.	mina	—	—	—	—	-mina (-inu)
3rd pers. cl. 1	jena	jo	joo	jani	jale	-hae
2	bona	ba	bao	bani	bale	-bona (-bo)
3	ona	wo	woo	wani	wale	-ona
4	jona	je	jeo	jani	jale	-jona
5	lona	le	leo	lani	lale	-lona
6	ona	a	ao	ani	ale	-ona
7	sona	se	seo	sani	sale	-sona
8	zona	ze	zeo	zani	zale	-zona
9	jona	je	jeo	jani	jale	-jona
10	zona	ze	zeo	zani	zale	-zona
11	lona	lo	loo	lwani	lwale	-lona
12	tona	to	too	twani	twale	-tona
13	kona	ka	kao	kani	kale	-kona
14	bona	bo	boo	bani	bale	-bona
15	kona	ko	koo	kani	kale	-kona
19	bjona	bje	bjeo	bjani	bjale	-bjona

NUMERALS

1. -ŋwe
2. -beli
3. -lalu } (adjectives)
4. -ne
5. -tanu
6. keta lizoho ka-( )ŋwe (finish the hand, add one)
7. keta lizoho ka-( )beli (finish the hand, add two)
8. keta lizoho ka-( )lalu (finish the hand, add three)
9. keta lizoho ka-( )ne (finish the hand, add four)
10. liʃumi (noun).

( ) = adjectival concord required.

Phrases, alternate to the above, for 6, 7, 8 and 9, are made with the verbs **zelela** (pass across, 6), **supa** (point, 7), **loba** (break two fingers, 8; break one finger, 9).

The COPULATIVE FORMATIVE is **ki-**.

APPENDIX V

KGALAGADI TABLES

KGALAGADI, spoken in the Bechuanaland Protectorate, has been described as 'one of the mixed dialects of Sotho'. It holds certain striking characteristics contrasting with the known literary forms in the group. These, with what are found in some other extreme Sotho types located in the Transvaal, such as Lobedu and Pai, seem to point to Kgalagadi as containing archaic elements of what might be called Proto-Sotho. For the tables given here I am indebted to the analysis by D. F. v. d. Merwe of textual material and notes collected by I. Schapera. This was published in the 'Communications from the School of African Studies' of the University of Cape Town, under the title of *A Comparative Study of Kgalagadi, Kwena and other Sotho Dialects*, in 1943.

THE VOWELS are: î, i, e(ε), a, o(ɔ), u, û, as in Sotho generally. In these tables the variant members of the e and o phonemes are not distinguished.

CONSONANTAL CHART

	Bilabial	Alveolar	Pre-palatal	Palatal	Velar	Glottal
EXPLOSIVE						
rad. .	p	t		c	k	
eject.					k'	
asp. .	ph	th		ch	kh	
voic. .	b			ɟ		
NASAL						
contin.	m	n	ɲ		ŋ	
syll. .	m̩	n̩	n̩̪		ŋ̩	
asp. .	mɦ	nɦ				
ROLLED						
contin.		r				
syll. .		r̩				
LATERAL						
contin.		l				
syll. .		l̩				
FRICATIVE						
unv. .		s	ʃ		x	h
AFFRICATE						
rad. .		ts	tʃ			
asp. .		tsh	tʃh		kxh	
voic.		dz	dʒ			
SEMI-VOWEL .	w		j		(w)	

Notes:
1. Only one word recorded with a click, and that ǃŋ.
2. Back labialization occurs, e.g. dʒw, lw, rw, cw, tʃw, kw, kxhw.
3. It is noteworthy that there are no denti-labials, no voiced fricatives, no lateral fricatives, and no implosives.

KGALAGADI TABLES

CONCORD TABLES

	N.P.	A.C.	R.C.[1]	E.C.	P.C.	S.C.	O.C.	Q.P.[2]
1st pers. s.	—	—	*	—	—	ki-	N-	no-
pl.	—	—	*	—	—	hi-	hi-	*
2nd pers. s.	—	—	*	—	—	u-	xu-	*
pl.	—	—	*	—	—	li-	li-	*
3rd pers. cl. 1	mu-, m̥-	jomu-	jou-	mu-	wa-	u-, (e-)	mu-	o-
1a	—[3], (o-)							
2	ba-	mba-	mba-	ba-	ba-	ba-, (be-)	ba-	bo-
2a	bo-							
3	mu-	omu-	ou-	mu-	wa-	u-	u-	o-
4	mi-	emi-	ei-	mi-	ja-	i-	i-	jo-
5	le-	dʒeli-	li-	li-	dʒa-	li-	li-	dʒo-
6	ma-	m̥ma-	ŋa-	ma-	a-	a-	a-	o-
7	ʃi-	ʃeʃi-	ʃeʃi-	ʃi-	ʃa-	ʃi-	ʃi-	ʃo-
8	bî-	dzebî-	dzebî-	bî-	dza-	bî-	bî-	dzo-
9	(i)N-[4]	eN-	ei-	i-	ja-	i-	i-	jo-
10	rîN-	dʒerîN-	dʒerî-	rî-	dʒa-	rî-	rî-	dʒo-
11	lu-	lolu-	lolu-	lu-	lwa-	lu-	lu-	lo-
14	bu-	dʒobu-	dʒobu-	bu-	dʒwa-	bu-	bu-	bo-
15	xu-	moxu-	moxu-	xu-	xa-	xu-	xu-	xo-
16	ha-	—	—	—	xa-	—	—	—
17	xu-							
18	mu-							

Notes:

* These forms have not been recorded.

[1] Relative suffixes used are -jo and -xo.

[2] Quantitative stems are: -the (all), and -ŋwi (only).

[3] Only one word recorded with prefix, viz. otʃwî (ostrich), pl. botʃwî; all other nouns of cl. 1a have no prefix.

[4] i is used with monosyllabic stems only, e.g. icwa (war), pl. rîcwa.

PRONOMINAL TABLES

	Absolute pronoun	Demonstrative pronouns			Poss. stem
		1st position	2nd position	4th position	
1st pers. s.	ŋna	—	—	—	-mi
pl.	tʃhona	—	—	—	-itʃhu
2nd pers. s.	wene	—	—	—	-xo
pl.	lina, ɲina	—	—	—	-inu
3rd pers. cl. 1	ena	jo, o	jowo(o)	jowa	-xwe
2	bona	m	mbo(o)	mbaja	-bo
3	*	wo, o	wowo	wowa, owa	-o
4	jona	je, e	(j)ejoo	jeja	-jo
5	dʒona	dʒe	dʒelejo	dʒeleja	-dʒo
6	ona	ŋ	ŋoo	ŋwaja, nwaa	-o
7	ʃona	ʃe	ʃeʃejo	ʃeʃeja	-ʃo
8	dzona	dze	dzebîjo	dzebîja	-dzo
9	jona	je, e	jejo	jeja	-jo
10	dʒona	dʒe	dʒerîjo	dʒerîja	-dʒo
11	lona	lo	lolowo(o)	lolowa	-lo
14	bona	dʒo	dʒobowo(o)	dʒobowa	-dʒo
15	xona	xo	xoxowo	xoxowa	-xo
16	hona	ho, ha mhano	hoo, mhoo	*	*
17	*	xo	xoxowo	xoxowa	*
18	*	mo	*	*	*

* These forms have not been recorded.

NUMERALS

1. **-ŋwi** (enumerative)
2. **-berî** ⎫
3. **-raru** ⎬ (adjectives)
4. **-ne** ⎪
5. **-thanu** ⎭
6. **-cîcani** (relative)
7. **-sûpa** (pointing)
8. **-hera (mino) ili miberî** (bending two fingers) ⎫ (7, 8, and 9 are verbal, used
9. **-hera (muno) uli muŋwi** (bending one finger) ⎭ with a participial construction)
10. **liʃume** (noun used in copulative construction).

COPULATIVE verbs **-ba, -li** and **-na** and the impersonal formative **ki-** are used.

APPENDIX VI

PAI TABLES

For information on this 'Eastern' type of Sotho, spoken mainly in the Pilgrim's Rest district of the Transvaal, I am indebted to notes supplied to me by Dr. D. Ziervogel, who has been conducting research in several little-known dialects of this area. Pai is still spoken by old people, but it not likely to survive long.

Vowels. Pai has five phonemes as in Nguni. In these tables only the five symbols **i, e, a, o,** and **u** are used, the variant forms of **e** and **o** not being indicated.

CONSONANTAL CHART

	Bilabial	Denti-labial	Alveolar	Retroflex	Pre-palatal	Velar	Glottal
Explosive							
eject.	p'		t'			k'	
asp.	ph		th			kh	
voic.	b			ɖ		g	
	mb		nd			ŋg	
Nasal	m		n		ɲ	ŋ	
Rolled			r				
Lateral			l				
Fricative							
med. unv.		f	s		ʃ	x	
med. voic.	β	[v]		(ʐ)			ɦ
lat. unv.			ɬ				
Affricate							
med. eject.	pf'		ts'	ʈʂ'	tʃ'		
med. asp.			tsh	ʈʂh	tʃh	kxh	
med. voic.				(ɳ)ɖʐ	dʒ		
lat. eject.						kɬ'	
Semi-Vowel	w				j	(w)	

Notes:
1. **r** and **ʐ** are dialectal alternatives.
2. Palatalized forms of bilabials and alveolars occur as follows: **pjh, bj, mj, βj, dj**; note that **dj** and **dʒ** are alternatives.
3. **v** is of foreign origin.
4. It is noteworthy that a homorganic nasal may occur before aspirated explosives and affricates, e.g. **mph, ntsh, ntʃh**, and **ŋkxh**; the nasals in these cases are presumed to be syllabic.

CONCORD TABLES

	N.P.	A.C.	R.C.	E.C.	P.C.	S.C.	O.C.	Q.P.
1st pers. s.	—	—	*	—	—	ki- / ŋ-	ki-	no-
pl.	—	—	*	—	—	ɦi-	ɦi-	ɦo-
2nd pers. s.	—	—	*	—	—	u-	xu-	we-
pl.	—	—	*	—	—	ni- / li-	ni- / li-	no- / lo-

* These forms have not been recorded.

PAI TABLES

CONCORD TABLES (cont.)

	N.P.	A.C.	R.C.	E.C.	P.C.	S.C.	O.C.	Q.P.
3rd pers. cl. 1	mu-	(ku-)mu-	ku-a-	mu-	wa-	u-	mu-	je-
1a	—			wu-				
2	βa-	(βa-)βa-	βa-βa-	βa-	βa-	βa-	βa-	βo-
2a	βo-							
3	mu-	(ku-)mu-	ku-u-	mu-	wa-	u-	u-	wo-
				wu-				
4	mi-	(ki-)mi-	ki-i-	mi-	ja-	i-	i-	jo-
				ji-				
5	li-	(li-)li-	li-li-	li-	la-	li-	li-	lo-
6	ma-	(ka-)ma-	ka-a-	ma-	wa-	a-	a-	o-
				a-				
7	hi-	(ʃi-)ʃi-	ʃi-ʃi-	ʃi-	ʃa-	ʃi-	ʃi-	ʃo-
8	βji-	(βji-)βji-	βji-βji-	βji-	βja-	βji-	βji-	βjo-
9	iN-	(ki-)i-	ki-i-	i-	ja-	i-	i-	jo-
10	tiN-	(ti-)ti-	ti-ti-	ti-	ta-	ti-	ti-	to-
14	βu-, βji-	(βji-)βji-	βji-βji-	βji-	βja-	βji-	βji-	βjo-
15	xu-	(xu-)xu-	xu-xu-	xu-	xwa-	xu-	xu-	xo-
					xa-			
16	fia-				fia-			
					xa-			
17	xu-	xu-	xu-xu-	xu-	xwa-	xu-	xu-	xo-
					xa-			
18	mu-				xa-			

Notes:
1. The 1st demonstrative prefacing the adjectival concord is commonly omitted.
2. Both strong and weak enumerative concords occur.
3. Class 11 has merged into cl. 5.

PRONOMINAL TABLES

		Absolute pronoun	Demonstrative pronouns						Poss. stem
			A			B			
			1st position	2nd position	4th position	1st position	2nd position	4th position	
1st pers.	s.	mini, ŋne, ŋni	—	—	—	—	—	—	-ka
	pl.	rune	—	—	—	—	—	—	-rune, -iru
2nd pers.	s.	weni, wena	—	—	—	—	—	—	-xo
	pl.	ḍune	—	—	—	—	—	—	-ḍune, -inu
3rd pers. cl. 1		jena, jeni	ku	kujo	kuwa	lo	lojo	loja	-x(w)e
2		βona	βa	βawo	βaja	laβa	laβo	laaβa	-βona
3		wona	ku	kuwo	kuwa	lo	lowo	lowa	-wona
4		jona	ki	kijo	kija	le	lejo	leja	-jona
5		lona	li	lijo	lija	leli	lelo	lela	-lona
6		ona	ka	kajo	kaja	la	lawo	lawa	-ona
7		ʃona	ʃi	ʃijo	ʃija	leʃi	leʃo	leʃa	-ʃona
8		βjona	βji	βjijo	βjija	leβji	leβjo	leβja	-βjona
9		jona	ki	kijo	kija	le	lejo	leja	-jona
10		tona	ti	tijo	tija	leti	leto	leta	-tona
14		βjona	βji	βjijo	βjija	leβji	leβjo	leβja	-βjona
15		xona	(xu)	(xujo)	(xuja)	(loxu)	(loxo)	(loxa)	-xona

PRONOMINAL TABLES (cont.)

	Absolute pronoun	Demonstrative pronouns						Poss. stem
		A			B			
		1st position	2nd position	4th position	1st position	2nd position	4th position	
3rd pers. cl. 16 17 18	xona	ɦa	ɦajo	ɦaja	laɦa	laɦo	laaɦa	-xona

Note: There are two sets of demonstratives; the first set is not susceptible to inflexion for the formation of copulatives, adverbs, &c., as is the second set.

NUMERALS

1. -ŋwe ⎫
2. -βedi ⎬ (enumeratives)
3. -raru ⎭
4. mune
5. hiɬanu
6. hiɬanu li-( )ŋwe
7. hiɬanu li-( )βedi ⎬ (nouns)
8. hiɬanu li-( )raru
9. hiɬanu limune
10. lisumi

( ) = enumerative concord required.

Note: There is a close pattern between these numerals and those for Chopi.

APPENDIX VII

PULANA AND KUTSWE TABLES

PULANA and Kutswe are closely connected dialects of Sotho spoken in the Pilgrim's Rest district of the Eastern Transvaal. They differ considerably from Pai of the same area, but their exact classification has not yet been determined. The following data were supplied by Dr. D. Ziervogel.

THE VOWELS are î, i, e(ε), ɑ, o(ɔ), u, û, as in Sotho generally. The variant members of the **e** and **o** phonemes are not distinguished in these tables.

CONSONANTAL CHART

	Bilabial	Alveolar	Retroflex	Pre-palatal	Pre-velar	Velar	Glottal
EXPLOSIVE eject.	p'	t'				k'	
asp.	ph	th				kh	
voic.			ɖ			[g]	
NASAL contin.	m	n		ɲ		ŋ	
syll.	m̩	n̩		ɲ̩		ŋ̩	
ROLLED		r					
LATERAL		l					
FRICATIVE unv.	ɸ	s		ʃ	ʰh		
voic.	β					ɣ	ɦ
AFFRICATE med. {eject.		ts'		tʃ'			
asp.		tsh		tʃh		kxh	
lat. {eject.		{tɬ'}				kɬ'	
asp.							
SEMI-VOWEL	w			j		(w)	

[ ] foreign sound.   { } occurring in Kutswe only.

Notes:
1. ʰh is the sound occurring in N.S.
2. Palatalized forms of bilabials and alveolars occur as follows: pjh, pj', βj, tjh (Kutswe only), dj.
3. The homorganic nasal is used with a wide variety of phones, e.g. (i) before ejectives: m̩p', n̩t', ŋ̩k', m̩pj', n̩ts', n̩tʃ', ŋ̩kɬ'; (ii) before aspirates: m̩ph, n̩th, n̩tjh, ŋ̩kh, n̩tɬh, m̩pjh, n̩tsh, n̩tʃh, ŋ̩kxh; (iii) before fricatives and continuants: n̩s, n̩ʃ, ŋ̩ʰh, ŋ̩ɣ, ŋ̩ɦ, n̩r, n̩l. In all these cases the homorganic nasal is syllabic.
4. The velar nasal is found in association with both velar and palatal glide, viz. ŋw, ŋj.

CONCORD TABLES

	N.P.	A.C.	R.C.	E.C.	P.C.	S.C.	O.C.	Q.P.
1st pers. s.	—	—	*	—	—	k'i-, ŋ-	N-	n̩t'o-
pl.	—	—	*	—	—	ri-	ri-	ro-
2nd pers. s.	—	—	*	—	—	u-	yu-	we-
pl.	—	—	*	—	—	li-	li-	lo-

* These forms have not been recorded.

CONCORD TABLES (cont.)

	N.P.	A.C.	R.C.	E.C.	P.C.	S.C.	O.C.	Q.P.
3rd pers. cl. 1	mu-⎫	je-a-	je-a-	mu-, u-	wa-	u-	mu-	je-
1a	—⎭							
2	βa-⎫	βo-βa-	βo-βa-	βa-	βa-	βa-	βa-	βo-
2a	βo-⎭							
3	mu-	wo-mu-	wo-u-	mu-, u-	wa-	u-	u-	wo-
4	mi-	jo-mi-	jo-i-	mi-, i-	ja-	i-	i-	jo-
5	li-	lo-li-	lo-li-	li-	la-	li-	li-	lo-
6	ma-	wo-ma-	wo-a-	ma-, a-	a-	a-	a-	o-
7	si-	so-si-	so-si-	si-	sa-	si-	si-	so-
8	d̥ɪ-	ts'o-d̥ɪN-	ts'o-d̥ɪ-	d̥ɪ-	ts'a-	d̥ɪ-	d̥ɪ-	ts'o-
9	N-	jo-N-	jo-i-	i-	ja-	i-	i-	jo-
10	d̥ɪN-	ts'o-d̥ɪN-	ts'o-d̥ɪ-	d̥ɪ-	ts'a-	d̥ɪ-	d̥ɪ-	ts'o-
14	βu-	βjo-βu-	βjo-βu-	βu-	βja-	βu-	βu-	βjo-
15	γu-	γo-γu-	γo-γu-	γu-	γa-	γu-	γu-	γo-
16	Φa-, ɦa-⎫							
17	γu-	ɦo-γu-	ɦo-γu-	γu-	γa-	γu-	γu-	γo-
18	mu-⎭							

Notes:
1. Both strong and weak enumerative concords occur.
2. Only one quantitative stem, viz. -ʃɪ (all), recorded.
3. Class 11 has merged into cl. 5.
4. In cl. 16, Φa- is Pulana prefix, ɦa- Kutswe prefix.

PRONOMINAL TABLES

		Absolute pronoun	Demonstrative pronouns		Poss. stem
			1st position	4th position	
1st pers. s.		ŋne	—	—	-k'a
pl.		rûne	—	—	-rûne
2nd pers. s.		wene ⎫ wenî ⎭	—	—	-yo
pl.		lûne	—	—	-lûne
3rd pers. cl. 1		jena	je	jela	-ye
2		βona	βo	βala	-βona
3		wona	wo	wela	-wona
4		jona	jo	jela	-jona
5		lona	lo	lela	-lona
6		ona	wo	ala	-ona
7		sona	so	sela	-sona
8		ts'ona	ts'o	ts'ela	-ts'ona
9		jona	jo	jela	-jona
10		ts'ona	ts'o	ts'ela	-ts'ona
14		βjona	βjo	βjela	-βjona
15		γona	[γo]	[γela]	-γona
16		yona ⎫	ɦo	ɦala	-γona ⎫
17		⎬			⎬
18		⎭	—	—	⎭

Notes:
1. It is remarkable that Pulana and Kutswe have demonstratives for two positions only.
2. Seldom-used forms in brackets [ ].

NUMERALS

(a) Pulana:
1. -ʃî (quantitative pronoun)
2. -βeḑî ⎫
3. -raru ⎬ (adjectives)
4. -ne ⎭
5. sikɬ'anu ⎫
6. mutshili │
7. βuʃûp'o │
8. mane maβeḑî ⎬ (nouns)
9. ŋk'uk'wane │
10. lisumi (archaic: lifiûmî) ⎭

(b) Kutswe:
1. -ʃî (quantitative pronoun)
2. -βeḑî ⎫
3. -raru ⎬ (adjectives)
4. -ne ⎭
5. sitɬhanu ⎫
6. sithup'a or sitɬhanu li-( )ʃi │
7. muʃûp'a or sitɬhanu li-( )βeḑî │
8. sitɬhanu li-( )raru ⎬ (nouns)
9. sitɬhanu li-( )ne │
10. lisumi ⎭

( ) = concord required.

APPENDIX VIII

KALANGA TABLES

This western type of Shona was sufficiently different from the other clusters to preclude its participation in the Shona unification. In these tables the two principal dialects of the cluster, Kalanga and Lilima, are treated, there being a very close resemblance between them. Information is based on my own language survey of 1929, as in *A Comparative Study in Shona Phonetics* (1931); and on the publication by G. Fortune, S.J., *Ndevo Yeŋombe Luvizho* ('Communications from the School of African Studies', University of Cape Town, 1949), as well as from concord tables kindly supplied by him.

The Vowels are as for general Shona, the five phonemes i, e, a, o, u.

CONSONANTAL CHART

	Plain consonants							Velarized consonants	
	Bi-labial	Denti-labial	Dental	Alveolar labialized	Pre-palatal	Velar	Glottal	Plain Velarizatn. Bilabial	Plain S-V. Velar, &c.
Explosive									
unv.	p		t			k		px	kw
asp.	[ph]		th						khw
voic.	b mb		d nd			g ŋg		bɣ mbɣ	gw ŋgw
Nasal									
contin.	m		n		ɲ	ŋ		mŋ	ŋw
syll.	m̩		n̩						
Rolled			(r)						
Lateral			l						
Fricative									
med. unv.	β	v	s [ns]	ṣ	[ʃ]		h		xw
med. voic.			z	ẓ	[ʒ]		ɦ		ɦw
lat. unv.			ɬ						
lat. voic.			ɮ						
Affricate									
unv.				tṣ	tʃ				
asp.					tʃh				
voic.			dz		[dʒ] ɲdʒ				
Semi-Vowel					j	w			

( ) rarely used.   [ ] found in Lilima only.

Note: The dental pronunciation (in place of alveolar) is not indicated here (i.e. t, n, not ṭ, ṇ).

CONCORD TABLES

	N.P.	A.C.	R.C.	E.C.	P.C.	S.C.	O.C.	Q.P.
1st pers. s.	—	—	ndi-	—	—	ndi-	ndi-	ndo-
pl.	—	—	ti-	—	—	ti-	ti-	to-
2nd pers. s.	—	—	u-	—	—	u-	ku-	wo-
pl.	—	—	mu-	—	—	mu-	mu-	mo-

KALANGA TABLES

CONCORD TABLES (cont.)

		N.P.	A.C.	R.C.	E.C.	P.C.	S.C.	O.C.	Q.P.
3rd pers. cl.	1	(u)N-	N-	u-	mu-, u-	wa-	u-	uN-	o-, e-
	1a	—							
	2	(a)βa-	βa-	βa-	βa-	βa-	βa-	βa-	βo-
	2a	βo-							
	3	(u)N-	N-	u-	mu-, u-	wa-	u-	u-	wo-
	4	(i)mi-	mi-	i-	mi-, i-	ja-	i-	i-	jo-
	5	(i)[li]-	[li]-	li-	li-	la-	li-	li-	lo-
	6	(a)ma-	ma-	a-	ma-, a-	a-	a-	a-	o-
	7	(i)tʃi-	tʃi-	tʃi-	tʃi-	tʃa-	tʃi-	tʃi-	tʃo-
	8	(i)ʒi-	ʒi-	ʒi-	ʒi-	ʒa-	ʒi-	ʒi-	ʒo-
	9	(i)[N]-	N-	i-	i-	ja-	i-	i-	jo-
	10	(i)[N]-	N-	dzi-	dzi-	dza-	dzi-	dzi-	dzo-
	11	(u)lu-	lu-	gu-	gu-	gwa-	gu-	gu-	go-
	14	(u)βu-	βu-	gu-	gu-	gwa-	gu-	gu-	go-
	15	(u)ku-	ku-	ku-	ku-	kwa-	ku-	ku-	ko-
	16	(a)pa-	—	pa-	—	(pa-)	pa-	pa-	po-
	17	(u)ku-	—	ku-	—	kwa-	ku-	ku-	ko-
	18	(u)mu-	—	mu-	—	(ma-)	mu-	mu-	mo-
	20	(u)ku-	ku-	ku-	ku-	kwa-	ku-	ku-	ko-
	21	(i)ʒi-	[li]-	li-	li-	la-	li-	li-	lo-
		(i)fii-							

Notes:
1. The possessive concord undergoes substitution of e before nouns with latent initial vowel.
2. Kalanga cluster lacks cls. 12 and 13, using suffix diminutives.
3. In cl. 21 (i)ʒi- is Lilima, (i)fii- is Kalanga.
4. Only Lilima uses the strong enumerative, and then only with stem -ŋwe (other).
5. In cls. 1 and 3, the N.P. consists of a syllabic nasal homorganic to the initial consonant of the stem.
6. In cl. 5 [li]- indicates initial vocalization, as generally described for Shona, see Ch. IX, p. 208. All concords of cl. 21 are as for cl. 5.
7. The ordinary possessive concord for cls. 16, 17, and 18 is kwa-, e.g. pakati kweŋumba (in the midst of the house); the forms pa-, kwa-, and ma- respectively are used in the indirect relative construction.
8. Participial concords are as S.C. except (i) that none are found for cls. 16, 17, and 18, and (ii) that the forms for cls. 1, 2, and 6 are e, βe- and e- respectively.
9. Quantitative prefix in cl. 1 is o- with stem -se, and e- with stem -ga.

PRONOMINAL TABLES

		Absolute pronoun	Demonstrative pronouns				Poss. stem
			1st position	2nd position	3rd position	4th position	
1st pers.	s.	imi	—	—	—	—	-ŋgu
	pl.	isi	—	—	—	—	-idu
2nd pers.	s.	iwe	—	—	—	—	-o
	pl.	imɲi	—	—	—	—	-iɲu
		iŋwi					
3rd pers. cl.	1	ije	oju	ojo	uno	oja	-e
	2	iβo	aβa	aβo	βano	βaja	-βo
	3	iwo	oju	ojo	uno	oja	-wo
	4	ijo	eji	ejo	ino	eja	-jo
	5	ilo	eli	elo	lino	lija	-lo
	6	iwo	awa	awo	ano	aja	-wo
	7	itʃo	etʃi	etʃo	tʃino	tʃija	-tʃo
	8	iʒo	eʒi	eʒo	ʒino	ʒija	-ʒo
	9	ijo	eji	ejo	ino	ija	-jo
	10	idzo	edzi	edzo	dzino	dzija	-dzo
	11	igo	ogu	ogo	guno	guja	-go
	14	igo	ogu	ogo	guno	guja	-go

PRONOMINAL TABLES (*cont.*)

	Absolute pronoun	Demonstrative pronouns				Poss. stem
		1st position	2nd position	3rd position	4th position	
3rd pers. cl. 15	iko	oku	oko	kuno	kuja	-ko
16	ipo	apa	apo	pano	paja	-po
17	iko	oku	oko	kuno	kuja	-ko
18	imo	omu	omo	muno	muja	-mo
20	iko	oku	oko	kuno	kuja	-ko
21	ilo	eli	elo	lino	lija	-lo

Notes:
1. There are many varieties of precisions and emphases among the demonstratives: the above are the simplest forms in each case. Lilima has -dʒa for -ja in the 4th position forms.
2. Absolute pronoun, 2nd pers. pl.: impi is Kalanga, iŋwi is Lilima.
3. With possessive stems of 2nd pers. s. (-o) and cl. 1 (-e), the prefixal element is double, e.g. ŋkadzi uwo (uwe), thy (his) wife; ŋombe dzidzo (dzidze), thy (his) oxen; &c.

NUMERALS

1. -ŋompela (= -ŋwe kupela) (enumerative)
2. -βili ⎫
3. -tatu ⎪
4. -nna   ⎬ (adjectives)
5. -ʃanu ⎪
6. -tathatu ⎭
7. Kl. -lumŋe gunotendeka (adj.); Li. tʃitendeka (noun, preceded by poss. concord)
8. Kl. -fianalume (adj.); Li. -li ʒanalume ⎫ (with copulative verb)
9. Kl. -fianakadzi (adj.); Li. -li ʒanakadzi ⎭
10. gumi (noun), followed by poss. concord.

INDEX

Absolute pronoun, 50, **56**; Chopi, 232; Kalanga, 253; Kgalagadi, 244; Kutswe, 250; Lozi, 241; Ngoni, 238; Nguni, **100**; Pai, 247; Phuthi, 235; Pulana, 250; Shona, **215**; Sotho, 133; Tsonga 189; Venda, **163**.

Abstract noun, 54; Nguni, 99; Shona, 213; Sotho, 131; Tsonga, 187; Venda, 161.

Adjective, 50, 60; comparative table of concords, 61; Nguni, 102; Shona, 217-18; Sotho, 135-6; Tsonga, 190-1; Venda, 166-7.

Adverb, **83-86**; affinity with conjunctive, 83; derived, 83, 112; Nguni, 111-13; primitive, 83, 111; Shona, 226-7; Sotho, 147-9; Tsonga, 200-2; Venda, 176-7; with non-locative formatives, 84; with prefixal locative formatives, 85; with suffixal locative formatives, 85.

Adverbial formatives: locative, 85; non-locative, 84.

Affixes, 50.

Affricate, 33; Nguni, 93; Shona, 206; Sotho, 122; Tsonga, 182; Venda, 156.

Affricative consonant, *see* Affricate.

Agentive adverb, 111, 148, 201.

— verb, 66.

Agglutination in Bantu, 47.

Alliteration, 47.

Alveolarization, Sotho, 40, 124-5; Southern Bantu, 40.

Appleyard, J. W., 12, 16, 41, 91.

Applied species of verb, **67-68**; Nguni, 105; Shona, 221; Sotho, 140; Tsonga, 194; Venda, 170.

Archbell, J., 12, 14.

Article: non-existence in Bantu, 48.

Aspect of verb, 71, 72; continuous, *see* Continuous aspect; indefinite, *see* Indefinite aspect; perfect, *see* Perfect aspect.

Aspiration of consonants, 31; Nguni, 92; Sotho, 122; Tsonga, 181; Venda, 156.

Associative species of verb: Sotho, 142.

Augmentative of nouns, 55; Nguni, 100; Shona, 210-11, 215; Sotho, 132-3; Venda, 163.

— species of verb: Sotho, 142.

Baca (dialect of Tekeza, q.v.).

Bantu: main morphological characteristics, 47; the term, 13.

Barnes, B. H., 230.

Barth, H., 13.

Beach, D. M., 17, 46.

Bennie, J., 14, 16.

Bennie, W. G., 46, 118.

Berthoud, P., 204.

Bieler, E., 230.

Bila (dialect of Tonga, Tsonga group, q.v.).

Bilabial fricative, 32; Kutswe, 249; Pai, 246; Pulana, 249; Shona, 207; Sotho, 122; Tsonga, 182; Venda, 156.

Birwa (dialect of Northern Sotho, q.v.).

Bishop, H. L., 184*n*., 202*n*., 204.

Bleek, W. H. I., 12, 41.

Bocha (dialect of Manyika, q.v.).

Bomvana (dialect of Xhosa, q.v.).

Bourquin, W., 13, 17, 48*n*., 118, 234.

Boyce, W., 12.

Brown, J. T., 153.

Brusciotto, G., 11, 14.

Bryant, A. T., 18.

Buck, H., 230.

Budya (dialect of Korekore, q.v.).

Bunji (dialect of Manyika, q.v.).

Bushman, 12.

Bvumba (dialect of Manyika, q.v.).

Callaway, H., 18.

Capell, A., 47*n*.

Cardoso, 11.

Casalis, A., 153.

Casalis, E., 14.

Case: non-existence in Bantu, 48.

Causative species of verb, 68; Nguni, 105-6; Shona, 221; Sotho, 140-1; Tsonga, 194; Venda, 170.

Central Orthography Committee, 15.

Cerebral, *see* Retroflex.

Chatelain, C. W., 204.

Chopi (Inhambane group), 25; concord tables, 232; consonantal chart, 231; dialects, 25; linguistic work, 231; numerals, 233; pronominal tables, 232-3; tables, **231-3**; vowels, 231.

Classes of nouns, 14, 15. *Cls. 1 & 2*, 53; Nguni, 96; Shona, 209; Sotho, 126; Tsonga, 184; Venda, 158. *Cls. 1a & 2a*, 53; Nguni, 96; Shona, 209-10; Sotho, 127; Tsonga, 184; Venda, 158. *Cls. 3 & 4*, 53; Nguni, 96; Shona, 210; Sotho, 127; Tsonga, 185; Venda, 159. *Cl. 5*, 53; Nguni, 97; Shona, 210-1; Sotho, 128; Tsonga, 185-6; Venda, 159. *Cl. 6*, 53-54; Nguni, 97; Shona, 210-11; Sotho, 128; Tsonga, 185-6; Venda, 160. *Cls. 7 & 8*, 54; Nguni, 97; Shona, 211; Sotho, 129; Tsonga, 186; Venda, 160. *Cls. 9 & 10*, 54; Nguni, 98; Shona, 211-12; Sotho, 129; Tsonga, 186-7; Venda, 160. *Cl. 11*, 54; Nguni, 98; Shona, 212; Sotho, 130; Tsonga, 187; Venda, 161. *Cls. 12 & 13*, 54; Shona, 213. *Cl. 14*, 54; Nguni, 99; Shona, 213-14; Sotho, 131; Tsonga, 187-8; Venda, 161. *Cl. 15*, 55; Nguni, 99; Shona, 214; Sotho, 131; Tsonga, 188; Venda, 162. *Cls. 16, 17, & 18*, 55; Nguni, 99, 113; Shona, 214; Sotho, 131-2; Tsonga, 188; Venda, 162. *Cl. 19*, 55; Shona, 214. *Cl. 20*, 55; Venda, 162. *Cl. 21*, 55; Shona, 215, Venda, 163.

Class-gender, grammatical, 47.

Classification: Bantu grammatical, 49-50; history of, 11-19; Southern Bantu languages, 20-25.

Clauses, relative, *see* Relative clauses.
Click consonants: Ngoni, 237; Nguni, 93; phonetic chart, 36; Phuthi, 235; Sotho, 121; Southern Bantu, 35; Tsonga, 182.
Cluster, 21; Chopi, 25; Kalanga, 22; Karanga, 22; Korekore, 21; Manyika, 22; Ndau, 22; Northern Sotho, 24; Ronga, 25; Southern Sotho, 24; Tekeza, 24; Tonga (Inhambane), 25; Tonga (Tsonga) 25; Tswa 25; Tswana 24; Xhosa 23; Zezuru, 22; Zulu, 23.
Coalescence of vowels, 29; Nguni, 94; Shona, 208; Venda, 157.
Cole, D. T., 48*n.*, 120, 125*n.*, 153.
Colenso, J. W., 15.
Collective noun, 54; Nguni, 99; Shona, 213; Sotho, 131; Tsonga, 187; Venda, 161.
Colyer, S., 240.
Comparative studies: history of, 11–19.
Comparison adverb, 112, 148, 176.
Compound consonants: heterorganic, 34; with semi-vowels, 34.
— nouns, 56.
— predicate, *see* Compound tenses.
— tenses of verb, 75; Nguni, 109; Shona, 225; Sotho, 145; Tsonga, 199; Venda, 174.
Concordial agreement, 47.
Concord Tables: adjectival comparative, 61; Chopi, 232; Kalanga, 253–4; Kgalagadi, 244; Kutswe, 249–50; Lozi, 241; Ngoni, 238; Pai, 246–7; Phuthi, 235; possessive comparative, 64, 65; Pulana, 249–50; relative comparative, 61.
Concords, 50; alliteral or euphonic, 14; objectival, *see* Objectival concords; predicative, 76–78; Nguni, 108; Shona, 223; Sotho, 144; Tsonga, 197; Venda, 172; qualificative, *see* Qualificative concords; subjectival, *see* Subjectival concords.
Conditional mood of verb, 74.
Conjugation of verb, 70–78; negative, 70; Nguni, 106–10; positive, 70; Shona, 222–5; Sotho, 142–6; Tsonga, 195–9; Venda, 171–5.
Conjunctive, 49–50, 87–88; derived, 88; followed by participial, 88, 115, 150, 203; followed by subjunctive, 88, 115, 150; Nguni, 115; non-influencing, 88, 115, 150, 202; primitive, 88; Shona, 227–8; Sotho, 150; Tsonga, 202; Venda, 177.
— adverb, 112, 148, 176, 200, 218, 226.
— verb, 66.
Consonant, **31-43**; affricative, *see* Affricate; aspirated, *see* Aspirated consonant; chart, *see* Consonantal chart; click, 35, 93, 121, 182, 237; compound, heterorganic, 34; with semi-vowels, 34, 182; ejected, *see* Ejection of consonants; explosive, *see* Explosive consonant; flapped, *see* Flapped consonant; fricative, *see* Fricative consonant; implosive, *see* Implosive consonant; lateral, *see* Lateral consonant; nasal, *see* Nasal consonant; Nguni, 92–93; palatalized, 155; retroflex, *see* Retroflex consonant; rolled, *see* Rolled consonant; semi-vowel, *see* Semi-vowel; Shona, 206–8; Sotho, 121–3; Southern Bantu, **30–37**;

Tsonga, 181–3; velarized, 155, 156, 206; Venda, 154–7; with prepalatal glide, 34, 182; with velar glide, 35, 182.
Consonantal chart, **30**; Chopi, 231; Kalanga, 252; Kgalagadi, 243; Kutswe, 249; Lozi, 240; Ngoni, 237; Nguni, 92; Pai, 246; Phuthi, 234; Pulana, 249; Shona, 206; Sotho, 121; Tsonga, 181; Venda, 154–5.
— phenomena, *see* Phonological phenomena with consonants.
— types, incidence of, 36.
Contactive species of verb, 70, 171.
Contingent mood of verb, 74; Nguni, 109.
Continuous aspect of verb, 71.
Contrast adverb, 112, 226.
Copulative, 50, **79-83**; base, 79*n.*; Nguni, 80, **110-11**; Shona, 82, **225-6**; Sotho, 81, **146-7**; Tsonga, 81, **199-200**; Venda, 81, **175**; verbs, 79, 200, 245.
Crisp, W., 153.
Cust, R. N., 13, 19.

Danda (dialect of Ndau, q.v.).
Davis, W. J., 14.
Declension, 14.
de Couto, 11, 16.
Deficient verbs, 49, **75-6**; Nguni, 109; Shona, 225; Sotho, 145–6; Tsonga, 199; Venda, 174–5.
Demonstrative pronoun, 50, **57**; Chopi, 232–3; Kalanga, 253–4; Kgalagadi, 244; Kutswe, 250; Lozi, 241; Ngoni, 238–9; Nguni, 100–1; Pai, 247–8; Phuthi, 235; Pulana, 250; Shona, 216; Sotho, 133–4; Tsonga, 189; Venda, 163–5.
Dempwolff, O., 13, 48*n*.
Denasalization of consonants, 157.
Denominative verbs, 66*n*.
Dependent mood of verb in Venda, 75, 174.
Derivatives, *see* Verbal derivatives.
Descriptive, 49–50.
Deverbative nouns, 56.
Dialect, in Bantu, 21.
Dias, 11.
Dieterlen, H., 18, 153.
Diminutive of nouns, 55; by prefix, 49; by suffix, 49; Nguni, 99; Shona, 213; Sotho, 132; Tsonga, 188; Venda, 162–3.
— species of verb, 70; Nguni, 106; Sotho, 141; Tsonga, 195.
Döhne, J. L., 18.
Doke, C. M., 15, 16, 17, 18, 19, 25, 46, 95*n.*, 117, 153, 210*n.*, 211*n.*, 230.
Domba (dialect of Manyika, q.v.).
Duma (dialect of Karanga, q.v.).
Dysart, J. P., 230.
Dzibi (dialect of Tswa, q.v.).
Dzonga (dialect of Tswa, q.v.).

Eiselen, W. M., 16, 204.
Ejection of consonants, 31, 92, 122, 156.
Elision of vowels, 28; Nguni, 94; Venda, 157.
Elmslie, W. A., 118, 237.

INDEX 257

Enclitic formatives, 50, 89; Nguni, 116; Shona, 228; Sotho, 151; Tsonga, 203; Venda, 178.
Endemann, C. H., 17.
Endemann, K., 15, 16, 18, 153.
Endemann, T. M. H., 18n., 153, 183n., 204.
Engelbrecht, J., 18.
Enumerative, 50, **62**; comparative table, **62–63**; Nguni, 103; Shona, 219; Sotho, 137–8; Tsonga, 191–2; Venda, 167–8.
Exclusive implication of verb, 71.
Explosive consonants, 31, 92, 122, 156.
Extensive species of verb, 69; Sotho, 142.

Feminine of nouns, 55; Nguni, 100; Sotho, 132; Tsonga, 189.
Flapped consonant, 32, 122.
Fortune, G., 252.
Fricative consonants, 32; Nguni, 93; Shona, 207; Sotho, 122; Tsonga, 182; Venda, 156.

Gaika (dialect of Xhosa, q.v.).
Gananwa (dialect of Northern Sotho, q.v.).
Garwe (dialect of Ndau, q.v.).
Gcaleka (dialect of Xhosa, q.v.).
Geographical position: Kalanga, 205; Karanga, 205; Kgalagadi, 243; Korekore, 205; Kutswe, 249; Lozi, 240; Manyika, 205; Ndau, 205; Ngoni, 237; Nguni, 91; Pai, 246; Phuthi, 234; Pulana, 249; Shona, 205; Sotho, 119; Tekeza, 91; Tsonga, 180; Venda, 154; Zezuru, 205.
Glides: prepalatal, 34; velar, 35.
Gluckman, M., 240.
Godfrey, R., 16, 118.
Gova (dialect of Korekore, q.v.).
— (dialect of Zezuru, q.v.).
Govera (dialect of Karanga, q.v.).
Grammatical classification, 49–50.
Grammatical outline: Nguni, **95–117**; Shona, **209–30**; Sotho, **126–52**; Tsonga, **183–204**; Venda, **158–79**.
Group: in Bantu languages, 20; Inhambane, 25; Nguni, 23, 91–118; Shona, 21, 205–30; Sotho, 24, 119–53; Tsonga, 25, 180–204; Venda, 25, 154–79.
Grout, L., 15.
Guta (dialect of Manyika, q.v.).
Gwamba (dialect of Tonga, Tsonga group, q.v.).

Hahn, C. H., 15.
Harava (dialect of Zezuru, q.v.).
Hera (dialect of Zezuru, q.v.).
Here (dialect of Manyika, q.v.).
History: of Bantu investigations, 11–19; of classification of languages, 11–19; of comparative studies, 11–19; of Southern Bantu languages, 14–19.
Hlanganu (dialect of Tonga, Tsonga group, q.v.).
Hlengwe (dialect of Tswa, q.v.).
Hlubi (dialect of Tekeza, q.v.).
Hoffman, C., 18.
Hortative form of subjunctive, 74.
Hottentot, 12, 13.

Hungwe (dialect of Manyika, q.v.).
Hurutshe (dialect of Tswana, q.v.).

Ideophone, 47, 50, **86–87**; Nguni, 114–15; Shona, 227; Sotho, 149–50; Tsonga, 202; Venda, 177.
Ideophonic derivatives, 66.
Imperative of verb, 71; Nguni, 106; Shona, 222; Sotho, 142; Tsonga, 196; Venda, 171.
Implication of verb, 71, 72; exclusive, *see* Exclusive implication; progressive, *see* Progressive implication; simple, *see* Simple implication.
Implosive consonants, 31, 92, 207, 231, 234.
Import of verb, 66.
Inclusive quantitative pronoun, 58.
Indefinite aspect of verb, 71.
Indicative mood of verb, **71–73**; Nguni, 107–8; Shona, 222–3; Sotho, 143; Tsonga, 196–8; Venda, 171–3.
Infinitive of verb, 71; Nguni, 106; Shona, 222; Sotho, 142; Tsonga, 195–6; Venda, 171.
Infixes, 50.
Inflexion: in Bantu, 47.
Inhambane group, 25, 231; classification, 25.
Initial vowel: latent in Shona, 28, Nguni, 28; Tsonga, 28, 184.
Instrumental adverb, 112, 148, 176, 200–1, 226.
— verb, 66.
Intensive species of verb, 68; Nguni, 106; Shona, 222; Sotho, 141; Tsonga, 195; Venda, 170.
Interjection, *see* Interjective, radical.
Interjective, 49–50, **88–89**; derived, 89; imperative, 116, 151, 178, 203, 228; Nguni, 115–16; radical, 88, 115, 151, 178, 203, 228; primitive, *see* radical; Shona, 228; Sotho, 151; Tsonga, 203; Venda, 178; vocative, 89, 115–16, 151, 178, 203, 228.
International Institute of African Languages and Cultures, 15, 46.
International Phonetic Association, 45.
Inter-University Committee for African Studies, 16.
Intransitive verbs, 66.
Invariable in Swahili, 50n.

Jacottet, E., 17, 18, 48n., 119, 153.
Jalla, A., 240.
Jankie, H. E., 153.
Jaques, A. A., 204.
Jena (dialect of Karanga, q.v.).
Jindwi (dialect of Manyika, q.v.).
Johnston, H. H., 13, 19, 25, 48n.
Jones, D., 16, 17, 44n., 46, 153.
Jonga (dialect of Tonga, Tsonga group, q.v.).
Junod, H. A., 180, 183, 204.
Junod, H. P., 231.

Kalanga (Shona group), 21; concord tables, 252–3; consonantal chart, 252; dialects, 22; geographical position, 205; linguistic work, 252; numerals, 254; pronominal tables, 253–4; tables, **252–4**; vowels, 252.
Karanga (Shona group), 21; coalescence of vowels,

B 2699 R

Karanga (Shona group) (*continued*) 208; consonantal charts, 206; dialects, 22; diminutive, 213; geographical position, 205; in unification, 205.
Karombe (dialect of Manyika, q.v.), 211*n*.
Kempe, A. R., 18.
Kgaga (dialect of Northern Sotho, q.v.).
Kgalagadi (Sotho group), 24; classification, 243; concord tables, 244; consonantal chart, 243; dialects, 24*n*.; linguistic work, 243; numerals, 245; pronominal tables, 244; tables, **243-5**; vowels, 243.
Kgatla (dialect of Tswana, q.v.).
Khambana (dialect of Tswa, q.v.).
Kololo, *see* Lozi.
Koma (dialect of Kgalagadi, q.v.).
Konde (dialect of Ronga, q.v.).
Koni (dialect of Northern Sotho, q.v.).
Korekore (Shona group), 21; dialects, 21; geographical position, 205.
Kriel, T. J., 153.
Kropf, A., 18, 118.
Kutswe (Sotho group), 24, 24*n*.; concord tables, 249-50; consonantal chart, 249; linguistic work, 249; numerals, 251; pronominal tables, 250; tables, **249-51**; vowels, 249.
Kuwe (dialect of Kgalagadi, q.v.).
Kwachikwakwa (dialect of Zezuru, q.v.).
Kwazwimba (dialect of Zezuru, q.v.).
Kwena (dialect of Northern Sotho, q.v.).
— (dialect of Tswana, q.v.).

Labio-alveolar fricative, 33; Shona, 207; Sotho, 123; Tsonga, 182; Venda, 156.
Lala (dialect of Zulu, q.v.).
Lateral consonants, 32, 93, 122.
— fricatives, 33; Nguni, 93; Sotho, 122; Tsonga, 182.
Leisegang, H. K., 18.
Lenge (dialect of Chopi, q.v.), 231.
Length: in ideophones, 44; in Southern Bantu, 43; Nguni, 95; Shona, 208; Sotho, 125; Tsonga, 183; Venda, 157.
Lepsius alphabet, 15, 45, 180.
Lestrade, G. P., 15, 17, 18, 46, 49*n*., 132*n*., 153.
Lete (dialect of Tswana, q.v.).
Lichtenstein, H., 11, 14.
Lilima (dialect of Kalanga, q.v.), 252-4.
Linguistic work, **11-19**; Chopi, 231; Kalanga, 252; Kgalagadi, 243; Kutswe, 249; Lozi, 240; Ngoni, 237; Pai, 246; Phuthi, 234; Pulana, 249.
Literary work, **11-19**; Nguni, 91; Shona, 205; Sotho, 119; Tsonga, 180; Venda, 154.
Locative, 85; by prefix, 49; by suffix, 49; Chopi, 231; Nguni, 112-13; Shona, 227; Sotho, 148-9; Tsonga, 201; Venda, 176.
Locative adverbs, *see* Locative.
— formatives, *see* Locative.
— demonstrative copulatives: Nguni, 111; Sotho, 147; Venda, 175.
— verbs, 66.
Louw, C. S., 230.

Lovedu (Sotho group), 24, 24*n*.
Lozi (dialect of Southern Sotho, q.v.), 24; characteristics, 240; concord tables, 241; consonantal chart, 240; linguistic work, 240; numerals, 242; pronominal tables, 241; tables, **240-2**; vowels, 240.

Mabille, A., 18, 153.
Makwakwe (dialect of Tswa, q.v.).
Malcolm, D. McK., 46.
Manner adverb, 112, 147, 176, 200, 226.
Manyika (Shona group), 21; dialects, 22; geographical position, 205; indirect relative construction, 229; in unification, 205.
Marconnès, F., 230.
Marsden, W., 12.
Masemola, *see* Tau.
Matthews, J., 231.
Mbire (dialect of Zezuru, q.v.).
McLaren, J., 15, 16, 17, 18, 118.
Meinhof, C., 13, 15, 16, 17, 41, 42, 46, 48*n*., 90, 157, 179.
Mfengu (dialect of Tekeza, q.v.).
Mhari (dialect of Karanga, q.v.): diminutive prefix, 213.
Mood of verb: **71-75**; conditional, *see* Conditional mood; contingent, *see* Contingent mood; dependent, *see* Dependent mood; indicative, *see* Indicative mood; participial, *see* Participial mood; potential, *see* Potential mood; subjunctive, *see* Subjunctive mood; temporal, *see* Temporal mood.
Morphology: main characteristics of Bantu, 47; Southern Bantu languages, **47-90**; special characteristics of Southern Bantu, 48.
Mpondo (dialect of Xhosa, q.v.).
Mpondomse (dialect of Xhosa, q.v.).
Mudau, E. F. N., 18*n*.
Müller, F., 13.
Mzamane, G. I. M., 17, 234.

Nambzya (dialect of Kalanga, q.v.).
Nasal consonants: 32, 92, 122.
Nasalization: Kutswe, 249; Lenge, 39; Nguni, 38, **93-94**; Pulana, 249; Shona, 38, **207**, 212; Sotho, 38, **123-4**, 130, 145; Southern Bantu, **37-39**; Tsonga, 38, **182-3**, 185, 187; Venda, 38, **156-7**, 160-1.
Ndau (Shona group), 21; dialects, 22; geographical position, 205.
Ndebele of Rhodesia, *see* Rhodesian Ndebele.
— of Transvaal, *see* Transvaal Ndebele.
Ndebele-Sotho (dialect of Northern Sotho, q.v.).
Ndlambe (dialect of Xhosa, q.v.).
Ndzundza (dialect of Transvaal Ndebele, q.v.).
Negative conjugation of verb, 70.
Neuter species of verb, 68; Nguni, 105; Shona, 221; Sotho, 140; Tsonga, 194; Venda, 170.
Ngologa (dialect of Kgalagadi, q.v.).
Ngoni (dialects of Zulu): click, 237; concord tables, 238; consonantal chart, 237; linguistic work, 237; literary form, 23; numerals, 239;

Nyasaland, 23, 237; pronominal tables, 238–9; tables, 237–9; Tanganyika, 23, 237; types, 237; vowels, 237.
Ngova (dialect of Karanga, q.v.).
Nguni group, **91–118**; adverb, 111–13; classification, 23–24; click chart, 93; clusters, 23; coalescence of vowels, 94; conjunctive, 115; copulative, 110–11; dialects, 23–24; elision of vowels, 94; enclitics, 116; geographical position, 91; grammatical outline, **95–117**; ideophone, 114–15; interjective, 115–16; length, 95; literary work, 91; locative formation, 112–13; nasalization, 93; notes on plain consonants, 92; noun, 95–100; numerals, 116; orthography, 91; palatalization, 94; phonetics, 92; phonological phenomena, 93–95; phonology, 92; plain consonant chart, 92; proclitic, 116; pronoun, 100–2; qualificative, 102–4; references, 117; relative construction, 117; stress, 94; substitution of *e*, 94; tone, 95; verb, 104–10; vowels, 92, 94.
Ngwaketse (dialect of Tswana, q.v.).
Ngwalungu (dialect of Tonga, Tsonga group, q.v.).
Ngwato (dialect of Tswana, q.v.).
Njanja (dialect of Zezuru, q.v.).
Nobvu (dialect of Zezuru, q.v.).
Nohwe (dialect of Zezuru, q.v.).
Nominal derivatives (verbs), 66.
Non-personal nouns, 56.
Northern Sotho (Sotho group), 24: dialects, 24; geographical position, 119; locative demonstrative copulative, 147.
Noun, 49, **50–56**; abstract, *see* Abstract noun; augmentative, *see* Augmentative of nouns; classes, *see* Classes of nouns; collective, *see* Collective noun; compound, *see* Compound nouns; derivation, 55, (nouns from nouns), 55, (nouns from verbs) 56; derivative, (non-personal) 56, (personal) 56; diminutive, *see* Diminutive of nouns; feminine, *see* Feminine of nouns; nature of, 51; Nguni, **95–100**; prefix table, 52, (Nguni) 95–96, (Shona) 209, (Sotho) 126, (Tsonga) 183, (Venda) 158; Shona, **209–15**; Sotho, **126–33**; suffixes, *see* Suffixes; Tsonga, **183–9**; Venda, **158–63**.
Nrebele (dialect of Transvaal Ndebele, q.v.).
Numerals: Chopi, 233; Kalanga, 254; Kgalagadi, 245; Kutswe, 251; Lozi, 242; Ngoni, 239; Nguni, 116; Pai, 248; Phuthi, 236; Pulana, 251; Shona, 228–9; Sotho, 151–2; Tsonga, 203; Venda, 178.
Numeration: quinary, 47.
Nyai (dialect of Kalanga, q.v.).
Nyamuka (dialect of Manyika, q.v.).
Nyatwe (dialect of Manyika, q.v.).
Nyongwe (dialect of Korekore, q.v.).
Nyubi (dialect of Karanga, q.v.).

Objectival concord, 78; Chopi, 232; comparative table, 78; Kalanga, 252–3; Kgalagadi, 244; Kutswe, 249–50; Lozi, 241; Ngoni, 238; Nguni, 108; Pai, 247; Phuthi, 235; Pulana, 249–50; Shona, 223; Sotho, 144; Tsonga, 197; Venda 172.
O'Neil, J., 118, 230.
Orner, A. J., 230.
Orthography: Nguni, 91; settlements, 15; Shona, 205; Sotho, 119–20, 121–2; Southern Bantu, 45; Tsonga, 180; Venda, 154, 155; Xhosa, 91; Zulu, 91.

Pacconio, 11.
Pai (Sotho group), 24, 24*n*.; concord tables, 246–7; consonantal chart, 246; linguistic work, 246; numerals, 248; pronominal tables, 247–8; tables, **246–8**; vowels, 246.
Palatalization: Nguni, 39, **94**, 100, 113; Pai, 246; Sotho, 40, **124**, 140; Southern Bantu, **39–40**; Tetela, 39; Tsonga, 188, 194; Venda, 155.
Paroz, R. A., 18, 153.
Participial mood of verb, 74; Nguni, 109; relative form, *see* Relative form; Shona, 224; Sotho, 144; Tsonga, 198–9; Venda, 173–4.
Parts of speech: fundamental, 49–50; secondary, 49–50.
Passive species of verb, 67; Nguni, 105; Shona, 221; Sotho, 140; Tsonga, 194; Venda, 169.
Passy, P., 16.
Pedi (dialect of Northern Sotho, q.v.).
Penultimate *i* (*e*), 29, 125, 208, 215.
Perfect aspect of verb, 71.
Perfective species of verb, 69; Nguni, 106; Sotho, 141; Venda, 171.
Peri (dialect of Kalanga, q.v.).
Personal nouns, 56.
Persson, J. A., 180, 183, 204.
Pfungwe (dialect of Korekore, q.v.).
Phalaborwa (Sotho group), 24, 24*n*.
Phani (dialect of Venda, q.v.).
Philip, J., 12.
Phonetic studies, 16.
Phonetics: Nguni, 92; prosodic elements, 43; Shona, 206; Sotho, 120; Southern Bantu, **26–46**; Tsonga, 180; Venda, 154.
Phonological phenomena with consonants, 37–41; Nguni, 93–94; Shona, 207–9; Sotho, 123–5; Tsonga, 182–3; Venda, 156–7.
Phonology: Nguni, 92; Shona, 206; Sotho, 120; Southern Bantu, **26–46**; Tsonga, 180; Venda, 154.
Phuthi (dialect of Tekeza, q.v.): click consonants, 235; concord tables, 235; linguistic work, 234; numerals, 236; plain consonantal chart, 234; pronominal tables, 235; tables, **234–6**; vowels, 234.
Pigafetta, 11.
Plaatje, S. T., 16, 17, 46, 153.
Portuguese writers, 11.
Positive conjugation of verb, 70.
Possessive, 50, **63–66**; concords, comparative table (type *a*) 64, (type *b*) 65; descriptive, 64, 103–4, 139, 168, 193, 220; direct, 64, 103, 138, 168, 193, 220; Nguni, 103–4; pronominal stems, 64, 103, 138, 168, 192, 219, (comparative table)

INDEX

Possessive (*continued*)
64; Shona, 219-20; Sotho, 138-9; Tsonga, 192-3; Venda, 168-9.
Potential mood of verb, 74; Nguni, 108; Shona, 224; Sotho, 143-4; Tsonga, 198; Venda, 173.
Potgieter, E. F., 118.
Predicative, 49-50.
Prefix, 50; adverbial, 50; auxiliary verbal, 50; disyllabic, 49; monosyllabic, 49; reflexive, *see* Reflexive prefix; substantival, *see* Prefixes of nouns.
Prefixes of nouns, *see* Classes of nouns: comparative table, 52; Nguni, 95; Shona, 209; Sotho, 126; Tsonga, 183; Venda, 158.
Prelocative -*s*-, 104.
Prepositions, non-existence in Bantu, 48.
Proclitic formative, 50, 89-90; Nguni, 116; Shona, 228; Sotho, 151; Tsonga, 183, 203; Venda, 178.
Progressive implication of verb, 71.
Pronominal tables: Chopi, 232-3; Kalanga, 253-4; Kgalagadi, 244; Kutswe, 250; Lozi, 241; Ngoni, 238-9; Pai, 247-8; Phuthi, 235; Pulana, 250.
Pronoun, 49-50, **56-60**; absolute, *see* Absolute pronoun; demonstrative, *see* Demonstrative pronoun; Nguni, 100-2; qualificative, *see* Qualificative pronoun; quantitative, *see* Quantitative pronoun; relative, *see* Relative pronoun; Shona, 215-17; Sotho, 133-5; Tsonga, 189-90; Venda, 163-6.
Prosodic elements, 43.
Proyart, Abbé, 11.
Pulana (Sotho group), 24, 24*n*.; concord tables, 249-50; consonantal chart, 249; linguistic work, 249; numerals, 251; pronominal tables, 250; tables, **249-51**; vowels, 249.

Qualificative, 49-50, **60-66**; Nguni, 102-4; Shona, 217-20; Sotho, 135-9; Tsonga, 190-4; Venda, 166-9.
Qualificative concords: Nguni, 104; Shona, 220; Tsonga, 193; Tswana, 139; Venda, 169.
— pronoun, 50, 59; Nguni, 102; Shona, 217; Sotho, 135; Tsonga, 190; Venda, 165.
Quantitative pronoun, 50, **58**; inclusive, 58; Nguni, 101; Shona, 216-17; simple, 58; Sotho, 134-5; table, **59**; Tsonga, 190; Venda, 165.
Quinary system of numeration, 47.
Qwabe (dialect of Zulu, q.v.).

Reciprocal species of verb, 69; Nguni, 106; Shona, 222; Sotho, 141; Tsonga, 195; Venda, 170.
Reduplication: of verb-stem, 70, 106, 141, 171, 195; of verb suffix, 69, 106, 141, 171, 195.
References: classification of Southern Bantu, 25; history of knowledge of Southern Bantu, 19; morphology of Southern Bantu, 90; Ndebele, 118; Ngoni, 118; Nguni, 117-18; Northern Sotho, 153; phonetics and phonology, 46; Shona, 230; Sotho, 153; Southern Sotho, 153; Tsonga, 204; Tswana, 153; Venda, 179.
Reflexive prefix with verb, 78.

Relative, 50, **61-62**; comparative table of concords, 61; Nguni, 102-3; nominal stems, 61; primitive stems, 61; Shona, 218-19; Sotho, 136-7; Tsonga, 191; Venda, 167; verbal stems, 61.
— clause construction, 62; direct, 117, 152, 178, 204, 229; elliptical, 230; indirect, 117, 152, 179, 204, 229; Manyika, 229; Nguni, 117; Shona, 218-19, 224, 229-30; Sotho, 152; Tsonga, 204; Venda, 178-9.
— form of participial mood, 75.
— pronoun, **60**; Venda, 165-6.
Repetitive species of verb, 70, 171.
Retroflex consonants: Kutswe, 249; Pai, 246; Pulana, 249; Tsonga, 182.
Reversive species of verb, 69; Nguni, 106; Shona, 222; Sotho, 141; Tsonga, 195; Venda, 170.
Rhodesian Ndebele (dialect of Zulu, q.v.): a literary form, 23; orthography, 91.
Rolled consonant, 32, 122, 207.
Rolong (dialect of Tswana, q.v.).
Ronga (Tsonga group), 25; dialects, 25; geographical position, 180.
Roots, 50; underlying unity in Bantu, 48.
Rozwi (dialect of Kalanga, q.v.).

Schapera, I., 17, 19, 243.
Schreuder, H. P. S., 15.
Schwellnus, P. E., 18.
Seleka (dialect of Tswana, q.v.).
Semi-vowels, 34.
Shanga (dialect of Ndau, q.v.).
Shangaan, *see* Tsonga.
Shangwe (dialect of Korekore, q.v.).
Shawasha (dialect of Zezuru, q.v.).
Shona group, **205-30**; adverb, 226-7; characteristics, 48; charts of consonants, 206; classification, 21-22; clusters, 21; coalescence of vowels, 208; conjunctive, 227-8; consonantal phenomena, 206-8; copulative, 225-6; dialects, 21-22; enclitic, 228; geographical position, 205; grammatical outline, **209-30**; ideophone, 227; interjective, 228; length, 208; literary work, 205; locative formation, 214, 227; nasalization, 207; notes on consonants, 207; noun, 209-15; numerals, 228-9; orthography, 16, 205; penultimate -*i*, 208; phonetics, 206; phonology, 206; proclitic, 228; pronoun, 215-17; qualificative, 217-20; references, 230; relative construction, 229-30; significance of prefixes, 215; stress, 208; tone, 208-9; unification, 205; velarization, 207-8; verb, 221-5; vocalization, 208; vowels, 206.
Simple implication of verb, 71.
Smyth, Bishop, 231.
Sotho group, **119-53**; adverb, 147-9; alveolarization, 124-5; chart of consonants, 121; classification, 23, 24; clusters, 23, 24; conjunctive, 150; consonantal phenomena, 123-5; copulative, 146-7; dialects, 24; enclitic, 151; geographical position, 119; grammatical outline, **126-52**; ideophone, 149-50; interjective, 151; length, 125; literary work, 14, 119; locative

INDEX

formation, 148-9; nasalization, 123-4; notes on consonants, 122-3; noun, 126-33; numerals, 151-2; orthography, 15, 16, 119-20, 121; palatalization, 124; phonetics, 120; phonology, 120; proclitic, 151; pronoun, 133-5; qualificative, 135-9; references, 153; relative construction, 152; strengthening, 123-4; stress, 125; tone, 125; velarization, 125; verb, 139-46; vowels, 120.
Sound-shifting in Southern Bantu, 41, 48; specimen chart, 42.
Southern Sotho (Sotho group), 24; dialects, 24; geographical position, 119.
Species of verb, **67-70**.
Spiss, C., 118, 237.
Stative species of verb, 69, 171.
Stems, 50; of verbs, 66.
Stilz, E. B., 39*n*.
Strengthening of consonants, 123-4, 145.
Stress: in ideophones, 43; Nguni, 94; Shona, 208; Sotho, 125; Southern Bantu, 43; Tsonga, 183; Venda, 157; with enclitics, 89.
Stuart, J., 19.
Subjectival concord, 76; Chopi, 232; comparative table, 77; Kalanga, 252-3; Kgalagadi, 244; Kutswe, 249-50; Lozi, 241; Ngoni, 238; Nguni, 108; Pai, 247; Phuthi, 235; Pulana, 249-50; Shona, 223; Sotho, 144; Tsonga, 197; Venda, 172.
Subjunctive mood of verb, 73; hortative form, 74; Nguni, 108; Shona, 224; Sotho, 145; Tsonga, 198; Venda, 173.
Substantive, 49-50.
Substitution of vowels, 29; Nguni, 94; Tsonga, 183.
Suffixes, 50; noun, (Nguni) 99-100, (Sotho) 132, (Tsonga) 188-9, (Venda) 163; substantival, 50; verb, 50.
Sumerian and Bantu, 18.
Swati, *see* Swazi.
Swazi (dialect of Tekeza, q.v.): consonantal distinctions, 93; copulatives from pronouns, 110; importance of, 24; relative concords, 103.

Tables: Chopi, 231; Kalanga, 252; Kgalagadi, 243; Kutswe, 249; Lozi, 240; Ngoni, 237; Pai, 246; Phuthi, 234; Pulana, 249.
Talahundra (dialect of Kalanga, q.v.).
Tande (dialect of Korekore, q.v.).
Tau (dialect of Northern Sotho, q.v.).
Tavara (dialect of Korekore, q.v.).
Tavhatsindi (dialect of Venda, q.v.).
Tawana (dialect of Tswana, q.v.).
Tekeza (Nguni group), 24; dialects, 24; geographical position, 91.
Temporal adverb, 112, 147, 177, 200, 201.
— mood of verb (Xhosa), 75, 109.
Tense divisions of verb (Nguni), 107.
Tenses of verb, 71, 73; compound, *see* Compound tenses.
Terminology, vernacular, 18.
Teve (dialect of Manyika, q.v.).

Textual material, 18.
Thembu (dialect of Xhosa, q.v.).
Time-action sequences of verb, 73.
Tlhaping (dialect of Tswana, q.v.).
Tlharo (dialect of Tswana, q.v.).
Tlokwa (dialect of Northern Sotho, q.v.).
— (dialect of Tswana, q.v.).
Tonal studies, 16.
Tone: Nguni, 45, **95**; Shona, 44, **208-9**; Sotho, 44, **125**; Southern Bantu, 44; Tsonga, 44, **183**; Venda, 44, **158**.
Tonga (dialect of Ndau, q.v.).
— (Inhambane group), 25, 231.
— (Tsonga group), 25; dialects, 25; geographical position, 180.
Torrend, J., 13, 41, 90.
Transitive verbs, 66.
Transvaal Ndebele (dialect of Zulu, q.v.).
Tshidi (dialect of Tswana, q.v.).
Tsonga group, **180-204**; adverb, 200-2; chart of consonants, 181; classification, 25; clusters, 23, 25; conjunctive, 202-3; consonantal phenomena, 182-3; copulative, 199-200; dialects, 25; enclitic, 203; geographical position, 180; grammatical outline, **183-204**; ideophone, 202; interjective, 203; length, 183; literary work, 180; locative formation, 201; nasalization, 182-3; notes on consonants, 181-2; noun, 183-9; numerals, 203; orthography, 180, 181; phonetics, 180; phonology, 180; proclitic, 203; pronoun, 189-90; qualificative, 190-4; references, 204; relative construction, 204; stress, 183; substitution of *i*, 183; tone, 183; verb, 194-9; vowels, 180-1, 183.
Tsunga (dialect of Zezuru, q.v.).
Tswa (Tsonga group), 25; dialects, 25; geographical position, 180.
Tswana (Sotho group), 24; dialects, 24; geographical position, 119; orthography, 16.
Tucker, A. N., 16, 17, 44*n*., 45*n*., 46, 120*n*., 234.

Ultimate -*na*, 29-30, 100, 106, 125, 189.
Unification, Shona, 205.
Unyama (dialect of Manyika, q.v.).
Ur-Bantu, 13, 41.

van der Merwe, D. F., 17, 24*n*., 243.
van Eeden, B. I. C., 17, 153.
van Warmelo, N. J., 13, 16, 17, 18, 24*n*., 25, 41*n*., 42*n*., 46, 48*n*., 158, 179, 231.
Varieties of the verb, 66-70; Nguni, 104-6; Shona, 221-2; Sotho, 139-42; Tsonga, 194-5; Venda, 169-71.
Velarization: Shona, 40, 206, **207-8**, 209, 210; Sotho, 40, 125; Southern Bantu, **40**; Tsonga, 184, 188, 194; Venda, 40, 155, 156, 157, 159, 169.
Velarized consonants: Shona, 206.
Venda group, 25, **154-79**; adverb, 176-7; chart of consonants, 154-5; coalescence of vowels, 157; conjunctive, 177-8; consonantal phenomena, 156; copulative, 175; denasalization, 157;

Venda group (*continued*)
dialects, 25; elision of vowels, 157; enclitic, 178; geographical position, 154; grammatical outline, **158–79**; ideophone, 177; interjective, 178; length, 157; literary work, 154; locative formation, 176; nasalization, 156–7; notes on consonants, 156; noun, 158–63; numerals, 178; orthography, 154, 155; phonetics, 154; phonology, 154; proclitic, 178; pronoun, 163–6; qualificative, 166–9; references, 179; relative construction, 178–9; stress, 157; tone, 158; velarization, 157; verb, 169–75; vocalization, 157; vowels, 154.

Verb, 50, **66–78**; agentive 66; applied, *see* Applied species; aspects, *see* Aspect of verb; causative, *see* Causative species; concords, 76–78, 108, 144, 172, 197, **223**; conjugation, *see* Conjugation of verb; conjunctive, 66; contactive, *see* Contactive species; deficient, *see* Deficient verbs; derivative species, **66–70**, Nguni 105–6, Shona 221–2, Sotho 140–2, Tsonga 194–5, Venda 169–71; diminutive, *see* Diminutive species; extensive, *see* Extensive species; implication, *see* Implication of verb; import, 66; instrumental, 66; intensive, *see* Intensive species; intransitive, 66; locative, 66; mood, *see* Mood of verb; neuter, *see* Neuter species; Nguni, 104–10; passive, *see* Passive species; perfective, *see* Perfective species; primitive stems, 66; reciprocal, *see* Reciprocal species; repetitive, *see* Repetitive species; reversive, *see* Reversive species; Shona, 221–5; Sotho, 139–46; stative, *see* Stative species; tenses, *see* Tenses of verb; transitive, 66; Tsonga, 194–9; varieties, 66, 104, 139, 169, 194, 221; Venda, 169–75.

Verbal derivatives, **66–70**; comparative table of suffixes, 66–67; Nguni, 105–6; Shona, 221–2; Sotho, 140–2; Tsonga, 194–5; Venda, 169–71.

Vernacular grammars, 18.
Vilakazi, B. W., 18, 117.
Vocative interjective, 89; Nguni, 115–16; Tswana, 151.
Vocalization: Shona, 41, **208**, 211; Southern Bantu, 41; Venda, 41, 157, 159.
Vowels: Chopi, 231; coalescence, 29; elision, 28, 94; initial, 28; Kalanga, 252; Kgalagadi, 243; Kutswe, 249; Lozi, 240; Ngoni, 237; Nguni, 92; Pai, 246; phenomena associated with Southern Bantu, 28–30; Phuthi, 234; Pulana, 249; Shona, 206; Sotho, 120; Southern Bantu, **26–30**; substitution, 29; Tsonga, 180–1; Venda, 154.

Wanger, W., 18, 117.
Ward, I. C., 46.
Welsh, G. H., 15, 17, 118.
Werner, A., 13, 47*n*., 90.
Westermann, D., 46.
Westphal, E., 157, 158, 174, 179.
Whistling fricative, *see* Labio-alveolar fricative.
Wookey, A. J., 153.
Word-division, 45, 180, 205.

Xesibe (dialect of Xhosa, q.v.).
Xhosa (Nguni group), 23; dialects, 23; early work in, 14; geographical position, 91; orthography, 91.

Zezuru (Shona group), 21; consonantal charts, 206; dialects, 22; geographical position, 205; in unification, 205.
Ziervogel, D., 17, 118, 153, 246, 249.
Zone: characteristics, 48; in Bantu languages, 20; South-central, **21–22**; South-eastern, **23–25**.
Zulu (Nguni group), 23; dialects, 23; geographical position, 91; orthography, 15, 16, 91.

For Product Safety Concerns and Information please contact our EU representative GPSR@taylorandfrancis.com
Taylor & Francis Verlag GmbH, Kaufingerstraße 24, 80331 München, Germany

www.ingramcontent.com/pod-product-compliance
Lightning Source LLC
Chambersburg PA
CBHW071819300426
44116CB00009B/1366